Getting Started with Oracle Policy Automation [2019 Edition]

Richard Napier

Published in 2019 by P8tech, an imprint of Play Technologies (England) Limited

Copyright © Play Technologies (England) Limited

ISBN: 978-0-9956565-9-8

P8Tech
6 Woodside
Churnet View Road
Oakamoor
ST10 3AE

www.P8Tech.com

About the Author

Richard Napier has been helping businesses and organizations in customer relationship management, business rules and related topics since 1993. He regularly delivers Oracle Policy Automation and Oracle Siebel CRM training courses as a contractor to Oracle University. Formerly of Siebel Systems, Inc. and InFact Group, he delivers training and consulting in French and English all around the world for private and public sector organizations in Policy Automation and Oracle Siebel CRM.

Passionate about constrained natural language and how it can be used to accelerate the adoption of business rule management systems, he can be found on LinkedIn and on his website at

https://theopahub.com/main

He is also to be found on the Siebel Hub, where he is Co-founder:

https://siebelhub.com/main

Table of Contents

Chapter 2: Functions | 51

Chapter 3: Entities | 67

Chapter 4: Word Tables | 89

Chapter 5: Excel Rules | 99

Chapter 6: Basic Interviews | 113

Chapter 7: Advanced Interviews | 129

Chapter 8: Working with Inferred Instances | 159

Chapter 9: Testing the Project | 165

Chapter 14: The Hub – Collaboration | 233

Chapter 15: Hub Deployments | 249

Chapter 16: Languages | 263

Chapter 17: Command Line Tools | 277

Chapter 18: OPA in Oracle Service Cloud | 289

Chapter 19: Web Services | 299

Chapter 20: OPA in Oracle Siebel | 319

Chapter 21: Custom Controls | 327

Chapter 22: Mobile | 339

Index

Foreword

It has been my great pleasure to see the Oracle Policy Automation community grow to the point where today it encompasses enthusiastic and knowledgeable employees and consultants on (almost!) every continent. As the first independent author of a book on Oracle Policy Automation, Richard Napier has played a key role in encouraging the growth and development of that community, and I am delighted that he asked me to contribute a short preface to this, the 4th edition of his authoritative *Getting Started with Oracle Policy Automation*.

The Oracle Policy Automation product team is passionate about empowering business users within any organization to easily capture, manage and deploy smart advice and decision-making services. Organizations that adopt OPA can then deliver agile, reliable and auditable service experiences to all their customers and employees.

By enabling natural-like language to be used to define rules and develop interview experiences, most steps between requirements – that is the original business policies – and implementation are eliminated, and the opportunities for miscommunication are dramatically reduced. Regardless of whether the policies are deployed via industry-standard web services, a mobile application, or through a self-service portal, the ability to show how the original rules were used in each case allows every organisation to be confident they are providing advice and making decisions that comply with regulations and other business obligations.

Richard's book is a great introduction to OPA for those that want to get a deeper appreciation for some of the reasons why OPA works the way it does, as well as containing lots of practical advice for how to go beyond the basics. Oracle, of course, assists our customers directly through Oracle University, Oracle Support, as well as on social channels and through the OPA Blog. But you have in your hands the benefit of Richard's many years of experience as a well-respected member of the OPA community, and I am sure you will enjoy getting started on your journey with Oracle Policy Automation by reading this book and trying OPA out for yourself.

I look forward to seeing you online or at one of our events in the near future.

Davin Fifield

VP Product Development, Oracle Policy Automation

Preface

What will I learn in this book?

This book, now in its fourth edition, aims to give the reader a broad overview of all of the functionalities of Oracle Policy Automation. As such, we will inevitably cover tasks which are typically the domain of several different types of user: business rule writer, screen designer, Hub administrator, Web Service tester, and even developer. The text tries to make clear both the context and the role associated with any particular task.

Since the title in this book includes the words "Getting Started", we will not go into great detail on more advanced technical topics, such as designing complex extensions in JavaScript or how to build custom integrations using Java or another programming language. However, you *will* learn enough about these features to understand the use cases so you can make intelligent choices as to which solution to choose for a given scenario.

Who is this book for?

This book is for anyone starting out working with Oracle Policy Automation. No previous experience is assumed. If you have worked with Enterprise software systems, such as customer relationship management systems then you will be familiar with certain ideas that underpin how you write rules in Oracle Policy Automation. Similarly, if you have worked in programming, you will find many of the structures and design patterns used to be similar to those you have worked with in the past.

Rule Authors will want to focus on the chapters on functions, rule writing, and interviews to begin with.

Consultants who define solution architectures will find the chapters on Connections and integration a good starting point.

Managers who want the big picture can focus on the first four chapters, and then look to Web Services, and Connections to understand the wider picture.

Hopefully, there will be something for everyone interested in Oracle Policy Automation.

What is Oracle Policy Automation?

Oracle Policy Automation is the name given to a family of applications concerned with the design, development and deployment of business rules. The solution aims to decrease the time it takes to write rules, as well as the effort it takes to update and deploy them.

The product is made up of five separate basic parts.

- A desktop tool for writing rules and designing ways to present them or their output to the end user known as Oracle Policy Modeling.

- A server-based web application to manage users, roles, and authorizations in respect of writing rules known as Oracle Policy Automation Hub.

- The same server-based web application is also used to manage how end users access rules that have been written (as Web Services or HTML pages, for example).

- A variety of development tools, software development kits, and API's to help developers embed Rules in their own applications or into existing enterprise software.

- The end result of your rule development will be an Interview (or *web determination*) that your end users interact with, Web Services (using the *determination server*) that enable your applications to communicate, and various other ways that your business rules can be consumed.

What Versions of Oracle Policy Automation are Available?

At the time of writing, in January 2019, Oracle Policy Automation is available in the following versions.

Oracle Policy Automation version 12 18D

This is the latest major version of OPA. It offers the same desktop modeling interface for both Oracle Policy Automation Cloud Service and private cloud / on-premise customers. It also provides the Policy Automation Hub application for visual management of the repository, external data source connections, deployments and Project collaboration. This version is the subject of this book. There are minor differences between Public and Private Cloud versions which will be highlighted.

Oracle Policy Automation version 10.4.x

Version 10.4.x includes a Windows-based modeling tool and is offered with a number of application-specific connectors (Siebel Connector, Connector for Oracle CRM On Demand, SAP Connector for Java). The majority of the examples of how to write rules will also work with this version. The latest version available is 10.4.7 (10.4 Update 7). This product is available in Private Cloud only. The Project Migration tool is introduced in this book, however the complexities of migrating integrations and custom controls are beyond the scope of this title.

In the Field

For readers whose primary job is consultancy, it is important to note that there are many customers still using version 10. Their reasons for not upgrading may be as diverse as custom integrations, complexity of rules, or indeed something as mundane as the old adage "if it ain't broke, don't fix it". Although this book does not try to explain all of the differences between versions 10 and 12, look out for a Glossary in chapter 1, outlining the major vocabulary and functional differences. You should of course refer to the online documentation for these products if in doubt.

Architecture Differences between 10 and 12

For readers who are moving from version 10 to 12, here is a brief summary of the changes in architecture. You are again encouraged to read the documentation for more details.

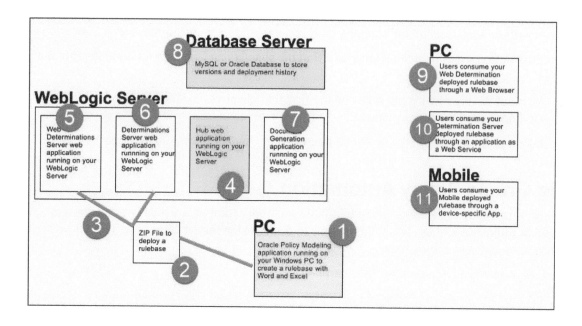

The following elements briefly show the main architectural differences between the two versions.

1. Oracle Policy Modeling has a revised user interface and more features related to collaboration, interview building, and data mapping.

2. Deployments are now performed using the Modeling client, in addition to version management.

3. The choices of deployment type are now managed using the Modeling client and the administrative interface.

4. The Hub web interface is completely new.

5. The Web Determinations application is fundamentally the same but the UX much improved.

6. The Determinations server is fundamentally the same.

7. Oracle BI Publisher is used to generate PDFs and other output.

8. These two database formats are supported for the Hub administrative database.

9. Interviews render as modern UX in client browsers.

10. New SOAP and Batch REST interfaces are available.

11. The OPA Mobile App and associated licensing offer new functionality and integration with Oracle Service Cloud.

Which parts of Oracle Policy Automation do I need to focus on?

The Oracle Policy Automation family can broadly be divided into two areas of interest: the design-time environment, where you will build business rules, design HTML interviews, or Web Services; and the run-time environment where your consumers will have their daily lives enhanced (we hope!) by using what you have built to get answers, explain policy, and provide useful information. In the following diagram, these areas have been aligned with the products of the family:

Oracle Policy Modeling

Ultimately, whatever OPA version you are working with, the modeling interface is the primary point of contact for those consultants whose job it is to write, review, or otherwise interact with business rules during design, testing or data mapping. In both guises it is Windows-based and provides the visual framework for the conception and delivery of rules, visual interviews and logic that can then be shared across applications.

This book concentrates on version 12 for Public and Private Cloud, as for most consultants, this is the easiest platform to install in order to create policy models. Consultants looking to work in a private cloud installation that includes the Oracle Policy Automation Hub can find installation instructions on the Oracle website.

> **NB:** A visual guide to setting up a Virtual Machine for Oracle Policy Automation can be found at https://theopahub.com/main/creating-an-opa-hub-self-study-platform-part-one/

The following screenshot shows the version 10 user interface upon running the program from the Start Menu in Windows. Notice the Project Explorer window on the left.

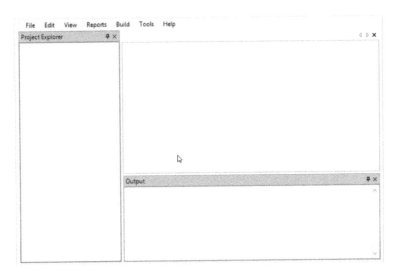

The next screenshot shows the version 12 application window. Notice the changed visual style more reminiscent of modern Microsoft Office applications, and the welcome pane of the Project tab displaying the version information, as well as some useful links.

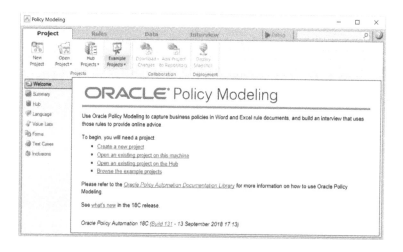

Although this book focuses on version 12, a fairly large percentage of the content relating to rule writing and Modeling usage will work, mostly without changes, in the earlier version. The Oracle OPA Website offers good advice for customers upgrading rule Projects from 10 to 12. In many cases, the process is without incident. In this book, Chapter 17 looks at the process of migration through the use of a command line tool called OPMMigrator and highlights some of the areas that might need attention.

Finally, although this book is focused on using Oracle Policy Modeling in English, there will be, where appropriate, both examples and commentary regarding potential differences that may occur when writing rules in other languages. Chapter 16 looks at languages and regions from a modeling perspective.

Oracle Policy Automation

In the previous section, you learned about the design-time tool: Oracle Policy Modeling. The name Oracle Policy Automation uses to identify the entire family of applications (both design- and run-time). The run-time platform is made up of tools that are deployed in either the Private or via Oracle Policy Automation Cloud Service (The Oracle Policy Automation Hub and the executable applications such as Oracle Policy Automation Web Determinations) or mobile devices (The OPA Mobile App for Android or Apple).

Oracle Policy Automation Hub

The family includes a web application called the **Oracle Policy Automation Hub**. As the name implies, it is a central location for the management of business rule Projects, their versions, and the roles of different users of the application suite. It is also used to manage the availability of these rule Projects to end users or applications:

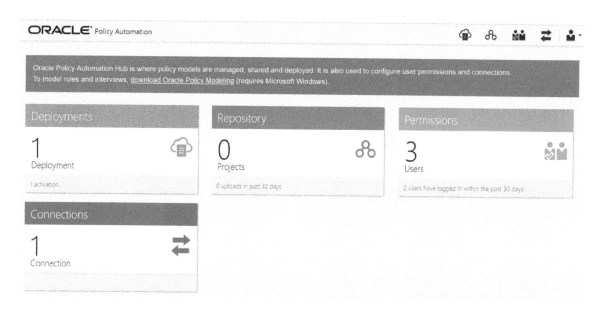

The Oracle Policy Automation Hub contains practical features such as logging statistics of rule usage and tracking versions of a rule Project, as well as more technical functions such as managing connectivity and data models obtained through integrations with other applications. This book looks at the management of users, deployments, the repository and all the associated management tasks.

Depending on the version of the Oracle Policy Automation Hub you encounter, and the licensing conditions of the purchase, you may find that you see a slightly different user interface. The example below comes from August 2017. Note the minor modifications:

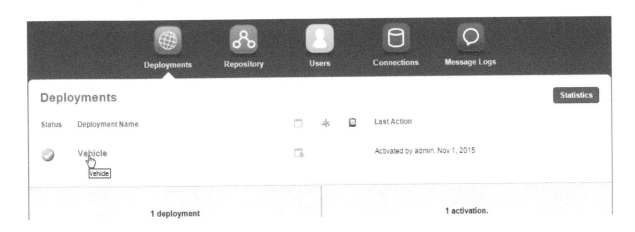

1. An icon toolbar replacing the colored sections shown in the previous image.

2. Users being used instead of Permissions to indicate how to manage access to the Hub.

Missing Icons or Non-functioning Icons

Depending on the licenses you or your company have acquired, some features may not behave as documented in this book.

For example, licensing the Oracle Policy Automation Cloud Service without the Collaboration features will cause the Repository to not be available, and all functionality related to it in the Oracle Policy Modeler will also be deactivated. Attempting to use this functionality will display a message to that effect:

Buying Oracle Policy Automation without the Oracle In-Memory Policy Analytics option will cause the Workspaces icon to not be visible in the Oracle Policy Automation Hub, and related functionality will be inaccessible:

NB: The Oracle In-Memory Policy Analytics option is outside the scope of this book. You will, however, discover the Batch Processor which is part of the Oracle In-Memory Policy Analytics solution, in Chapter 17.

Oracle Policy Automation – Web Determinations

The **Web Determination** web application is a big part of end-user deployment of Oracle Policy Modeling rule Projects. Users access a URL that displays the series of screens that make up your rule Project, and displays other features such as the final summary screen and links to any documents that may be made available by the rule designer.

In version 12, modifying the look and feel is achieved through a set of clearly defined **styles**, and more advanced rule designers have many design options and sophisticated layout tools. Much can be achieved without recourse to customization (e.g. JavaScript or custom external controls) as you will discover in Chapters 6 and 7. In Chapter 9, you will learn about the testing and debugging tools available.

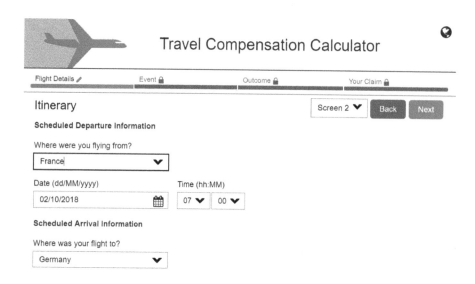

An example web determination session is shown above. The bottom line is: *web determinations* display web pages to let the user view, edit, and submit information in order to get an outcome. For example, when you go online to pay your taxes, you enter salary and other data, some of which may be pre-populated from an external system, and the outcome is your expected tax bill.

Interviews are often accompanied with PDF output (which are called Forms in Oracle Policy Automation) and you will learn how to enrich your web determination experience with these in Chapter 12.

Oracle Policy Automation – Web Services

Web Services provide access to your business rule Projects in a different way to web determinations; the rules are available in XML, not HTML. Communication with the Server is in the form of a SOAP request and response mechanism, making it practical for integration with software which needs to leverage a Policy Automation project's rules.

Although writing application code to take advantage of the XML-based interface is beyond the scope of this book, you will get a good understanding of the deployment process in Chapter 15. There are several different ways to access Web Services depending on your requirement:

Assess Service

If you are looking to use Oracle Policy Automation as a back-end, zero user interface platform, then the Assess Service is going to probably be one of your chosen solutions. It has methods dedicated to passing in data and receiving the response. Of course, it is up to you to provide the mechanism (coded as a process or library) that is going to actually handle the input and output. This is pretty much the same service as exists in version 10.

Answer Service

Newer than the Assess Service, the Answer Service has methods relating to the use of Connection objects in Oracle Policy Automation (see the chapters on Web Services and Deployment). In short, if you have used Oracle Policy Modeller to map inputs or outputs from (and to) another application and you want to access this business rule Project using a Web Service, then the person responsible for calling your business rule Project in their code will need to know the data model that your Project is expecting, so that they can build the right input. Some examples are the `GetInputDataDefinition` Action which responds with a data model, followed in all probability by the `GetAnswer` action which attempts to get an outcome from the business rules. This is fundamentally a "zero user interface" integration, the consumer of the service does not use any Interview created in Oracle Policy Modeller.

Interview Service

There may be situations where developers need to use the structure of your Project user interface (how many screens you have designed and what they display) but they need to display the screens using something other than HTML – perhaps a native format for a mobile application, or adjusted in some way to take advantage of an external user interface. As the name shows, this service allows us to work though the screens in your Project, and to handle all the different user interactions (back, forward, save, close, and so on) that can occur.

This service is used, for example, with Oracle Siebel CRM IP15, and fancy techniques used to (re)generate the screens of your Project in native Siebel Open UI. Look out for `GetInputDataDefinition`, `StartInterview`, `Investigate`, `EndInterview`, `GetFiles` and `SnapshotSession` actions. If you see them, then you are looking at the Interview Service.

Server Service

Last but by no means least, the Server service gives access to things like Timezone settings as well as a list of deployed Projects. This can be useful to understand what a particular server is providing.

In most of the above cases, the WSDL file can be accessed through the Oracle Policy Automation Hub web application, and the file can be simply downloaded from your Web Browser, as shown for example below.

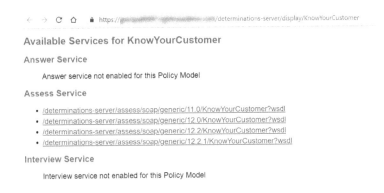

Oracle Policy Automation – Mobile Application

Starting with version 12, Oracle Policy Automation Projects can be deployed to a mobile device that uses Apple or Google Android as its operating system. The rules that are viewed on the mobile device are retrieved from the Oracle Policy Automation Hub. The use of the mobile application is not, however, a pre-requisite for using Oracle Policy Automation on a mobile device – if the web determination URL is accessible, then it can be reached on your tablet or phone.

This application is available for download from both the Apple Store and Google Play sites. An example screen is reproduced below. In chapter 22, you will learn how to give a user access to a Project on their mobile app.

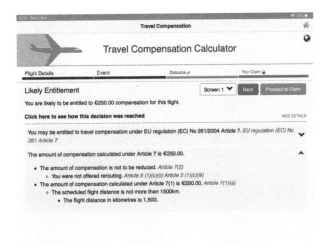

Oracle Policy Automation Mobile Cloud Service provides an enhanced mobile experience in the following areas:

- An optimized visual experience in the app.
- Full control of which Projects are available to which users.
- Out of the box integration with Oracle Service Cloud through the Assessment object in Service Cloud, allowing assessments to be assigned to field agents.

Developers can also use the Oracle Policy Automation Mobile SDK to build custom mobile applications. More information was available at time of writing at: https://blogs.oracle.com/opa/opa-mobile-sdk-get-started

An important note about licenses

Oracle Policy Automation products are available for download from the Oracle Software Delivery Cloud, currently at the web address https://edelivery.oracle.com or from the Oracle TechNet website at https://www.oracle.com/technetwork/apps-tech/policy-automation/overview/index.html As a user of these sites, remember that is it *always* your responsibility to make sure you respect the license agreements you and your organization has, and any conditions attached.

In addition, as already mentioned, some functionality is licence-based. You may not have access to all the features and functionality described in this book.

A note about the images used in this guide

For the sake of space, some images in this guide have been truncated or had irrelevant white space removed. Where appropriate, colored icons will guide you to the important aspects of the image.

First Principles

Writing Rules in Microsoft Word

This chapter is all about writing simple rules in Microsoft Word. Before you jump right in, some thoughts about getting ready.

Preparing for Oracle Policy Modeling

This section is divided into two parts. In this first part, you will discover the practical steps to get ready to work in Microsoft Word. In the second part, you will learn about the important things you need to think about *before* you start writing.

Preparing to Write Rules

Getting Ready to Write Rules in Microsoft Word

Writing rules in Oracle Policy Modeling is probably the first way a lot of people experiment, and Microsoft Word (because of its familiarity) is the first place people go. However there are some things to keep in mind before you start. Microsoft Word has a number of features that may be quite counterproductive when you write, edit or format the text of your policy. This is especially true when copying and pasting.

Microsoft Word AutoCorrect

Automatic formatting can sometimes conflict with the formatting that is necessary for your rules to function correctly. You will find these options, depending on your version of Microsoft Word, in a variety of locations. The most recent versions of the product have these options inside the Office Button or the File menu. In Word 2013, for example, File > Options provides the following dialog box.

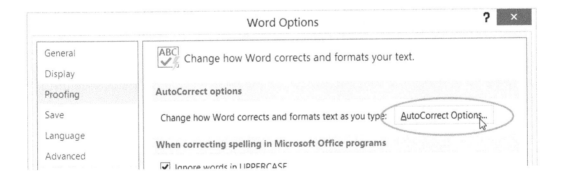

Clicking the button highlighted above leads to a second dialog, where there are two main areas to focus on.

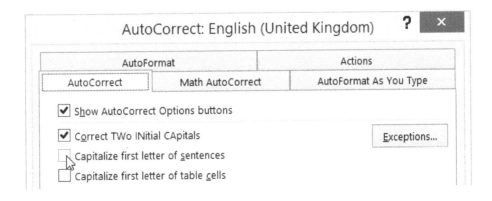

In AutoCorrect, you may wish to switch off the capitalization of the first letter of sentences and table cells. As you will discover later on, a feature of Oracle Policy Modeling uses the text you type to create links with other text. If text capitalization does not match – this can stop the linking from happening.

Microsoft Word AutoFormat as You Type

As you will learn in detail in this book, formatting text correctly is one of the key steps of getting your rule Project to work properly. So the following tab which contains various options will require attention.

AutoFormat		Actions	
AutoCorrect	Math AutoCorrect	AutoFormat As You Type	

Replace as you type

- [ ] "Straight quotes" with "smart quotes"
- [x] Fractions (1/2) with fraction character (½)
- [ ] *Bold* and _italic_ with real formatting
- [x] Internet and network paths with hyperlinks
- [x] Ordinals (1st) with superscript
- [x] Hyphens (--) with dash (—)

Apply as you type

- [ ] Automatic bulleted lists
- [x] Border lines
- [ ] Built-in Heading styles
- [ ] Automatic numbered lists
- [x] Tables

Automatically as you type

- [ ] Format beginning of list item like the one before it
- [x] Set left- and first-indent with tabs and backspaces
- [ ] Define styles based on your formatting

[OK] [Cancel]

Particularly important, for example, is the "Straight quotes" with "smart quotes" option – Oracle Policy Modeling needs you to use "these quotes" and not "these quotes". In addition, automatic formatting such as bulleted or numbered lists, or any option which formats following items like the one before should be switched off for best results.

Microsoft Word Settings

To be perfectly clear, most of these options will make your life easier in Oracle Policy Modeling, but you may find they make your life less comfortable when you use Microsoft Word for other purposes.

Returning these settings to their previous value is something you will either have to do by hand, by reopening Word and changing them, or by using another method. The relevant data is held for the most part in the Windows Registry. You can find the correct Registry Keys to modify them manually, at your own risk, or you can try and find a mechanism to do it for you.

Since Microsoft Office 2007, there has no longer been a built-in Save Settings Wizard so you will have to consider an external tool to do the job. I have not tested the following tool but have read good things about it.

Mirinsoft CloneApp

http://www.mirinsoft.com/index.php/download/viewdownload/39-cloneapp-portable/180-cloneapp

Before you consider doing anything to restore settings, please remember to make sure to back up the registry before you modify it. Make sure that you know how to restore the registry if a problem occurs.

How to Approach Rule Writing

New users of Oracle Policy Modeling are generally enchanted by the freedom it appears to offer the rule writer. Using natural language in a famous word processor sounds too good to be true – and it is – to some extent. To avoid issues later on, the rule writer needs to keep some simple rules in mind. You will of course discover these through practical exercises in this book, in a hopefully interesting and educational way. But there are a few things you need to do before getting started.

Structure and Organize your Projects

The above title sounds like a lot of work. However, I simply mean that the writer of a rule has a responsibility to the other members of the team to structure and organize work to make it clearly accessible. Everyone in the team needs to be aware of mutually agreed standards such as the following (and these are only common examples):

Table of Contents

Word documents that you use to write business rules can also contain non-Oracle Policy Automation elements. You should therefore take advantage of the Table of Contents feature on Microsoft Word and create one for your rule documents.

Links

In the same manner as Tables of Contents, your Word documents can contain other non-Oracle Policy Automation elements such as links to source materials, web sites, SharePoint sites, and so on. Make sure that any – and all – source material is referenced for easy access.

Naming Conventions

Just like normal business Projects when multiple people are involved, you need conventions to define what kind of names you will use, and what different folders you might use. This is just as true inside Oracle Policy Modeling as it is on your own PC. Having a set of rules will save a lot of time when you move to a different rule Project.

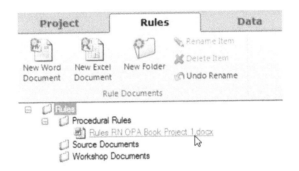

Document Headers

Given that many other people (legal teams, subject matter experts, project colleagues, and so on) will refer to your documents, it is of primary importance to have an agreed method for defining the rule scope, the business requirement they are solving, and related topics in the form of a header or heading page that is added to your documents every time one is created. It could be as simple as a set of headings in a Table or something far more complex: but it needs to be systematically used.

Document Name:		Document Author:	
Date of Creation:		Last Updated:	
Description:			

Later in this book, you will learn about the version control features of the Oracle Policy Automation Hub, but good document management practices will never go out of fashion.

Glossary

Your Oracle Policy Automation efforts will perhaps involve integrations with other applications such as Oracle Siebel Enterprise or Oracle Service Cloud. In this case, you will be involved to some degree in the mapping of key terms as either input(s) or output(s) of your rule Project. In this case, it is good practice to maintain an up-to-date list of the different terms in both of the applications. Once again this is beneficial to all members of the team. For example:

CRM System	Oracle Policy Automation	Source Document A	Source Document B
Contact	the contact	the citizen	the taxpayer
Account	the establishment	the company	the organization

Writing Styles

As you will discover in the upcoming chapters, there are often several different ways to express a concept in Oracle Policy Automation; to avoid confusion, especially where multiple rule writers will collaborate closely, define and stick to guidelines about how rules should be written.

Clear Goals

Writing an Oracle Policy Automation rule requires a laser focus on the goals of your rule:

Writing a rule means having a clear vision of the expected *goals for the end user*.
- What will the end user expect to receive at the end?
- What further information should be highlighted or proposed?
- What information can be provided as attached documents?

At the same time, writers need consider not just goals like these, but *goals for the user interface*.
- What order will the input be requested (either logical or to match current practices)?
- What documents are to be considered true sources of information?
- What assistance will be provided to help the user?

Similarly, what are the goals in respect of *interview management*?
- New rules that become necessary to aid processing of the data (intermediate rules).
- The information needed to ensure document generation is successful (public names for example).
- Mapping the source documents to the written OPA rules.
- Tracking and documenting the testing process.

What are the goals of the *data model*?
- Interaction with an external system like Oracle Service Cloud or standalone.
- Upsert or Insert and which objects will be impacted in the external system?
- How will it be exposed, through which Web Services?

What are the policy goals for the *organization*?
- Enforce laws or legislation.
- Provide a customer service.
- Encourage Self-Service to reduce reliance on other channels.

All through this book you will be encouraged to focus on the goals as you discover the details of working with Oracle Policy Automation, but ultimately you and your project team need to be working closely to ensure you have the right information you need to create successful rules.

Getting a Team Ready

Getting your team up to speed is not just a matter of throwing them in at the deep end, giving them Microsoft Word, and telling them to write natural language business rules. All projects are different, but there are some simple rules that you should bear in mind when starting out.

Training

Investing in good training from Oracle University and working with Oracle Policy Automation experts are just two more ways to ensure that your team gets a head start. The currently available courses are listed in Chapter 19.

Evangelisation

Don't assume that Oracle Policy Automation will be met with complete understanding and open arms just because people have been trained. There is a strong need to accompany people, guide their efforts, and act as a point of contact, promoting the correct use of different parts of the product and the best practices.

In addition, expect to be able to identify when Oracle Policy Automation is a good choice for a business problem, and when it is not.

NB: There is an excellent presentation called *Is Oracle Policy Automation a Good Fit for My Business?* currently available on the Oracle Website at this location: https://www.oracle.com/technetwork/apps-tech/policy-automation/learnmore/isopaagoodfitformybusiness-1653261.pdf

Demystification

When working in a Project where English is not the first language, you will find that you need to develop techniques and vocabulary to facilitate discussion. Sometimes this can be quite a challenge. Even if you don't speak French, the example below might be quite easy to understand. This is an extract from the **Online Function Reference** for French:

*Utilisé comme conclusion pour inférer qu'une instance de **entity** existe et est membre d'une relation **relationship***

Aside from the mixture of English and French which renders it hard to understand for non-English speakers, the verb *inférer* is unfamiliar to some (to infer, in English) and during our discussion we settled on *déduire*, to deduce, or *determiner* (to determine) as a good alternative.

Please do not misunderstand my intention. I am not condescending or criticising the Function Reference – I am simply trying to point out that although Word and Excel are known to many, the vocabulary of Oracle Policy Modeling may not be.

NB: At the time of writing, the latest Function Reference can be found here: http://documentation.custhelp.com/euf/assets/devdocs/cloud18d/PolicyAutomation/en/Content/Guides/Policy_Modeling_User_Guide/Work_with_rules/Function_references/Function_references.htm

Writing Rules in Microsoft Word

Assuming you have not been put off by all the above, now you can turn your attention to the user interface of Oracle Policy Modeling. Writing rules in Policy Modeling means adapting and getting used to the constraints of the rule Project concept, and the different features available. The following sections of this chapter will walk you through what you need to know to be up and running quickly. You will be given text to type and tasks to accomplish. All of these are tailored to accelerate getting to grips with Oracle Policy Modeling.

Rule Writing – Getting Set Up with Oracle Policy Modeling

Open Oracle Policy Modeling from your PC. If the start-up is correct then you should see something like the following screenshot. Of course the language you see in the user interface might be slightly different depending on how the installation was performed and how the program is launched.

As an example, on my computer I have the following command line to run the program, where XXX is typically the release version, for example "18C":

```
"C:\Program Files (x86)\Oracle\Policy Modeling\XXXX\bin\OPM.exe" --language=fr-FR
```

The addition of the switch `--language=fr-FR` allows you to start Oracle Policy Modeling with the user interface in French (as an example) irrespective of your Windows language. The application is available in a number of languages; you should consult the documentation to find out which, for your version. The choice of user interface language has no effect on the languages or regions you select for your projects.

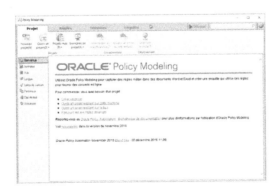

> **NB:** Sometimes when I encounter an error in a non-English version of the product, I switch to English to investigate the behaviour, for example when uploading work to the OPA Hub (see chapter 14).

Other Useful Command Line Switches

There are a few other command line switches that you might need from time to time.

`--diagnostics`

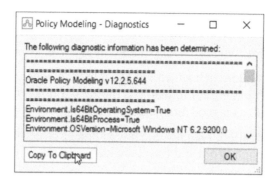

The above report can be useful to ensure, for example, that the program has been installed correctly and that your versions of Microsoft Word and Excel have been successfully identified and the compiler used by the application correctly installed. Support personnel may ask you to provide this.

In recent versions of the Oracle Policy Modeler, you can also access these details by clicking the *build number* on the Welcome tab of the application, as shown below, and selecting Full Diagnostics.

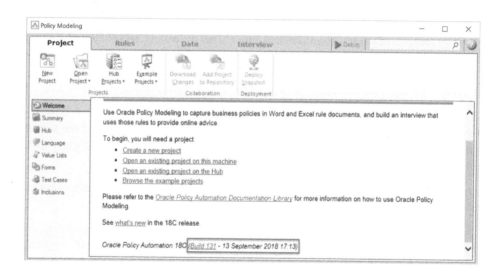

`OPM.exe [<project-path> --language=<locale>]`

Starting the Oracle Policy Modeling application as shown above, the project-path variable can be used to open an existing rule Project directly, and in combination with the language switch you can open the rule Project with an appropriate language user interface for the rule designer. You will learn about other command-line tools in Chapter 16.

Keeping Multiple Versions of Oracle Policy Modeling

Since Oracle Policy Modeling changes regularly, as updates are released, when you install the product on your hard disk, you can happily have multiple versions living side-by-side since they will be in different directories.

When you open a Project, the application will switch to the version that was used to create the Project, assuming that you have it installed. At any time, you can view the version number and other details on the Welcome tab of Oracle Policy Modeling.

In the screenshot below, you can see another clever feature at work. If you have a version of Oracle Policy Modeling open and you attempt to create a **New Project**, the application will warn you if you have a more recent version installed – as you can see in the background image with five different versions installed on this computer. The version that is open is August 2015, but there are several other versions available including August 2016. That is the version that will be used if the user clicks Yes in the dialog shown below.

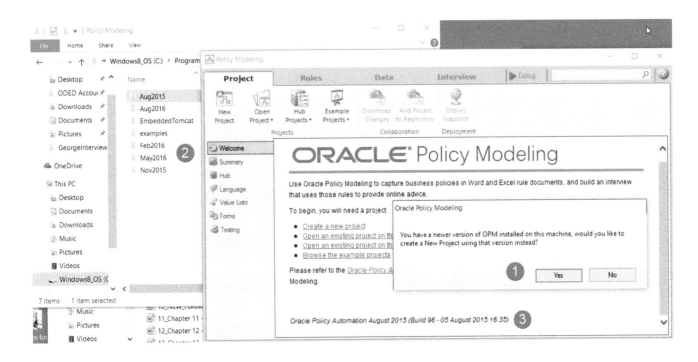

It may help to create shortcuts to each of the versions on your Windows Desktop, especially if you are working with different customers, Cloud or On Premise, that use different versions.

> **NB:** The OPA Hub, which we will discuss in Chapters 12, 13, and 14, is also version-sensitive and will refuse to interact with your Oracle Policy Modeling unless you have a matching version number. Although Projects can be upgraded (as you will learn in Chapter 16) keep a close eye on your version and ensure that you have a strategy in place for managing upgrades, migration and testing of Project(s).

Creating a First Project

Any work you do in Oracle Policy Modeling needs to be within the context of a rule Project. Each of these Projects can contain any number of Word or Excel files, as well as definitions of PDF output, data mappings, and so on.

So to get the first practical steps underway, create a New Project right now, and call it `Basic Rule Principles`.

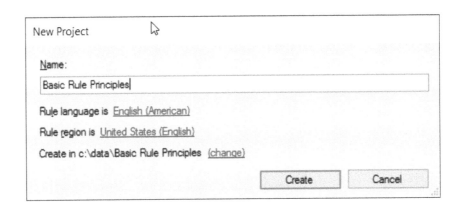

Notice that the rule language is set to English (American) so that (in these exercises) you will write in English, and the Rule region is set to United States (English). Oracle Policy Modeling should default to the language of your installation of Microsoft Windows, and the region should also default to the region of Windows. The setting for Rule region will impact how region-sensitive data like dates are displayed.

Creating a new Project and setting the file Location

The name of the Project needs to be a valid filename in Windows, and cannot have more than 260 characters. In addition it should not end in a "." character as this can cause issues with deployment on Internet Information Services (IIS from Microsoft).

The default location for the Project is situated under the My Documents folder of the current user of Windows. You can change this to another valid location. As you can see in the screenshot above, any valid folder is fine (but remember to have a backup strategy in place for the folder in question).

Opening Existing Projects

When clicking the Open Project button from the ribbon, Oracle Policy Modeling will default to showing Projects in the folder mentioned above, but you can always search for Projects that are elsewhere on your computer (for example on a USB stick) by clicking the Other... button in the top right corner of the files list, as shown below.

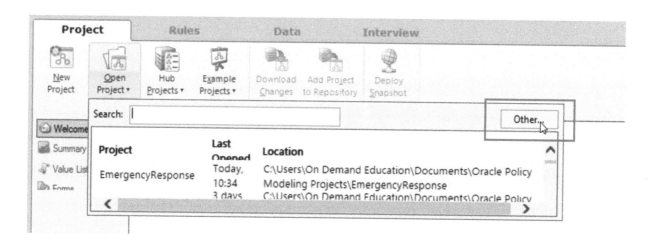

The list of files will grow over time and will show your recent work. If a project has been moved or deleted from your disk, Oracle Policy Modeler will prompt you to remove it from the list of projects if you click on that project in the list.

About Project Files

Project files are **XPRJ files**, and do not contain any information that can be manually edited. You can review what information you have entered by checking in two different views of the Project tab. Firstly the basic information about your Project is in the Summary View.

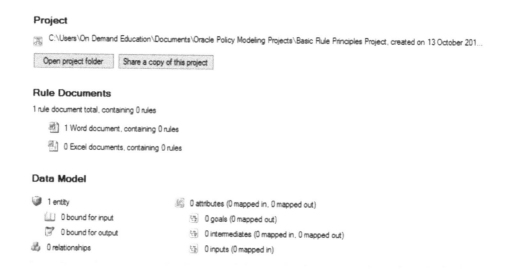

As you can see above, the Project already contains one Word document; this file is added automatically as soon as you click the Create button in the New Project dialog. In addition, you can see a Project file's location and can navigate there quickly through the shortcut button Open project folder. We'll discuss why you would want to create a copy of a Project a little later.

The second place you can find useful information is in the Language View of the Project tab.

Here you can see the region – which controls how information like currency is displayed – and the language you chose to write your rules in. We will look at the other options on this page later.

Rule Writing - Concepts and Vocabulary

To begin writing rules, you will work with a series of example rules to learn from. Consider the management of candidates in an interview process. Your employer would like to automate the processing of the results of the first series of interviews in order to identify candidates that are going to be continuing in the interview process.

The idea of automating a decision is right at the heart of Oracle Policy Automation – if you can "teach" the Determination Server to process candidates correctly, then the organization can gain a lot of time. And, of course, you can write those instructions in natural language. Go to the Rules tab and double-click the Word document in your Project tab.

Enter the following text in your document. Our goal is to test whether a candidate for a job is accepted or not:

> the candidate is accepted if
>
> the candidate's references are valid and
>
> the candidate's interview was a success

The text is on three separate lines (hit Return after each) and is written without *any* formatting. When text is written without formatting, it is essentially ignored by Oracle Policy Modeling. Two things need to happen before it becomes "visible".

1. Format the text.

2. Validate your work. (This is also called Compile, depending on the version).

Format and Validate Rule Text

Using the Policy Modeling Ribbon in Microsoft Word, select the first line of text (or just put the cursor at the beginning of the line) and click the button labelled Conclusion. Your text should now look like this:

the candidate is accepted if

the candidate's references are valid and

the candidate's interview was a success

Select the other two lines of text. Using the Policy Modeling Ribbon in Microsoft Word, in the Levels drop-down list and choose Level 1.Your document should now look like the text shown below.

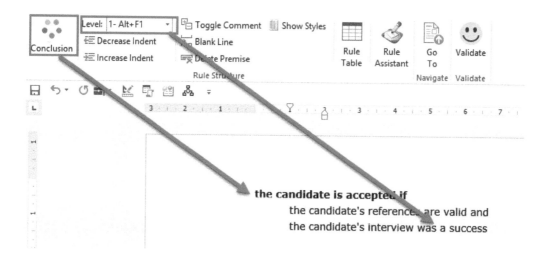

Having formatted the text, it needs to be validated. Validating your work is much more than just checking your spelling or clicking on a smiley face. Once you have clicked on the Validate button, and hopefully received a message that no errors were found – switch back to Oracle Policy Modeling (you can leave the Microsoft Word document open for now) and go to the Data tab.

You should see something like the example below. All your hard work has paid off. Your simple text has been processed and Oracle Policy Modeling has identified some data based on your typing.

Type	Attribute Text	Role
Boolean	the candidate is accepted	Goal
Boolean	the candidate's references are valid	Input
Boolean	the candidate's interview was a success	Input

Notice the key elements in this window – the text has been split into separate parts (two Input(s) and a Goal) and all three have been identified as **Boolean** (yes/no) types. If you cannot see the word Boolean, make the first column large enough to see both the icon and the text describing your data type. One of your goals is to manage a clear and efficient data model, and this window will allow you to review the current one for this Project.

From the simple example above, several important conclusions can be drawn:

1. Every rule must be formatted correctly to be parsed by Oracle Policy Modeling
2. Every element of a rule that represents data is called an **Attribute**.
3. The **Attribute Text** is written in natural language
4. Every attribute has a **Role**.

Attribute Roles in the Data Tab

The Role will change depending on the usage of your data item, or attribute; later you will see roles such as Joining, Top as well as Goal, Input, and others. The Role column can be a useful way to get an understanding of what a Project is trying to determine. For example, if you have defined **the candidate's age** as a piece of data that is calculated from their date of birth, you would not expect it to be listed as an Input but rather as a Goal, meaning that the input (the candidate's date of birth) is used to determine the age (the goal).

Oracle Policy Modeling uses the term **Input** to signal that the data has to come from somewhere – the user or an external system – rather than a Goal, which is to be inferred or determined. Be on the lookout for incorrect roles appearing in the attribute list as this can help debug issues.

Inputs and Goals

Any time you write a simple rule, you need to focus on the inputs and the goal. Bear in mind that a Project might contain many different inputs and many goals. Frequently, a Project without a goal may not be very useful – why ask lots of questions without an actual point to your conversation? Without a goal, you cannot expect to determine anything. Take the following questions, asked to you by someone else.

What is your name?

What is your age?

Why are you being asked those questions? Is it to join the library, or to sign up for a space journey to Mars? Now consider the following version which specifies the goal.

The person is accepted for a library card if

the person's name is recorded and

the person's age is recorded

With this structure, the reason becomes clear, the **goal** becomes clear as does the relationship to the inputs. The process is now ready to be automated – Policy Automation can accelerate the work of recording names and ages if they are forthcoming, and can accept people who wish to join your library, if they meet your conditions (which we have not added to the example above for the sake of brevity).

Writing Rules - Basic Structure

The candidate-based rule you built has a very simple, yet powerful structure: two inputs that are needed to reach the goal of determining whether the candidate can continue the interview process. Everything you write in Oracle Policy Modeling documents must have a clearly-defined structure. If the goal is not clear, or an input is unclear, then something will need to happen before you use the Project to automate your process.

Writing in another language, the process would have been exactly the same. Take the same example, this time in French.

le candidat est accepté si
les références du candidat sont valables et
le candidat a fait un bon entretien

Notice how the formatting is identical. Perhaps the only appreciable difference is the absence of apostrophes in the text – nothing to do with Policy Modeling and everything to do with the chosen language. The result in the Data tab is exactly the same in terms of data model, types and roles.

The similar formatting and the structure of the text has given us the same result. Writing rules for Oracle Policy Modeling requires close attention to sentence structure, and this is the first example.

Writing Rules - Conclusions

In Microsoft Word, you will need to use the **Conclusion** format to identify your goal, and the goal needs to be written in a certain way. Our current example is what is known as a binary or **Boolean** goal – it's yes or no. In order for your text to be acceptable as a Boolean goal, certain things must be in place. Here is a checklist for you to work with.

- The Boolean **Conclusion** or Condition *must* use a verb that is understood by Oracle Policy Modeling.

- The **Conclusion** must have a subject – in this case "the candidate".

- The **Conclusion** should end in "if" or the equivalent keyword for readability (it's not mandatory).

- The **Conclusion** must be formatted correctly.

You'll learn about other types of goals and data shortly.

Writing Rules – Negative Conclusions

In Oracle Policy Modeling, and this will feel strange at first, a Boolean goal can be written in the positive *or* the negative. If you change the text of this document to the following negative version then click the Validate button again:

> **the candidate is not accepted if**
>> the candidate's references are not valid and
>> the candidate's interview was not a success

…the Data tab will remain *completely unchanged*. You have made the conclusion a negative one, as well as the other two lines. But there is absolutely no difference except in the way the rule is written. There are still two inputs, they are still Boolean, and the goal is still Boolean. The way you write the rule is up to you, but there are several things to consider – readability, ease of maintenance, and how it compares to the original documentation to name just three – before you should decide to use the negative version.

Now you will review the four bullet points above.

The Boolean Conclusion and Condition must use verbs

This often catches new rule writers out. You write Boolean text using a verb, not with a "=". Using an equals sign to assign a value is signalling that it is definitely *not* a Boolean. Furthermore, the list of verbs understood by the Oracle Policy Modeling engine is not limitless – you have to ensure you use one of the accepted verbs, or that you have added any specific verbs to the verb list. At the time of writing, Oracle Policy Modeling has a list of 392 verbs as standard in English.

> **NB**: You will find out how to add extra verbs to your project, for example to reflect a domain-specific concept, in Chapter 15.

The Conclusion must have a clear subject

Writing rules without a subject will confuse Oracle Policy Modeling and you as well. Properly structured sentences are the basis of the validation process. As you will see throughout this book, it is important to build sentences correctly, using complete phrases, as in "the candidate is accepted" *not* "they are accepted".

The Conclusion should end in "if" or the equivalent keyword

Think of your Conclusion – it can only be reached *if* the Conditions are met. The presence of the "if" is not actually required in your Word document, but it will be easier to get started this way.

The Conclusion must be formatted correctly

Painting it so it looks like a Conclusion is not accepted. If you are ever in doubt about what formatting you have applied, use the Show Styles button on the Policy Modeling Ribbon in Microsoft Word to check:

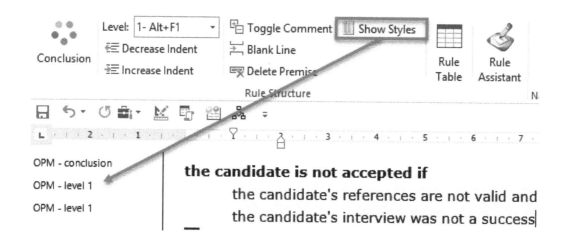

To remove the Styles from your page view, switch to View > Print Layout or the equivalent in your version of Microsoft Word.

About Rule Validation

When you click the Validate button, your text is parsed. Errors will usually be obvious but it is worthwhile remembering that unformatted text is ignored, so will not generate an error.

The validation step is at the heart of everything you do in Oracle Policy Modeling. If you learn the subtleties of how your text is validated (and each supported language has unique 'parsing' challenges) for your language then you are well on your way to getting comfortable. Some of the typical issues with parsing are covered in this book, and others will be specific to your language. I encourage you to read Chapter 15 and to consult the latest documentation for notes about what may not be parsed correctly in your language.

So far you have discovered the basics of writing Boolean conclusions and conditions so that the parser understands them. Now you will look at the other data types and how to approach them. You will also look at some common traps when writing rules with them.

Number and Currency Attributes

Numbers and currency introduce several new features into your Project. Furthermore, as a consultant you must decide whether the number or currency is best for your situation. Let's take a look at an example, by extending the existing Word document to include the following rule:

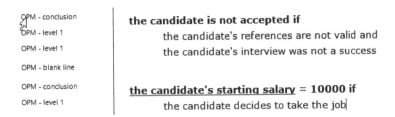

Don't forget to Validate after writing your text and formatting it. Notice the underline showing you that the parser has identified a new, non-Boolean piece of your "Data Model". If you switch to the Data tab you will see the following:

The new Goal has been added to the list, with a type of Number.

Creating a new **attribute** in this way can appear fun and easy: the data attributes show up "as you type"; but there are a number of pitfalls for you to watch out for, which are listed below.

Data Type

In this case, it has assigned a type of Number. It may be more appropriate to use a currency attribute instead – you will investigate this in a moment. In any case, *always* check that your attribute has been given the correct type.

Attribute Text

Is this a yearly or monthly salary? When you read this again in six months' time, will you remember? Will you need another attribute with similar text?

Number or Currency?

Number attributes have one big advantage over currency attributes. The currency that is assumed, when a rule requires a currency attribute, is the currency of the Project region (English – United Kingdom; or French-France; and so on) whereas the number display format is invariable – it is a number.

If your rule Project contains only one currency and it is always the currency of the Project region then you are in luck. But otherwise it might require different handling.

Based on the above, you can amend your Word document to look like this:

OPM - conclusion	**the candidate's initial yearly salary in British Pounds** = 10000 if
OPM - level 1	the candidate decides to take the job
OPM - conclusion	**the candidate's initial yearly salary in Canadian Dollars** = 30000 if
OPM - level 1	the candidate has to move to Canada
OPM - conclusion	**the fixed costs in British Pounds of hiring the candidate** = 1000

Units of Measurement in Attribute Names

This introduces several new principles for smart working in Oracle Policy Modeling. Firstly, as mentioned, we have clearly defined the underlying unit of measurement (GB Pounds, Canadian Dollars). This is good practice – always provide clarity in your attribute text.

Secondly, we have introduced a new type of conclusion: the fixed costs line with no conditions attached shown at the end of the text. It is perfectly acceptable, within reason and when required, to assign a fixed value to an attribute. This might be a value referenced elsewhere in your project.

Consider, for the purposes of reinforcing the next steps, changing the fixed cost line so that it mentions the currency of your own Project region. Leave the other two as they are.

Return to the Data tab after validating your work and you should see the following changes. Notice the (Auto) suffix after each of the numeric attribute Type definitions. Since these attributes could be something other than a number, Oracle Policy Modeling highlights this in order to prompt us to verify the choices.

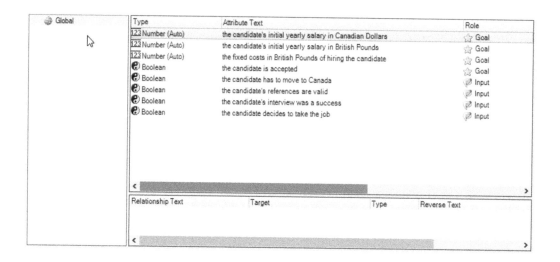

Automatic Type Assignment

While reviewing attributes, in much the same way as described above, the Edit Attribute dialog shows the suffix Automatic for any attribute whose type is not immediately detectable.

You should confirm the Type of each of the attributes in turn, by double-clicking each one and selecting the correct Type from the drop-down. It is good practice to verify the Type straightaway while you are concentrating on these attributes. There are some occasions, as you will see, where Oracle Policy Modeling prohibits us from performing an action unless the Types have been confirmed in this way, so it is good to get it done now.

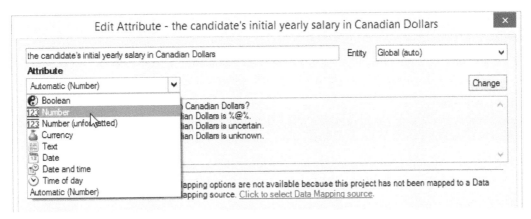

After changing all of the attributes, your Data tab should look like this. Displaying the Type Column fully provides you with both an icon and a text reference point to check your work.

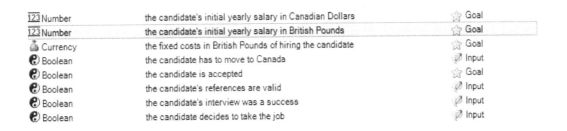

These three new attributes are all goals. They all produce an output. From the *input* information you provide, Oracle Policy Automation will be able to deduce the values that need to be assigned to them. Two of them are deduced through conditions, and one is a fixed value.

Unformatted or Formatted?

You can specify the Type of Number (unformatted) if you need to *not* inherit the regional display of numbers but instead want to use a standardized format. The integration with Oracle BI Publisher described in Chapter 11, for example, exposes unformatted values.

> **NB**: A table showing unformatted values of the different attribute types can be found online at
> http://documentation.custhelp.com/euf/assets/devdocs/cloud18d/PolicyAutomation/en/Default.htm#Gui
> des/Policy_Modeling_User_Guide/Attributes/Formatting_of_attribute_values.htm?Highlight=Unformat
> ted

Attributes without a Type

From time to time you may see the following Type icon displayed in the Data tab or the Attribute Editor. It is a sign that whatever you have written cannot be assessed as any particular type at all, so Oracle Policy Modeling creates the attribute but without a type.

In addition you will see a further error at the top of the Data tab.

This error should be the cue for you to return to your Word or Excel file in the first instance to look at the text featuring the word "chocolate" in this case – it's *probably* where you have gone wrong. Perhaps you have a piece of information that in one place you treat like a number, then in another place you treat like a date, and so on. Or perhaps you were simply not clear in your text. You will discover all manner of ways of writing clear text in this book.

In general, once you have got past the stage of building your basic data model – setting types and removing spelling mistakes – you will want to investigate your work further: it is time to turn to the Debug button.

More Attribute Advice

There are a good number of basic, good practice ideas that you can impose on yourself and other people who work with you when creating Oracle Policy Automation projects. Here are just a few to get you started.

Boolean Attributes should represent one single expression – if you intend to work with both of the following highlighted concepts, as separate elements, then create two attributes not one.

The parcel is ready to ship and **the shipping can be calculated** if
The products are picked

Avoid shortened versions or unclear references to other elements in your Oracle Policy Automation project.

The parcel's ready to ship and **the shipping can be calculated if**
The conditions are satisfied

In the example above, the first concept is written in informal English which is not appropriate for a policy document, and the second concept is unclear to the reader as to what exactly you are referring to.

Rule Writing – First Steps in Debugging

Debug Often

The Debug button in the top right-hand corner allows the rule writer to test the work that they have done. So rule designers should debug their work often as part of their normal workflow.

The Debug button introduces new vocabulary and concepts into the Oracle Policy Modeling experience. In the next screenshot, there are six areas to consider to become familiar with the Debugger. This window allows you to visualize your rules *from Oracle Policy Automation's standpoint*. The Debugger will attempt to automate your rules and produce an efficient visual interview to determine what answer(s) to give you, based on the rules you have written. If you have given Oracle Policy Modeling correctly-formed text and valid attribute definitions, then the Oracle Policy Automation Debugger will let you demonstrate that.

To make it sound even more dramatic, let us say that you will be demonstrating the expert system you have built with Oracle Policy Automation, based on the natural language rules you provided. After the following screenshot, we will review the different numbered icons shown below:

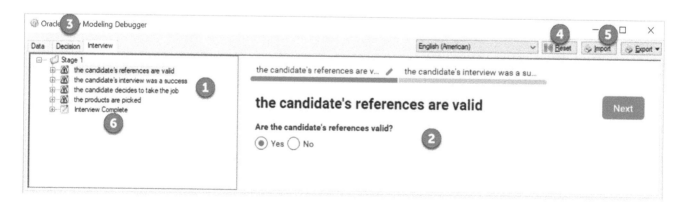

1. The list of screens and stages.

By default, the list on the left will be of all of the inputs in the Project. Policy Modeling will have transformed each one into a separate screen, or page, to show to you. Inputs that help you reach defined goals are shown here, as you will learn in a short while. These are gathered into something called a *stage* which approximates to a visual chapter.

   2. The current Interview screen content.

The current question is displayed for data input. Depending on your version and any configuration, you may also see, as shown, a coloured bar for the active screen, and icons for any completed / uncompleted screens.

   3. The Data, Decision and Interview Debug tabs.

These tabs allow the user to switch between the different ways to view the debugging content.

   4. The Restart button.

This button lets you clear all the answers to all questions and start again. If you just want to go back and look at a question again, simply click the screen on the left-hand pane. Note that in some versions of Oracle Policy Modeller, this is labelled the Reset button.

   5. The Import and Export Buttons.

It becomes useful very quickly to be able to re-test a Project with the same data. When you restart the debugger, or close Oracle Policy Modeling, your data is forgotten, so exporting and importing can save you lots of time. It also helps you build up a library of scenarios to show to colleagues or to illustrate weaknesses in your rules.

   6. Interview Complete.

This is the final screen – where you will end up, if you just follow the Screens and click Next each time.

Understanding the Parsing Process

So where did all that text come from? You have no text corresponding to "Are the candidate's references valid?" in your Word document. The text was *generated automatically* by the parser, when you entered those Boolean conditions. You can find it quite easily in the Edit Attribute dialog we referenced earlier:

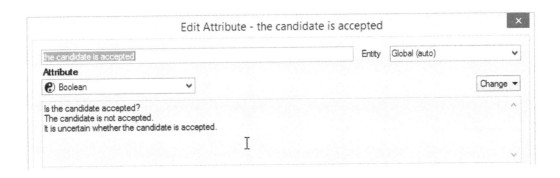

Parser Garbage In, Parser Garbage Out

The importance of getting your Word document in good shape should by now be clear – the parser uses each Boolean attribute to generate three further pieces of text automatically. So if your original text is badly structured or phrased, then the three further pieces of text may well be so too.

Check out the following example of a phrase that was not clear to begin with, on account of using a verb that is difficult to negate.

the candidate must provide a copy of their passport if
the candidate isn't Canadian

At first glance it looks just fine, doesn't it? If you try entering it yourself, remember to format it correctly before validating the text. Now look at the Data tab and see what you have created by double-clicking the attribute shown below:

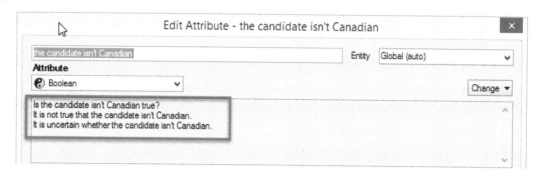

Taking shortcuts, writing 'sloppy' text, and generally not focussing on your structure will be a sure-fire way to introduce issues like this into your rule Project.

> **NB**: In version 10, both the conclusion and the condition produce bad phrasing. In version 12, although "must provide" is a challenging phrase to negate, "need not" is correctly proposed by the parser.

These kinds of issues affect you, as the rule writer and debugger, but they will also affect the end users who one day may be confronted with your strange text!

The issues just described are absolutely not reserved for the English language parser. Consider the following:

le salaire annuel initial du candidat en livres Sterling = 1000 si
    le candidat accepte la proposition d'emploi

le salaire annuel initial du candidat en Dollars Canadiens = 1000 si
    le candidat doit s'expatrier au Canada

les frais fixes d'embauche en Livres Sterling = 1000

le candidat doit fournir une photocopie de son passeport si
    il n'est pas de nationalité canadienne

This is more or less a translation of the rule Project used previously. Two issues have been introduced in order to illustrate the challenges. In the last line, a 'sloppy' wording has introduced "il" (he) – who is he? Is it a he or a she? We mean the candidate of course:

Est-ce qu'il est de nationalité canadienne?
Il n'est pas de nationalité canadienne.
Il n'est pas certain que il est de nationalité canadienne.

In the associated conclusion, we use "doit" to indicate "must". The French parser gives us the following automatically generated text for the negative: "le candidat ne doit pas fournir une photocopie de son passeport".

But "the candidate *must not* provide a copy of their passport" is most certainly not what was intended. We mean that they *don't need to provide it* which is not the same as not being permitted to provide one! So we see a distinct difference here between the English and French parsers. In Chapter 15, you will find a (non-exhaustive) list of the kind of differences you might find in other language parsers in Policy Modeling. You should however always refer to the documentation for complete details.

In this case, and in many others, a conscious attempt to provide clearer phrases and to choose more appropriate verbs, will result in less time spent "fixing" attribute text. Using "obliged to" produces a clear, and cleanly expressed, phrase in both positive and negative forms.

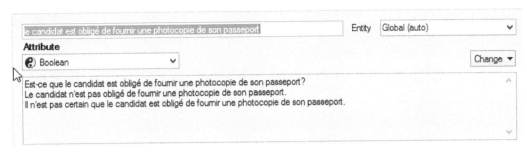

Even if you don't ever intend to write anything except English, hopefully the point is clear enough. If you have entered the example with the illustrated problems, correct it to look like this before continuing.

The candidate is obliged to provide a photocopy of their passport if

The candidate is not of Canadian nationality

Debugging the Interview

As you learned in the first chapter, one way to deploy an Oracle Policy rule Project is to create a visual interview, sometimes referred to as a **web determination**. When you select the Interview tab of the Debug window, this is precisely what you are looking at. Of course, right now there is absolutely no configuration of the interview, so the process feels quite raw. Oracle Policy Modeling simply displays a set of automatically generated screens for you to navigate through to complete the determination process.

Debug Window Interview Tab

The Interview tab will be useful in understanding the process of determination. It can reveal the concept of pertinence or relevance which will be important when your rule Project is more complex.

Start the Debug window and make sure the Interview tab is active. Now enter a value for the first piece of information – click No to indicate that the candidate's references are *not* valid.

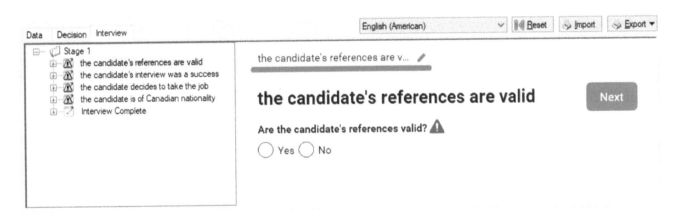

You will learn more about Interviews, Screens, and the other visual components on display here in Chapters 6 and 7. For now, you can use the Interview tab to navigate visually in your rules and enter data as an end-user will.

Relevance

When you click Next, watch what happens to the second screen in the list – it is greyed out. If you hover your mouse over the screen and click the details icon, you will be told the information on this screen is not relevant.

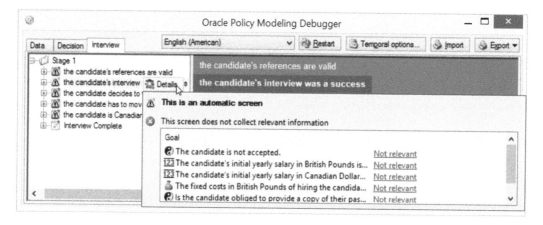

The question on this screen, regarding the interview success *is not relevant*. It is not relevant in the context of the goal that was set (to find out if the candidate was accepted) because the conditions were connected with "and", meaning both have to be met for your candidate to be accepted. The information on this screen will not change the policy results or the outcome of this interview. So the Web Determination skips the screen completely. Of course you can click on it and change the value, but from a logical point of view, the goal outcome will not change.

> **NB**: The concept of relevancy underpins much of Interview behaviour, and contains several complex ideas. You can find the documentation on this subject here:
> http://documentation.custhelp.com/euf/assets/devdocs/cloud18d/PolicyAutomation/en/Default.htm#Guides/Policy_Modeling_User_Guide/Design_interviews/Definition_of_relevant.htm?Highlight=relevancy

Determination

The process of determination means not just determining an answer, but using the most efficient way to do it. You can say that Policy Automation is always looking for the most efficient way to get your job done – and sometimes this can be both confusing and useful. Confusing because when you begin working, it can feel strange that the Interview experience is not as linear as designing, for example, a set of database forms, and useful because it can help you identify attributes that don't work, or which are not behaving as you expect.

If you now click the Reset or Restart button in the Debugger, and enter Yes for the first question, notice how the second Screen does not go grey – because now you have said that the candidate has met one half of the conditions, it becomes relevant to show the second screen since the candidate might have met the other criteria as well, in which case they *would be* accepted.

Debug Window Data Tab

The Data tab in the debug window shows you the raw data of your interview. If you are looking for a more methodical way to enter information and test the outcomes of your determination, the Data tab will be useful. Notice how questions that have been answered show both their *value* and their corresponding *text*. It can be confusing at first, but by examining an example we can clarify things.

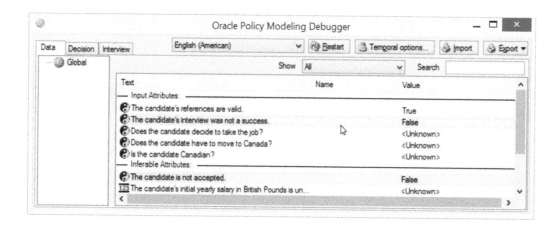

In the example above, the question "Was the candidate's interview a success?" was answered with a "No". So the *value* of the attribute is False. At the same time, the Data tab of the debug window displays the negative version of the *attribute text*: The candidate's interview was not a success.

If you are not yet comfortable, switch between the Data and Interview tabs in the debug window to observe the changes. Finally go to the Data tab in the main Oracle Policy Modeling window and double click the attribute to review the generated text:

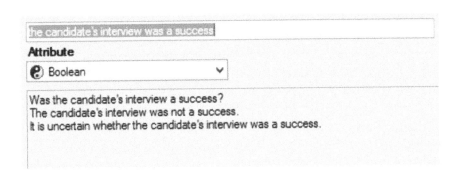

Unknown Values

The Data tab of the debug window shows Unknown for the majority of your attributes at the moment. Unknown here means that the question has not been asked yet. When using the Data tab, you can reset the value of an attribute to Unknown by double-clicking the attribute and selecting Unknown from the pop-up window:

The concept of Unknown values will become more important, later on, as we work with situations where you might not have every piece of information to hand and your business policy needs to be able to cope.

Uncertain Values

If you look at the Set Attribute Value dialog shown above, there is a fourth possible value called Uncertain. If Unknown means the question has never been answered, then Uncertain means the question has been asked, but the answer is uncertain. Again, a demonstration will help. In your Debug window, click Restart. Then using the Data tab and the Set Attribute Value dialog, set the first two values as follows:

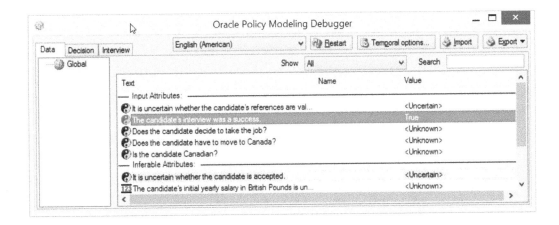

Notice that the inferable attributes (those that can be deduced from your data entry) now tell us that is *uncertain* whether the candidate is accepted. They *might be accepted*. But the information available does not allow a definitive "yes" or "no". Uncertainty is a powerful tool in Oracle Policy Automation since it can help identify situations where more information might be required before a decision can be taken, or where the addition of another rule may help clarify the situation or perhaps the interview can conclude successfully without *all* the information being available.

There are some excellent resources on the Internet to help understand the concept of Uncertain and when it is applied.

> **NB:** A good site is http://www.varsitytutors.com/hspt_verbal-help/determining-whether-a-statement-is-true-false-or-uncertain

Debug Window Decision Tab

The Decision tab is blank, until you decide what exactly you wish to *investigate*. You investigate, in normal circumstances, some output from Oracle Policy Modeller. For example, in the screenshot below, the inferable attribute "the candidate is accepted" can be investigated since it is deduced from the rules you have created. To investigate, just right click the inferred attribute in the Data tab of the debugger and select Show Decision.

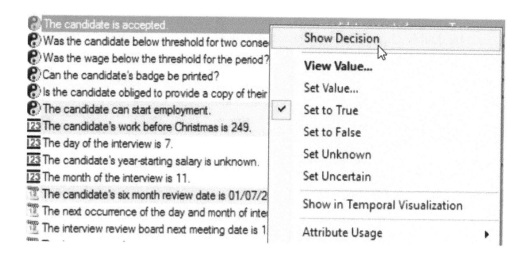

Once you have selected it, the Decision tab of the Debugger will open and reveal the reasoning behind the decision of the Debugger. In the screenshot below, notice how the Debugger puts the relevant information at your disposal to better understand the process and the result. The context menu allows you to change values and even to visualize where in your rule documents you have mentioned the attribute. This is a great tool for working out what happened, and where and why it happened!

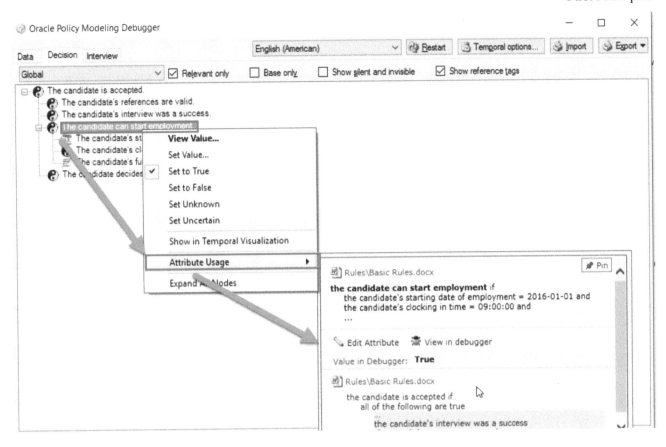

NB: I can't stress this enough – the debugger Decision tab is a really useful tool not just for debugging but for understanding rules and logic in a Project. Use it often!

NB: The View Decision menu item will be replaced by Investigate when you are investigating an attribute whose value is unknown.

Region in the Debugger

Switch back to the Interview tab in the Debugger. Enter all the information requested, answering "Yes" to every one of the questions. The process will navigate to the Interview Complete Screen.

You will notice there is a difference in the display of those numbers and currency. The currency attribute is displayed, in my case, with a £ symbol – the currency symbol for my chosen region in my rule Project. The numbers are not showing any currency symbol, but they are showing "," as the thousands separator and both types use "." as the decimal point.

The currency symbol is going to be useful if you *always* intend to have only one currency in the interview, but additional currencies might have to be formatted as numbers, to either include the currency in the attribute text, or perhaps (using techniques discussed in Chapters 8 and 9) to display the symbol graphically using another method.

> **NB**: To learn more about where the regional formats are managed in Oracle Policy Modeling, read Chapter 15 "Languages and Regions".

More Data Types and more Debugging

Oracle Policy Modeling attributes can be of several different types:

Number (unformatted) attributes

Unformatted numbers do not show any separator. They are used by Oracle Policy Modeling itself in the Debugger and they are used in integration with Oracle BI Publisher to display raw numbers. You will learn more about the role of Oracle BI Publisher in Chapter 7.

Date attributes

Date attributes are also affected by the notion of regional formatting. In the Date tab of the debugger window, you will need to enter dates in a region-neutral format YYYY-MM-DD (for example 2019-02-09 in the Data tab of the debugger). The values will display in the same tab as per your region. In the Interview tab as well as the Data tab *text* column, you will see and work with them in region-specific format. "The candidate's starting date of employment is 09/02/2019." (If you have the same region as the example shown earlier in this chapter.)

Date Time attributes

As above, only with the inclusion of the time in HH:MM:SS z (where z is the time zone of your Project which you visualized earlier on the Oracle Policy Modeling language pane). So you might enter 2019-02-09 10:35:00 GMT in the debugger as the region-neutral value but the text will display (if you have the same region as shown earlier) "The candidate's date and time of interview is 09/02/2019 10:35 GMT."

Time of Day attributes

Time of day attributes are written HH:MM:SS and you will enter them in your interview in this way.

Text attributes

Text attributes such as the candidate's last name will require "straight quotes" to define their value if you are writing in rules. As you will discover later, they will also need special handling in Microsoft Excel.

Extending Your Example Project

Adding new attributes and rules to our document

To demonstrate these attribute types you will extend your current Project. To enable you to view the parsing of the different attributes and to create attributes in a more structured fashion, you should use the Oracle Policy Automation Data tab. You should close the debugger before you begin these steps. Use the New Attribute button on the Data tab to enter the following further attributes directly.

Type	Attribute Text	Role
Time of day	the candidate's clocking in time	Goal
Text	the candidate's full name	Goal
Date and time	the candidate's date and time of interview	Goal
Date	the candidate's starting date of employment	Goal

> **NB**: Entering attributes in this way is easier to control and allows for immediate verification of their text, type, and the generated phrases, *before* you begin writing in Microsoft Word.

Enter the following new rule into your document. Feel free to adjust the date and time to something else. This is purely for instructional purposes.

the candidate can start employment if
>> the candidate's starting date of employment = 2016-01-01 and
>> the candidate's clocking in time = 09:00:00 and
>> the candidate's full name is certain

In the above example, there are three things to note.

1. In your document, the attributes are underlined once you have validated them. If they are not underlined, double-check your spelling and compare with the attribute text you provided.

2. The rules use region-neutral dates and time as part of their definition.

3. The final line is a Boolean condition, since there is a verb. The certain operator can be used to reliably respond if the information is certain, by means of a true or false value.

Launch the debugger and see how the data you enter is managed in the Interview tab, and how it is displayed in the Data tab.

These new attributes can be used for self-study in later sections of this book.

Rule Writing – Linking Rules

Building Links into your documents

The rule Project you have been working on is now beginning to resemble a stream of consciousness. Lots of good ideas, all written down on paper one after the other. This can be a risk since the more you write in this way, the more it becomes difficult for you, and especially for other people, to read and understand the complete picture.

This is definitely one area of your Project where you will need to be especially careful. As a learning exercise, this Project is acceptable. But it will soon resemble spaghetti.

Writing rules requires rigorous use of features like headers, comments and descriptive text as we have already mentioned. In addition, rules need to be structured in more efficient ways in order to deliver the results you need. Take a look at the following extended rule document.

the candidate is accepted if
>> the candidate's references are valid and
>> the candidate's interview was a success and
>> the candidate can start employment

the candidate's initial yearly salary in British Pounds = 10000 if
>> the candidate decides to take the job

the candidate's initial yearly salary in Canadian Dollars = 30000 if
>> the candidate has to move to Canada

the fixed costs in British Pounds of hiring the candidate = 1000

the candidate is obliged to provide a copy of their passport if
>> the candidate is not Canadian

the candidate can start employment if
>> the candidate's starting date of employment = 2016-01-01 and
>> the candidate's clocking in time = 09:00:00 and
>> the candidate's full name is certain

The two red-highlighted areas of text match exactly (except for the "if"). In this way, two parts of the document have become linked. The *conclusion* that the candidate can start employment is itself a *condition* of the candidate being accepted. This is one way of creating connections between parts of your rule Project.

Switching to the Oracle Policy Modeling Data tab, there is now a visual reminder of the new construct. This is what is known as an intermediate attribute.

Intermediate Attributes

This linking feature is extremely powerful. It is not based on the order of the text, indeed the text can be in completely different *documents* in the same Project. This is a powerful tool for making your project more structured and clearer to the unfamiliar eye – documents in Word can become self-contained units of a wider project, that all link together.

Joining Attributes

If you wish to experiment with moving the paragraph to another document (to add a second document, click the New Word Document on the Rules tab) within the same Project, then cut and paste - not forgetting to validate both documents (so as to update the information about moved attributes). You will notice the following changes to the visual cue to the associated icon:

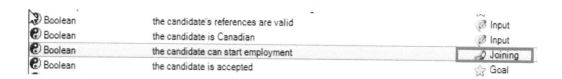

At any time, for any attribute in your Data tab you can right-click the attribute to discover where it is used. In the case of the attribute above, this returns the following (the names of the files may be different in your case).

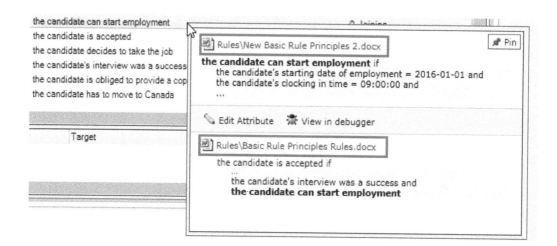

Rules Writing - Organize your Project Folders

The concept of linking can help you keep on top of linked attributes and multiple documents in your Project. Bear in mind that, in a Project, you will need to create several different documents unless it is a trivial exercise.

Keeping Types of Rules Separate

As you will discover in this book, and as you may have seen in other products, there are several different kinds of rule that you might be called upon to create. For example

1. A rule to calculate the benefit someone is entitled to.

This is a business rule, directly related to the business objective.

2. A rule to decide whether to display a particular question to the interviewee.

This rule manages the interview procedure.

3. A rule to set the exchange rate, which is modified once a month.

Create Folders for Clarity

The above examples hopefully show you that these different kinds of rules exist (let's call them business, procedure and system rules) and it makes absolute sense to separate them into different documents and/or folders in your Project. Create them right at the start so you don't forget!

Rule Writing – Avoiding Loops and Issues

The structure of the goal "the candidate is accepted" now looks something like the diagram on the following page.

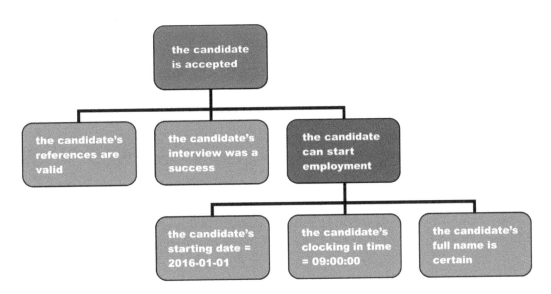

In the diagram above, the *top-level* attribute is displayed in pink. It represents the goal. The blue boxes represent *base-level* attributes. They must be either acquired from the end user or some other source. The brown box represents your intermediate attribute, whose value can be inferred from the three base-level attributes below it in the picture.

Users of version 10 are extremely lucky since they can produce documents like the schema shown, directly from Oracle Policy Modeling. For more information, see the section on differences with version 10. Whatever version you are using, identifying base-level attributes is very useful since they need to be provided as input in order for your process to be automated.

Logical Loops

Linking text together can be a source of logical loops if you accidentally get mixed up. For example, something in your rule Project cannot be a condition of itself. The rule below shows an example:

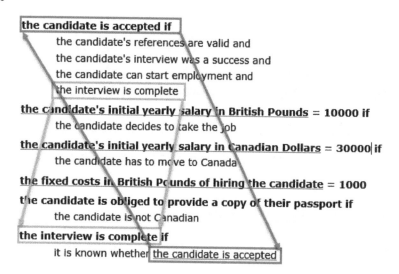

The candidate is accepted is the goal. The candidate is accepted is also a condition of the interview being complete, which is a condition of the candidate being accepted. Upon validation (with no error visible in your Microsoft Word document), Oracle Policy Modeling highlights the issue with:

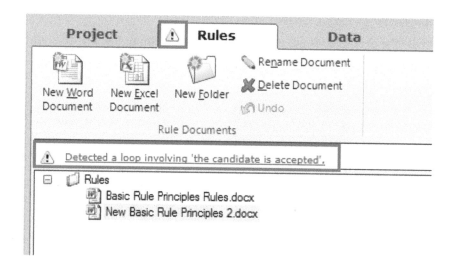

There *are* situations where a logical loop may be actually correct, but they are beyond the scope of this introductory book.

Other Common Issues

Probably the most common way to introduce errors involving failed links into your documents is simply to not be rigorous and sticking to conventions such as:

- Always using the correct apostrophe to show possession in English.

- Always writing with the definite article ("the", "le", "Der" and so on).

- Always looking for the underline that shows you have matched original text.

- Always commenting and documenting *why* something is where it is, and what it does.

These rules may not apply for all languages (especially apostrophe usage) but similar ground rules will benefit all rule writers – make sure all your team members look out for them.

Rule Writing – Grouping for Clarity

Before looking at the next way to better organize your rules in a rule Project, it's time to make a few changes to your rule document. These changes introduce an intermediate attribute based on some of the existing text, and make a few simple comments in green to help you follow the different steps.

For simplicity, although in a previous example we discussed placing text in two different Microsoft Word documents, to make it easier for you to read here, the text has been placed in one single file. To delete the file, first ensure that all the text has been copied from the file into the remaining one, then click Delete Document. You can undo your deletion with the Undo Delete button. The undo operation is available for a short time, before the button becomes greyed out. The deleted file is stored in the folder `C:\Users\...Oracle Policy Modeling Projects\Project Name\.undo` with a filename like `d1`, `d2` before it is automatically deleted.

Here is the file as you will work with in this series of practical examples:

Interview Completion Goal

the interview is complete if
> it is known whether <u>the candidate is accepted</u> and
> it is known whether <u>the candidate has to move to Canada</u> and
> it is known whether <u>the candidate is Canadian</u>

Candidate Evaluation Goal

the candidate is accepted if
> the candidate's references are valid and
> the candidate's interview was a success and
> the candidate can start employment and
> the candidate decides to take the job

Candidate Starting Employment Evaluation

the candidate can start employment if
> <u>the candidate's starting date of employment</u> = 2016-01-01 and
> <u>the candidate's clocking in time</u> = 09:00:00 and
> <u>the candidate's full name</u> is certain

the candidate is obliged to provide a copy of their passport if
> the candidate is not Canadian

Salary and Costs Calculations and Fixed Values

<u>**the candidate's initial yearly salary in British Pounds**</u> = **10000 if**
> the candidate decides to take the job

<u>**the candidate's initial yearly salary in Canadian Dollars**</u> = **30000 if**
> the candidate has to move to Canada

<u>**the fixed costs in British Pounds of hiring the candidate**</u> = **1000**

Note that the above is not a very likely interview assessment in real life – most of the goals have been added to simply demonstrate functionality. Several features (fixed salary values, fixed dates, fixed times) would not be necessarily a good approach in real life.

The areas in green are formatted using traditional Word tools, and are invisible to Oracle Policy Modeling and the parser. Although the layout of the file is better, the main sections suffer from an excess of operators. It is not natural to see "and..and..and" everywhere. So that's your next exercise: grouping.

Grouping AND

As an alternative to writing like the example above, you make use of the following to make a rule document easier to read. You replace the initial section concerning the completion of the interview with this alternative:

Interview Completion Goal

the interview is complete if
> all of the following are satisfied
>> it is known whether <u>the candidate is accepted</u>
>> it is known whether <u>the candidate has to move to Canada</u>
>> it is known whether <u>the candidate is Canadian</u>

Candidate Evaluation Goal

the candidate is accepted if
> all of the following are true
>> the candidate's references are valid
>> the candidate's interview was a success
>> the candidate can start employment
>> the candidate decides to take the job

Both of the variations shown above are acceptable in English, as is the shortened version all. In languages other than English, the operator will take a similar form:

l'entretien est terminé si
> tous dans la suite sont vrais
>> il est connu ou pas que <u>le candidat a accepté</u>
>> il est connu ou pas que <u>le candidat doit s'expatrier au Canada</u>
>> il est connu ou pas que <u>le candidat est de nationalité canadienne</u>

le candidat est accepté si
> tous dans la suite sont satisfaits
>> les références du candidat sont valables
>> le candidat a fait un bon entretien
>> le candidat peut être signé |
>> le candidat accepte le poste

The wording of the all grouping operator is a little more clumsy in this language (French).

Grouping text has required the use of **Level 2** formatting. You can simply select existing lines and click the **Increase Indent** button on the Policy Modeling ribbon to move the text slightly to the right and format it with the different colour shown. The list of five levels can also be accessed using the levels drop-down on the ribbon.

Debug your Work

Debug the rule Project as it stands and ensure that there are no issues. Enter values for all the base attributes and verify in the Data tab of the debug window that all inferred attributes are displayed with suitable values. Now is a good time to click the Export button in the debugger to save an XML data set (XML File, with XDS extension) for later use.

In the next section, we will study it in more detail. For now, we can say that the line in yellow is proved by the lines in pink. all of the items are true refers to the following pink lines.

Grouping "OR"

The same facility exists for writing rules that use the OR logical operator. In the following example, two conditions are connected with the OR operator. One or other of the conditions must be met for the conclusion to be true. Consider an example of OR below:

the candidate is obliged to provide a copy of their passport if
> the candidate is not Canadian or
> the candidate's driving license has expired

This can equally be restructured to the grouped version using the following text:

the candidate is obliged to provide a copy of their passport if
    at least one of the following is true
        the candidate is not Canadian
        the candidate's driving license has expired

So if you are not Canadian, or you are Canadian and your driving licence has expired, then you will be obliged to provide a copy of your passport.

Truth Tables

At the time of writing, the Oracle Policy Automation documentation for version 10 contains examples of truth tables https://docs.oracle.com/html/E27551_01/Content/Reference/Truth_tables.htm

For help with visualizing truth tables and entering AND, OR style logic, there is a good interactive tool at the following address http://turner.faculty.swau.edu/mathematics/materialslibrary/truth/. There are many other resources on the Internet.

Rule Writing – Structured Levels in Word

The previous section introduced the concept of different levels within your Word document. The coloured levels offer another opportunity to visually clarify your rule structure.

Writing Rules with Levels

Writing rules in your Project with multiple levels offers a powerful and effective way to structure your document. To begin, we can add the following paragraph to our Word rule document. This example concerns the assigned clocking in time, and the actual arrival time of the candidate on their first day on the job.

the candidate's first day at work gets off to a good start if
    the candidate arrives on time
        the candidate's arrival time <= the candidate's clocking in time

In the above example, the level 1 line (in yellow) is proven by the level 2 line below it. Now compare that with the alternative method you saw earlier:

the candidate's first day at work gets off to a good start if
    the candidate arrives on time

the candidate arrives on time if
    the candidate's arrival time <= the candidate's clocking in time

The examples above will form the basis of the next set of practical tasks designed to familiarize you with Oracle Policy Modeling. Compare how they display in your Word document and the debugger.

Common Parsing Problems

The rule above has deliberately included some unclear text. Unclear, in the sense that the validation and parsing process will have difficulty extracting the verb, and thus the meaning, from your phrase.

To start with, enter the single paragraph version with only one conclusion line and both level one and two (pink and yellow) condition text. Validate your work and navigate to the Data tab of your main window and review the generated text for the attribute:

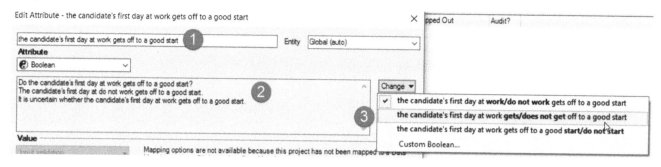

1. This is the text you entered in the Word document.

2. The parsed text provided by default is incorrect.

3. Use the Change button, as shown, to select the correct parsing of your text.

Repeat the process for the attribute the candidate arrives on time. Observe the attribute text that has been generated is, again, not correct. Simplify your attribute to read `the candidate is on time` and click the OK button. Oracle Policy Modeling will display a warning message:

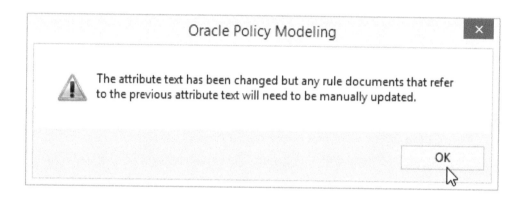

Bear this in mind when changing attribute text in the Data tab. Rework could be required in other documents.

4. Take a moment to also change the **Type** of the attribute the candidate's arrival time to Time of Day from Time of Day (Auto).

Compare your work with the result shown below:

the candidate's first day at work gets off to a good start if
      the candidate is on time
          the candidate's arrival time <= the candidate's clocking in time

---

NB: It is vital that when you write rules that *seem* simple to you, that you check your work. This example with two lines required multiple corrections to provide a working solution.

Leveraging Levels in the Debugger

Start the Debugger and if necessary, either click Restart or if you have previously exported your data set, Import it now. Enter any remaining base attributes to ensure all inferences are made. Your Data tab in the debug window should look like this:

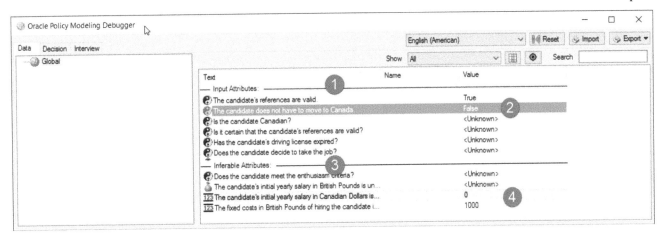

In the screenshot, you should be clear on the following points:

1. Data needs to be inputted, either by importing or entering data, for your Input Attributes.
2. As you enter values, they are displayed here.
3. Inferable Attributes are deduced or determined based on your input.
4. Any changes to deductions will be highlighted by a green bar which will flash when a result is changed.

The inferable attributes are useful for you to see *what* has been determined, but there is an even more useful feature designed to help you understand *why* something has been determined. You briefly looked at it earlier. Now, right-click the interview is complete and select Show Decision. Your debugger should now switch to the Decision tab.

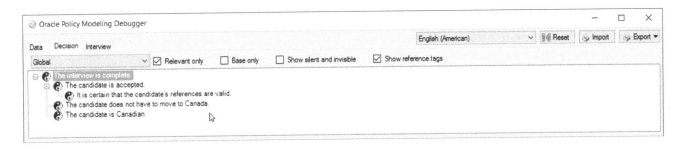

The content of this window is the decision report, or the explanation of why the determination was made. It helps visualize how an answer was reached. You will, of course, have seen that this also displayed in the Interview tab when the interview is complete, in the form of a clickable icon:

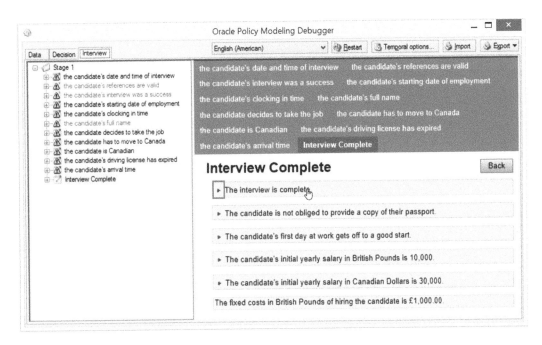

The exact layout of the Interview Complete screen will look slightly different in later versions of Oracle Policy Modeling. Here is a screenshot from a more recent release, notice how the icons have been replaced with text labels marked Show Details or Hide Details. Notice also the stages of the Interview are shown either as blue tabs (above) or blue bars with text labels (below). You will learn all about Interviews in Chapters 6 and 7.

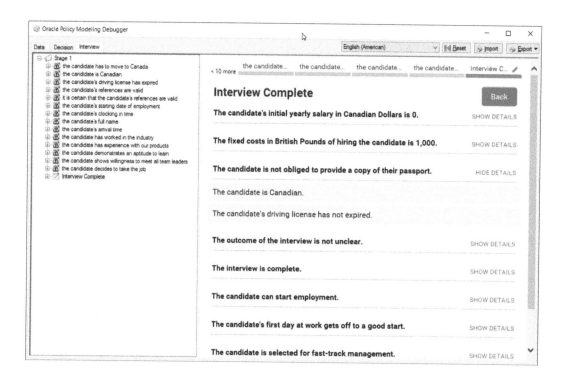

The notion of a decision report, or **explanation** as it is known in this version, is an important part of understanding the behaviour of your rules, and also an important resource for the end user. In Chapter 8, you will find out more about the role of explanations and how to use them in both Projects and also in documents – such as PDF files for output.

Multiple Levels in a Document

The use of levels in your documents allows a more structured approach to writing, perhaps at the price of losing some natural readability. However a cleanly written, level-based paragraph should be quite easy to follow. Consider the following example.

> **the candidate is selected for fast-track management if**
>   the candidate meets the experience criteria
>   all of the following are satisfied
>   the candidate has worked in the industry
>   the candidate has experience with our products
>   or
>   the candidate meets the enthusiasm criteria
>   all of the following are satisfied
>   the candidate demonstrates an aptitude to learn
>   the candidate shows willingness to meet all team leaders

The candidate will be selected based on two sets of criteria, and they only have to meet one set. The output in the Decision tab of the debugger would look something like this, assuming you have entered the relevant attribute values.

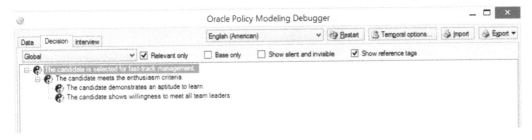

Notice how in the Word text, the structure must both "open and close". The first set of criteria, based on experience, drops down as far as level three. Prior to the next section, the OR logical operator must return to the level of the initial line defining the experience criteria as a Boolean, and so must the line defining the Boolean for the enthusiasm criteria. Building this structure can at first give you a headache, but just remember the following

- If you have two or more sets of criteria, they must be set up on the same level (here, level 1).

- No matter what levels you use, when you switch to the next set – in this case by using the OR operator – remember to return to the initial level (here, level 1). The operator (here, OR) needs to be on the same level as the sets of criteria.

- The OR (or other operator) should be on a separate line.

Debugger Information

Notice that in the debugger there is also the ability to display non-relevant information by unchecking the checkbox Relevant only. This feature allows us, in this case, to review the alternative criteria at the same time. It also demonstrates that the debugger is performing the determination in the same way, irrespective of the use of the Interview, Data or Decision tabs.

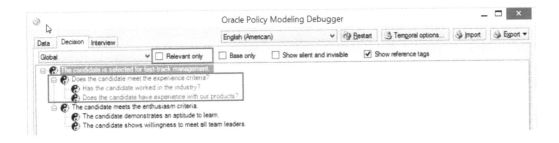

Showing Base attributes only can be useful as a shortcut to seeing the data provided by the end-user or your external system. The other options will be detailed in a forthcoming chapter.

Rule Writing – Toolbar Icon Helpers

Sometimes rule writing requires parts of your document to be temporarily hidden from the parser and Oracle Policy Modeling. The Toggle Comment button in the ribbon allows you to do just that.

Toggle Comments

For this button to function correctly, you must have already formatted the text in some way using standard Oracle Policy Modeling styles. Selecting the line or lines and clicking the Toggle Comment button applies special styles, prefixed by **Comment**.

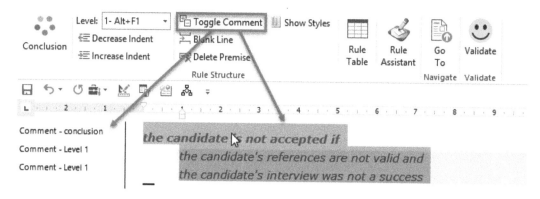

When you click it again, the original style is reapplied. This is much more efficient, in this context, than using Blank Line (see below).

Clear Formatting

Similarly, if you just want to wipe all the formatting from a piece of text in Word, select the text and click the Blank Line button also shown in the previous screenshot. All formatting will be removed from the selection.

Delete Premise

A premise is a conclusion or condition for one of your rules. Placing the cursor on your condition and clicking the Delete Premise button shown above, should delete the text and formatting of the entire line.

There are some specifics to be aware of, however, which are designed to protect the writer from removing something that is potentially not yet ready for deletion. In the diagram below, the numbers correspond to different cursor positions. Placing the cursor on the line indicated produces the actions and /or warnings listed.

1. The Conclusion cannot be removed as it still has conditions.

2. The Level One line is deleted, all other related lines are moved up one level.

3. The premise cannot be deleted as it still has sub-premises.

4. The grouping operator all of the following are satisfied is deleted and the selected Level 3 (blue) line is deleted. The remaining Level 3 line is moved up to Level 2.

5. The OR operator line is removed.

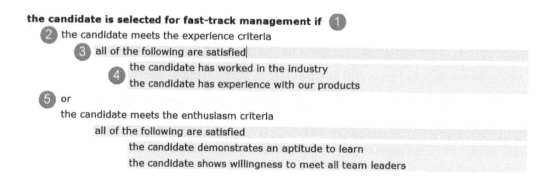

Rule Writing – References

Creating References to Documentation

When creating rule Projects and documents, it is quite possible that the rules you are planning to write are themselves based on existing documents. Perhaps a colleague has forwarded you the legal text in a PDF file and you wish to base your outcomes upon it. Or, more specifically, perhaps articles or paragraphs needs to be referenced. The references can be added using a simple notation.

Adding References

Add a reference using [] square brackets at the beginning of the relevant phrase in the Word document. Oracle Policy Modeling will automatically format the text in grey when the Validate button is clicked.

or

[Criteria B]the candidate meets the enthusiasm criteria

all of the following are satisfied

[Criteria B1]the candidate demonstrates an aptitude to learn

[Criteria B2]the candidate shows willingness to meet all team leaders|

Viewing References in the Debugger

When the debugger is launched, the correct references are displayed in the Interview Complete screen when the user clicks on the explanation icon:

▾ The candidate is selected for fast-track management.

⊟ The candidate meets the enthusiasm criteria. *Criteria B*

☐ The candidate demonstrates an aptitude to learn. *Criteria B1*

☐ The candidate shows willingness to meet all team leaders. *Criteria B2*

They are similarly displayed, in italics at the end of the text, in the Decision tab of the debugger.

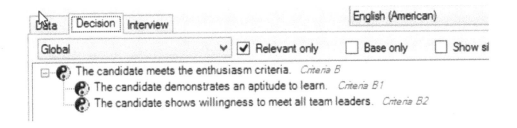

Advantages of References

Adding references in this way can contribute positively to the maintenance of the document, the alignment with source material, as well as the overall understanding of the content of your Word document.

Combined with the previously described comments, styling and other tools, Oracle Policy Modeling gives you everything you need to write clear, efficient and easily referenced rules.

Rule Writing – Names

When writing rules and creating attributes in Oracle Policy Modeling, the writer should pay attention to the need to create reliable methods to share information with the outside world. Given that an attribute text can be translated into many different languages, Policy Automation needs an alternative, language-independent way to reference it.

Thus, for every attribute in your rule Project, you should ensure that a valid Name is added. Names are required for many things, including

- Creating Forms.

- Mapping data to external sources.

- Working with Substitutions.

Edit Attribute - the candidate is accepted ✕

the candidate is accepted | Entity | Global (auto) ⌄

Attribute
ℓ Boolean ⌄

Name

candidate_accepted

Use %candidate_accepted% to show this attribute's value on a screen

OK | Cancel | Explanation options...

An example of an attribute with both text and a name is shown above. Each of the described uses will be explained in this book. As a matter of course, you should ensure that your attributes have Names defined. A Name cannot contain spaces or special characters other than the underscore and the period. Names will also be needed for other elements of your Project as you will learn in Chapter 8.

NB: All through this book, it is good practice to take backups of your work – particularly at the end of a chapter. This book will remind you when there are large numbers of modifications to be applied. In a real world project, you can also use the Repository to store versions of your work, as you will find out in later chapters.

To create a backup copy of this Project follow the steps below:
- Make sure all documents in your Project are closed.
- Navigate to the Summary Pane of your Project.
- Click the Share a Copy of this Project button.
- The resulting Zip Archive can be placed somewhere safe.

The screenshot below shows the button. You should be aware that this button was only introduced in February 2016's release of Oracle Policy Modeling.

Rule Writing – Version 10 Differences

Bearing in mind that you may find yourself working on the previous version of Oracle Policy Modeling, version 10, it is useful to list here the major differences. Going into too much detail is beyond the scope of a book such as this, however this should be enough to get started working with version 10.

Working with Project Files

In version 10, the Project is created in much the same way with the same options before you begin. However the following changes should be noted, which are highlighted in the next screenshot. In the course of the other chapters of this book, other differences will be highlighted.

- Various folders are created by default. They can be added to or deleted.

- Rules documents are added manually. No default Word file is added.

- The Data tab is replaced by a **Properties** file. The file is added manually.

- Existing Word, PDF or other Windows documents can be added to a Project, for example scope documents or other items of interest. External files cannot be edited in Oracle Policy Modeling but double-clicking opens the registered application, for example Adobe Acrobat Reader.

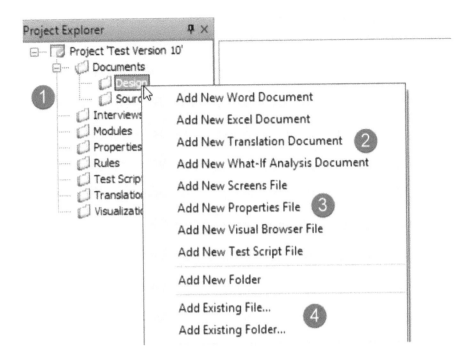

Working with Attributes

Writing rules in version 10 is similar, with one fundamental difference. *Any* non-Boolean attribute must be explicitly declared. The process should be undertaken once the Properties file described above has been added to the Project.

In the following example, a new rule has been added to version 10 and the formatting applied. The conditions involve non-Boolean attributes which must be declared.

The validation button is replaced with the **compilation button** showing the same icon. Failing to declare attributes in this way results in the error shown. To correct the error, follow the steps as shown below:

1. Select the attribute text using the mouse, click Add Attribute from the ribbon.

2. Add and Public Name, and select the correct Type.

3. Select the Properties file from the File drop-down.

4. Click OK.

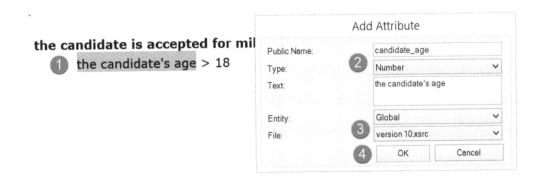

5. Click Compile to complete the process and confirm the new attribute. The presence of compiled text and attributes is clear from the hidden text that is shown on screen (but not printed, by default).

[b1] the candidate is accepted for military service if
[p1 > 18] the candidate's age > 18

The new attribute should now be visible in the Properties file. Accessing the Properties files in order to review attributes in your Project is done via the main window.

1. Double-click the Properties file to open it from Oracle Policy Modeling.

2. Further attributes can be added directly to the Properties file by right-clicking and choosing Add Attribute.

3. Existing attributes can be modified by double-clicking.

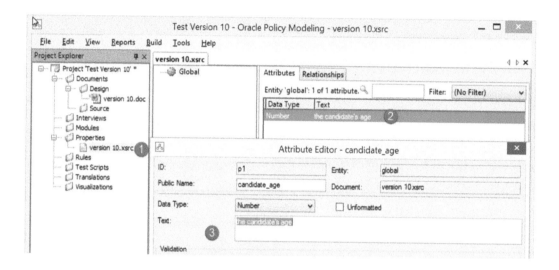

Working with the Debugger

The debugger in version 10 comes in two different forms. From the Build menu, click Build > Build and Debug. To access the debug window and Data and Decision tabs, click Without Screens. To access the Interview tab as well, click With Screens. The rule Project is automatically deployed to a built-in debugging server and the Interview tab is displayed.

To stop the debugger, select Build > Stop Debugging

Working with References in Version 10

To add references to your rule document, add them at the start of an existing condition or conclusion lines between the hidden marker text and your own, followed by a single tab character.

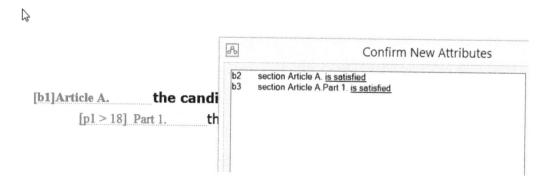

NB: The references are cumulative, and Part 1 becomes Article A. Part 1. When the debugger is used, or the interview deployed, the references are shown in the explanation which is accessed by clicking the icon next to the relevant conclusion.

Vocabulary

It may help to have a summary of the major differences in vocabulary. This table attempts to align wording with either similar or identical functionality. It is intended only as an aid to migration.

Version 10	Version 12
Properties File	Data Tab
Translations Folder	Project Tab Language Pane
Build and Debug (two choices)	Debug button
Decision Report	Explanation
Public Name	Attribute Name
Document	Form
Screen File	Interview Tab
Test Script	Project Tab Testing Pane
Question Screen	Interview Screen
Screen Flow	No longer used. Not migrated.
Screen Order	Interview Stages
Visualizations	N/A
N/A	Inclusions
Modules	N/A
File > Project Properties	Project Tab Summary Pane
Output Window	Warning Pane
List of Values	Project Tab Value Lists Pane

About live Debugging in Version 12

In the latest versions of Oracle Policy Modeler, starting in August 2016, the debugger is "change aware". This means that if you have a debugging session open, and you make changes to Word or other documents or attributes in your project, then the debugger will instantly be aware of these changes. A message will be displayed, in the top of the Debugger window, that changes have been detected.

Clicking the Apply link, as in the example above, will cause the debugging to refresh to reflect your new changes. This is a time-saving feature that avoids you having to close or reload the debugger to see your latest changes.

> **NB**: Remember we said that you should make backups of Projects while working with this book? Well now is a good time to do so with your first Project. If you need a reminder of how to do it, you will find it on page 42.

Writing Rules with Functions

This chapter shows how to use the power of Oracle Policy Automation's Functions. They increase the amount of processing we can perform in rule documents and create more complex rules.

You will continue to work with the existing attributes from the previous chapter, and will learn how to improve their behavior.

What this chapter is

This chapter will explore a variety of useful functions in different categories through practical examples you can follow yourself. By the end of the chapter, you will be able to work with any Oracle Policy Automation function.

What this chapter is not

This chapter is not a function reference. You can find them online, at the time of writing, at the following Internet URL:

http://documentation.custhelp.com/euf/assets/devdocs/cloud18d/PolicyAutomation/en/Default.htm#Guides/Policy_Modeling_User_Guide/Work_with_rules/Function_references/Function_references.htm

Links in the body of this page give links to all available languages. This URL will change over time, and can be accessed through the main Documentation link for Oracle Policy Automation:

http://www.oracle.com/technetwork/apps-tech/policy-automation/documentation/index.html

Writing Rules with Functions – Basic Principles

Some ideas in Policy Modeler cannot be achieved by simply asking questions – or, they would take such a long time for the end user to work out, they would wonder why they were using an "automation" tool at all.

Functions work with your attributes to execute more complex determinations. As always, it is better to start with an example. It would be a good idea to take a copy of your previous project from chapter 1, and work from that. Let us begin by investigating probably one of the simplest categories: numeric functions.

In your current Project, add a new Word Document and name it Functions and Calculations. Your Project should look like this:

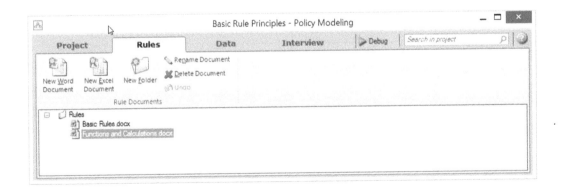

Open the new Word document. To begin this chapter, we are going to use a feature that is designed to help novice rule writers get things done more quickly. I can hear you murmuring "But I'm not a novice anymore!"

and although I agree, let me show you how useful this feature is by asking you a simple question: can you remember the spelling and detail of all of your Project attributes? I think the answer is, probably not.

Of course you can switch between the Policy Modeler data tab and the Word document, but that isn't very user-friendly. The Rule Assistant feature helps improve spelling, avoids common errors, and also provides helpful hints to get rules written more rapidly.

The Rule Assistant

Open the Rule Assistant. Start typing the candidate and watch what happens. If you need to, you can move the Rule Assistant window around using the mouse to be able to view your Word text at the same time.

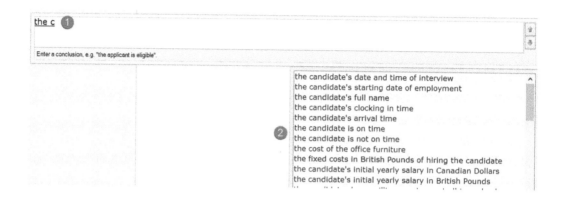

1. The text that you type in the main Rule Assistant window brings up…

2. …all the attributes containing the text in the drop-down list on the right. (An *instant* time saver!)

Rule Assistant – Improving Spelling

So, with the Rule Assistant, we have a pretty cool way of reminding ourselves of the text used for our attributes. But the Rule Assistant is even more flexible as you will discover in just a moment. In the Rule Assistant window, enter the text shown below, using the drop-down demonstrated above to select attributes that already exist:

Rule Assistant – Function List

To further illustrate the usefulness of the Rule Assistant, after you have accepted the text above (which you do just by hitting the *Enter* key), you can try entering the following on the next free line in your Word document. The Rule Assistant has displayed the lesser of value and value in its drop-down window.

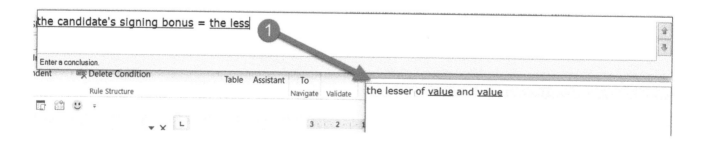

This is your first exposure to the built-in functions of Oracle Policy Automation. There are a large number of functions accessible in your Project rules, to make expressing complex policy ideas possible, using Modeler-provided functions.

Functions generally (this is not a hard and fast rule) exist in two versions, sometimes even more. We can divide these into two types: **long form** and **short form**. As an example, review the following paragraphs:

the candidate's signing bonus = the lesser of the default signing bonus and (the candidate's initial yearly salary in British Pounds /12)

the candidate's signing bonus = Minimum(the default signing bonus ,(the candidate's initial yearly salary in British Pounds /12))

Both of the examples above would work just fine and are functionally identical. They are the long and short forms of the same function – which you can find in the Function Reference mentioned at the start of the chapter.

Rule Assistant – Other Languages

The Rule Assistant is capable of displaying localized versions of the functions as well, for example in the case of a Project whose language is French.

la prime d'embauche du candidat = le plus petit des frais fixes d'embauche en Livres Sterling et du salaire intial en Livres Sterling du candidat

Enter a conclusion.

The Rule Assistant is also language-aware in reference to operators and other keywords, so if you are entering rules in a Project whose language is set to French or another supported language, then the Rule Assistant will display operators in that language, as shown below. The exact display will also depend on the language of Microsoft Word and Windows.

pour chacune des dépenses, le type de la dépense est renseigné

Enter a condition.

	Table	Assistant	To					
			Navigate	Validate				

Accept condition and add another condition et condition

Accept condition and add another condition ou condition

Rule Assistant – Formatting Help

The Rule Assistant is useful, even if it does not fulfil the role of a fully-fledged Wizard – since you have to know the function you wish to use. You should also bear in mind that some of the long form, non-English, functions do not display the list of attributes once you have begun typing your phrase. But it's a great start, and it can also help novice rule writers with formatting challenges. For example, writing the rule shown above in the Rule Assistant will ensure that the Condition is correctly formatted for you, automatically. The Assistant will add the correct level formatting to conditions and will similarly format conclusions correctly.

Writing More Complex Rules

So far, in summary we have learned that

- The Rule Assistant helps us write attributes and functions (although it won't tell us the right ones to use).

- Functions usually exist in long and short forms. Short forms typically (but not always) use brackets and a regional separator (a comma, or another punctuation mark) to define the different parts of the function.

- In mathematical expressions, brackets are acceptable to indicate items to process first. In fact, the traditional **B**racket **O**rder **Di**vision **M**ultiplication **A**ddition **S**ubtraction sequence is respected.

Writing Rules with Date and Time Functions

Now that you have the basics sorted, it is time to build a more interesting example. You will use **Date** functions and functions relating to the time of day. Working with dates and their functions will help you perform calculations like this:

1. What date and time is it right now?

2. How many (days/weeks/months) have elapsed since a certain date?

3. What is the date X (days/weeks/months) from now?

4. The Saturday following the interview is what date?

5. How many days work did the employee do last month?

Working with the current date and time

In the previous chapter, you created an attribute called `the candidate's date and time of interview`. Now you can add the following line to the Word document to calculate automatically the time of the interview, or determination session.

the candidate's date and time of interview = the current date time

The current date time is in fact a function in its long form. `CurrentDateTime()` is also acceptable, if less readable. The date and time returned will be the time of the session in Policy Automation. The companion function "the current date" or in short form `CurrentDate()` will return only the date portion.

In the case of a non-English project, you may experience difficulty formulating the above phrase in your language. This is because functions are not always translated into both natural language and short versions in all languages. In French, for example, the following is the equivalent of the previous screenshot:

la date et heure de l'entretien du candidat = DateHeureActuelles()

There is no equivalent long form function for "the current date time" in French. This is a difference that you may come across in many different languages, not just French.

Checking the Function in the Debugger

If you validate and debug your Project now, the attribute should have moved into the **Inferable Attributes** at the bottom of the window, since it is now being populated through the function, and the value will be the current date and time.

—— Inferable Attributes: ————————————————————

The candidate's date and time of interview is | 13/02/2016 16:28 GMT. | 2016-02-13 16:28:47 GMT
Is the candidate on time?   <Unknown>

Or in French:

—— Inferable Attributes: ————————————————————

La date et heure de l'entretien du candidat est 01/07/2016 13:03 GMT.   2016-07-01 13:03:11 GMT

Working with elapsed days, weeks, months and years

To calculate the difference in days, weeks, months or years between two dates, rule designers can take advantage of the function series **DayDifference**, **WeekDifference**, **MonthDifference** and **YearDifference**.

It should be kept in mind that the goal of many Policy Modeling efforts is to produce a document that should be readable to non-technical contributors, so there are also long form versions which we shall use mostly in these examples.

Viewing the function in the Rules Assistant shows us the required arguments – two dates or dates and times. By cross-referencing with the Function Reference we can see that the order of the two dates is not important. So a new line in this Word document can be written thus:

the waiting period of the candidate in days = daydifference(the candidates date and time of interview, the candidate's starting date of employment)

the waiting period of the candidate in days= the number of days from the candidates date and time of interview to the candidate's starting date of employment

Looking at the long form it should already be clear just how important it is to use the definite article ("the") in your attribute names to maintain readability. Think how unfriendly it would be to read "from candidate's date and time of interview to candidate's starting date of employment". If your goal is natural language, then make it as natural as you can without sacrificing clarity or maintainability.

In other languages, the same problem of readability will occur but not necessarily for the same reason. Here is the same rule in another language:

la durée de la période d'attente du candidat en jours = DifférenceJours(la date et heure de l'entretien du candidat; la date d'embauche du candidat)

The biggest challenge with the above example is its readability. Since the function in question does not have a French natural language version available, non-technical users might find this quite difficult to read.

Types, Arguments and Outputs in Functions

Working with functions in Policy Modeler requires attention to detail, and one area that requires attention is the *type* of the arguments required. Take, for example, the following scenario. We wish to calculate the difference in time between the specified clocking in time and the actual arrival time of the candidate. We may, for example, wish to give someone a bonus if they arrive early, or a warning if they are late. You might be tempted to try the following:

the time bonus accrued by the candidate = the candidate's clocking in time – the candidate's arrival time

And if you did, Policy Modeler would simply show you the following message in the main Window.

⚠ Argument 1 for - is TimeOfDay but is required to be Number (OPA-E00348)

1 error ⌃⌄

Clicking on the error will take you to the offending line in your Word document. A closer look in the Function Reference reveals that **SecondDifference()** and **MinuteDifference()** also exist, which would give you the answer to your problem. The functions are organized into tabular format in the reference so remember to look into all of the relevant tables.

the time bonus accrued by the candidate = SecondDifference(the candidate's clocking in time , the candidate's arrival time)

NB: These functions return a positive number irrespective of whether the candidate is early or late, so just by calculating this you won't know whether to give them a bonus or a warning. Note also that the function accepts either a `DateTime` or a `TimeOfDay` as inputs.

Looking ahead with Dates

AddMinutes(), AddHours(), AddDays() and other related functions let the writer find dates in the future or past, based on a date that is already known. For example, if you wished to calculate the date of the six month anniversary of hiring a candidate in order to review their progress, you could use either version of the following function:

the candidate's six month review date = AddMonths(the candidate's starting date of employment,6)

the candidate's six month review date = the date 6 months after the candidate's starting date of employment

NB: A common trap is to write "six" instead of 6, or to use the word "from" instead of "after".

NB: If you are using the short form while working in languages other than English, it is important to note that the function arguments may be separated by another character. In French, for example, the function example we just looked at would be as follows; observe the semi-colon after the first argument:

la fin de la période d'évaluation du candidat = AjouterMois(la date d'embauche du candidat; 6)

If, however, you are writing in the long form, the more natural approach avoids such issues:

la fin de la période d'évaluation du candidat = la date 6 mois après la date d'embauche du candidat

Looking for the next specific day of the week

Sometimes your rules need to find out the next occurrence of a certain day. Perhaps the review board meets every Thursday, and the company needs to tell the candidate when their case will be reviewed after their interview, which can take place on any work day. Policy Modeler lets us achieve this with a whole battery of functions that follow the theme of the following example:

the interview review board next meeting date = NextDayOfTheWeek(the candidate's date and time of interview, "Saturday")

the interview review board next meeting date = the next Saturday on or after the candidate's date and time of interview

NB: In the above example, the function will return today's date, not next Saturday's date, if the interview is on a Saturday. The long form includes the text "on or after..." or "on or before..." making it clearer.

NB: The `"Saturday"` must be in quotes, and must correspond to the correct word in the localized rule language. Otherwise you will see "What is Saturday?" appearing in your debug session.

Counting Weekdays

Assuming the person works on weekdays only, we can calculate how much work they will do between two dates in the following fashion. It is highly unlikely you would want to hard-code a date in this function, it is in this example for simplicity only.

> **the candidate's work before Christmas = the number of weekdays (inclusive) between the candidate's starting date of employment and *2016-12-15***

Writing Rules with Text Functions

Writing rules and using text functions is relatively uncommon. There are, however, a number of standard functions that a rule designer might need from time to time, for example concatenation of words to create a text attribute, or for converting numbers into text and so forth.

Text manipulation

The example below shows you **concatenation**, finding a **substring**, finding the **length** and converting a number into **text**.

> **the candidate's employee code = the concatenation of "EMP-" + the candidate's last name + "-" + the candidate's first name + SubString(the candidate's place of employment , 0, 2) + "/" + Text(the length of the candidate's full name)**

NB: Note that the concatenation symbol is "+" not "&".

Writing Rules with Logical Functions

In an earlier chapter, we discussed how in Policy Automation, the concept of *unknown, uncertain* and therefore *known* and *certain* data had an important role in the logic of your rules. It follows therefore that there is a set of functions allowing us to perform tests on your rule attributes to understand their logical state.

The use of *known* functions requires quite careful handling. Some concrete examples will help explain. Firstly, you should be aware that there are two versions – currently known and known – as well as the negative unknown version.

[Currently] Known or Unknown Functions

The commonest usage is to simply require that a piece of information be collected, for example as part of a procedural goal to ensure that attributes are collected from the user.

> **the interview is complete if**
> it is known whether <u>the candidate is accepted</u>

The above function will evaluate to true if the underlined attribute in the condition has any value, otherwise it will return a value of *unknown* when the underlined attribute has no value.

> **the interview is complete if**
> it is currently known whether <u>the candidate is accepted</u>

The above example will evaluate to true if the underlined attribute in the condition has any value, otherwise it will return a value of *false* when the underlined attribute has no value. This version tests the current state of the attribute.

> **the interview is complete if**
>> it is currently known whether <u>the candidate is accepted</u>

Confusingly, in the case of [currently] unknown, whether you use the word currently or not, the behaviour is identical. In both cases, the test of the attribute will return either *true* or *false*.

Certain and Uncertain

The example below will create a condition that returns *true* if the value of the attribute is not uncertain.

> **the candidate is accepted if**
>> it is certain that the candidate's references are valid |

In this final example, the uncertain function (used here with the optional `whether` in place of `that`) helps by returning *true* if the underlined attribute value is uncertain.

> **the outcome of the interview is unclear if**
>> it is uncertain whether <u>the candidate's references are valid</u>

Logical Functions Summary

In the face of so many variations, here is a summary to help guide you. The attribute `the candidate's references are valid` used with the different functions, and different possible values, results in a table like this:

The Operator	The candidate's references are valid (*true*)	The candidate's references are not valid (*false*)	Are the candidate's references valid? (attribute is *unknown*)	It is uncertain whether the candidate's references are valid (*uncertain*)
It is **certain** that the candidate's references are valid	TRUE	TRUE	TRUE	FALSE
It is **uncertain** whether the candidate's references are valid	FALSE	FALSE	FALSE	TRUE
It is **known** that the candidate's references are valid	TRUE	TRUE	UNKNOWN	TRUE
It is **currently known** that the candidate's references are valid	TRUE	TRUE	FALSE	TRUE
It is **[currently] unknown** that the candidate's references are valid	FALSE	FALSE	TRUE	FALSE

NB: Writers who build rules in languages other than English should check vocabulary and phrasing as it is easy to get confused!

Writing Rules with Number Functions

Working with number attributes means you will perhaps need to perform some of these tasks:

1. What is the largest or smallest value?

2. What is this value, truncated to *n* decimal places?

3. What is this value, rounded to *n* decimal places?

Number Functions – an example

It might surprise you that the example for **maximum(x,y)** and **minimum(x,y)** is going to be about dates. The functions in both accept numbers, dates, or dates with times for the *x* and *y* pair of arguments. The following paragraph provides us with some useful function examples:

the candidate's physical checkup date = the latest of **the candidate's starting date of employment** and NextDate(ExtractDate(**the candidate's date and time of interview**), ExtractDay(**the candidate's date and time of interview**),ExtractMonth(**the candidate's date and time of interview**))

Functions and Readability

As a side note, the whole rule is difficult to read – and this should be a reminder to you that readability is one of your goals as a rule writer. This is most certainly *not* natural language. Let us break it into parts and rebuild it with a different structure. Several functions can thus be identified.

the date of the interview = ExtractDate(**the candidate's date and time of interview**)

the month of the interview = ExtractMonth(**the candidate's date and time of interview**)

the day of the interview = ExtractDay(**the candidate's date and time of interview**)

the next occurrence of the day and month of interview = NextDate (**the date of the interview, the day of the interview, the month of the interview**)

Clearly the reader would benefit from the rule being less verbose. By breaking up the different constituent parts, it becomes clearer what we are trying to achieve. (At the same time, there is no excuse for not adding commentary text to explain the goal of the rule).

ExtractDate / ExtractMonth / ExtractDay to a Number

The first three lines use **ExtractDate**, **ExtractMonth** and **ExtractDay** – all similar in concept and useful for retaining only part of a date or a date/time combination. Note that these functions do not have a natural language alternative. The day/month of the interview is a *number* attribute as these functions return numbers.

Maximum and Minimum

In the final section, the rule designer is attempting to find the latter of two dates, namely the date the candidate was hired and the next occurrence of the day and month of the interview.

the candidate's physical checkup date = the latest of **the candidate's starting date of employment** and **the next occurrence of the day and month of interview**

When you try and validate the above, Policy Modeler will throw an **ambiguous expression** error. The attribute names are causing a problem. It is unwise on principle to have the word "and" (since it is a logical operator) in an attribute name. So to get around the problem in the short term, as the error message advises, you could use parentheses.

the candidate's physical checkup date = the latest of **the candidate's starting date of employment** and (**the next occurrence of the day and month of interview**)

The maximum function (seen here in long form `the latest of`) is used to compare two dates, and since our second date attribute contains `and`, the Modeler advises us to use parentheses... which we do. In a real situation, this would call for a change in the naming strategy of the attribute – adding operators into attribute text can only add confusion for readers.

NB: Think carefully *before* you write *anything*. Break the rule down into constituent parts and identify the *clearest* path to your goal. Writing quickly will produce long, unwieldy rules and over-complicated text and functions. The examples here are for demonstration only and are sometimes deliberately unwieldy as I try to highlight potential issues "in situ".

NB: Have a clear strategy for attribute text, and avoid using operators and other words that have ambiguous meaning(s) as part of your attribute wording.

Writing Rules with Validation Functions

Validation Events are best described as methods to raise a flag to the end user, that something is not right. They come in two forms, an **Error** and a **Warning**.

As in the previous example, you will use these as a focus for furthering your knowledge of attributes and general Policy Modeler behaviour.

Warning("the candidate appears to be rather old") if
the candidate's age > 100

As the job requires a degree of physical work and a certificate of aptitude, this will warn us of a potential issue in respect of the candidate's age. The warning will appear in the debugger with a triangle. The value will be accepted, however, *even if* you enter a value greater than 100.

If you edit your rule and replace `Warning` with `Error`, following validation and a new debug session, you will no longer be able to enter a value above 100 – the attribute will remain with the value unknown until you enter a number that is acceptable.

This illustrates the fundamental difference between these two – one is a warning, but you may continue with the value you have entered, whilst the other will not let the session continue. This will become even more useful when you use Policy Modeler to create your own customized interviews.

Other Data Validation Options

The above functions might appear quite simplistic for managing data entry. Data validation functionality can also be found on the Edit Attribute dialog back in the Policy Modeler main window.

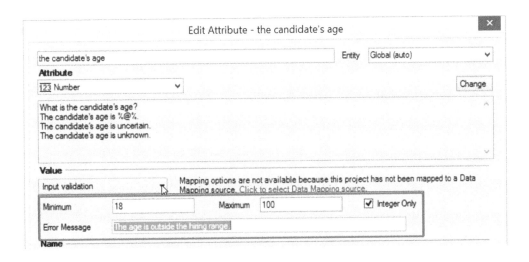

Creating entry ranges is a fast and efficient way to configure your attribute, and in this case you might use the Integer Only checkbox to ensure the user can only enter whole years for the attribute. The same options are available for Date, Time of Day, and Date Time attributes (without the Integer Only checkbox). Note that when editing a Text attribute, a different option is available:

61

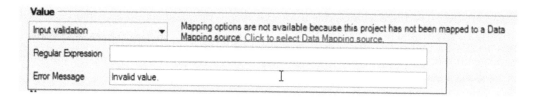

Using regular expressions to control the data entry mask is a powerful tool for controlling data quality. There are many good resources on the Internet to discover their (sometimes very complex) syntax. If the value entered by the user does not match the expression, the message is displayed.

Temporal Functions

Temporal reasoning is a powerful feature of Policy Automation which allows the rule designer to work with points in time. This can be quite confusing at first. Let's begin with a very simple example. *How old are you?*

The answer to this question will depend on the day I ask it. Perhaps tomorrow is your birthday. In any case, if I ask you in a few days' time, you will technically be older than when I asked you before. Both answers you gave to me would be valid at that specific point in time.

This concept is extremely powerful; when using Oracle Policy Automation, we can begin to look at temporal reasoning as a way to answer questions whose answers depend on when you ask them. Another simple example, common to most people is, *How much money do you have in the bank?*

In a Policy Modeling Project, you can create an attribute to test this concept. For the purposes of demonstration, the example below includes the word *temporal* in the attribute text. This is not necessary.

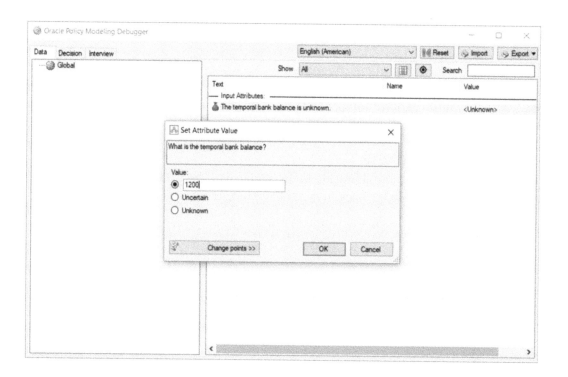

In the image above, the value is 1200 (the units are not specified in this demonstration). But what does that value actually mean? *When* did you have that money in your account?

Let's add some more data to our Debugger session. Open the Change points >> dialog and add three lines. This data will help us begin to see the concept of temporal reasoning.

Add three change points (1000, 1100, 1500), for the first, second and third of a particular month (July is used in the example above). Looking at the data, we can now use some Oracle Policy Automation Functions to understand how useful temporal functions can help us work with data that changes over time.

The bank balance on the first of july = ValueAt(2018-07-01, **the temporal bank balance**)

The bank balance on the second of july = ValueAt(2018-07-02, **the temporal bank balance**)

The bank balance on the third of July = ValueAt(2018-07-03, **the temporal bank balance**)

The bank balance on the last day of june = ValueAt (2018-06-30, **the temporal bank balance**)

The bank balance today = ValueAt (the current date, **the temporal bank balance**)

Now, return to the Debugger:

Text	Name	Value
— Input Attributes:		
The temporal bank balance is {£1,200.00, £1,000.00 fro...		{1200, 1000 from 2018-07-01, 11...
— Inferable Attributes:		
The bank balance today is £1,500.00.		1500
The bank balance on the first of july is £1,000.00.		1000
The bank balance on the second of july is £1,100.00.		1100
The bank balance on the third of july is £1,500.00.		1500
The bank balance on the last day of june is £1,200.00.		1200

Observe how the values for the three days in July are perhaps exactly what you are expecting. The `ValueAt` function has provided you with the value on the date you specified.

The bank balance today (assuming today is a date after the third of July and that you used the same data as my example) is listed as 1500. In this case, Oracle Policy Automation has found that the last change point was July 3rd, and gives you that value. In summary – *according to the data you entered* – there was no change after the 3rd.

Finally, the amount on June 30th, *outside the data points you gave*, is the amount you entered in the debugger right at the beginning. If you right-click the temporal bank balance, and select Temporal Visualisation, then click the Temporal Visualisation tab on the left, the data is displayed visually:

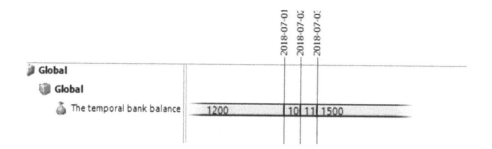

You will investigate another example of temporal reasoning later in this book following an in-depth look at tables in Word documents in Chapter 4.

> **NB**: The temporal functions do not have long forms, so make sure that the documented comments clearly explain the rule and the determination.

Other Functions

In recent versions of Oracle Policy Automation, a number of extra functions have been added, notably the function `CurrentLocale()` which returns the language locale of the current session. You will learn more about using Oracle Policy Automation in different locales later; but this function will come in very handy when you want to display content (for example a website link) that changes depending on the language of the user.

Here are some more of the most recently added functions:

`NewLine()` – this function adds a new line marker to your text attribute.

`Contains()` – this function searches for a substring in a text attribute.

`Quote()` – this function returns true or false depending on whether the attribute contains a quote (") mark.

The customer's burger size = Default (the burger supplied size, "Extra Large")

The customer's burger size = DefaultWithUnknown (the burger supplied size, "Extra Large")

The milkshake size = If (the burger has cheese, "Large", "Extra Large")

`Default()` – used to set an attribute value in a Web Service call where none was provided. If the customer's burger size is uncertain, the default will be "Extra Large". If it is *unknown*, the function will return *unknown*.

`DefaultWithUnknown()` – Used to set an attribute in a Web Service call where none was provided, including unknown values, thus always returning a result. If the chosen size is unknown, the function will return "Extra Large".

`If()` – Simplifies rules to test conditions without separate rules. This is similar in syntax to the Microsoft Excel function: *condition*,value if true, value if false. So in the above example, the milkshake size will be "Large" if the burger has cheese.

> **NB**: Remember to provide comments in your documents to help readers understand the context and goal of your rule. In longer rule documents, use the standard Microsoft Word Table of Contents feature to provide easy navigation for readers.

Separators

In the examples used in this chapter, whenever there have been several arguments to a function, these arguments are separated with a comma. Be aware that this *separator* is dependent on the region setting of your Policy Model. For example, in a France-French project, it will be a semi-colon. Check which separator is used in your region by referring to your function reference using the links given earlier in this chapter. Bear this in mind if you have teams working on different projects using different regions (but perhaps the same language) as this may cause confusion.

> **NB**: Changing region in an existing project will require you to check all separators, and of course change any region-specific notation (for example, the symbol for a decimal point). Don't underestimate how much checking you might have to do!

Summary

There are many functions in Oracle Policy Automation. The few that have been showcased in this section have been chosen to help you get to grips with syntax, pitfalls, and common issues when getting started with rule writing.

We will investigate more functions when we discuss Entities and Entity reasoning, as they have a complete set of entity- and relationship-focused functions.

Entities

Working with Entities

Most consultants and rule writers will be familiar with the concept of an **Entity** – a single thing, defined with different attributes. Given that Policy Automation might be used in conjunction with other Enterprise software such as Oracle Siebel CRM or Oracle CX Cloud which often contain many different entities, it is important to be able to model such structures in the Policy Modeling.

Once you can model entities and their relationships in Policy Modeling, then you are ready to build rules and make determinations based not on flat structure, but on something much more powerful, an **entity model**. This will also, from a conceptual perspective, help you understand how Policy Automation can be used with other application.

When do you use Entities?

A simple answer is, you use entities whenever you have the same attribute (for example, *the order number*) that can have multiple values during one interview or determination server session.

If you know that your CRM System sends Oracle Policy Automation a customer, their orders and the relevant order lines for processing at the start of each interview, then how will you cope with having multiple orders for a given customer? How will you deal with orders having any number of lines? The short answer is, by creating entities and relationships to structure your work.

An Entity Example

To illustrate the principles, begin by creating a new Project in Policy Modeling and make sure you set the language and region accordingly. Open the Data tab and review what is visible. On the left-hand side of the window you will see Global, with a world icon.

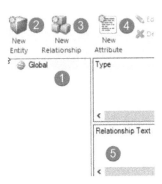

In the screenshot above:

1. The Global Entity. All attributes, unless otherwise stated, are part of the Global Entity. It cannot be removed.

2. New entities can be added to your model. They will be logical children of Global.

3. New relationships can be constructed to define how your entities interact. Some relationships are created automatically.

4. Attributes can be created for your new entities.

5. Relationship details appear here.

The Global Entity

Even without knowing it, you have already been working with entities. There is automatically one entity in *every* Policy Modeling rule Project.

All attributes that you have created so far have belonged to the Global entity. Recall the following screenshot from the previous chapters:

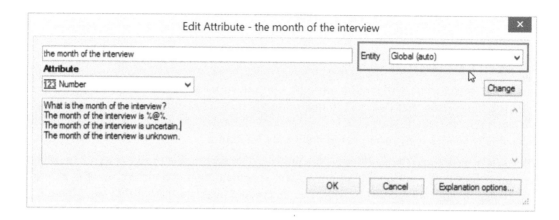

The Global entity acts as a container for all Project attributes if another entity is not explicitly identified. Every attribute in the Global entity can only have one value per interview.

Now consider the following entity model, shown in a **Data Model View** from Policy Modeling version 10. This is a *partial* model for demonstration purposes. The customer is represented by Global. There is no need to create a separate entity for Customer – since in our model your Project will evaluate one customer per session, with orders and order lines, thus Global can occupy the role of this "singleton" customer entity.

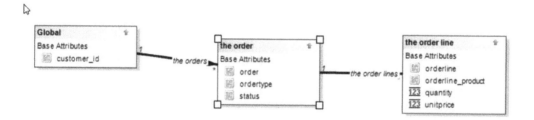

There are relationships that have been defined and named "the orders" and "the order lines". Attributes have been created and assigned to the relevant entities. The nature of the relationships has been defined (as can be seen by the "1" and "*" at each extremity of an arrow).

To create the same entity model in Policy Modeling in version 12 (although we cannot visualize it in the same way), perform the following steps.

1. In the Data tab, click the New Entity button. Enter the order as the name of the new entity.

2. With this new entity selected, click the New Entity button again. This new entity will be called the order line.

3. Select the Global entity in the left pane. With the entity selected, click the New Attribute button. Add a new text attribute called the customer id.

NB: *Always* include the definite article "the" (or the language-specific word as appropriate) where possible when creating an entity. This will result in clearer phrasing and it will be easier to identify to which entity you are referring. This concept holds true for any language that uses articles.

NB: Never create an entity using the plural ("the order" and never "the orders"). We will see how to deal with plural items in a moment.

If you have followed the steps above you should have something like the following in your Project. It might have seemed very simple but a lot of very important things have been happening.

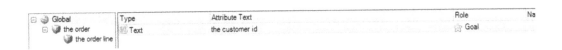

During this creation of entities, some key concepts have been uncovered. To review the process in more detail and investigate, select "the order line" entity and click the Edit Entity button. Notice the details of this dialog box, specifically the following:

Containment

The Contained By field; Policy Modeling automatically creates these relationships as you add entities, and your entity is contained by its parent in the structure you created, the order. In Policy Modeling you will see reference to the notion of containment to describe parent and child relationships between your entities. The concept of containment and whether data is complete or not will be useful later on in this chapter.

Close the Edit Entity dialog box for now.

Entity and Attribute Text

When working with entities and attributes, it is very important to maintain a strict approach to how you write attribute names. To demonstrate the potential trap, follow along with this practical example.

1. Select the order in the left hand pane.

2. Click the New Attribute button.

In the attribute text, notice how the order is already selected for you. For demonstration purposes, edit the relationship text to read the order line quantity. Notice that the entity field in the right-hand corner changes immediately to the order line. *Policy Modeling uses the attribute text to determine to which entity an attribute belongs.*

NB: You write your attribute text carefully to avoid attributes being assigned to the wrong entity. If you create an attribute called "the order amount" or "the order's amount", both of these contain the text "the order" which is the entity you created previously, so Policy Modeling will assume the attribute is to be placed in the definition of that entity. Always use the entity name in the attribute to make it clear. So "the order line quantity" belongs in "the order line" and "the order status" belongs in "the order".

Containment Relationships

When you create an entity, Policy Modeling automatically creates a **Containment Relationship**. Because your entity is always a child of some other entity (Global, or another custom-created entity) then it is always true that your entity is contained by a parent entity. To examine an automatically created containment relationship, select the Global entity and then select the relationship which appears in the lower part of the right-hand pane:

Notice the relationship type Containment (One to Many). This is logically true, since Global acts as a container for the order and you can have multiple orders in your interview, but only one Global. The text proposed is all instances of the order. This is not natural language, and you can correct it.

Entities in the Debugger

We have not yet created any Word document rules, but you can still start a new debug session. One of the uses of the debug window is to test the structure and definition of your entity model, even before the Project contains any rules.

In the screenshot above, I have selected the all the instances of the order icon on the left-hand side. The only features available to me are the Add Instance button and the Delete Instance button. After clicking the Add Instance button three times in succession, the display shows the following if you expand the tree view:

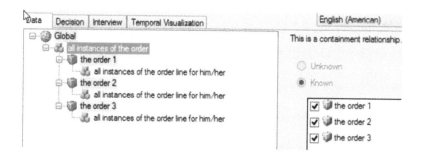

The debug window helps rule designers to understand the structure of the model they are creating and, at the same time, highlight issues that need to be dealt with as they strive to achieve the stated goal of writing clear rules in English or another language. The following items are going to need further attention.

Improving Relationship Text

1. The text describing the set of orders and order lines uses all instances which is not natural. Relationship text will often be used in your Word or Excel documents, so it is best practice to rename them to something more meaningful.

Recall that in the section on the previous pages, you learned that Policy Modeling automatically generates the containment relationship text. You can edit this to meet your requirements.

Return to the Data tab and select the relationship all the instances of the order. Click the Edit Relationship button from the ribbon. Change the *relationship text* to the orders.

Repeat for the relationship all the instances of the order line and change the text to the order lines.

2. The different orders are hard to tell apart; order 1 and order 2 is not realistic and not very friendly.

3. Later you will also discover how to fix the "him/her" problem and tell Oracle Policy Modeler that an order is not a person.

Entity Identifiers

As you create "instances" of our entities, the debugger displays each instance in the left-hand pane marked the order 1 and so on to enable you to identify them. There are several ways to improve this:

In the Data tab, select the entity the order and click the Edit Entity button.

Edit Entity Identifiers

Each entity has an "identifying attribute". In real life, you might have an order number that was unique, which would be the "identifier". In Policy Modeling, an identifying attribute is automatically created for you as soon as you create a new entity. The "identifying attribute" is used for identification purposes and, also by default, for substitution, which you will discover shortly.

Close the Edit Entity dialog and return to the Data tab. Select the *attribute* the order and click Edit Attribute.

- Change the attribute text the order to the order number.

Start a new debug session and switch to the Data tab.

- Click Add Instance. Select the order.

- In the right-hand pane, double-click the order number. Enter 1-111 and click OK.

- Your debugger should look something like this. Notice how the left-hand pane shows the identifying attribute value to help you see which order you are working on.

To experiment with identifying attributes one last time, close the debugger and return to the Data tab.

- Select the order entity.

- Click Add Attribute and add the order type as a text attribute.

- Select the order entity.

- Click Edit Entity.

- Change the identifying attribute to the order type.

- Click OK.

- Start a new debug session and create a new instance of the order.

- Enter an order number as before, and enter Sales Order as the order type.

After these steps, your debug session should look like this. In this case the order type would not be a useful identifying attribute since lots of orders will have the same type. Before continuing:

- Change the identifying attribute back to the order number.

Bear in mind that sometimes the choice of the identifying attribute may be imposed by an integration with another system that supplies the input data for your sessions.

Substitution

In the debugger, you have begun to see that in certain situations, the *value* of an attribute is substituted in place of the attribute *text*. It can be seen in action by implementing, for training purposes, the following sequence of steps.

- In the Data tab, return to the order type attribute.

- Click Edit Attribute and enter a name. Recall that names are used to identify attributes and other elements of your data tab when external applications need to reference them.

- Update the Name as shown below. Notice the remark, underneath, concerning using the name in screens.

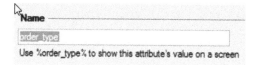

- Click OK to save your changes.

- Still in the Data tab, now select the order line entity.

- Select the order line *attribute* and click Edit Attribute.

- Change the default text that is used to present the attribute to the user by clicking the Change button on the right-hand side.

- Edit the Custom Attribute Form dialog as shown below. Recall that Policy Modeling automatically generates text for your attribute, corresponding to the different logical states.

- Notice that as soon as you type % Policy Modeling presents you with a list of attributes that have names, ready for you to select one.

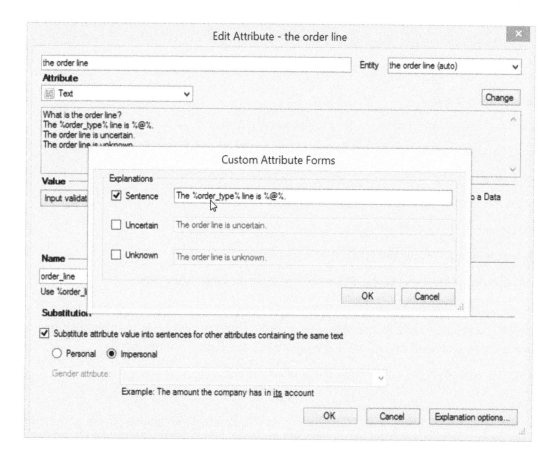

- Click OK twice to close both dialog boxes.

- Start a new debug session.

- In the Data tab, create a new order instance. Enter the Order Number as 1-111 and the Order Type as Sales.

- Select the text the order lines on the left-hand pane and click Add Instance.

- Edit the value of the order line attribute to 1.

- View your work. You should be able to see that Sales (the value of the Order Type attribute) is repeated in the Order Line attribute text as shown below. You have successfully used %name% to insert the *value* of one attribute into the *text* of another.

The use of %name% in this fashion is extremely useful in building friendly interviews. For example Hello %first_name% as a greeting (assuming you have an attribute with that name) would produce Hello Richard which is much better than Hello Customer.

You will return to this concept when building interactive interviews in Chapter 6. For now, return the attribute text shown above and the entity identifying attribute to their original values. In a real life situation, unnecessary editing and mixing of attribute substitution will often confuse readers as to what you are referring to.

Relationship Types

Our model currently only has *containment relationships*. Recall that Policy Modeling creates these relationships automatically whenever a new entity is added to the Data tab. Containment relationships are implicit.

Adding Relationships to the Entity Model

As a rule writer, you often need to express relationships that are not implicit – rather, they form part of your business model. These relationships need to be created manually. To provide an example, firstly create a new entity, and edit the containment relationship created for you:

- In the Data tab, select Global.

- Click New Entity.

- Enter the invoice.

- Click OK to save the new entity. Policy Modeling automatically creates the identifying attribute the invoice and the containment relationship.

- As good practice, immediately select the relationship at the bottom of the Data tab and click Edit Relationship.

- Edit the text all the instances of the invoice to the invoices.

You should now have an entity model in your rule Project that looks like this.

If you have accidentally placed the invoice as a child of another entity, you can change it by returning to the Edit Entity dialog and selecting the appropriate entity in the top right-hand drop-down list. Make sure it is contained by Global as shown in the next screenshot. You can now further edit your data model by adding new relationships.

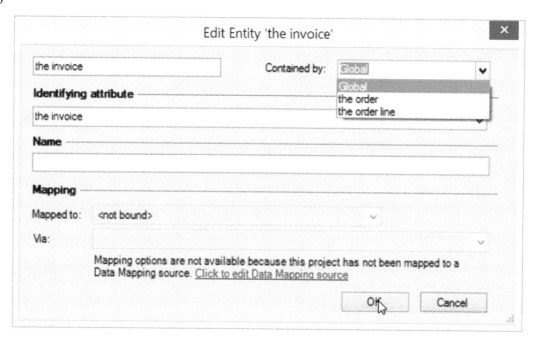

Reference Relationships

A reference relationship is any relationship that is not implicit, that is added to your model for the purposes of describing a business context. So in the case of invoice entity, if you need to establish a relationship with an entity other than the logical parent, then this *reference relationship must be created by the rule designer manually.*

Reference relationships come in many types (one to one, one to many, many to many) that can be configured when creating the relationship. Key to the successful creation of a reference relationship is selecting the correct source and target. In the following demonstration scenario, the invoice will be placed in a one to one relationship with the order.

Create Reference Relationship

Select the order entity in the Data tab and click the New Relationship button. In the annotated screenshot shown below, the following points are noteworthy.

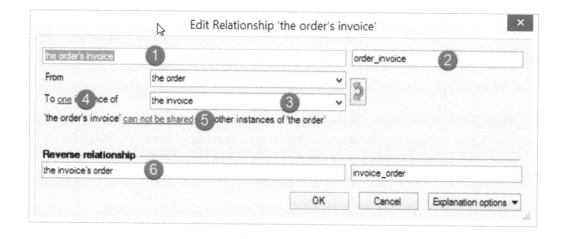

1. Ensure that the relationship text accurately describes the nature of the relationship. In this case, with a one to one, there is no plural involved. In the case, for example, of a many to many relationship, the invoices of the orders might be more appropriate since it reflects more succinctly the nature of the relationship. As always, your goal is to create rules that are easy to follow and clearly understandable.

2. The relationship name is used in features such as integration and when creating end-of-interview documents, both of which will be discussed later.

3. The target entity should be specified here.

4. The hyperlink can be clicked to cycle between many and one.

5. The hyperlink can be clicked to cycle between can be shared (to many) and can not be shared (to one).

6. If you need to create rules that work with the relationship in the reverse direction, fill in the reverse text and the reverse relationship name.

Debugging Reference Relationships

Start a new debug session and review the Data tab of the debugger. Create, if necessary, an order, and an invoice.

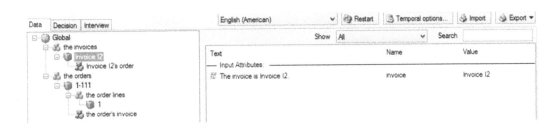

As in the screenshot above, you should be able to see your different entities and create instances. By default, since this is a reference relationship that must be manually invoked, the invoice and the order are not related. Select the target that you defined in your relationship (the order) and expand the order until you see the order's invoice.

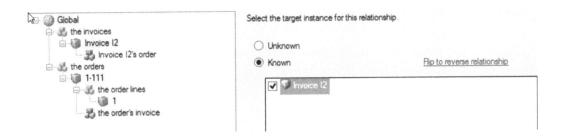

The selection of the invoice becomes possible after you select Known. The connection is now made. You can review the reverse relationship by clicking the hyperlink. Notice that you cannot change the reverse relationship; it is inferred.

Removing and Editing Reference Relationships

Relationships that you create can be edited (the text, the name, and so on) or deleted. It will not be possible to delete the relationship if it is used in an interview screen. This is also true of conclusions and attributes as you will discover in Chapter 6 when you build interactive interviews.

> **NB**: Bear in mind that as you discovered in this chapter, the generated text can be modified (for example by adding %attributename% as shown in a previous practical exercise). If you make modifications to your relationship name, or indeed an attribute name, check to see that your customized text forms are updated and that the newly generated text actually makes sense. For example:
>
> The %customername%'s order (Bob's order) may not make sense if it is changed to a many to many relationship. It might be more appropriate to say "Bob's orders".

Creating Rules with Entity Functions

So far you have experimented with creating and manipulating entities and relationships in the debugger. You are now ready to create rules in Word documents that leverage this structure to determine outcomes. Working first on the entity model then on the Word document ensures that you have tested your model and ironed out any issues before you begin writing rules.

Entities in rule documents are used in conjunction with entity functions. These functions leverage the entities and relationships defined in your data tab to make determinations.

Entity Quantifier Functions

Before you begin using them, you should be clear in how these functions are written. Many of them require you to provide details of the model you have built, such as the *relationship text* rather than, as in earlier examples, an attribute text. The function reference should be at your side when creating these rules.

As a first example, a rule will test to see for a given order, if there are any order lines that have a quantity of greater than one item – perhaps someone is ordering multiple copies of a product. This will involve us using an entity function and a new attribute.

> **the order has lines with multiple units if**
>   Exists(the order lines, the order line's quantity > 1)
>
> *the order has lines with multiple units if*
>   *for at least one of the order lines, the order line's quantity exceeds one*
>
> *the order line's quantity exceeds one if*
>   *the order line's quantity > 1*

For educational purposes, the above screenshot shows the same resulting determination twice. The second part, in grey, has been commented out using the Toggle Comment button in the Oracle Policy Modeling Ribbon. The entity function is available in long form as for at least one of and in short form as Exists().

Close inspection of the function reference reveals that there is a difference in the acceptable arguments depending on the form used.

The long form requires a Boolean condition as second argument, so attempting to write the rule in one statement with a single condition whilst using the long form instead, will cause an error in Policy Modeling.

To implement the long form would require two lines, one to create the intermediate Boolean attribute and the other line to use it in the Exists(). This is shown below.

> **the order has lines with multiple units if**
>   for at least one of the order lines, the order line quantity exceeds one
>
> **the order line quantity exceeds one if**
>   the order line quantity > 1

NB: Beware functions whose accepted arguments change between the long and the short form.

Exists Function

The Exists() function returns true if there is at least one instance of the relevant entity that meets the condition. So if there is at least one line in the order with a quantity greater than one, the rule will return True.

In the debugger, starting a new session and creating the order and order line instances with the relevant attribute values will produce something like the following, whichever form of the function you decide to use:

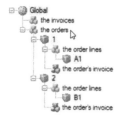
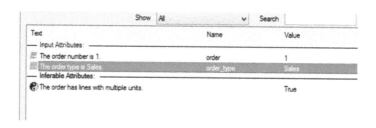

NB: The Decision tab has a feature that helps clarify the concept of entities and instances. In the example above, there are two orders, 1 and 2, each with one line A1 or B1. The values of the attributes are such that order 1 has multiple units, but order 2 has not.

Selecting an inferable attribute and right-clicking provides the context menu to go to the Decision tab. Now *the list of instances* appear in a drop-down, making it easy to understand that the rule you just created will provide an instance-level conclusion – each order is evaluated separately.

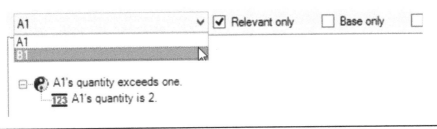

ForAll Function

The previous function returned true when at least one of the order lines had a quantity greater than one. But what if we want to only return true if *all of the order lines have a quantity greater than one*?

The `ForAll()` function, or *for each of* in its most common long form, does exactly that:

> **the order has only lines with multiple units if**
> for each of the order lines, the order line quantity exceeds one
>
> **the order line quantity exceeds one if**
> the order line quantity > 1

As before with `Exists()` there is an identical difference in the implementation of the arguments between the short and long form. The long form is shown above.

For Function

The previous examples dealt with how to leverage the relationship between the order and the order lines. Functions in Policy Modeling are sometimes specifically designed to work with certain kinds of relationship. You should always check to see if the rule you're trying to build, the relationship that exists, and the function you are using, are compatible.

In this next practical example we will use the **For** function, used in this case with a one to one relationships.

> **the order is ready for closure if**
> in the case of the order's invoice, the invoice is paid

The long form example, above, can also be written `For(<relationship>, <value>)`. The For function also works with many to many and many to one relationships.

Aggregation and Counting

There are several functions that allow rule writers to build determination logic based on the instances available in a session. These functions will help you determine useful information like the following:

- How many lines are there?

- How many lines whose list price is greater than 100?

- What is the average order line amount in this order?

- What is the average order line amount for all the orders for this customer?

InstanceCount Function and Variations

The `InstanceCount()` function, or the long form which is *the number of* allows the rule writer to find out how many instances of an entity are in the session, using the relationship specified. To find out therefore the number of lines in an order:

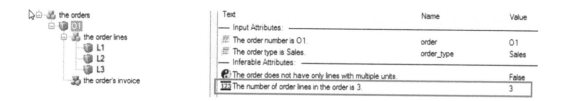

the number of order lines in the order = the number of **the order lines**

The output to the debug window Data tab is as follows, assuming three order lines:

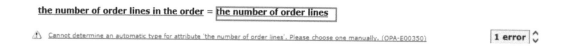

Common Errors with Entity Functions

Once again, the formulation of the rule's text is critical to the result. In the interest of exploration, if the text of the rule changes to the following…

the number of order lines in the order = **the number of order lines**

⚠ Cannot determine an automatic type for attribute 'the number of order lines'. Please choose one manually. (OPA-E00350) | 1 error |

…the relationship text was not found, the context is lost and the Policy Modeling attempts to interpret the last part of this rule as a new attribute, which is most certainly not what we intended.

The `InstanceCount()` function comes as part of set : `InstanceMaximum()` and `InstanceMinimum()` to find the lowest or highest value in the data set, plus `InstanceSum()` to add a numeric attribute. Here is an example of InstanceMaximum in the long form:

the largest quantity in the order = the greatest of **the order line quantity** for all of **the order lines**

> **NB**: Oracle Policy Modeling in version 12 uses underlining to indicate that non-Boolean attributes or relationships have been discovered. In the above example, it allows the rule writer to clearly distinguish between the text of the long form function (*the greatest of….for all of…*) and the attribute and relationship text.

The other members of this set of functions add an extra input argument; specifically they allow us to perform *conditional* aggregation. Perhaps it is required to only count the number of lines that have certain products; to do this you can additionally leverage a product attribute in a count function. To implement this example, begin by adding a new attribute to the order line entity:

The rule you will implement will only consider order lines where the product is "OPA Product". All other lines will be ignored.

The long form:

> **the total number of OPA lines in the order** = the number of **the order lines** for which it is the case that **the order line product is an OPA product**

> **the order line product is an OPA product if**
> the order line product = "OPA Product"

The short form:

> **the total number of OPA lines in the order** = InstanceCountIf(**the order lines, the order line product** = "OPA Product")

NB: Notice that the function will return Unknown until you provide an order line product for each of your order lines, and should any lines contain a product whose value is *uncertain* then your total number of lines will also be *uncertain*.

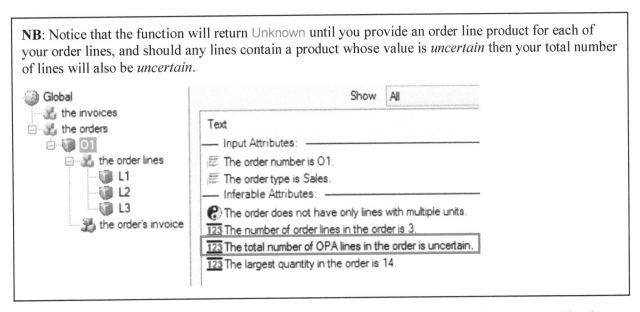

The InstanceCountIf function is accompanied by others that all have the same basic structure, with minor adjustments:

InstanceSumIf Function

Create the following rule in your Word rule document for this rule Project. For this example use the short form. Notice that this function takes three arguments; the relationship, the numeric attribute, and the conditional expression. It is also possible, as in this example, to perform simple mathematical operations.

> **the order value of OPA Products** = InstanceSumIf(**the order lines, the order line amount * the order line quantity, the order line product** = "OPA Product")

Assuming your order contains some OPA Product and has an amount and quantity entered, then you should be able to see the result in the debugger as shown below.

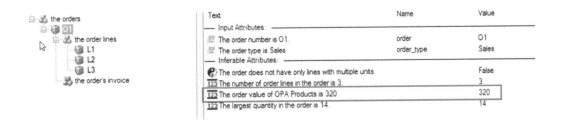

> **NB**: The fact that the new attribute – *the order value of OPA Products* – contains the entity text *the order* ensures that the attribute is correctly associated with *the order* entity; so we see a value *per instance* of the order.

InstanceValueIf Function

If you need to retrieve a value from a number attribute in a specific order or order line, then `InstanceValueIf` will allow you to specify how Policy Modeling can find that unique value.

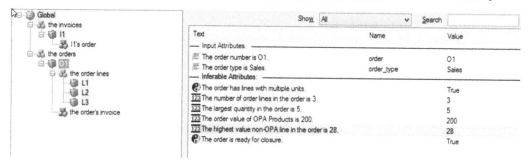

the highest value non-OPA line in the order = InstanceValueIf(the order lines, the order line amount * the order line quantity, the order line product <> "OPA Product")

If the data in your session does not allow the debugger to identify the unique value in question – because there are two or more that have the same value, or none meet the condition, then the function will return *uncertain*.

Multi-level Entity Models

Writing rules with entity functions so far, we have only leveraged a single pair of entities (the order and the order lines, the order and its invoice, and so on) each time. But in complex models, especially those inherited from external applications, it is likely that the rules we write will need to traverse several levels of entities.

If this is the case, the notion of entities in scope will become of the utmost importance. To learn about this through a practical example, consider the following business rule:

An order is considered ready to close if the order lines all have a shipment that is marked as having been delivered.

To implement this, firstly we need to revise the Project data model to reflect the existence of another level of entity. This entity will be a child of the order line; you can name it the shipment.

Ensure that you:

- Update the containment relationship text to the shipments.

- Create a one to one relationship with the order using the shipment order line as the relationship text.

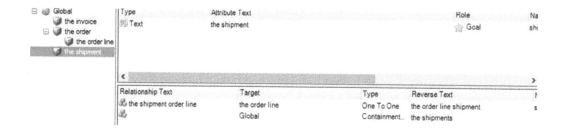

Entity Structure and Rule Design

Now visualize this as a rule in a Word document. The Policy Modeling reads the text, one line at a time for processing purposes. In order for any policy to validate properly, any mentioned entity must have been introduced in the current line of text, or in any parent lines. Additionally the Global entity is *always* available.

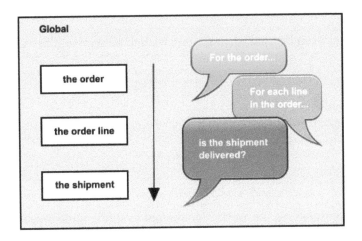

Reflecting Structure in Rules

So just by visualizing it in this way, you probably have already guessed at the way forward. Rule text will have to step down the entity hierarchy, ensuring that the correct entities are brought into scope, in order that the rule will work as expected. The rule is thus written in a series of steps or levels, with each level bringing the relevant entity into the text, using special functions.

ForScope and ForAllScope Functions

the order is ready for closure if
  ForAllScope(the order lines)
    ForScope (the order line shipment)
      the shipment is marked as delivered

The above example shows the role of the **ForScope** and **ForAllScope** functions – they bring information you need into *scope*, so that you can determine something successfully. Each step brings the relevant entity into scope. The final element to resolve is – why do we use `ForAllScope` for the order lines and `ForScope` for the order line shipment?

`ForAllScope` is used when you want to refer to all the members of the target to see if they meet the conditions (in this case, it is one order to many order lines), and `ForScope` brings a target in a one to one relationship into scope (the shipment for the order line).

As mentioned above, the correct structure of your entity model must be respected. Here are some examples of what *will not* work:

the order is ready for closure if
  ForAllScope(the order lines)
    the shipment is marked as delivered

The example above tries to jump from *the order lines* to an attribute of *the shipment* without bringing *the order line shipment* properly into the line of text.

the order is ready for closure if
  ForScope (the order line shipment)
    the shipment is marked as delivered

The second example, above, tries to jump from *the order* to *the order line shipment* without bringing *the order line* into the structure.

ExistsScope Function

In the same style, `ExistsScope` can be used when we just wish to determine if at least one order line meets a condition:

the order is on hold if
>   ExistsScope(<u>the order lines</u>)
>   ForScope (<u>the order line shipment</u>)
>   the shipment is marked as delayed |

As seen in the various examples that did not work, any attempt to shortcut the process of referencing entities failed. It is by experimenting with this kind of visualization exercise that the power and importance of your relationship definitions becomes clear.

Inferring Instances of an Entity

Sometimes within rule logic, you need to identify instances as belonging to a relationship purely through reasoning, or to simply deduce the existence of instances because of logic – for instance, you have a large pet food bill I can deduce the existence of an instance of a pet.

Infer Instance as a Conclusion

Consider the following example. If an order qualifies for a special gift (through some unspecified logic such as value of the order, certain products or whatever), then the gift should be automatically added to order – it's existence can be inferred.

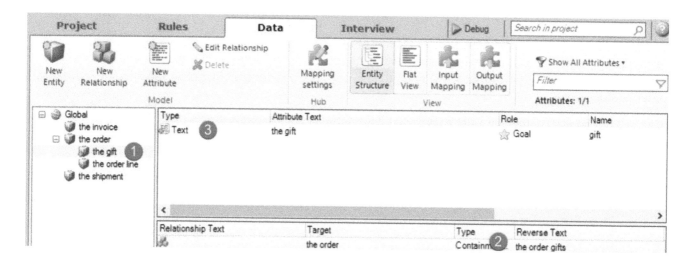

In the above screenshot, notice the new entity, and relationship text. Finally, there is only one identifying attribute for simplicity.

Now you can add the following rule to a Word document in your Project:

InferInstance(<u>the order gifts</u>, "a free gift teeshirt") if
>   the order qualifies for a gift

In this case, you are simply inferring the existence of a gift. The text *a free gift teeshirt* is simply the identifying attribute text. Running the above in the debugger, should produce the following result.

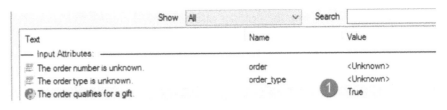

If the order qualifies for a gift, the order gifts shows a single inferred instance.

> **NB**: For reference, the above function is also available in a long form of the type *the order gifts ("the free gift tee-shirt") exists if...*
>
> We will return to the subject of inferring instances in your Projects later, in the chapters on Word tables (4) and Excel Spreadsheets (5).

Inferring Membership of a Relationship

Inferring membership of a relationship follows a similar pattern. As a simple, non-business example, I can infer that in the global context of "everyone", you belong to the group of people "fans of OPA". Fans of OPA is, in a sense, a subset of people in my Global context.

For a more business-like example, consider the requirement to analyse an order, and to process order lines for the product we called OPA Product in a different way in some back-end system. So you need to split orders into two parts.

> **the order line** is a member of **the special processing order lines** if
> > the order line product is an OPA product

The `IsMemberOf()` function is shown above as a conclusion.

> **NB**: The relationship *the special processing order lines* must exist as a reference relationship in your Project Data tab. Without it, you will find Policy Modeling has created another Boolean attribute instead.

Membership as a Condition

In the same way as membership can be inferred, membership can be used as a condition.

> **the order will cost more to process if**
> > for each of the order lines
> > > the order line is a member of the special processing order lines

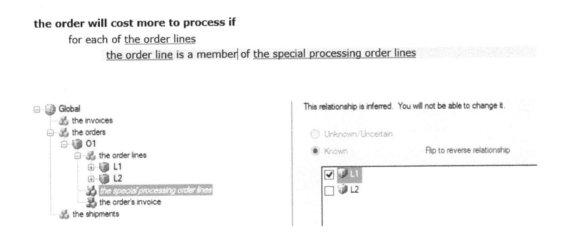

The debugger shows the inferred relationship in yellow, and we are not able to change it since it is inferred.

The Debugger – investigating Relationships and Members

The debugger – both the Data and the Decision tabs – provides plenty of feedback to the rule writer in respect of inferred and reference relationships. For example, in the case of an inferred relationship like the example above, if an order line is missing the product information (the order line product is *uncertain*) then the inferred relationship will itself be shown in the debugger thus:

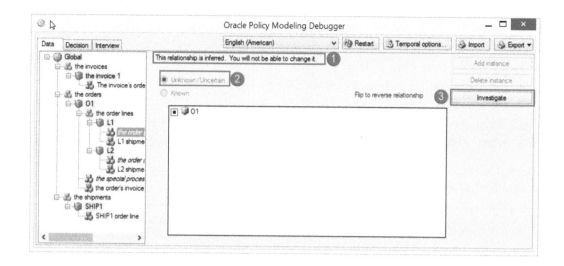

1. Inferred relationships cannot be manually edited.

2. Because information is missing, the inference is not behaving as the business expected, and the relationship displays unknown.

3. Clicking the Investigate button as highlighted, will cause the debugger to display the uncertainty that is, in this case, causing the problem:

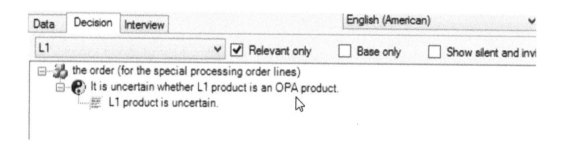

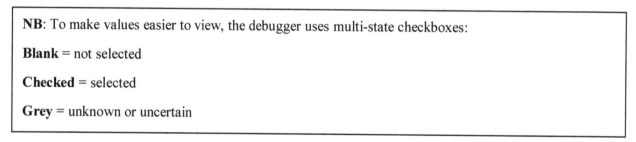

If the rule designer provides a *certain* value for the product of order line 1, it will change the relationship to *known*.

> **NB**: To make values easier to view, the debugger uses multi-state checkboxes:
>
> **Blank** = not selected
>
> **Checked** = selected
>
> **Grey** = unknown or uncertain

On a more general level, the debugger displays the usage of a relationship when we select Relationship Usage from the context menu in the Data tab.

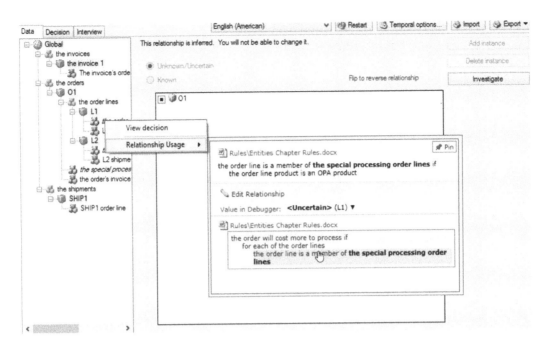

Containment Relationships and Completeness

Up to now you have leveraged the containment relationships in functions. But what does containment actually mean or do? If you have an order and *n* order lines, how do you know the data actually represents *all the order lines for this order*? The answer comes from the notion of containment being complete or not.

Containment Complete

Certain functions, particularly those that aggregate information from entity instances, can produce different outputs depending on whether containment is said to be complete.

This concept is best described with an example from our existing rule Project. We calculate the total number of lines in the order. To do this, Policy Automation must assume that the list of order lines present is the complete set – the containment relationship the order lines represents the entire order.

- Using a new session of the debugger, create a new instance of the order; do not add order lines. The value of the number of order lines in the order is unknown at this stage. Investigating the attribute will show:

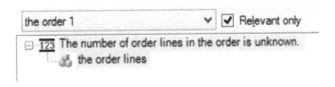

- Add three order lines. Do not worry about entering any attributes. The number of order lines should provide the following in the debugger Decision tab:

This determination resolves, as Policy Automation is sure that the three lines entered are the complete set of order lines. In other words, that the containment relationship *the order lines* is complete.

Now, using the Data tab, right click the relationship – notice the Containment Complete context menu item is checked.

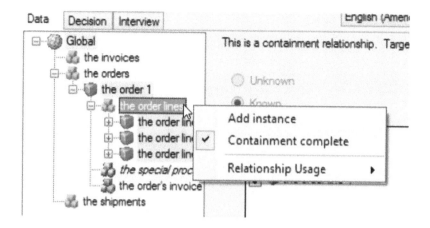

Uncheck the menu item and return to the debugger Decision tab and now the number of order lines is once again unknown.

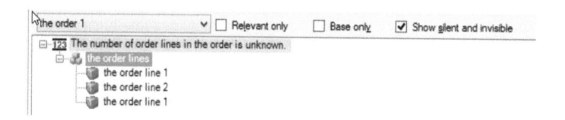

Whilst it might seem odd to need to handle this situation, if you are planning to use your rule Project in a non-interactive way (with a Web Service and not with an interview) then data sent to Policy Automation from external systems might need to signal whether all items in a set were present. Some Application Programming Interfaces supplied with Oracle Policy Automation require a **Containment Complete** flag for a containment relationship to be set in data sent to Policy Automation.

When writing rules, you might add intermediate levels to act as indicators of partial data:

> **the number of order lines in the order can not be calculated if**
> the number of order lines in the order is currently unknown

You could also use a rule or function to assign a value of zero instead of unknown. Recall that the previous chapter introduced these functions: `Default()` and `DefaultWithUnknown()`.

Identifying Scope Errors

One of the main purposes of this chapter is to get used to writing rules using entity functions. In each of the cases you examined, the text of the rule was important for other reasons.

When the conclusion line contained the order, which is entity text – it identified the *context* for the conclusion. If the condition line contained the order lines, Oracle Policy Automation detected a relationship where the order is the source and the order line is the target. Your condition worked as expected since the context was available (the order line is a logical child of the order, and the relationship the order lines was found by Oracle Policy Modeling exactly according to the text provided).

In writing complex rules with many different relationships it is all too easy to make mistakes. To take the example to an extreme, the following deliberate mistake shows what happens when the Policy Modeling is unable to understand the context and/or the relationship appears to not be the correct target or source:

the **customer** has lines with multiple units if
for at least one of the order lines, the order line quantity exceeds one

Validation Errors
×

'the order' is not available here. You may need to use an entity function to refer
to 'the order lines'. (OPA-E00209)

Go To

Close

The customer does not exist as an entity, and the order lines are not related to it in the way Policy Modeling expected. So the error is presented. Notice the error gives us a hint as to what has happened – the Policy Modeling is looking for the order since the order lines refer to it as the source. Thus the order lines cannot be evaluated for the customer since it does not exist and there are no relevant relationships that can help.

> **NB**: Remember if an entity is not in scope, Policy Modeling will be unable to validate the associated part of your policy. Pay close attention to the text of your entity rules!
>
> **NB**: Draw an entity model, and complete it with examples of entity text and relationship text, ensuring that all rule writers have access to it.

Summary

Working with entities and entity-level attributes requires clear structure and a rigorous approach to relationship, entity and attribute text. To avoid errors later on, it is good common sense to adopt a specific style of naming and ensure that it is used all the time.

In addition, as many of these functions do not have a long form, it becomes once again incumbent upon the writer to ensure that all aspects of the determination logic are clearly documented.

Furthermore, when working with relationship functions, failing to bring the relevant entities into scope can result in extraneous attributes being created in your data model.

Finally, partial information may affect the outcome of your rules and may need to be managed within your rule logic.

If you intend to rework these examples, or you want to take a ZIP file as a backup, now is a good time to do it, this backup can be called Chapter Three.

Word Tables

Writing Rules in Word Tables

Certain rules are easier to write in Microsoft Word tables. If you find yourself writing a succession of scenarios with the same attribute, then you will, most likely, be better off using a table.

In addition, working with Word tables allows you to leverage entities and inferred instances as well as work efficiently with temporal reasoning. All of these topics are investigated with practical examples in this chapter.

Why Use Tables

Word Tables are useful when you need to run through a series of conditions to set an attribute. A good analogy might be that you change the shipping charges on an order, depending on the number of order lines. You could write a series of conclusions, one for each price, or you could put the different prices in a table.

Create a Simple Table

To begin working with tables, create a new Project and give it a name like `4 - Working with Tables`. Set the language and region and open the newly created Word file. The **Rule Assistant** is of great help when starting out with Word Tables as the following procedure shows:

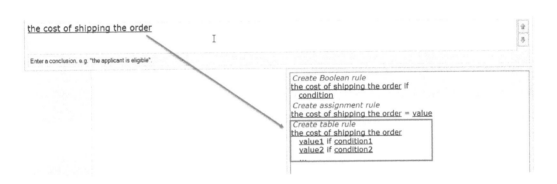

As soon as a potential or existing attribute has been entered, the Rule Assistant proposes, amongst the different options, to create a rule in a Word Table. Selecting that option creates the basic table:

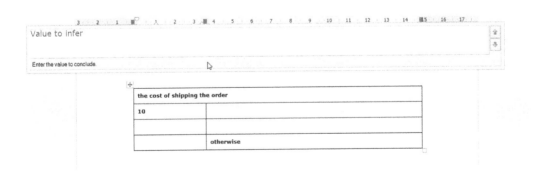

To further assist in the creation of the table, the Rule Assistant takes away some of the doubt as to how to fill the table in. For example, by placing your cursor in the left hand series of cells (where I have already entered the figure 10 above) and clicking the Rule Assistant again, you can see in the commentary zone on the left-hand corner Enter the value to conclude. The **values** of the shipping cost should go in this column. Likewise you can summon the assistant when the cursor is in the right-hand column and you will see the following in the Rule Assistant.

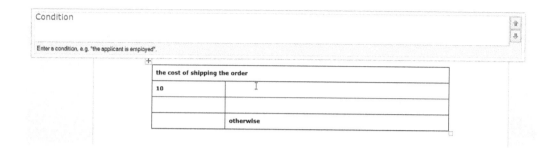

Thanks to the Rule Assistant, it is clear that the right-hand portion is for the **conditions**. The other relevant, and so far unique, aspect is that the Word table has an otherwise statement.

Otherwise in Tables

The **otherwise** element in the table helps us to understand the manner in which this table will be processed during your interview sessions. First, you should complete the table – empty rows will cause validation errors.

the cost of shipping the order	
10	the order value < 30
15	the order value < 50
20	otherwise

In the example above, when in the debugger, entering a value of 30 for the order value correctly outputs the conclusion as 15. The processing of the table is from top to bottom, with each line being disproved before moving to the next line.

Thus, when the second line is reached and found to be true, the expression that results is "the order value is not less than 30 and the order value is less than 50". If all the rows are exhausted then the *otherwise* statement allows us to capture this situation by providing an alternative conclusion even when all the other conditions are false. So if the order value is 51, then the *otherwise* row will be used, as all the previous lines are false.

This ability to respond with an alternative conclusion is one of the attractions of the Word table.

> **NB**: The Policy Modeling Ribbon also has a **Create Table** button if you just want to get stuck in without the Rule Assistant.

Conditions in Tables

Adding more rows to the table is perfectly acceptable, and there is a degree of complexity which can be introduced to provide for more complex tables. As always there is a need to avoid creating something that is overly difficult to read.

Taking the example further, using the data model of the previous chapter (the order, the order line) the following example illustrates a sample document designed to illuminate several features of tables in Word.

- The left cells can be used to contain expressions.

- The right cells can contain grouping, structured levels and functions.

- The Word document can contain further, non-tabular rules, and can also contain multiple tables reaching entirely unrelated conclusions based on further attributes or expressions that leverage the conclusion from the first table.

the cost of shipping the order	
the size of the order * 2	the order is not high value and all the order is intra-EU the order is not for fresh produce
the size of the order * 4	the order is high value or any the order is for fresh produce the order is for the airport the order is for zone three
uncertain	otherwise

<u>the date of shipping</u> = AddDays(the current date, 2)   (2)

the amount of packing material for the order (3)	
0.5	<u>the cost of shipping the order</u> < 5 (4)
1	<u>the cost of shipping the order</u> < 10
2	otherwise

Two tables are used to demonstrate the following points of functionality:

1. Structured levels can be added to your Word table, just like in your normal Word paragraphs. But it may not improve readability.

2. Interspersing text and tables is perfectly acceptable.

3. Having more than one table is perfectly acceptable.

4. Referencing attributes in one table that are inferred in another table (in this case the cost of shipping of the order) is perfectly acceptable.

The Order of Rows

The order of the *tables* in the document is not important. When building Word tables, it is essential to bear in mind the nature of the processing that is performed on your table *rows*. As the table is read vertically from top to bottom, conditions that are disproved cause the processing to move to the next line. In the example above, if the order is high value then the first conditions are disproved, the second row is then processed. So, the order of *rows* is important.

Careless construction of tables leads to situations like the following, where the desired result cannot be reached:

the cost of shipping the order	

**the size of the order
* 2**
	the order is not high value and
	
	all
	
	      the order is intra-EU
	
	      the order is not for fresh produce

**the size of the order
* 4**
	the order is high value or
	
	any
	
	      the order is for fresh produce
	
	      the order is for the airport
	
	      the order is for zone three

the size of the order * 10	the order is air freight
uncertain	**otherwise**

In the above table, an order for air freight will never be priced correctly. If you review the debug window, step by step, it becomes clear why this table is in need of restructuring:

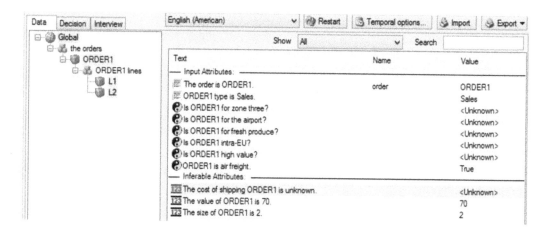

Initially you update the air freight Boolean attribute to true. The cost of shipping remains unknown, since there are a number of other conditions that are, as yet, unknown value. The Decision tab of the Debugger confirms this if you ask to investigate the inferable attribute the cost of the shipping.

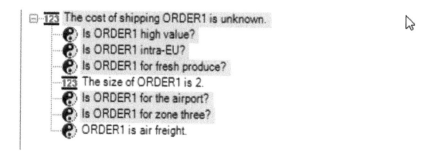

If you now select the high value attribute and assign a value of true, then the cost is calculated on the basis of the high value. The air freight tariff is never reached as the processing of the follows the schema shown in the simulated table below:

the cost of shipping the order	
the size of the order * 2	LINE ONE IS FALSE
the size of the order * 4	LINE ONE IS FALSE AND LINE TWO IS TRUE : INFERENCE MADE
the size of the order * 10	THIS LINE NOT REACHED
uncertain	otherwise

NB: Ordering the data in your table is important for correct behavior and also improved readability.

In addition, *unknown* attributes in a Word table row will stop the evaluation of the table, even if there are rows further down in the table that can be evaluated.

Create a Table to infer Entity Instances

Word tables are also used in Policy Modeling to create instances of an entity. To demonstrate this technique, you can continue to work with the above table as the starting point. If you are unsure about entities, you can go back and revisit Chapter 3.

You need to add a new Entity into the Project model. This entity will represent packing slip information that must be added to the order, according to the destination. You wish to determine the packing slip and create it as an instance of an entity, automatically, according to the situation. This kind of inference is quite common when you have an external system receiving your output from Oracle Policy Automation.

For example, the analysis of your current situation may give rise to you receiving three government benefits. These benefits are inferred by business logic, and inserted into the benefit system as three records.

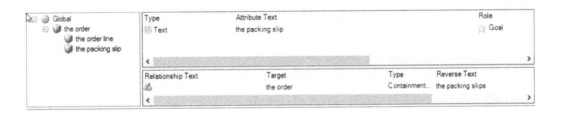

Note the relationship Text has been changed to the packing slip for readability – telling you also this is a one to one relationship since both sides of the relationship are singular. The requirement is to infer the type of packing slip from the attributes already present in the Word document. So you can create a new table to perform this determination.

the packing slips	
"EU 28"	the order is intra-EU
"WW"	the order is not intra-EU

The structure of the rule table is similar to previous examples, with two main differences:
- The conclusion is not an attribute, rather it is relationship text.
- There is no *otherwise* row, as there is no alternative conclusion.

> **NB:** This is known as an inferred entity instance rule. Inferring instances in this way can prove extremely powerful – inferring the services a customer needs based on the products they have purchased, for example.

Start the debugger; create the necessary data for your order, ensuring that the value is entered for the Boolean "is the order intra-EU?" The rule infers an instance of the packing slip for your order.

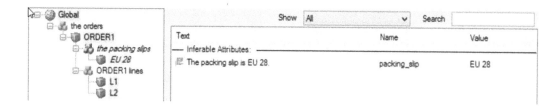

Inferred Entity Instance Attributes

The entity used in this inferred entity instance rule has only one attribute at the moment – the identifying attribute the packing slip which was automatically created when the entity was added.

In early versions of Oracle Policy Automation 12 (and indeed 10), further attributes cannot be added to the entity; they cause an error:

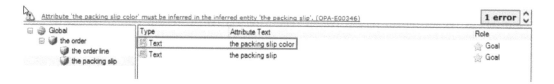

This causes confusion at first – why can't you add another attribute to your simple entity? That's because in many versions (up to November 2016) in an inferred entity, *all* attributes needed to be inferred. In order to add the required attribute to our entity you needed therefore *infer* it through rules.

the packing slip color	
"red"	the order is intra-EU
"blue"	the order is not intra-EU
"green"	**otherwise**

the packing slip date	
the current date	the order is for the airport
the date 3 days after the current date	the order is intra-EU
the date 2 days after the current date	**otherwise**

Although the two examples shown are in table format, attributes can be inferred in normal text-based rules.

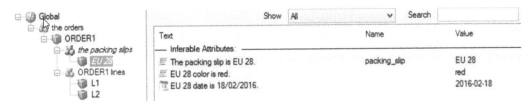

The screenshot shown above illustrates the result, with the inferred instance now containing three inferable attributes.

As mentioned above, the limitation was removed in November 2016's release. You will see some examples in chapter 6. You should however bear in mind that if you are responsible for upgrading or recycling an existing Project, it might have been written at a time when these limitations were in place. Upgrading might require some rework to take the changes into account and optimize the rules.

Limitation of Word Tables

The screenshot of two attributes in *separate* tables highlighted one limitation of Word tables. In an ideal world, it would be have been far more readable to merge the two tables into one in order to keep both conclusions together since they refer to entity-level attributes in the same entity.

This is not possible in Word in current versions of Oracle Policy Automation. The design of a Word table is limited to one conclusion and one condition column. For a flexible layout, involving many columns of conditions and conclusions, read the following chapter.

Temporal Functions in Word Tables

As discussed in the chapter on function usage, temporal functions (which use change points to infer conclusions, such as when a customer last had a certain amount of money in their bank account) will be effective when arranged in Word tables.

Once again, an example will help to explain why Word tables may be convenient in this case. Consider a business that prides itself on shipping produce very fast. They offer money-back guarantees to customers, so that when an item is delivered late, a deduction is made off the value of the order.

Let's imagine that the amount deducted increases, as the length of time to deliver increases. For example, for the first five days, it's only 2 percent of the order value per day. But after five days that rises to 5% per day.

Temporal Reasoning in a Table

Translating that timeline into Word produces the following table, with an explanation below it.

The money lost on the delayed shipment	
The order value * 0.02	TemporalBefore(AddDays(the date of shipping, 1))
The order value * 0.02	TemporalBefore(AddDays(the date of shipping, 5))
The order value * 0.05	TemporalBefore(AddDays(the date of shipping, 10))
The order value * 0.10	TemporalBefore(AddDays(the date of shipping, 15))
The order value * 0.20	**otherwise**

The money lost as of today = IntervalDailySum(the date of shipping, the current date, The money lost on the delayed shipment)

The residual money less the money lost = the order value – the money lost as of today

The table sets up the initial logic. According to how many days have elapsed since the date of the order being shipped, different loss rates apply. The calculations below the table show the money lost, and the residual.

Assuming an order value of 100, then using the shipping date you can visualize the impact in the Debugger. Firstly, the daily loss percentage, shown here in Temporal Visualization:

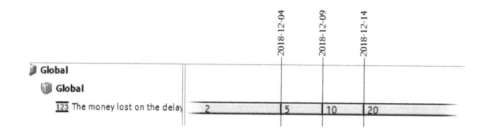

Secondly the Decision view of the attribute that calculates the money lost as of today's date.

123 The money lost as of today is 20.
    The date of shipping is 11/29/2018.
123 The money lost on the delayed shipment is {2, 5 from 12/04/2018, 10 from 12/09/2018, 20 from 12/14/2018}.

Finally, you can view the information in an Interview Screen.

What is the order value?

100

What is the date of shipping?

11/29/2018

20 - Lost so far

80 - Residual

Change Points

The functions `TemporalAfter()` and `TemporalBefore()` allow the rule writer to define the rate of change by creating change points using business logic. In effect, in your table this creates change points after 1, 5, 10 or 20 days.

The textual rule under the table takes the different deductions and calculates the current total amount of money lost, based on the shipping date and the current date. So a shipment that was shipped ten days ago would have five days where you lost 2% of the order value, followed by five days at the higher rate of 5%.

Remember to view the results of your debug session using the **Temporal Visualization** tab as described in the chapter on functions.

> **NB**: The business, armed with such information, might create rules to flag orders whose delivery has not been delivered after *n* days once the current total depreciation reaches a critical percentage of the value of an order.

Summary

Working with tables in Word reveals new functionality – the ability to stack different conclusions in a vertical list is an efficient way of selecting a value from a series of choices, depending on various conditions. It is generally more efficient to place this kind of rule in a table than to try and write all the iterations manually.

Word tables also handle *alternative conclusions* in an easy-to-follow way – if a situation is not handled in your table, then *otherwise* will apply.

You also saw useful applications of Word tables to infer instances of entities and to collect information for change point creation in temporal logic.

Although Word tables are powerful, they lack the ability to handle extra *columns* of information, whether it be to define conditions or conclusions. The next chapter explains how to overcome these limitations, by switching to Microsoft Excel to create rule spreadsheets in a rule Project for the first time. All of the features you investigated in this chapter are available in Excel, as well as exciting new capabilities.

> **NB**: That completes your initial Table exercises. In the next chapter, you will begin a new Project so (if you want to) don't forget to save your work and make a backup Zip of your Project.

Excel Rules

Writing Rules in Excel

In the previous chapter, Microsoft Word was used to create rule tables. As well as saving time in maintaining a list of possible outcomes in a tabular form, Word offered a means to create instances in a table, and to use time-based or *temporal* functions to create new business rules that change over time.

In spite of this, several limitations were exposed. Now, in chapter 5, you will use Microsoft Excel to not only go beyond Word tables, but to discover some unique functionality as well.

Getting Started with Microsoft Excel

Microsoft Excel occupies a number of key roles in a rule Project – it is the tool for managing translations (see Chapter 15) and the basis for automated testing (see Chapter 8). In this chapter, you shall work exclusively with Microsoft Excel as a rule document, much as you did with Microsoft Word.

Adding your first Excel Spreadsheet

For the purposes of getting familiar with Microsoft Excel it's time to start a new Project in Policy Modeling and navigate to the Data tab. There, begin by clicking the New Excel Document button, adding the file to the Project.

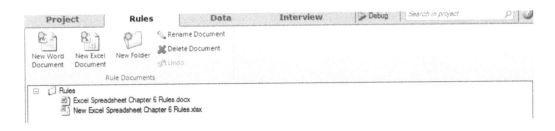

In practical terms, the presence of an Excel file does not change the general maintenance tasks or management of a rule Project. It does however reinforce the importance of good documentation and comments, since an Excel spreadsheet can be challenging to interpret. It can contain multiple tabs, some of which have unique properties.

Before you begin working with this Excel file, it is necessary to examine the differences and the new ways you need to approach the Excel rule-building experience.

The two Standard Worksheets

Opening the Excel file you just created shows that, by default, there are only two tabs created. The **Declarations** tab, and the **Rule Table** tab.

The Rule Table tab, as its name suggests, is the place where most of the policy design work will take place. Note, you are not limited to a single Rule Table sheet, as you will see later in the chapter. For now just begin working on a new table.

Formatting in Excel

The principle of rule writing in Excel is exactly the same as that for Word, namely the content of your document must be correctly formatted in order for it to be validated. The formatting in Excel is contained in a ribbon similar to that in Word. There are, however, some differences that can make it hard to adapt at first.

The Heading Formats and Cell Formats

The example Rule Table that is added automatically to your Excel file contains five different formats. The column headers each have formatting, the cell contents have formatting, and lastly the **else** cell, reserved as in

Word ("otherwise") for the alternative conclusion. The location of the different formatting buttons is shown in the screenshot below.

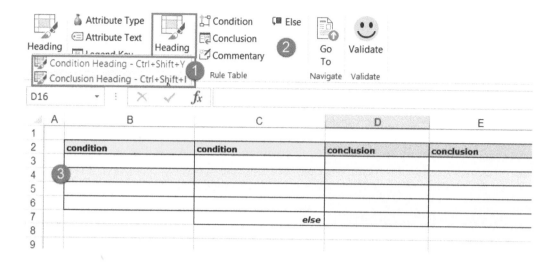

1. These are the two formats for the Condition Heading (the brighter green) and the Conclusion Heading (the darker brown).

2. The Condition, Conclusion and Else buttons provide the main body of the table, light green and light brown respectively.

3. The Commentary button allows cells to be marked in order to place comments, remarks or other non-parsed information. Commentary is not required in a table.

The remaining formats are reserved for the Declarations tab which will be discussed in a few pages time.

Orientation and Order

The exact order of the columns is not important, since every column type has its own specific formatting. This also means, for example, that a table can be rotated to switch from the standard X-Y to Y-X orientation.

The standard layout is presented with the headings on the top of the relevant columns, as shown in the very simplistic table shown below.

the weight of the cargo	the product color code	the kind of packaging	the storage temperature
100	red	"small"	"hot"
100	blue	"small"	"cold"
200	green	"big"	"wet"
	else	uncertain	uncertain

The table shown in the screenshot below is functionally identical to a standard one, however the headings are on the left rather than on the top.

the weight of the cargo	100	100	200	
the product color code	red	blue	green	*else*
the kind of packaging	"small"	"small"	"big"	uncertain
the storage temperature	"hot"	"cold"	"wet"	uncertain

More Excel Formatting Specifics

When working with Excel, in the same manner as with Word in Oracle Policy Modeling Version 12, attributes are detected and added to the Data tab of your Project. Microsoft Excel may fail to propose a Type, however, and you will be instructed to select the correct Type before you can debug your rule Project.

This will be made clear when you save the Project for the first time.

The Project will contain a number of erroneously interpreted attributes, as demonstrated above, until you correct the Type of the attribute referenced in the error message. Errors of this kind may also occur, as you saw in an earlier chapter, when an attribute or condition text is poorly constructed.

Improving the Detection of Attribute Types

To accelerate your Excel file creation, you can use several techniques to make the attribute type easier for Policy Modeling to interpret:

- Create the attribute in the Data tab prior to using it in Excel.

- Format Currency Attributes before saving for the first time.

To highlight cells as being of Policy Automation Currency format, select all the cells, including the heading cell, and apply the Currency from the Format Cells context menu command. This will signal to Policy Modeling that the data is of type Currency. In order for this to work properly, however, your PC's region should match that of your Policy Modeling Project.

To provide further precise information about your attributes if they are not created in the Data tab, you can use the Declarations tab in Excel.

The Declarations Tab

The Declarations tab in Excel has two main functions. The first is arguably a legacy of Oracle Policy Modeler version 10:

To stipulate the Type of new attributes (should you choose not to create them in the Data tab or the Properties File for version 10), you can enter the corresponding attribute text and attribute type directly in the Declarations tab as guidance for the Policy Automation engine. For example, consider that the attribute shown in the previous screenshot (the weight of the cargo) has not been previously entered in the Data tab of your Project. Entering it in the Declarations tab as follows will ensure the correct type is selected for you. This is effective for numbers and currencies particularly.

Attribute Type	Attribute Text	Legend Key
number	the weight of the cargo	

Boolean attributes do not normally need any attention, they are detected and handled automatically when you validate your work irrespective of your version of Policy Modeling.

The Legend Key Cell in the Declarations Tab

The Declarations tab in Excel has a second use. Although Excel provides for a great deal more horizontal space than a Word document, it is often good practice to shorten the width of columns and to use truncated text in your column headers. To do this, add a legend text in your Declarations tab as follows:

Attribute Type	Attribute Text	Legend Key
number	the weight of the cargo	weight

You are then able to reference your attribute just by using the legend key, which will improve manageability and lessen scrolling in many cases:

weight	the packaging type	the pallet size
< 100	"light"	120
< 200	"medium"	220
< 300	"heavy"	350
< 400	"heavey"	450
else	"reinforced"	500

Working with Condition and Conclusion Columns

There are two ways to use the conclusion or condition columns in Excel. Either reference an attribute text or legend, as we have shown in the screenshots up to now, or use the following strategy, where appropriate.

Condition Heading

The condition columns can simply be headed condition as shown below. The heading must be accompanied, in that case, by valid expressions or Boolean statements.

Conclusion Heading

Likewise the conclusion column can be headed conclusion. In this case the conclusion must be a Boolean as shown.

weight	conclusion	the pallet size
< 100	the packaging is light	120
< 200	the packaging is medium	220
< 300	the packaging is heavy	350
< 400	the packaging is heavy	450
else	the packaging is reinforced	500

In both cases, as shown above, it is possible to mix the two methods in different columns in the same table.

A Practical Example

Now that you have seen the various ways to work with an Excel spreadsheet, to reinforce these ideas we can build a working example.

> **NB**: To avoid confusion with existing attributes, if you have already used an Excel sheet in your Project to work with the different items explained above, save and close that file now. Using the method described in chapter 1, take a backup ZIP copy of your Project in case you wish to review it later.

Create a new Project and add another, new Excel file. When using Excel, as we have seen, it is perfectly normal to want to extend or reduce the column count on either part of the table. Your table needs to have three condition columns and three conclusion columns as shown below.

value	assessment	assessment	reimbursement	reimbursement date	conclusion
		else			

Your table will calculate the different amounts to reimburse customers when something goes unexpectedly wrong in the order management process. Reimbursements will be issued to customers when certain criteria are met.

In the Declarations tab enter the following information to specify the desired attribute text, attribute type and shortened legend for the table shown above.

Attribute Type	Attribute Text	Legend Key
currency	the value of the order	value
datetime	the date of assessment	assessment
currency	the reimbursement amount	reimbursement
datetime	the date of reimbursement	reimbursement date

Entering Ranges of Data

The Excel spreadsheet allows us to create data ranges easily, since (as in the example shown) it is possible to have two columns with the same attribute or legend text.

value	assessment	assessment	reimbursement	reimbursement date	conclusion
	>=2015-01-01	<2015-06-30			
	>=2015-06-30	<2015-07-31			
	>2015-07-31	<2015-08-31			
	>2015-10-31	<2015-11-30			
	>2015-11-30				
		else			

Once the range of dates is entered, you might also wish to merge the column headers (using the standard Excel Merge formatting) so that it becomes easier to review the table.

value	assessment		reimbursement	reimbursement date	conclusion
	>=2015-01-01	<2015-06-30			
	>=2015-06-30	<2015-07-31			
	>2015-07-31	<2015-08-31			
	>2015-10-31	<2015-11-30			
	>2015-11-30				
		else			

NB: When you attempt to 'un-merge' columns that contain information, Excel may remove important information from the cells. Both here, and later, when we discuss merging in more advanced situations, be careful not to merge or unmerge before you have made sure you are aware of the consequences.

Using Conclusions to infer multiple Boolean attributes

In the case, as above, where the table uses conclusion as the heading, it is possible for each of the lines to infer a different Boolean attribute. This can be very useful where a single set of input needs to produce multiple, different, Boolean results.

In your Excel rule table, add the following text to demonstrate this capability:

value	assessment		reimbursement	reimbursement date	conclusion
	>=2015-01-01	<2015-06-30			the customer is on the old watchlist
	>=2015-06-30	<2015-07-31			the customer is on the summer watchlist
	>2015-07-31	<2015-08-31			the customer is on the late summer watchlist
	>2015-10-31	<2015-11-30			the customer is on the autumn watchlist
	>2015-11-30				the customer is on the winter watchlist
		else			

Complete the initial table structure by adding the following elements to demonstrate (for training purposes) the different functionalities of decision tables in Excel.

Adding Functions to Excel Tables

Next you will enter a new function in the reimbursement date conclusion column using the `AddDays()` function, to indicate when reimbursement should have been issued by.

Notice that the function arguments change depending on the line in the table. It's easy to imagine that criteria were changed to reflect operating conditions in the business.

The `AddDays()` function adds a certain number of days to another date or date time attribute.

reimbursement date	con
AddDays(the date of assessment, 10)	the
AddDays(the date of assessment, 10)	the
AddDays(the date of assessment, 10)	the
AddDays(the date of assessment, 20)	the
AddDays(the date of assessment, 10)	the

NB: In the case of text attributes, be careful not to get mixed up and accidentally create Boolean attributes. In the screenshot below, the left conclusion column is inferring Booleans. The right-hand column is inferring text for a text attribute. Pay attention to the Data tab and eliminate spelling errors.

conclusion	the customer statement
the customer is on the old watchlist	"yellow list customer"
the customer is on the summer watchlist	"yellow list customer"
the customer is on the late summer watchlist	"yellow list customer"
the customer is on the autumn watchlist	"orange list customer"
the customer is on the autumn watchlist	"red list customer"

Adding Expressions to Excel Tables

Expressions, for example a calculation for a number attribute, can be entered in the same way as Word rule documents in your Project. Enter the following information to add more conditions to your Excel file. For ease of reading, only the conclusions are shown.

reimbursement	reimbursement date	conclusion
the value of the order * 0.10	AddDays(the date of assessment, 10)	the customer is on the old watchlist
the value of the order * 0.10	AddDays(the date of assessment, 10)	the customer is on the summer watchlist
the value of the order * 0.10	AddDays(the date of assessment, 10)	the customer is on the late summer watchlist
the value of the order * 0.11	AddDays(the date of assessment, 20)	the customer is on the autumn watchlist
the value of the order * 0.15	AddDays(the date of assessment, 10)	the customer is on the autumn watchlist

Rationalizing Tables Using Merge

The merge feature proved useful in an earlier section to highlight two Excel columns used for a range of values. Merge is also available to rationalize data in conditions or conclusions. For example, the first condition column at the moment shows the same data for every line (let's assume the table is not yet complete, and that other values will be added later). So merging them will improve readability.

type	value	assessment		reimbursement	reimbursement date	conclusion
	> 100	>=2015-01-01 09:00:00	<2015-06-30 17:00:00	the value of the order * 0.10	AddDays(the date of assessment, 10)	the customer is on the old watchlist
	> 100	>=2015-06-30 09:00:00	<2015-07-31 17:00:00	the value of the order * 0.10	AddDays(the date of assessment, 10)	the customer is on the summer watchlist
	>100	>2015-07-31 09:00:00	<2015-08-31 17:00:00	the value of the order * 0.10	AddDays(the date of assessment, 10)	the customer is on the late summer watchlist
		>2015-10-31 09:00:00	<2015-11-30 17:00:00	the value of the order * 0.11	AddDays(the date of assessment, 20)	the customer is on the autumn watchlist
professional	>150	>2015-11-30 09:00:00		the value of the order * 0.15	AddDays(the date of assessment, 10)	the customer is on the autumn watchlist
			else			

Merging Conclusions

As we discovered when working with Word tables, unknown attribute values in a row causes the processing of the table to stop. So consider the following situation, where you have two attributes in your conditions:

the order type	the order quantity	the order can be shipped
sales		TRUE
	100	TRUE

If the order type is unknown, but the order quantity is known, the evaluation would not proceed – even though we have enough data to prove the second line. What we are trying to indicate is that either of these two combinations is enough to prove the conclusion.

the order type	the order quantity	the order can be shipped
sales		
	100	TRUE

Merging conclusion cells indicates that the table rows associated with the merged conclusion are logically combined using an OR to create a single row. This can be useful if you are faced with two conditions, as shown above, where one of them may be *unknown*.

In this domain, users of version 10 have a slight advantage; they can call up an extra window called the **Rule Browser**. In version 10, creating the same Excel spreadsheet as the example shown above and right-clicking allows the rule writer to see the generated result after Policy Modeling has performed compilation / validation:

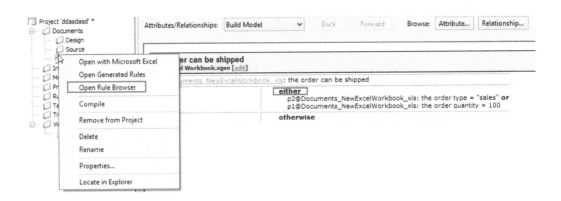

The screenshot shows that the Excel content is evaluated using a logical *either...or* as in the example above.

Blank Cells in a Table

Sometimes in an Excel table you need to indicate that a criterion is not relevant for a given line. For example, in the fourth line of the table you entered at the start of this section, there is no value. Similarly there is no "end date" for the assessment condition.

In the case of the order value, you might need to indicate that during a particular period of assessment, *any* value of order was accepted for processing. In the case of the assessment date, the last line is open-ended and there is no "end-date" at the moment. Blank cells are used for this purpose.

Avoiding Misinterpretation

When you are using Excel spreadsheets and working with Boolean operators, you may need from time to time to enter values such as `true` or `false` into your spreadsheet. When entering them, be sure to enclose them in brackets to avoid them being interpreted as text strings. You will need to do this also for references to other text attributes as show in a new example below:

the law is subject to revision	the points of l	the classification of the law
(TRUE)	L627	(the classification of law article L627)

Using Multiple Worksheets

It is entirely possible to have multiple tables on one Worksheet, just as it was possible to have several completely unrelated goals in the same Word document in your rule Project. It is also possible to have multiple Worksheets. You may wish to leverage multiple Worksheets to create copies of a table for date-based determinations, as described in the next section.

Creating Multiple Tables for Date-based Selection

Suppose you have several tables, all with the same rule structure – but with different conditional expressions or different conclusions – that need to be selected, based on a date attribute. For example, for orders that were received in 2015, a different set of reimbursement values apply than for 2016, and so forth. Another example might be the tariffs for 2015, 2016, and 2017 which all use the same criteria but different calculations.

Implementing this kind of date-related functionality requires three steps:

1. Creating copies of the relevant Worksheet.

Once you have created the copies, you can update the values and work on each table individually.

2. Naming the Worksheets in a clear way.

Each Worksheet should have a clear name and you should make sure that they identify the reason for selection.

3. Referencing the Worksheets in a special **Master Table** of the Declarations tab.

Create a new table in the Declarations tab. Make sure you format it with the correct headings (Conclusion Heading, Condition Heading) and that you populate it with the criteria for selection of your Worksheet, and the name (case-sensitive) of the Worksheet involved. The screenshot below gives a example of what this looks like.

Attribute Type	Attribute Text	Legend Key
currency	the value of the order	value
datetime	the date of assessment	assessment
currency	the reimbursement amount	reimbursement
datetime	the date of reimbursement	reimbursement date

the date of the order	Apply Sheet
>2016-01-01	2016
>2015-01-01	2015
else	Earlier

Declarations | 2015 | 2016 | Earlier | ⊕

The text Apply Sheet is reserved and you should not use this in your Worksheet names or as a column header.

NB: You might be surprised that this works – you were expecting an error perhaps, telling you that it is not allowed to have attributes that are proven multiple times. Instead, the extra condition is consolidated at validation time. Again version 10 users can review the Rule Browser to have confirmation of this.

```
both
    p5@Documents_ExcelExample_xls: the order type = "professional" and
    p1@Documents_ExcelExample_xls: the value of the order > 100 and
    either
        both
            p2@Documents_ExcelExample_xls: the date of assessment >= 2015-01-01 09:00:00 and
            p2@Documents_ExcelExample_xls: the date of assessment < 2015-06-30 17:00:00
    or
        both
            p2@Documents_ExcelExample_xls: the date of assessment >= 2015-06-30 09:00:00 and
            p2@Documents_ExcelExample_xls: the date of assessment < 2015-07-31 17:00:00
    or
        both
            p2@Documents_ExcelExample_xls: the date of assessment > 2015-07-31 09:00:00 and
            p2@Documents_ExcelExample_xls: the date of assessment < 2015-08-31 17:00:00
and
    p1@Properties_DataTab_xsrc: the date of the order > 2016-01-01
```

The screenshot above shows the extra condition as a logical and at the end of the compiled rule.

Using Entities with Excel Tables

Writing rule tables with entity text

There are some restrictions when working with entities and entity functions in Excel spreadsheets.

Entity Attributes as Conclusions

When using Excel to infer entity-level attributes in a table, then all conclusions must come from the same entity. To demonstrate this, create a new table in your existing Workbook and Worksheet and enter the following excerpt from another rule table:

condition	the wire transfer type	the wire transfer amount	the wire transfer can be issued by a non-manager
the number of the wire transfers <=10	national	<500	TRUE
the number of the wire transfers <=5	national	>500	FALSE
		else	FALSE

This also assumes that in your Data tab, you create the entity the wire transfer and you rename the relationship text from all the instances of the wire transfer to the wire transfers.

Although this rule table is not complete, start a debug session to view the Data tab of the debugger. Enter several wire transfers. The rule table functions without error.

Notice however that the number of wire transfers, one of your conditions, is not visible in the debugger data. This is a slight disadvantage of using a generic "condition" heading in Excel. To rectify this you could use normal Policy Modeling techniques:

1. Create an attribute in a Word File, and use an entity function to infer a value

$$\underline{\textbf{the total wire transfers}} = \textbf{InstanceCount(}\underline{\textbf{the wire transfers}}\textbf{)}$$

2. Change the Excel spreadsheet to include the attribute text, as shown in the leftmost column. Don't forget to adjust the condition text as appropriate

the total wire transfers	the wire transfer type	the wire transfer amount	the wire transfer can be issued by a non-manager
<=10	national	<500	TRUE
<=5	national	>500	FALSE
		else	FALSE

The total wire transfers joining attribute is now visible both in the Data tab of the debugger, and in the View Decision context menu item for the Decision tab, as shown in the inset image below.

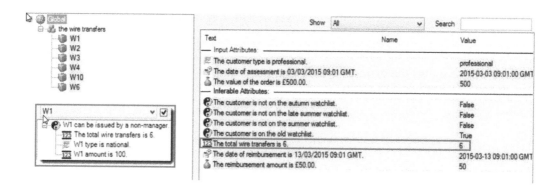

If it wasn't already obvious, hopefully this last example has served to illustrate that rules in Excel can leverage attributes inferred in Word and vice-versa.

> **NB**: Now is a great time to create a ZIP copy of this Project as described in Chapter 1. You can call this backup copy `Chapter Five Part Two`. A new Project will be used in the next section.

Inferring Instances in Excel

One of the most interesting and powerful features of Excel is the ability to infer instances. Although the same concept was introduced in Word, due to the limitations in place it really is much more useful when performed in Excel.

Example Entity Model

To examine this functionality, we need to create a new Project, and we will use the following entity model.

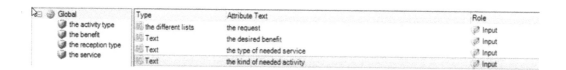

In this more complex example, there will be four different entities. Citizens will come to an online portal or kiosk, and they can choose from a series of options: they can request a list of benefits, or services, or activities. Or they can ask for a lists of clubs or other reception centres. All of the above might be related to childcare in your neighbourhood – so this rule Project helps you, the citizen, find out what is available, and what the different centre names and centre codes are – which will help the citizen fill out the paperwork when requesting a service.

There might be different kinds of user; parents might request a list of services, activities, benefits or reception centres in order to help them organize and get the childcare they need, or perhaps government personnel will use the portal to obtain codes and abbreviations used to request a package of services.

Take care to update the containment relationship text from the default all instances of... to a more appropriate text such as the activity types or the services. Then you are ready to build the first Excel table.

A Request for Activity Types

The following small table illustrates the principle. A condition column called *the request* – which is a text attribute of the **Global** entity) is used to infer two instances of an entity called the activity type. The second column header uses the relationship text. Thus when a citizen asks for a list of activity types, the two activity types will be inferred. In user interface terms, selecting "List of Activity Types" will return two values.

the request	the activity types
	"YOUNG_PERSON_LEISURE"
"List of Activity Types"	"INFANT_RECEPTION"

A Request for Services

The example can be extended with a second table in the same worksheet. This time we will use *two* conditions, both attributes from the **Global** entity, to instance multiple services and to provide not just the identifying attribute, but also a second attribute at the same time.

the request	the type of needed service	the services	the service's name in text
		"AFH"	"After School Hours"
		"OOTT"	"Out of Term Time"
	"YOUNG_PERSON_LEISURE"	"YPC"	"Young Person Centre"
		"MSR1"	"Multi-Service"
		"MCRCH"	"Micro-creche"
"List of Services"	"INFANT_RECEPTION"	"COMMCRECHE"	"Community Creche"

Asking for a list of available services (column 1) and specifying the needed service (column 2) infers the services with their codes (column 3) and the text-based name for each service (column 4).

In the above table, if the request is "List of Services", and the type of needed service is "YOUNG_PERSON_LEISURE" then the conclusions AFH, OOTT and YPC can be inferred. Recall that the heading of the first conclusion column is not an attribute but is *a relationship text*. This will cause Policy Modeling to infer the existence of the services. In addition, the service's name in text form is also inferred.

A Request for Benefits

the request	the type of needed service	the kind of needed activity	the benefits
			"OPA EX YOUNG_PERSON_LEISURE"
		"After School Hours"	"GRANT"
			"OPA EX YOUNG_PERSON_LEISURE"
		"Out of Term Time"	"GRANT"
	"YOUNG_PERSON_LEISURE"	"Young Person Centre"	"OPA EX YOUNG_PERSON_LEISURE"
			"OPA EX INFANT_RECEPTION"
			"GRANT"
		"Multi-Service"	"NEW CHILD STARTER"
			"OPA EX INFANT_RECEPTION"
			"GRANT"
"List of Benefits"	"INFANT_RECEPTION"	"Micro-creche"	"NEW CHILD STARTER"

In the third example, above, the request for a "List of benefits", once the three condition attributes have been populated with values, infers instances of benefits. Once again the benefits is not an attribute name but a *relationship text*.

A Request for a List of Activity Centres

This concept can be extended to provide any number of inferred attribute values – something that was not possible in a single Word table. For example, the following is a third table, detailing a third request for a list of reception types (youth centres, after-hours clubs). It has been broken into two parts for ease of printing. First the conditions:

the request	the type of needed service	the kind of needed activity	the desired benefit
		"After School Hours"	"OPA EX YOUNG_PERSON_LEISURE"
		"Out of Term Time"	"OPA EX YOUNG_PERSON_LEISURE"
	"YOUNG_PERSON_LEISURE"	"Young Person Centre"	"OPA EX YOUNG_PERSON_LEISURE"
		"Multi-Service"	
		"Community Creche"	
"List of Reception Types"	"INFANT_RECEPTION"	"Micro-creche"	"OPA EX INFANT_RECEPTION"

And now the conclusions; the first column creates the instances and the other columns populate the attributes:

the reception types	the reception type's characteristic	the reception	the reception type's age grou	the reception type's	the reception type in detail
"OPA-PER-36-AVC"	"After School Hours"			"Before Class"	Variable
"OPA-PER-36-PM"	"After School Hours"			"Lunchtime"	"RN-PERISCO"
"OPA-PER-36-APC-T1"	"After School Hours"		"3-6"		"RN-PERISCO"
"OPA-PER-612-APC-T2"	"After School Hours"		"6-12"	"After Class"	"RN-PERISCO"
"OPA-TAP-36"	"After School Hours Grant"		"3-6"		"RN-TAP"
"OPA-EXT-PV-TOU-36"			"3-6"		"RN-EXTRA-PV"
"OPA-EXT-PV-TOU-612"			"6-12"		"RN-EXTRA-PV"
"OPA-EXT-PV-TOU-1217"	"Easter Holidays"	"Halloween"	"12-17"		"RN-EXTRA-PV"
"OPA-EXT-V-SUMMER-36"	"Holidays"	"Summer"	"3-6"		"RN-EXTRA-PV"
"OPA-ACC-1217"	"Young Person Centre"		"12-17"		"RN-ACC-YOUNG"
"YOU-MUL-CRECO-06"	"Junior Creche"		"0-6"		"RN-MULTI-CRECHE"
"YOU-MUL-CREFA-06"	"Multi-service Creche"		"0-6"		"RN-MULTI-CREFA"
"YOU-MUL-CREPA-06"	"Junior Creche"		"0-6"		"RN-MULTI-CREPA"
"YOU-CRECO-06"	"Multi-service Creche"		"0-6"		"RN-CRECO"
"OPA-MICRO-06"	"Micro Community Creche"		"0-6"		"RN-MICRO"

> **NB**: In these examples, you are inferring attribute values for instances of an Entity. For the purpose of simplification, the attributes are all inferred and the results, essentially, are read-only – which corresponds to this scenario. In recent versions of Oracle Policy Automation, the possibility to mix inferred attributes with non-inferred attributes in an entity has become possible, and you will learn more about this in chapter 6.

Notice once again that, with Excel, we can infer as many entity attributes as we need in each table.

Debugging the Project

The debugging session will require you to enter only the various Global attributes. Once you have entered a request (List of Services, List of Activity Types etc.) and specified the nature of your request, then the inferred instances should automatically appear in the Data tab.

For example, below I have asked for Reception Types, for young persons after school hours. Five inferred instances are created in the debugger. If you encounter issues, make sure that you have not confused *relationship text* with attribute text.

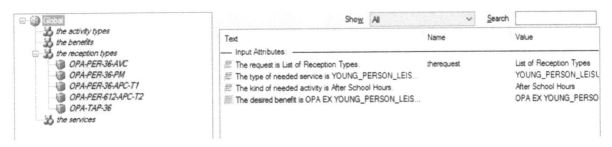

Summary

Microsoft Excel tables provide a very structured environment in which to create both tables to infer conclusions and to infer the existence of entity instances. The fact that Excel and Word cooperate so easily in Oracle Policy Automation lets the rule writer concentrate on picking the best tool for the job at hand.

Excel's versatility means that you will be using it for several other purposes in Oracle Policy Automation. These other roles will be met in later chapters.

> **NB**: When using Excel to create tables that infer instances, no *else* line is required.
>
> If you have not already done so, now is a great time to take a ZIP copy of this Project as described previously. You could call it `Chapter Five Part Three` for example.

Basic Interviews

Creating Interviews

So far in your investigation of the functionality of Policy Modeling you have focused on writing rules and entity models. In this chapter, you will learn how to create vibrant, easy-to-use interviews so that an end-user can benefit from the policies being automated.

Interviews are used to interact with users, and can be displayed on any modern browser. The OPA Mobile App also leverages the interview structure you create but displays it in a device-optimized way.

Before we go any further, you should remember that this is only one way of using Oracle Policy Automation to determine the answer(s) to your policy goals. It is also perfectly possible to work with the *determination server* in another way: using a SOAP Web Service and XML, rather than HTML as shown in these chapters. Both meet different customer needs.

Getting Started with Interviews

Interviews are the front end view of a determination session. End users need to get a job done or to find out information quickly, so your goal should be to create a user experience that lets that happen.

Version 12 users have a significant advantage over version 10 – the interface for creating interviews is much more streamlined and the workflow is simplified. At the same time, it is more mouse-friendly and, most importantly of all, the result is easy to style using modern Web standards.

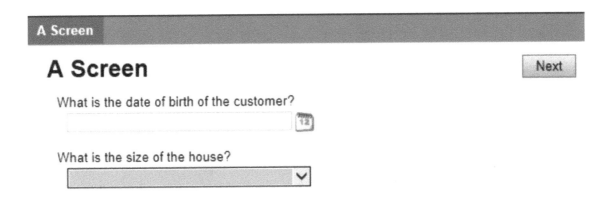

Above is an interview screen from one of the 2015 releases.

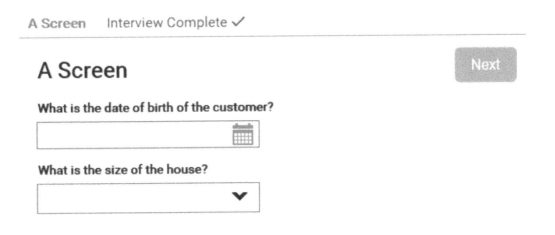

And for comparison (above), the same information in a more recent release with new icons, buttons and fonts. These are continuously evolving, producing ever more attractive user experiences.

To enable you to work on different scenarios, your first Interview will require you to load up one of your backup Projects. For this first example, use the project from chapter 1.

Screens

The basic unit of your interview is the **Screen**. Put simply, a screen is a page in your browser, designed to collect or view Global or entity attributes. There is already one screen in your interview, which serves as the end point to allow for the display of the explanation (see Chapter 9). Go ahead and start the debugger and switch to the Interview tab. Enter some appropriate data and you will observe that *each* new attribute that needs to be collected, appears on a *separate* screen. This is the default behaviour when no work has been done to improve the interview – Policy Automation creates these screens automatically to enable the user to at least complete all the required inputs, even if the layout is very unfriendly.

On the left-hand side of the screenshot, above, you can see a series of *automatic* screens. The icons you see in your debugger may be different however; they are highlighting the fact that you have not designed any Screens for your interview.

You will also notice that the screen real-estate is quite empty, apart from a button to move forward or back. The debugger does, however, provide lots of information "on demand". On the left-hand side of the window, selecting a screen and clicking the Details floating button reveals the following window:

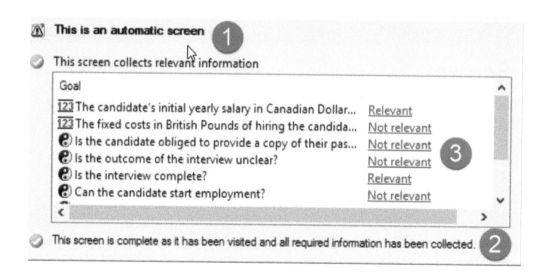

In the above image, the following points are notable for future reference:

1. Screens that are generated by the Oracle Policy Automation inference engine are called *automatic* screens.

2. The status of the data entry in the screen can change the colour of the Stage at the top of the page during the interview (see the next page).

3. The data on this page is relevant to your interview Goal (see the next page).

Organizing your interview into screens that you build yourself (rather than just using the *automatic* screens), is the first step towards making it easier to use. Deciding what information is displayed, and ensuring that it is relevant to the goal(s) of the interview, is part of that process.

Goals

Your rule Project might contain more than one goal; there is more than one top-level attribute. Which one(s) will be the goal(s) of your interview? Deciding on which goals to focus on will help you identify what is relevant or not relevant, and will clarify the process for the end user. Oracle Policy Modeling helps you define these attributes by allowing you to select what your interview goal is, and by highlighting whether an attribute is pertinent to the selected goal(s) of your interview, as shown in the screenshot above. In simple Projects where, for instance, you calculate a single number, it is easy to define the goal. In complex Projects, there may be many goals at different levels (Has the order shipped on time? Was the discount applied?).

Stages

In the case of a longer interview, the end user needs to know, where they are in the flow. We are all familiar with the idea of breaking a process into sections. These are called **Stages** in Policy Modeling. Screens can be organized into stages. The Web Determination displays the Stage in the interview for reference. Stages can have their own styling and can be displayed horizontally, vertically or not at all.

Above, you see Screens, Stages (displayed horizontally to the user) and styling for the active Stage.

Checkpoints

In recent versions of Oracle Policy Modeling, a feature known as Checkpoints has been introduced. This allows users to save and resume an interview, for example because they were interrupted. This kind of "suspend and resume" functionality requires a specially configured Connection.

Below is an example of how the different screens in an interview can be selected as checkpoints, allowing the user to save at that point.

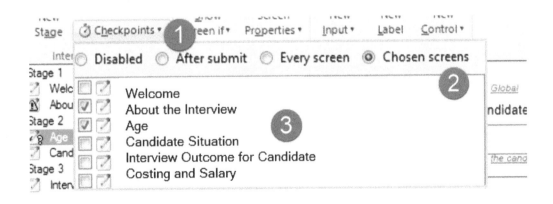

1. Click Checkpoints from the Interview tab.

2. Select the option you need – for example, allow saving only after certain screens.

3. Select the Screens as appropriate.

Checkpoint Usage

The use of checkpoints is only possible in Interviews that have defined Connections that support this functionality. Users of Oracle Service Cloud who load or save CRM data in Oracle Policy Automation must configure their Service Cloud to permit checkpoints. Users of a CRM system with Oracle Policy Automation must code or otherwise configure their Connection to support this behaviour. In standard, non-configured Projects, users of the Modeling will see the following message instead:

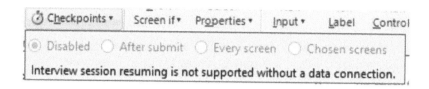

The structured data that is captured during the Checkpoint Save is converted into **Base64** text, to simplify storage in a typical database column. It is reconverted and reinserted into the relevant screens by the Resume Session functionality.

Building a Screen

Now you have seen the basic components available, let's get started working on your interview.

In your Project, switch to the Interview tab and select New Screen from the ribbon. You should also close the debugger if you have it open, as you will not need it for a few minutes and by the time you debug again, the interview will hopefully look very different.

As shown above, the order of the screens can be altered by dragging and dropping the icon in the interview explorer window. Notice also that your interview already has a single stage and a single screen *before* you add your own.

Define Interview Goals

For now, the initial focus will be on setting up the **Goal**. In the Interview tab ribbon, click the Goals drop-down control. The list of current goals in your Project appears.

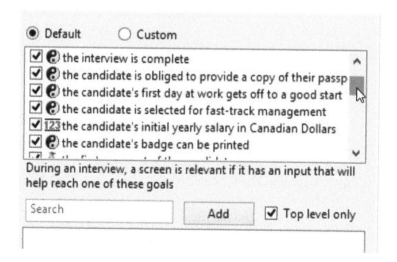

Select one of the goals, so that your list looks like the example shown below. In the screenshot below of the Project, the interview is complete goal has been selected. Note the useful explanation in the lower portion of the window – to be considered relevant, an input attribute must help the inference engine reach one of the defined goals.

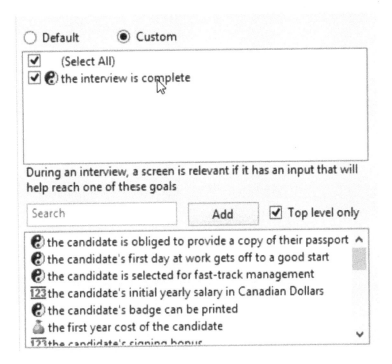

Interview Goal Testing

Now, as a proof of concept, start the debugger again. Notice that the automatic screens have lessened in number, and they all relate to the goal selected. Selecting the right goal will already give you a good idea as to what information you will need to collect or display.

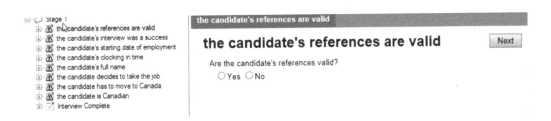

> **NB**: Selecting a goal in this way, and testing it in the debugger, is a quick way of finding out what is relevant – useful if you are discovering a rule Project written by someone else!

In your interview, this is the goal you will work with to begin building a new improved user interface.

Modifying the General Appearance

While working with the goals and screens, before you get into the detail of working with the visual elements on each page; now is a good time to access the Styles… dialog via the Ribbon and review the Appearance tab inside.

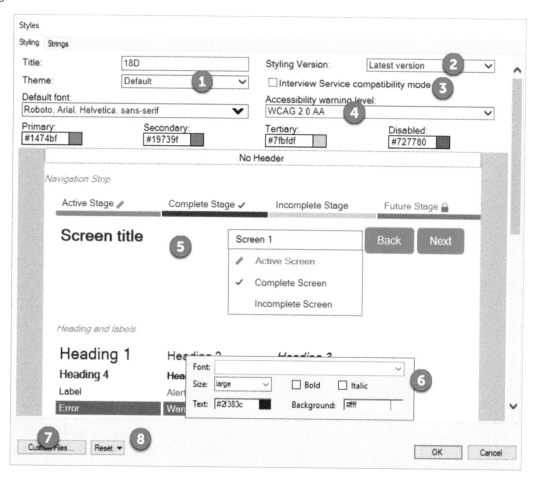

As the picture above makes clear, you have latitude to modify the user experience to a considerable degree without having to resort to any kind of *coding* such as JavaScript.

1. Two themes or "skins" are provided. The standard one used most of the time in this book, and another Theme that reproduces the look and feel of Oracle Engagement Cloud.

2. Significant user experience enhancements were introduced in August 2016, and this allows the designer to remain in "August 2016" mode or to use all the new features. For information on the complete list of features, consult the online documentation for your version, for example http://documentation.custhelp.com/euf/assets/devdocs/cloud18d/PolicyAutomation/en/Default.htm#Gui des/Policy_Modeling_User_Guide/Design_interviews/Switch_to_Latest_Version_interviews.htm .

3. You will learn about the Interview Service later in this book.

4. If you need to design your Interview to be accessible to those with assistive technologies, then you can set the required level of compliance. The Interview Designer, and other parts of the Oracle Policy Modeling interface, will warn you if your Screens do not respect the constraints you have selected.

5. Most of this area is clickable, in order to make changes to the look and feel. You will gain some experience of working with these options later in this chapter.

6. As an example, the Header 2 style has been clicked, and the editing dialog is displayed ready to accept the new values for this text size and colour.

7. In more advanced scenarios, Style Sheets and other files can be added to the resources used by your Interview.

8. If you have made changes to the Styles and wish to revert, you can click this button.

You will learn more about all these features in the coming pages.

Basic Controls

An interview Screen, at a simple level, lets the rule writer group questions onto a page, rather than having one question per page as per the *automatic* behaviour. Begin your work by stopping the Debugger, going to the Interview tab and adding a New Screen with the button on the ribbon.

Screens can be dragged and dropped in the explorer window on the left. Make sure your screen is above the Interview Complete screen.

The last screen in the interview will display a red dot – or another icon depending on the exact action to be taken when this screen is reached – to indicate it is the end. Notice also, on the right-hand side, that it says the last screen will not have a next button. Information text appears regularly in the design window, and it can prove very useful. In your new screen, double-click the New Screen text and edit it to read About the Interview.

At the same time, the explorer window will update to show the same text. All screens have a **Screen Title** which serves to identify it in this way.

The configuration of the buttons, can be modified within the Styles... dialog accessible from the Interview Ribbon and also by clicking directly on the Button and editing it.

Input Controls

Of course, if you want to let the user actually interact with this interview, the screen needs to ask for their **Input**. To add input controls, click the New Input button on the ribbon. A list of **uncollected attributes** appears. Inputs can be attributes, entities or relationships.

Gradually over the course of building the interview, items that have been added to a screen or screens will be removed from this list, so that you can focus on finding only the items that have not been collected already.

The Show All checkbox in the top right-hand corner will switch back to showing all the attributes if you need it.

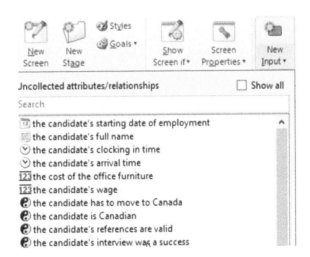

To start working with your interview, double-click the following attributes to add them to your screen:

- The candidate's full name.
- The candidate's age.

The result should be something like the following. The exact rendering will depend on the language used to write the rules and the version of Oracle Policy Automation you are using. Even if you have the correct text in front of you, the following example of incorrectly displayed text is a good learning experience.

As you can see in the example above, the text relating to the candidate's full name is not appropriate. In fact there are several issues that we will deal with in this section:

- Text Attribute Personal Form Interrogative.
- The label text in an interview in general.

Text Attribute Issues

Policy Modeling thinks this text attribute needs to be phrased using personal interrogative format (who?) and not impersonal format (what?)

To correct this for the attribute, return to the Project Data tab and edit the attribute:

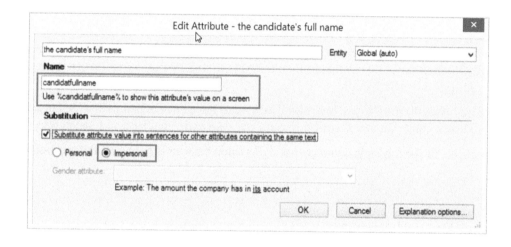

The important change at this stage is to choose Impersonal. The name, which was mentioned in an earlier chapter, will be used in substitution which is especially useful to make interviews more personal; you will examine that in a moment.

The same issue will occur in other languages for text attributes, the highlighted label is also incorrectly formulated in the personal interrogative:

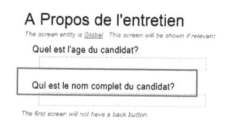

Label text in an Interview

The other issue is more simply explained: it is far too wordy and long. In a typical computer-based form, the end-user would expect to have much simpler data entry labels:

Labels in your interview can be modified simply by double-clicking and editing them directly. This affects only the label, *not* the attribute text that you defined in the Data tab.

NB: Whilst it is important to know that attribute labels can be changed and made more concise or more appropriate, you should remember that the default text is derived from the attribute text itself. So if you write more concise and appropriate attribute text, then you will have less editing to do in the Interview Screen.

Label Controls

When selecting an attribute to add to a screen, Policy Modeling essentially adds both an **Input Control** and a **Label Control** to hold the Question Text, such as we have been modifying in the previous steps.

You can significantly improve usability by adding *extra* labels, to inform the user of the context or provide other useful information. Clicking New Label allows the writer to do just that, and the label text is editable as before:

1. Change the label text to Candidate Information.

2. Select a standard **Style** from the drop-down to alter the look of the text. You will learn how to change these standard styles later in this chapter.

Having added a first screen, create a second new screen and add the following Input Controls to the new screen:

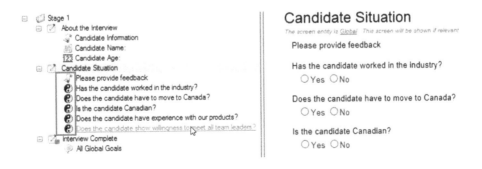

It should be obvious from the screenshot shown above that just adding more inputs to a screen does not actually improve the user experience.

Notice on the left-hand window that the different icons, and their position in the vertical list, helps the rule builder see the structure of the page. Items can be dragged and dropped in this list to change the order.

Changing Input Styles

Select the first attribute in the new screen using the mouse. You may find it easier to use the Explorer to select items.

In the ribbon, notice the **Radio Button** option is currently selected. Change the Input Control to a **Checkbox**. Repeat for the next Inputs except the last one (Does the candidate show willingness to meet all team leaders?). We will come back to the other choices in due course.

This is better, but still not very good. The layout is excessively vertical, which brings you to the Container control.

Other Controls

Aside from the basic data entry controls, one particular element of the Interview will allow you to improve the page layout significantly. This is called the Container control. Readers familiar with HTML can think of this as a <DIV> or <SPAN> with specific, easily-changed properties accessible from the Interview tab.

> **NB**: You can nest Containers inside each other and create exciting layouts. Beware, however, making too complex a layout. It will make updates more difficult and may affect responsive display.

Container Controls

Using a container control is a good way of making your interview less vertical. As the name implies, it is a control that can contain other controls. Drag a **Container Control** (from New Control > Container) onto your screen. You should see something like this in your explorer:

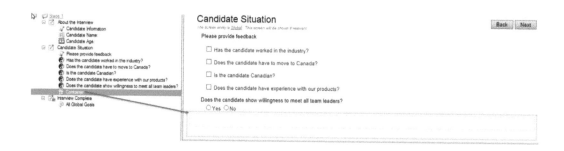

Now with the container in place, drag and drop the Boolean attributes on the screen *into* the container. When dragging using the mouse, make sure you drag the Booleans into the container and not above or below it.

> **NB**: You can adjust the size of the Container, and other controls, using the mouse.

Repeat for all except the Boolean that still uses radio buttons. Your screen will look like the following screenshot. Notice that the default layout of the container is horizontal, but can be altered. In addition, if you resize the Policy Modeling window, the number of checkboxes displayed horizontally will change – the container is *responsive* to the window size.

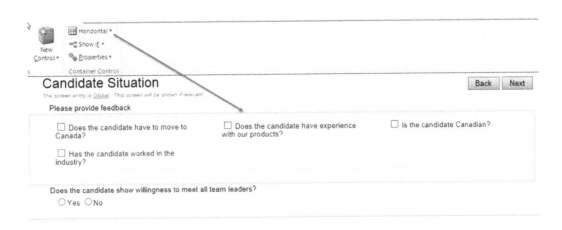

The Ribbon has various features, as you have now seen, that change according to your selection – certain options, like the one highlighted above, will only display if the correct type of control is selected.

> **NB**: Rule designers planning to integrate their Project with Oracle Siebel CRM using Open UI (version 15.5 or later) should be aware that not all controls are supported, and the Container cannot be mapped to the Siebel User Interface. They should instead focus on the alternative integration method described in the White Paper at this address https://blogs.oracle.com/opa/combining-siebel-ip-2016-and-native-opa-12x-interviews-answer-service .

Image Controls

It can be useful to create images – either static or dynamic – that add value to the interview. Create a New Screen and add the following items to the screen:

- Container Control.
- Input Control for The candidate decides to take the job.
- Image Control, referencing an image of your choice.

> **NB**: If you need an example image to work with, use this https://www.ondemand-education.com/corp/files/GREENTICK.png (assuming you have an Internet connection).

Customizing When and How to Display an Attribute

Now you will customize how the attributes are displayed using the options on the Ribbon. Select the last Boolean that still has radio buttons and notice the different options, as described below.

In the Show if configuration, with the image selected, set the following properties:

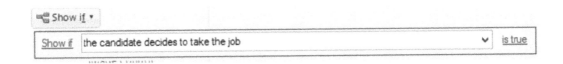

Your image will be invisible unless the above attribute is true. Choose to right align the image if you wish.

Your screen should look something like this:

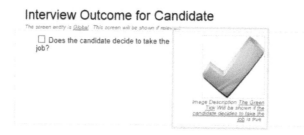

Interview Outcome for Candidate

Default Value

The Default Value has two separate choices – static and dynamic. For now, we will choose static, and a default value of *false*. Dynamic default can drive the default from another Boolean attribute by inferring that the candidate was willing to meet all team leaders if the interview was a success, for example.

Show if

We saw above that an image control could be rendered invisible using this dialog. For the Boolean attribute, further options are available. Complete the configuration of this control by selecting the Mandatory button and adjusting the following properties:

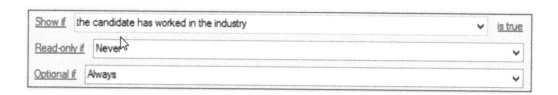

When you close the dialog box, the control should add a third radio button. With the attribute entry now optional, the Uncertain radio button appears.

A control does not have to be a radio button to be optional.

Control Visibility

These three options all function in the same way – select an operation (show, hide, read-only, and so on) and then select either a value (never, always) or a Boolean attribute (The candidate has worked in the industry) followed by a value (true, false, certain, uncertain, unknown).

The resulting screen is shown below. Notice the useful information displayed under each configured control, describing its behaviour.

CAPTCHA Control

The automated test to distinguish a human from a computer program is a common way of ensuring that public domain data entry (such as signing up for something on the Web) is actually from a human. In the case of an Interview from Policy Automation this may be also useful for the same reason. To add a CAPTCHA control, we will create a new screen and place it in the front of your interview.

- Add a New Screen.

- Add a Label Control.

- Add a CAPTCHA Control as shown in the next screenshot.

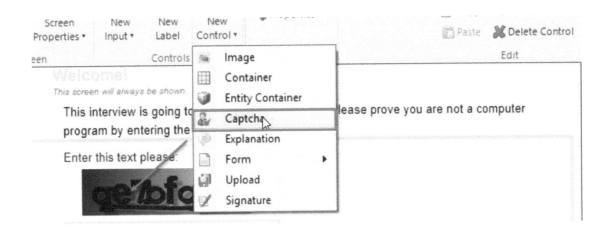

In most cases you will then wish to customize the label and display relevant text to personalize the interview screen.

The entering of the correct text will allow the user to click the Next button and therefore continue the interview.

Signature Control

The signature control allows the end user to electronically sign an Oracle Policy Automation interview session. The image of the signature is saved as part of the session data, as an image. This behaviour is preconfigured to work with Oracle Service Cloud and to save the data to the Attachments tab of the **Agent Desktop**. The Connection feature can enable saving of Signature images to other back-end systems. They are typically converted to a text-based format (Base64 or MIME encoding) and then decoded by the receiving system.

Your screen can have multiple signature controls, but one signature per context (one for the customer, one for the purchase order and so on).

When working with the Mobile App, the user can sign with their finger. In a desktop browser, the user can sign using the mouse.

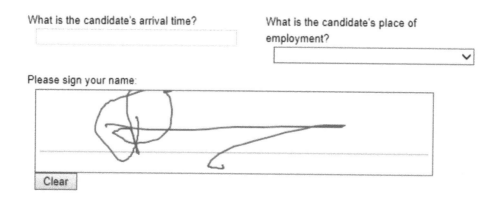

Upload Control

The file upload control does exactly what you would expect – allows the end user to upload files. These files are either uploaded to Oracle Service Cloud (in the case of an Oracle Policy Automation Cloud Service installation) or are uploaded to another Connection data source configured by you (in the case of a Private Cloud installation).

In both cases, the upload control is ideal to facilitate uploading proof (copies of scanned documents, receipts or whatever is required in the business scenario) to be associated with a record in a back-end system. The upload of documents is supported in the Oracle Policy Automation Mobile SDK as well.

You will learn more about data mapping and external systems in a later chapter.

Creating an Upload control or controls for your Project requires two distinct steps. Firstly, upon clicking New Control > Upload > New Upload Group, you are presented with the following dialog.

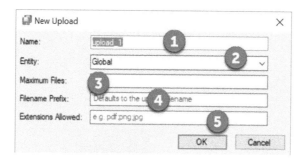

1. Each Upload Control is identified by a name. You might use the name to illustrate the purpose or type of documents that are to be uploaded.

2. As you learned about in chapter 3, entities allow the rule designer to reflect a data model. Uploaded files can be associated with a particular entity.

3. You can restrict the number of files the user can upload with this control. Perhaps the control is destined to let the user upload the recto-verso copy of their work permit, so only two files are needed.

4. Files can be prefixed with text you specify.

5. Only certain extensions can be uploaded, as you specify here.

At the end of this process, upon closing the dialog, your new Upload control is displayed in the Interview Screen, as shown below.

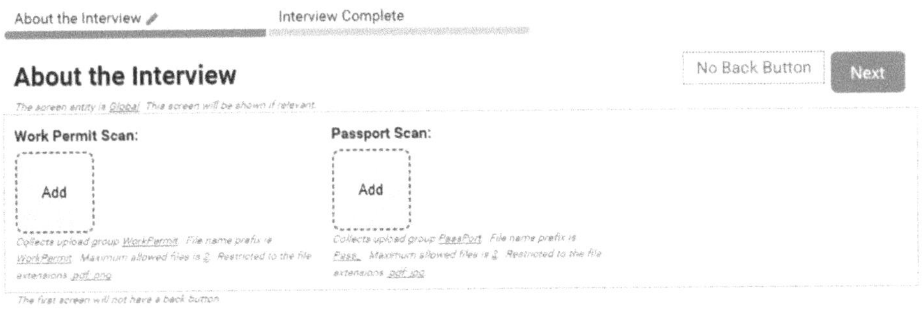

In the screenshot above, you can see two Upload groups with different names and prefixes. Both accept a maximum of two files and have the same file type restrictions. They have been placed in a Container as you learned earlier in this chapter, to give a horizontal layout.

NB: All of the above controls can be configured to Show if using logic as in the previous examples for the image and Boolean controls.

Summary

The Interview tab provides you with a very powerful yet easy to use set of options to create a truly personalized experience for the end user. In this respect, less is often more – adding too much customization will dazzle the user and will increase your chances of having a difficult migration in the future.

In this first part of the investigation you focussed on the mechanics of creating interviews and building simple layouts. In the next part you will add more complex features.

NB: If you have not already done so, now is a good time to create a ZIP backup copy of the Projects you have used in this chapter.

7

Advanced Interviews

In the previous chapter, you learned the role of the interview in Oracle Policy Automation and then you practiced using the basic components to create your own basic flow. In this, the second chapter about interviews, you will learn some of the more advanced features that you are likely to need in order to make your interview as pleasant and efficient as possible for your end customers. Be careful to ensure that when you look to enhance your interview, that you select options that will improve the user interface but not at the cost of a complex or costly migration.

Improving the Experience

As each version of Oracle Policy Modeling hits the shelves, the developers make enhancements to the styles, colours and functionality of the Interview process. Don't worry if the colours of your Interview do not match those seen in this book exactly.

The main areas you will focus on in this chapter are entering and selecting data from lists, working with calendars, optimizing the display logic so that nothing but the essential is displayed, and finally how to take your interview to the next level with custom content and controls.

Dealing with Lists

In the interview screens we have been building, you probably will have noticed one area where end user data entry is particularly unfriendly in style; any control that requires the display of a list of values.

In the most recent versions of Oracle Policy Modeling there are two ways for the rule builder to create lists of values: as part of the interview, or as part of the Project.

Lists for an Interview

If you are building a list of values that occurs only once in a Project and is only used in an Interview (not in any other determination) then it is possible to create a **List of Values** in the Interview tab. For example, in your current rule Project there is an attribute called the default signing bonus.

1. Display the default signing bonus as an Input in a screen in your interview.
2. Select the control and choose either List or Drop-Down to change the type.
3. Select Values.
4. Enter Values for your attribute (as appropriate).

The screenshot below shows the steps, and the resulting display, in the interview designer.

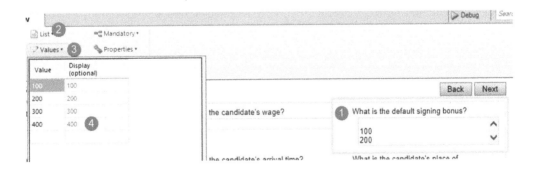

The disadvantage, here, is the list is associated explicitly with one input, and only that input.

Value Lists in Projects

In many rule Projects you might find that the same list is reused in several places. For that reason the solution given above would not be appropriate, as it would lead to unnecessary duplication.

Create a Value List

You will find Value Lists on the Project tab of Policy Modeling. To create a re-usable list, follow the steps below. Select the Project tab then…

1. Select Value Lists.
2. Click New (the button may be hidden if the window is too small).
3. Choose the Type (text or number).
4. Enter a Name to recognize the list later.
5. Enter the values (the actual value recorded and the displayed values can be different).

For example, this Project contains an attribute that defines the location where the employee will work. End users will find data entry easier if you create a suitable list of locations: London, Toronto, Quebec, and Vancouver.

The numbers above refer to the steps in the previous paragraph. Once the list is created and named, you can reference it in multiple attributes. In this example scenario, you will now associate it with the relevant attribute(s).

- In the Data tab, select the attribute and click the Edit Attribute button.
- In the Type drop-down, select the Value List you just created.

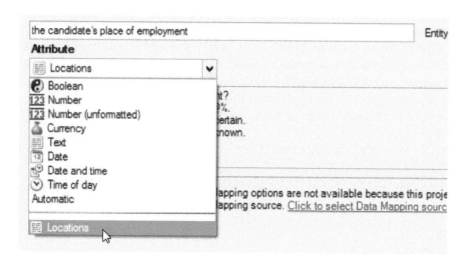

The Value List entry has changed slightly in later versions of Policy Modeling. You may see instead the following:

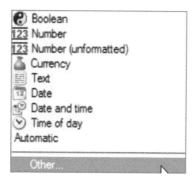

Clicking on the Other link will open the list of Values Lists and you can proceed to select the right one.

Switch to the Interview tab; if your attribute is already visible on a screen it will have adapted to correspond to a value list input control. You may change its behavior only in the following ways:

1. The Interview editor displays the current style of control.
2. Change to a list, drop-down, a filterable drop-down or radio button; set and define it as mandatory or not.
3. Edit the Value List to add or remove values.
4. Set Defaults by picking from the Value List.

The different ways to configure the Value List are highlighted in the next screenshot.

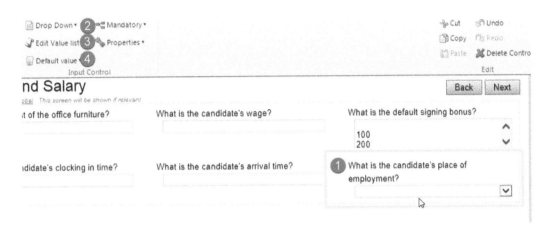

Changing Input Style

As you design your Project, build Screens and so on, it is quite likely that you will have inputs that switch from being simple text boxes to drop-downs, and perhaps vice-versa, as you consider the best way to obtain information from the user. As a result, you will often see the following error:

Either switching the control to a Text Box , or adding Values to the list input from the Ribbon, will remove the error.

Converting Lists to Value Lists

If you create a Screen-based list, and then decide to use it in several locations in your Project, you can convert it at the click of a button. Shown below is an example. Clicking the Convert to Value list will prompt you for a name, and the values will be copied into the Project tab.

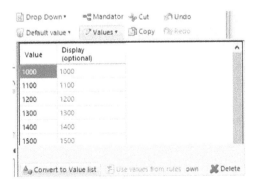

Obtaining List Values from Rules

Given that a rule may exist long before any Interview Screens are built, sometimes it becomes clear that the actual list values are already present in Word or Excel files in the Project. In this case, the Oracle Policy Modeler will detect them automatically and propose to populate the list automatically. In the example below, a Word table contains values for the candidate's starting salary. The Ribbon proposes to use them as the values displayed to the user.

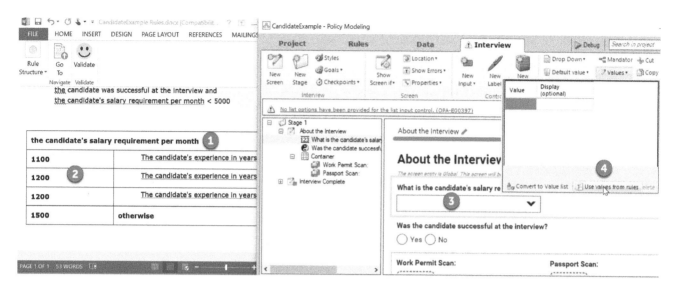

1. The attribute is used in a Word table or Excel spreadsheet.
2. The values are provided in the table.
3. The Control chosen is a drop-down or similar.
4. The Ribbon proposes to copy the values from the rule table.

Hierarchical Lists

Hierarchical lists are a very common feature of computer systems. Choose a product line then choose a (relevant) product. Choose a brand, choose a model. It can be frustrating at first, but the Oracle Policy Modeling interface does not let you build a hierarchical list structure directly. You must build each list in turn then perform manual editing to create the structure you require. For the purposes of demonstration let's take two lists, each defined in your Project as Value Lists in the appropriate manner, with a type of Text.

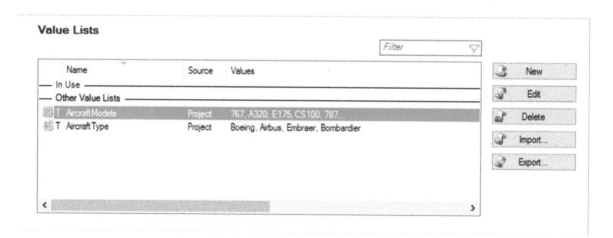

It does not take too much imagination to imagine that these two, Aircraft Type and Aircraft Model, need to be arranged in a hierarchy. But there are no buttons to allow you to do so directly. Follow the next few simple steps to get this structure built. If you want to build this example, you should create a stand-alone Project for the purpose.

- Use the Export Button to export the Parent list (whichever is the top part of your two levels).
- Edit the XML file to add the necessary children to your XML hierarchy.

```
<value>
  <text-val>Boeing</text-val>
  <child-values>
    <text-val>787</text-val>
    <text-val>777</text-val>
    <text-val>767</text-val>
    <text-val>757</text-val>
    <text-val>747</text-val>
    <text-val>737</text-val>
  </child-values>
</value>
```

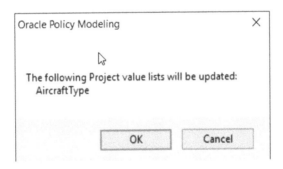

In the example above, the list of Aircraft Types has been exported, and the corresponding Aircraft Models added to the XML file. The steps are indicated in detail below:

1. Add a new structure called <child-values> - which must also have a closing tag.

2. Double check your child <text-values> are in closed tags and that they match values in the child list.

3. Verify that the child values are inside the parent <value> tag.

- Add an extra attribute to the top of your XML file in the main value-list tag called <child-list-name>:

```
<value-list name="AircraftType" type="text" child-list-name="AircraftModel">
```

- Now you are ready to *re-import* the XML file you just modified, *back* into your Project. You should see a message like this one. If you do not, there is an error in the XML file, perhaps you have mis-typed a value or list name.

Oracle Policy Modeling ✕

The following Project value lists will be updated:
AircraftType

[OK]   [Cancel]

- Revisiting the Value Lists will now reveal a new button in your Oracle Policy Modeling user interface.

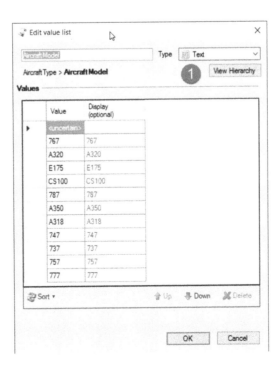

As you can see above there is now also a visual reminder of the hierarchy on the left. Clicking the button highlighted above will display a simple window for testing your new structure. Any further edits to the relationships will have to take place in your XML file and be re-imported again.

Even though this demonstration has completed the update of the two lists and created a hierarchy, a few final steps are required to display the hierarchy successfully.

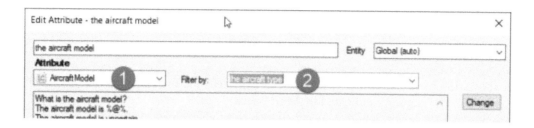

1. Apply the child Value list to the child attribute.
2. Select the correct Value List which will filter the choices available.

Finally add two controls needed to display the above information (assuming you have made them pertinent to your overall objective), then display them thus:

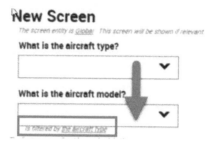

You will see the hint text is reminding us of the filter that is in place. In Debug mode you will see the second list is left inactive until you select a value from the parent. As soon as a parent value is selected, then the relevant values are displayed in the Child List.

Date Entry

Inputting a date in Policy Automation interviews can be performed in three different ways. Upon adding a date attribute to your screen, select the attribute and choose either Multi-input date, Multi-input Text or Calendar.

The multi-input date controls use three fields to collect the information, in a style similar to the user interface of version 10, whereas the Calendar input control uses a more standards-based JavaScript calendar which may be more familiar to end users.

In your Project, there is a date in reference to the starting date of employment. Configure the Input Control to use either Date or Calendar and observe the differences:

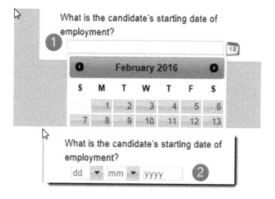

Depending on your version of Oracle Policy Modeling, you may be presented with a Calendar control that is styled differently. For example the screenshot below shows a more recent version of the Calendar Control.

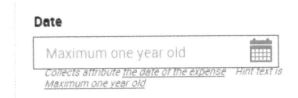

Note the different icon, and the corresponding Calendar uses a new look and feel at runtime.
In the example above, you can see the "Hint Text" reference below the Calendar mentions "Maximum one year old". Should you wish to give your end user a hint as to the underlying limits for this data entry, you can do so in the Interview Ribbon once you have selected the Calendar Control (or indeed any standard entry control):

The items above correspond to the following bullet points:

1. The hint text to be shown to the user.

2. The hint text will be shown in the data entry field at runtime.

3. Other default information can be entered at the same time in the Interview Ribbon.

Attribute Input Validation

Any input validation that has been put in place in the attribute definition will be reflected in the interview and the handling of data entry for that attribute.

In the attributes of the current Project, the minimum age for hiring was 18, and an error message was associated with failure to validate an entry.

The interview respects this constraint if the attribute is placed on one of the screens and the user is stopped from continuing until the error is repaired:

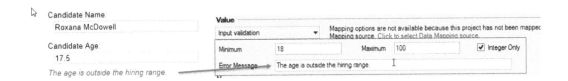

Interview Logic and Flow

In the previous section we have seen that the concept of chosen goals for an interview modifies the automatic screens that are created. To put it simply, selecting a goal for your interview tells Policy Automation what is relevant.

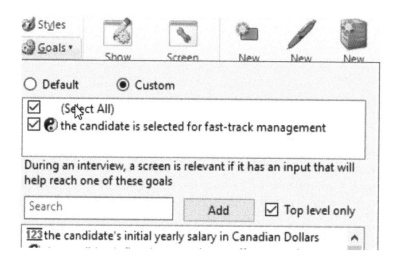

You will already have noticed that on each screen, there is a message confirming that it will be displayed, if relevant. In order to optimize the interview experience, Policy Automation tries to avoid displaying irrelevant information requests.

Screen Logic

In the event that you wish to display a Screen even if it is not truly relevant, for example a disclaimer screen that does not actually collect any information relevant to the goal but needs to be displayed, you can make use of the Screen Properties button from the ribbon.

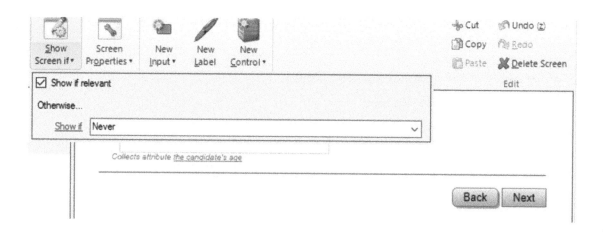

In the above example you might change the Show if relevant checkbox or use the drop-down to link the display of the Screen to another Boolean, for example:

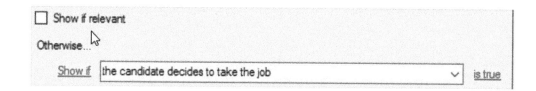

Screens and Controls thus have similar Properties to enable the interview designer to customize the display of attributes and screens.

Geolocation

It is now possible to use latitude and longitude, via the Browser, to capture the location of the user. This is quite common in modern Web Browser applications and is supported by the majority of modern platforms. To set the scene for a simple example, in the Project shown below, there are two attributes to store the latitude and longitude. The presence of attributes ready to store the location data are a prerequisite to using the new Location control.

Locating the User with Attributes

Through the new Location option in the Interview Ribbon, you can implement geolocalization by mapping to the two attributes just mentioned. This will allow the information from the Web Browser to be passed into the Oracle Policy Automation Interview.

To assist the rule designer, the same concept is brought into the Debugger through a small icon on the toolbar, allowing for the manual entry of data to simulate a Web Browser geolocation.

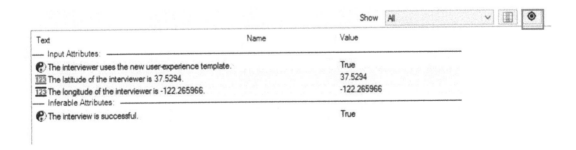

Deploying the Rule Project that contains the new Location control will now prompt the user to confirm access to the Location features of the Web Browser being used, when the Interview is started. The security dialog is mildly different depending on Operating System and Web Browser.

Locating users in this way allows rule designers to implement fencing logic to provide relevant advice and conclusions according to location, without the need for complex JavaScript.

> **NB**: Not all national authorities permit geolocalization, and some Internet providers may not return valid information. Be prepared to provide alternative means (such as a manual address entry) for capturing location in your Interview.

Image Group Control

In previous versions of Oracle Policy Modelling, to achieve a visual image group (such as the following example) required a Value List, a set of Radio Buttons, Image Sprites, and some customized CSS rules:

Quel est votre type de logement ?

Appartement   Maison

With the arrival of the Image Group in recent versions, when creating a Value List, the rule designer sees the option is available to add checked and unchecked images to your values:

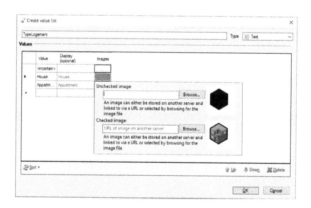

Secondly, when the time comes to display the Value List, new options allow for the images to be used either as standalone items or with their corresponding text displayed at the same time. In the image below, the Value List is associated with a text attribute and the Image Group displayed with the text, to ensure the user understands the option values.

1. The Text *and* Image can be displayed.

2. The orientation of the images can be modified.

3. The images are shown in the Interview design, using the *unchecked* image.

Upon running the Interview in the Debugger, the new Image Group works as expected and the end user can select a value simply by clicking the corresponding image. The unchecked image is replaced by the checked image dynamically, as shown in the next screenshot.

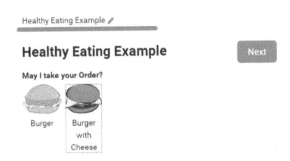

Other new controls include a slider for numerical values where a number attribute has been defined as having a range of acceptable values; in this case, a range between 0 and 6. In recent versions, images can be associated with sliders as well.

These new controls allow for a fresher, more modern look and feel to the Interview session. The rule designer can create these effects without any need to write JavaScript or CSS Style rules.

Dynamic Control Refresh

In November 2016, a new feature was introduced to allow for the seamless update of a control on an Interview Screen, even if the control needs to read data from the same screen.

In the example shown, the first two input attributes drive the goal placed underneath. The goal is directly derived from the attributes through a calculation. Therefore changing the data in the first two text boxes must update the third. In previous versions, this was not possible. Now, changing the first two will dynamically change the third, without the need to move to another page.

Show Errors Immediately

In addition to the dynamic layouts and refresh capabilities mentioned already, the designer of the Interview can configure, via the Interview Ribbon, when to display errors: immediately, or upon navigation away from the active Screen.

Restrict File Extensions

Designers can globally restrict the types of files that will be accepted by the File Upload using the **Styles** dialog. Recall from the previous chapter that you can also control this per Upload Group.

Entity Controls

So far we have looked at how to improve the general experience of entering or modifying data in respect of Global attributes. When working with entities however, it can take more effort to produce a flowing user interface.

To examine the different approaches, close your current Project and prepare to open another backup from the previous exercises.

Displaying and Collecting Entity Instances

To display instances, the rule writer will need the Entity Container. This example will use the Project from chapter 4, which had four different entities on the theme of orders and shipping.

The easiest way to understand the structure of an interview screen that must show entity attributes is to work in the same manner described for functions that work with entities: focus on the available scope.

For example, the first screen in this interview might collect the Customer Id, as well as allow the creation of the basic order information (the order type and the order number for instance).

This combination will be accepted by the interview designer, as we begin by adding a Global attribute. The scope of the interview screen is thus set to Global.

Now, still using New Input, we select the orders – the *relationship text* displayed with a yellow entity icon. We add two more attributes, the order number and the order type.

The interview designer detects they are from the entity (the order) and adds them inside the entity container. If you drag them outside, you will receive an error. Now your interview screen hierarchy should look like this:

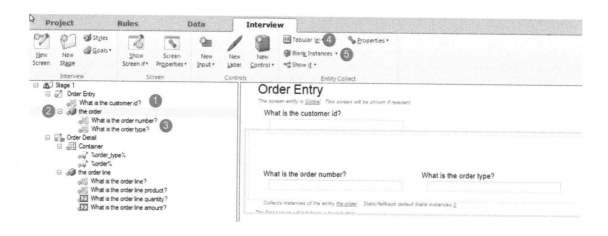

The numbers shown in the screenshot refer to the following points

1. The Global attribute.

2. The Entity Container.

3. The Entity-level attributes.

4. The layout options of the Entity Container. To collect limited numbers of attributes, as in this case, the Tabular layout is useful.

5. You can display several blank lines automatically if you know the end user will need to create several instances.

The first screen will now look like this in the debugger Interview tab.

In this first screen, we can continue to add relationships that have Global as their containment source – respecting the scope of the interview screen. For example, it would be acceptable to add *the invoice* on the same interview screen:

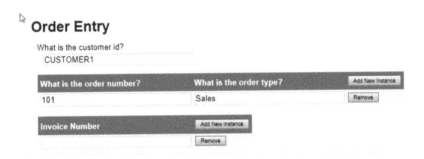

In fact, any of the entities that are in scope could be added. In such a situation, your screen contents will soon become cluttered, and it will be necessary to add labels to inform the user of what is going on, as shown in the screenshot below:

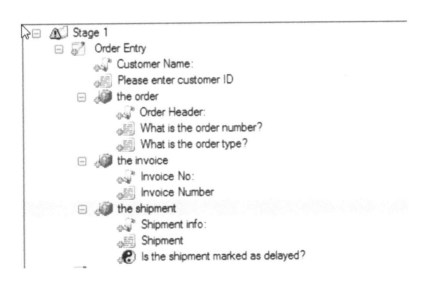

> **NB**: If your interview screen icons are not the same – specifically if the green plus signs and warning triangle are not present – do not worry. This is because the above screenshot was taken from an environment with an OPA Hub. We will learn about the Hub in Chapters 11 and beyond.

It will also become necessary to edit the default buttons proposed for entity instance creation. In the screenshot below, the text of the buttons has been modified to identify their purpose appropriately.

To edit the button text, just double-click the button and type the new text. An example is given below with the three entity collection buttons visible with custom text.

To display the order and allow the creation of *the order lines* however, we will add a second screen – the interview – whose screen entity will be *the order*, thus allowing us to add the child entity via the relationship text. To build this new screen:

- Add a new Container (New Control > Container). Add two Input Controls (the order number, the order type) to the container. Arrange the container as you wish. The screen entity will be the order.

- The relationship the order's invoice is available from this context. Adding it from New Input will add an entity selection drop-down.

- Add the order lines relationship (New Input).

- Add attributes for the order line such as the quantity and so forth (New Input).

- Optionally, add the order line shipment relationship on the same level as the order line attributes, to respect the structure of the data model (New Input).

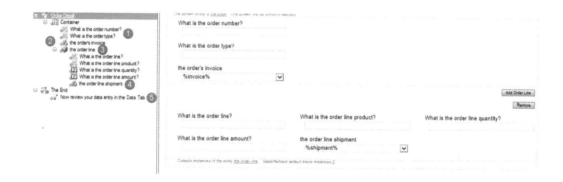

In the example above, note the following useful pointers to help you build your screen:

1. The first attributes set the screen entity to the order.
2. The one to one relationship the order's invoice is acceptable here.
3. The relationship the order lines is also acceptable here.
4. The relationship the order line shipment is also acceptable, at the level of the order line itself.
5. The final screen is necessary for this training example, as data is only stored in the session once the Next button is clicked.

Displaying Inferred Entity Instances

In a previous chapter, you worked on inferred instances. These instances were inferred in rules using Excel or Word. In your interview, since this information is essentially created for viewing only, the initial goal is to ensure this information is simply displayed.

Given that the rule writer may need to display several instances, it is necessary to find a convenient way to display rows of data. As such, the container which we viewed earlier, thanks to its horizontal layout may be ideal. The following example is just one way of achieving the desired effect.

You will use the Project you backed up from your work in chapter five, part three – where you inferred public services such as after-school activities for citizens to discover. Thus your interview establishes various inferred entity instances.

Before you can begin building the Screens, ensure that all the attributes in each of the entities has been given a *name*. Remember, a name is used between % marks to indicate a substitution should be made at run-time. We will use labels and **%name%** to display the information from the inferred instances.

Create two new screens, with the following titles:

- Information Center.

- As the second screen title, use whatever *name* you created for the Global attribute called *the request* – which in my case was `%therequest%`.

In the first screen, Information Center, add the four main attributes from the Global entity.

- Optionally, you can create Value Lists or Lists of Values for your attributes to facilitate data selection.

The resulting screen should look a little like this, assuming you have created drop-downs with values to display.

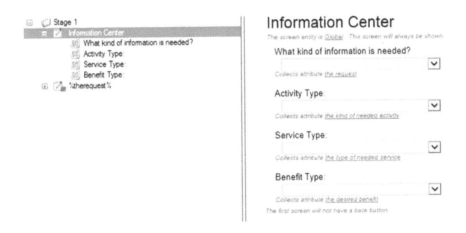

The second screen should only have the title at this stage, using the substitution as described previously. Now you can work to display the inferred instances. Add a container control then follow the steps:

- Inside the container control, add four entity containers (New Control > Entity Container), one for each entity in your Project.

- Under each entity, add at least one attribute *using a label control and % to select the relevant name for substitution.* Inferred entities cannot display input controls.

- Under the Reception Type, add another container. In the container, arrange the different attributes using the same technique as described in the previous bullet point – *use labels and substitutions.*

The end result of your work should look a little like this; your substitution names may be different of course, but your screen has only labels, containers and entities.

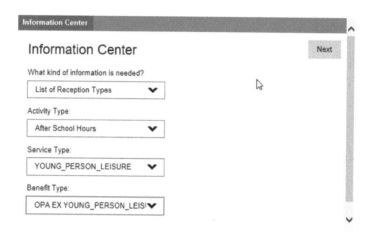

If you have not already done so, delete the Global Goals control since we do not have any applicable goals to display. The inferred entity instances are the only "output".

Running your interview in the Debugger should produce something like this for the first screen:

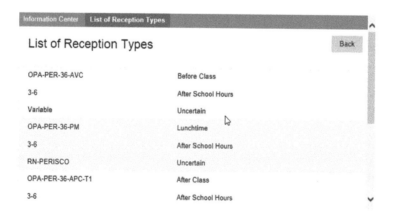

And the second screen, which leverages % attribute value substitutions both in the title and the content, should look like this. The instances are inside a horizontal container, ensuring that they look good when the page is resized.

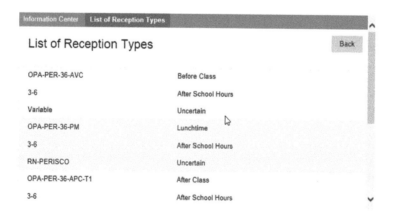

Entities in Interviews - Summary

Of course there is a lot more to be done, but the basic mechanism for displaying and entering entity instances depends upon a close attention to the visual structure of the page, which must respect the structure of your data model.

Enhancing the Interview

Substitution

On several screens in this chapter you have used %names% to substitute values of attributes directly into an interview. Substitution is available throughout the interview, and the % key automatically displays the list of available elements for the current context:

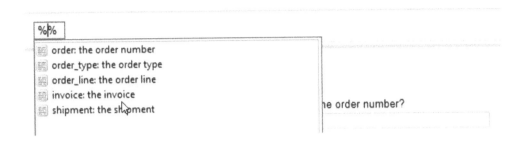

Gender

Previously you observed that some attributes had been incorrectly assigned as impersonal (what is?) or personal (who is?) by the validation engine. In languages, where the pronoun depends on the gender of the subject (his car, her car), you may wish to automatically substitute the correct word (his, her) depending on the gender of the person. This is known as gender substitution. It requires several simple steps to configure:

Create an attribute to ask the gender (the gender of the customer) with appropriate list of values:

Assign it to the attribute that you wish (for example, the customer).

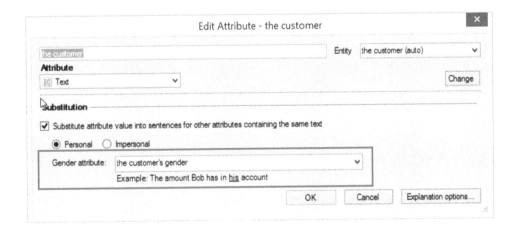

Display the customer in other attribute text using phrases that would normally need a gender-specific pronoun:

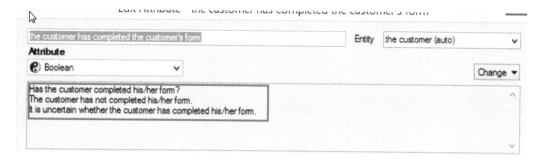

Visualize it in the interview.

> **NB**: In languages where the agreement with the gender is object-based (a car is always feminine in French for example – *sa voiture*) then this feature may not be useful.

Second Person

In the same style as the previous example, in certain interviews you will need to address the interviewee directly "You have qualified for a license". This is known as second person substitution. There is no need to write rules in this way, you can simply request Policy Modeling to perform substitution using the second person. For example, if a Global attribute called "the customer" exists, and has normal substitution enabled, select it for second person substitution from the Language pane of the Project tab.

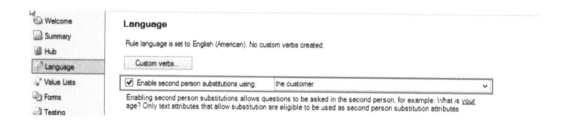

Create further attributes that use the same text "the customer", phrased in the normal way.

Display these attributes in your interview and observe the new text.

Style the Interview

In Policy Modeling interviews, interview designers have a wide range of choices that can change the visual styles and colours used in an interview. Beyond these choices, advanced customization options allow for complex HTML and JavaScript to be introduced into the interview.

Working with the Styles Dialog

As you saw earlier in this chapter, the Styles dialog contains a wide variety of options to change colours, fonts, images and placement of visual real-estate.

Changing Appearance and Styles

With the Interview tab of your Project open, click the Styles button on the ribbon. This dialog has many options, and most of them are accessed in the same way as shown below. Clicking on the Styling tab displays a dialog with the corresponding properties.

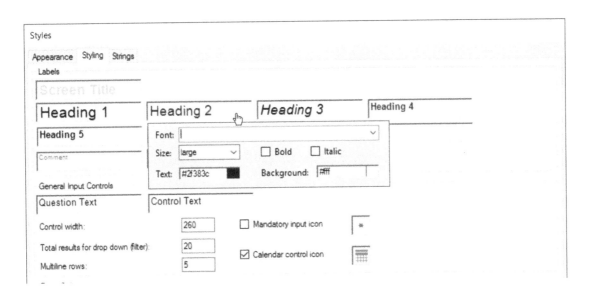

Customizing the font, colour, the styling of text, or the editing of standard sizes and icons is all performed in this dialog through the Styling tab. Changes made will show in your debug session for the interview in question.

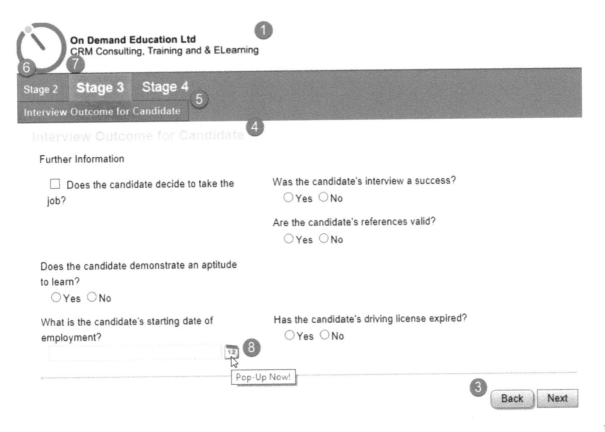

In the screenshot, above, the following elements have been customized:

1. The Header image.

2. The Footer content and style.

3. The style of the Back button.

4. The style of the Screen Title.

5. The style of the active Screen.

6. Show Progress Stages and the style of the past Stages.

7. The style of the active Stage.

8. The text string of the Calendar icon.

HTML Validation

The HTML that is produced from your interview is validated according to specifications that are documented b Oracle on the Oracle Policy Automation Documentation website. The page includes information about how to display reserved HTML characters like "<" and ">" as well as a list of permitted HTML tags.

> **NB**: At time of writing the URL is
> http://documentation.custhelp.com/euf/assets/devdocs/cloud18d/PolicyAutomation/en/Default.htm#Guides/Policy_Modeling_User_Guide/Design_interviews/HTML_validation_for_interviews.htm
>
> HTML tags that are on the *allowed list* can be added, for example, to label controls to enhance the look of the interview.

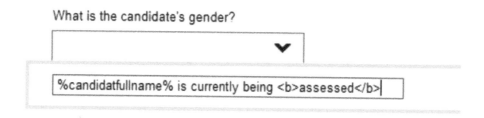

As a general rule however, it is much more efficient and better practice to control the advanced visual appearance of items in your interview using CSS, if you have exhausted all the standard styling options in the Styles... dialog.

Adding Custom Interview Files

Although it potentially goes far beyond the stated goal of this book, *Getting Started with OPA*, you should know that custom files of various types can be used in Projects. This is not without risks for the Project, since you can potentially introduce all sorts of errors and upgrade challenges through badly conceived external files. Putting that aside, to create the necessary folder requires simple steps.

1. In the Styles dialog, click the Custom Files... button that you can see in the bottom left-hand corner of the screenshot on the previous page. The application will warn you of the risks by displaying the following message:

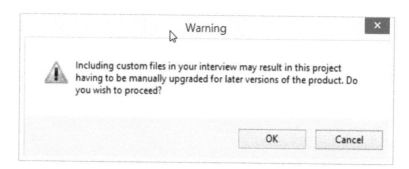

2. When you click the Custom Files... button, the folder that is created is named as the *resources* folder. It contains external files you might have written, but it can also be used to store *images* for your Project as well as other external content such as fonts and so on.

The resources folder

There are several sorts of file that you can store in this folder. The commonest is the **Cascading Style Sheet** format, used by Web Developers to customize the look and feel of a Web page. An example is shown below:

```
75   .opm-radio {
76     background-image: url(${resources-root}/images/chair_sprite.png) !important;
77         -webkit-background-size: 622px 138px !important;
78           background-size: 622px 138px !important;
79           width: 78px;
80           height: 150px;
81   }
```

This screenshot shows a custom Style Sheet which changes the look and feel of the standard radio button in Oracle Policy interviews. It loads a custom image and uses various styling to position it correctly. The image location uses ${resources-root} a permitted special symbol, to ensure that the file can be found later even if the Project is deployed on another server, provided the *resources* folder exists (along with any child folders you might have created, of course).

CSS Style Sheets could be a complete synchronization of your Project's visual style to match existing Internet real-estate. Modern browsers offer the developer plenty of tools to identify the standard Oracle Policy Automation styles, but here are a few just to get you started.

- opm-input *a basic input control*
- opm-radio *a group of radio buttons*
- opm-radio-item *a single radio button*
- explanation *the explanation on the final page*
- explanation_caption *the label associated with the explanation*

As you can no doubt see, the naming conventions are relatively easy to follow.

Although the above may seem an easy solution to the challenge of adapting the look and feel of Oracle Policy Automation interviews, in reality it has a variety of negative effects, and should therefore be limited to perhaps prototyping and edge cases where no other method is available. Here are just some of the downsides to consider:

1. The above style changes require significant cross-browser testing.

2. The above style uses a specific image which needs to be included in the project.

3. The style rule also uses the "!important" modifier which, when overused, can make debugging styles very difficult.

4. The Styles dialog, coupled with the Web Interview Styling Extensions (discussed later in the book) offers a robust and easier-to-maintain solution for Interview styling needs.

The appearance.properties file

Also in the resources folder is the `appearances.properties` file, which contains a number of parameters in relation to CAPTCHA and other global Project formatting options. You will notice that the different parameters in this file are all currently disabled through the use of the "#" character. Should you wish to take advantage of these advanced features, you should selectively enable and modify the settings.

```
#specifies the number of characters per CAPTCHA
# captcha-length = 6
#The CAPTCHA image dimensions
# captcha-image-height = 50
# captcha-image-width = 200
#specifies whether line noise should be added to a CAPTCHA. Valid values are none,
‗‗‗‗‗‗‗‗‗‗‗‗‗‗‗‗‗‗‗‗‗‗‗‗‗‗‗‗‗‗‗‗‗‗‗‗‗‗‗
#specifies the background style for the image CAPTCHA. Valid values are Colour, Gradient
# captcha-image-background = Gradient
#specifies the icon to use for the CAPTCHA
# captcha-audio-ico =Speaker_ico.png
```

JavaScript Files

In the recent past, the usage of JavaScript files in a Project has evolved from the following choices, prior to the August 2016 release:

- JavaScript
- Custom Controls

The current version of the documentation mentions the following, by comparison.

- RuleScript
- Custom Controls
- JavaScript Extensions

Project designers also have a number of decisions to take in respect of custom controls to let the users interact in novel ways with your interview. In the following paragraphs, you will learn about the different options available, and when to use them.

RuleScript

RuleScript is a feature introduced in the August 2016 version of Oracle Policy Modeling. RuleScript allows the definition of Oracle Policy Automation rules in JavaScript rather than Word or Excel. As such, it is not designed to be used by business users and it requires a level of familiarity with JavaScript and programming in general.

In the screenshot below, you can see that New Script Document is present in the Ribbon on the Rules tab.

If you cannot see this in your own Oracle Policy Modeling, do not be concerned. The feature is currently in an experimental phase and is not available by default. According to the documentation, permission must be requested through an Oracle Support account. You will be expected to provide a use case and explain why you wish to use this feature.

When to use RuleScript

RuleScript can be useful when there are non-business concepts (such as data conversions, mathematical algorithms) that need to be in your Project, but they should not distract business users from their job of writing policy in Word and Excel documents. In addition, since RuleScript is essentially JavaScript, certain programming techniques can be applied to information in your Project (such as Benford's Law, probabilities) that would not be very easy or possible in Word or Excel.

The biggest advantage of being able to create RuleScript files within the context of a Project is the ability to easily access the different attributes of your Data tab. As a very simple example, the following lines of RuleScript will place the value of the attribute shown in the console of your browser.

```
// RulesScript Example : using global attributes
function candidate_name(global) {
    console.log("Assessing " + global.candidate_fullname);
}
```

Using similar syntax and standard JavaScript it is also possible to reference and access entity attributes, as in the second example below.

```
// RulesScript Example : using entity attributes
function order_total(global) {
    //Retrieve a containment relationship
    var orderset = global.the_orders.get();
    var total_orders_value = 0;
    //Loop through the members
    for (var orderid in the_orders) {
        total_orders_value += the_orders[orderid].order_value;
    }
    //Set a global attribute
    global.total_orders_value = total_orders_value;
}
```

There are also limitations to the use of RuleScript, some technical and some practical. It is not possible to derive an Explanation from a RuleScript, nor is it possible to use the audit report feature for attributes whose values have been changed by a RuleScript.

Since, at this stage of its development, RuleScript is not yet generally available, it would be advisable to watch for announcements in the future. In any case, bear in mind that solutions designed prior to the arrival of RuleScript may require reworking to be made compatible.

Custom Controls

In the previous paragraphs you learned that custom styles can be added to your interview. It is possible to go even further and add custom controls to your Project. There are several different kinds of custom control.

Embedding static content

A Custom Control in Oracle Policy Modeling is a snippet, or portion of HTML. It is not an entire HTML page. This makes it easy to use as a way of inserting a piece of content (for example, a video, or some textual content that is not being developed by your team) and maintaining a link to it even while it is developing and changing. Follow the example below to see how this can help you.

Consider the following snippet of HTML, written in a simple text file:

```
<h2>Thanks for reading this book!</h2>
<p>Click <a href="https://theopahub.com/main">to join the OPA Hub Website</a></p>
```

If this external content is being developed by another team, to be inserted into your Project, you can create a Custom Control to do that. If the content is stored somewhere that your Oracle Policy Automation interview session will be able to access it, it will be displayed seamlessly to the user. To demonstrate this, add a new label to your interview, for example on the final summary page.

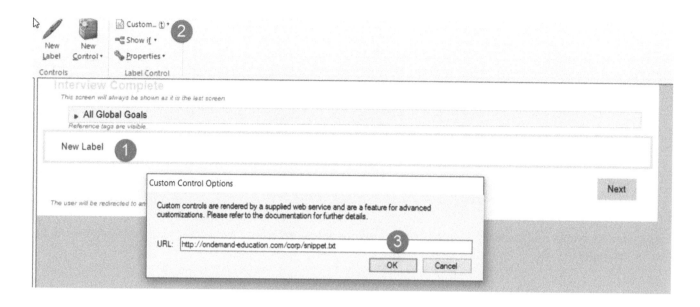

In the screenshot above, I have added a new label, then selected Custom from the dropdown and finally I have added the link to the snippet of HTML you saw in the previous screenshot.

Upon execution of the interview session and navigation to the relevant page, you will observe the following (assuming you have linked to your own snippet). The HTML now is part of the page.

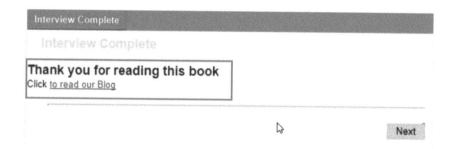

Creating labels in this way is an efficient way to streamline content creation by another team.

Writing JavaScript or PHP

Labels, as just demonstrated, allow you to create custom controls with static content. However you can also create a custom control that is based on an Input Control. In this scenario you are more likely to make use of a programming language such as PHP or JavaScript.

A good example of the power of such a Custom Control is the ability to replace a standard Input Control with something more adapted to the business or organization context. Consider the following example:

The interview currently contains an Input Control for the end-user to enter the salary:

Age

The screen entity is *Global*   This screen will be shown if *the candidate decides to take the job* is true

Age

Collects attribute *the candidate's age*

Next

This basic Input Control could be replaced by something altogether more interesting such as a sliding control like the one below:

Users of the interview can use the mouse to slide the correct value for the age of the candidate. Users of tablets can use their finger.

The functionality shown above is a custom control. The custom control can be written in PHP or other languages and can include JavaScript as well. Although this book does not intend to give you a complete detailed implementation plan, here are the basic design principles.

> **NB**: The code shown in the following pages is absolutely *not for production use*, it is simply to provide a learning foundation. You should refer to the Custom Control documentation for your version of Oracle Policy Automation before starting a real implementation.

The Oracle Policy Automation engine will provide a set of HTTP POST parameters to your custom code. For example, in PHP the $_POST variable reveals the following in the above example from the candidate Project. You can see the name, id and value are highlighted.

Languages such as PHP can access the POST parameters and can build content for your HTML snippet based on these items of data. For example, the PHP code below shows some simple steps to create a custom visual experience.

```
custom_age.php
1   <?php
2   echo '<script src="http://ondemand-education.com/corp/files/jquery.knob.js"></script>';    1
3   echo '<input name="' . $_POST["name"] . '" id="' . $_POST["name"] . '" class="dial" value="'. $_POST["value"] . '">';
4   echo "<script type=\"text/javascript\">";
5   $(\".dial\").knob({    3
6   'release' : function (v) {document.getElementById(\"" . $_POST["name"] . "\").value= v } });";
7   echo '</script>';
8   echo '<script type=\"text/javascript\">';
9   echo '$("#' . $_POST["name"] . '").populate({"' . $_POST["name"] . '" : "' . $_POST["value"] . '"});';
10  echo '</script>';
11  ?>
```

1. This line loads a standard jQuery visual widget library.

2. This line builds a string of HTML to create an Input Box, whose ID and NAME will use the information passed by the Oracle Policy Automation engine about the Custom Control you added to the interview. The class has been set to "dial" as instructed by the widget designer.

3. This section of code is provided by the widget author and follows the instructions on how to handle the releasing of the mouse button on the slider.

4. This line will populate the Control with any existing value when the page is displayed.

At the time of writing the above code was available for you to test in the Oracle Policy Modeler debugger at the following address: http://ondemand-education.com/corp/custom_age.php. Loading this custom control against an input of type number and running the debugger should provide you with an output like the following:

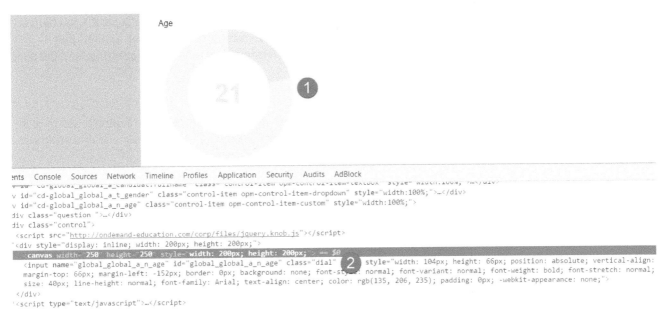

```
ints  Console  Sources  Network  Timeline  Profiles  Application  Security  Audits  AdBlock
v id="cd-global_global_a_t_gender" class="control-item opm-control-item-dropdown" style="width:100%;">...</div>
v id="cd-global_global_a_n_age" class="control-item opm-control-item-custom" style="width:100%;">
div class="question ">...</div>
div class="control">
  <script src="http://ondemand-education.com/corp/files/jquery.knob.js"></script>
  <div style="display: inline; width: 200px; height: 200px;">
    <canvas width="250" height="250" style="width: 200px; height: 200px;"> == $0
    <input name="global_global_a_n_age" id="global_global_a_n_age" class="dial"  2  style="width: 104px; height: 66px; position: absolute; vertical-align:
    margin-top: 66px; margin-left: -152px; border: 0px; background: none; font-style: normal; font-variant: normal; font-weight: bold; font-stretch: normal;
    size: 40px; line-height: normal; font-family: Arial; text-align: center; color: rgb(135, 206, 235); padding: 0px; -webkit-appearance: none;">
  </div>
  <script type="text/javascript">...</script>
```

1. The dial is displayed and can be manipulated using the mouse. The debugger Data tab displays the value once you move to the next page. If you return to the page by navigating backwards, the value is repopulated for you to modify.

2. The HTML includes the name and id attributes that have been populated dynamically from the HTTP POST attributes retrieved by the PHP script.

There are many more ways to use Custom Controls to change how labels and inputs are displayed and react to the end user. Consult the documentation and the Sample projects provided with Oracle Policy Modeling for more information.

JavaScript Extensions

The third available option for adding custom content to your Project is officially described in the documentation as the **Interview Extension** and **Control Extension** objects. In simple terms, a JavaScript object called `OraclePolicyAutomation.AddExtension` allows developers to create new user experiences for almost any part of the Interview. For example you can create the following (as of December 2018).

- Styling Extensions to add a custom look and feel to text inputs, calendars, and signatures, combined with CSS rules in a documented framework.

- Control and Interview Extensions to change the behaviour of the controls and navigation of your Interview using JavaScript, jQuery, and other plugins and libraries that you wish to implement.

These extensions were introduced in November 2016, and this explains why many of the user experience options are documented in terms of what was possible and typical *before* and *after*.

Consultants working on projects designed before this release are likely to be confronted with *custom controls for labels and inputs, stand-alone JavaScript to manipulate the page look and feel,* and potentially tasked with the job of migrating these to *Control or Interview Extensions and Styling Extensions* all using the documented framework.

The topic of Control and Interview Extensions in JavaScript is large enough to warrant a separate chapter, towards the end of this book.

Completing the Interview

Appropriately enough, the final section of this chapter will deal with the end of the Interview. You may configure the following on all except the final Screen.

Next Button

You can choose to display or hide the Next button. If you remove the Next button, the Screen becomes a potential navigational dead end for your user. Depending on the goal of the interview, that may make sense (perhaps to highlight an inappropriate scenario for your user to follow). You can also reinstate it if you change your mind, by selecting the No Next Button placeholder and selecting Back once more. Bear in mind that making the navigation too complex will have side-effects; your Interview will require more testing, and the user experience may suffer.

Submit and Redirect Button

Submit and Redirect submits your Interview to your Connection to a Data source, and then redirects the user to another site. Choosing this option displays the following dialog to enter the URL of the other site. Substitutions are allowed in the URL, making it dynamic.

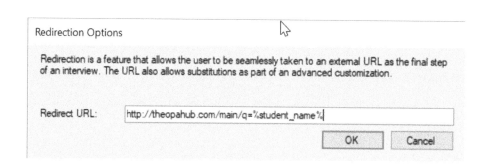

In the example above, the student name forms part of the URL.

Submit

The Submit button sends the Interview content to the Connection data source.

No Button

Removing the "forward motion" button leaves the possibility that your end-user might find themselves on this page and have no way to move forward. Testing would need to determine that built-in relevance functionality means this would not happen. Recall relevancy was seen in the chapters about Explanations and in the previous chapter about Interviews.

The following Buttons are available on the last Screen of your Interview, with the same functionality as just described:

- No Button

- Submit and Redirect

- Redirect

As an example, review the following Screenshot and identify the icons, before reviewing the guidelines beneath the image.

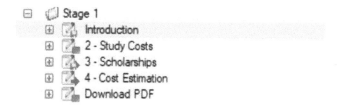

1. The Introduction Screen has a Submit Button specified. Data is sent to the Connection. A diskette icon is shown.

2. The Study Costs Screen has No Next Button specified. Only a Previous button is visible. A Stop icon is displayed.

3. The Scholarships Screen has a Submit and Redirect specified, and a diskette icon with an arrow is visible.

4. The Cost Estimation Screen has a Redirect specified, and an arrow icon is displayed.

5. The Download PDF Screen has no Button specified, and it is the final Screen. The Stop icon is again displayed.

> **NB**: The Back Button is also configurable; the options available are Back or No Button.

Summary

The Interview tab provides you with a very powerful yet easy to use set of options to create a truly personalized experience for the end user. In this respect, less is often more – adding too much customization will dazzle the user and will increase your chances of having a difficult migration in the future. Be especially careful to ensure that your custom controls and JavaScript do not break the ability to upgrade in the future.

Developers should pay particular attention to how *changes in the November 2016 release* may affect their custom controls if they are working on a migration project.

> **NB:** If you have not already done so, now is a good time to create a backup copy of the Projects you have used in this chapter.

Working with Inferred Instances

Inferred Entity Instances

In the last two chapters, you discovered the Oracle Policy Automation functionality known as inferring entity instances or inferring entities. In earlier versions of Oracle Policy Automation, there were some restrictions in respect of the behavior of these instances. This chapter examines the process of inference in more detail, and shows how these instances behave in versions of Oracle Policy Automation after November 2016.

Understanding these features will provide you with new avenues of rule design, and may affect the upgrade or modification of existing rules from previous versions. In addition, Rules that infer relationships and entity instances make for easier mapping to an external application, and the potential to insert records in that application.

So why another chapter on the subject of inferred entities? Because I am often asked for clarification as to the capabilities and functionality in this area, and because it offers a good opportunity to practice both Word, Excel and Interview Screens all in one place.

Accessing the Scenario

To work through these examples, you will need a new Project. Unlike previous examples – where you build the Project from scratch – in this instance you will use one of the example Projects provided in Oracle Policy Modeling.

Finding an Example Project

I cannot stress enough how useful it is to be able to study example Projects from my laptop. These examples are fully functional, detailed Projects that often showcase advanced or complex features. In addition, they are built for a variety of different uses, industries and deployment types (Interview, Web Service).

To access them, in the Project tab, click the Example Projects button. Notice the search facility which lets you look for industry-specific examples and functionality-specific demonstrations.

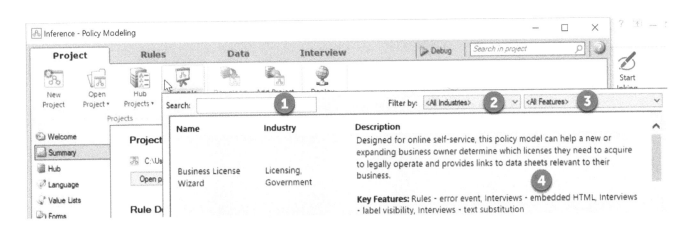

1. You can search directly if you know the name of the Project.

2. You can filter by industry or view for all industries.

3. You can filter by functionality or feature.

4. Details of each project are given to help you understand the background of the example.

In this chapter, you will use the RetailDiscount example. When you select it from the list, a copy of the Example is saved in your normal Project folder. Should you wish to modify the example, as in this chapter, you can always use the Zip feature to save a copy of your modified version.

Working with Entities in Retail Discount

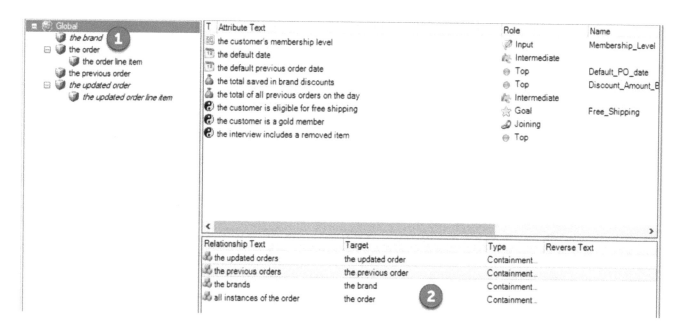

Above is a screenshot of the data model used in this example. There are many valuable learning points, shown below.

1. There are a number of inferred entities, as identified by the italics.

2. All the Containment relationships have been adjusted to display natural-sounding text.

Now take a look at the Relationships, with the following as your guide:

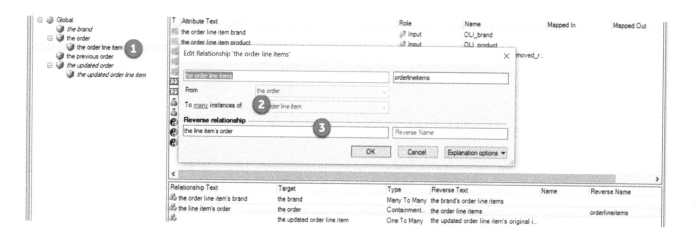

1. Select the order line item entity.

2. Observe this is a standard Containment relationship.

3. However, reverse text has been added to allow functions to reference the relationship from the opposite perspective.

Infer Instances of an Entity

Using the information shown above, the rule designer can leverage functions you discovered in chapter 4 in novel ways. For example, adapted from the example Word document `Brand Discounts.docx`.

InferInstance (<u>the order line item's brand</u>, <u>the order line item brand id</u>)

The rule above can be read, in pseudo-language, as "for every line item, find the brand and create a new line in the list of brands based on the brand id". So if you create an order in the Debugger, with three order line items *but only two different brand ids*, you will find you have two instances of the Brand entity.

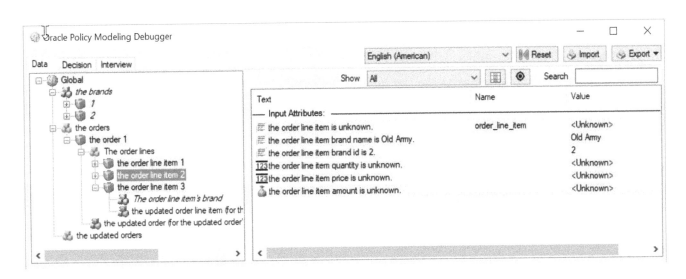

In this way, as orders are being entered, instances of the brand entity are inferred and appear in the Debugger. This concept is used in several ways in this example project. Firstly to create a copy of each order:

<u>the updated order</u> exists for <u>the updated order's original order</u>

Secondly, to create order lines in the copy. Notice the conditions added to this, so that only valid lines are copied (lines whose quantity is zero, for example, are not copied).

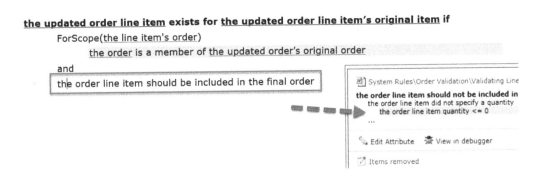

Visualizing Non-Inferred Entities

This example project is also an excellent opportunity to review the differences in display between an Entity Collect Control and an Entity Container. Consider the following Screen, displaying the Previous Orders. Recall that Previous Orders is *not* an inferred entity, rather it is entered manually or captured from an external system such as Oracle Engagement Cloud.

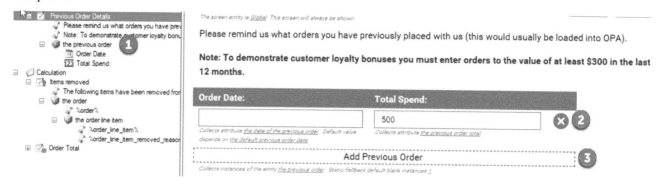

In the screenshot above, the following points reflect the display of a non-inferred entity for the purposes of data capture.

1. The icon displayed is yellow, with red streaks.

2. The control offers the ability to show or hide the delete button.

3. Similarly you can choose not to display the Add button, change its text, or change the number of blank records displayed by default.

Visualizing Entities

The Items Removed Screen in the same Project demonstrates how to display Entity data (either inferred or non-inferred) for review purposes.

1. Notice the icon does not have red streaks. This is an Entity Container, not an Entity Collect.

2. Although not obligatory, the Interview designer has chosen to show all information in the form of labels, which are inherently read-only and a good choice in this instance.

Visualizing Inferred Entities

Now that you have had the opportunity to review some of the features of this example, you will experiment with some of the entities in order to learn the restrictions in place regarding display and capture of data. For this, you will add a new Screen in your Interview, anywhere except the last Screen.

On the Screen, add the following element using the screenshot as your guide:

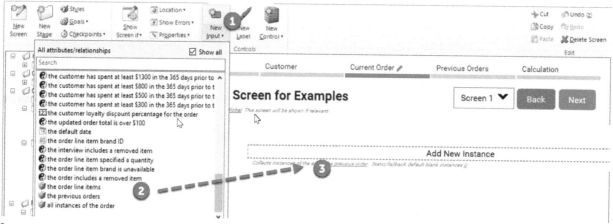

1. Select New Input. Ensure you select Show All.

2. Notice only how non-inferred Entities are present.

3. Notice the Entity Collect immediately displays Add New Instance.

Now delete the Entity Collect from your Screen. Choose, instead, to visualize one of the inferred Entities. Using the screenshot as your guide, add the following elements.

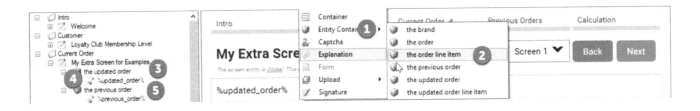

1. Add an Entity Container for the previous order entity.

2. Add another for the updated order. You can use Entity Containers for both normal and inferred entities.

3. Add a label in each Entity Container.

4. Use the label to display information; recall that a label can contain one or more substitutions.

The Entity Container, therefore, is able to display both entities – and the effect is identical.

For a final example, you will perform just a few more steps to discover the behaviour of the entities in another common scenario.

Using the screenshot displayed below as your guide, complete the Screen as follows:

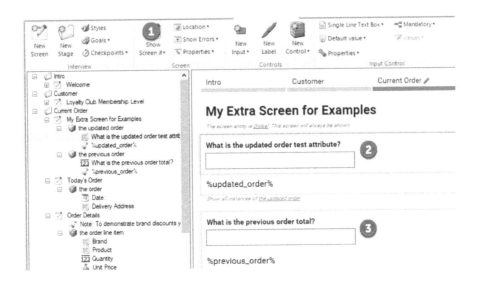

1. Set the Screen Show If... to Always. As our Screen is purely for testing purposes and does not display information that is uncollected or relevant to the Interview, it would be hidden by default.

2. Create a new attribute *the updated order test attribute* of type Text. Add this Input to *the updated order* Entity Collect. Recall that *the updated order* is an inferred entity.

3. Repeat for *the previous order* entity, which is not inferred.

Now run your Project in the Debugger and enter the following information.

- Enter an order, with order lines. Ensure you enter a quantity and the order line item undiscounted price for each of your items.

- Manually enter a Brand for the first line. Select the Yesterday's Brand from the drop-down for the second line.

- Enter a Previous Order with an order date less than six months ago. Ensure it has an order total.

- Enter the loyalty card level as Gold.

- To help you identify each item, use the identifying attribute to provide a name, such as P1 for the Previous Order, O1 for the order, OL1 for the first order line and so on.

Now using the Interview tab of the Debugger, navigate through the Screens until you reach your test Screen.

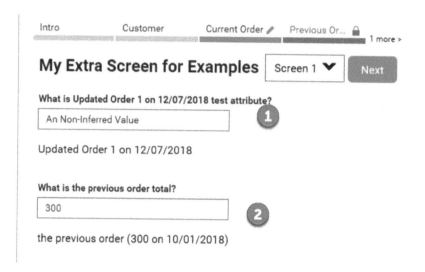

1. The inferred entity instance can also have *non-inferred* attributes that are inputted manually. Observe that you are permitted to enter data in this non-inferred attribute of an inferred entity.

2. The non-inferred entity, as expected, allows modification of the attribute value.

As you have just learned, an Entity Container can be used to display *or* update information. For example, in the above Screen, *both* entities are displaying an input control as well as a read-only label.

Data Collection in Entities

This functionality has always, by design, been available for non-inferred entities but was introduced for inferred entities in November 2016. Now you can infer an entity instance, including some of its attributes, but those entity instances can also have other, non-inferred attributes (like the test attribute that you added in the exercise), that are populated with data collected or modified by an end user.

This was not the case in earlier versions of Oracle Policy Automation.

Summary

In this short chapter, you have learned several very useful points:

- The importance of using the example projects to learn Oracle Policy Automation.

- The use of relationship text in reverse form to allow for more flexible use of Entity functions such as InferInstance()

- The behavior and display of entities for data entry, modification, and reviewing.

The next chapter introduces the testing feature of Oracle Policy Modeler, to allow rule designers to go beyond the Debugger and into more strategic testing of their rules.

Testing the Project

Testing the Project

So far we have used the debugger to 'unit test' rules in your Project. It provides screens that enable designers to analyze behavior, see problems and understand decisions, as well as visualize the interview that will be presented to the end-user.

But if you need to move beyond unit testing, to a broader approach – then you will need another tool to track test cases and results. You probably will need to be able to run much larger numbers of sessions, and to track both the actual results and the expected results, in order to study any reasons for divergence. Once you have identified any problems, return to the debugger for further analysis.

Getting Started with Testing

The testing process in Policy Modeling can be broken down into several stages. Before you begin testing, there are a number of things to put in place. In this chapter, you will initially use the backup copy from Chapter 1 – the original Project with the candidate and a large number of Global attributes.

Testing is organized on the Testing Pane of the Project tab. The basic outline of the window is displayed below, with a set of comments underneath.

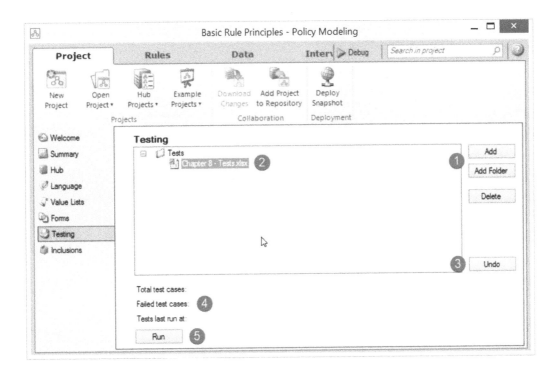

The icons above represent the following:

1. Adding new Test files and folders. You can add as many files as you need, and organize them in folders. The same folders will appear on your hard disk, in the Project folder under the Tests sub-folder.

2. Test Files are Excel worksheets.

3. If you have added or deleted a file momentarily and wish to undo that action, this button will be available for a short time.

4. Here you can view information about the different test case results.

5. The run button will execute all of the test cases in the selected Excel file. You can also execute tests by opening the Excel file and working with individual test cases.

Creating Your First Test File

1. Create an Excel Test file in the Project.

The Excel file used for testing purposes in Policy Modeling has a different ribbon to the files we have used so far. We use these buttons to work with the worksheet.

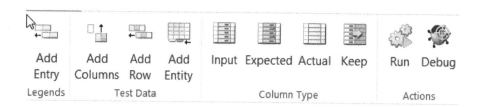

> **NB**: In version 10, testing can take place in two different ways: the **What If Analysis** document can be added to your Project, or a **Test Case** document can be added. Broadly speaking, version 12 brings this under a single file type. Not all version 10 functionality is available in version 12 at the present time.

2. Open the Excel Workbook.

The file is mostly empty at first. To begin your first example of testing, select a small part of a rule Project to analyze. In the Chapter 1 Project, there is an intermediate conclusion structure that infers whether a candidate has accepted the job offer. A fragment of this Project is reproduced below in case you wish to recreate it in a new file.

Candidate Evaluation Goal

the candidate is accepted if
    all of the following are true
        the candidate's references are valid
        the candidate's interview was a success
        the candidate can start employment
        the candidate decides to take the job

Candidate Starting Employment Evaluation

the candidate can start employment if
    the candidate's starting date of employment = 2016-01-01 and
    the candidate's clocking in time = 09:00:00 and
    the candidate's full name is certain

3. In the Excel file, click the Add Columns button on the ribbon.

As a first step to testing a simple rule Project, you must add some columns to this worksheet. The Test Cases Dialog opens. The features are detailed in this screenshot:

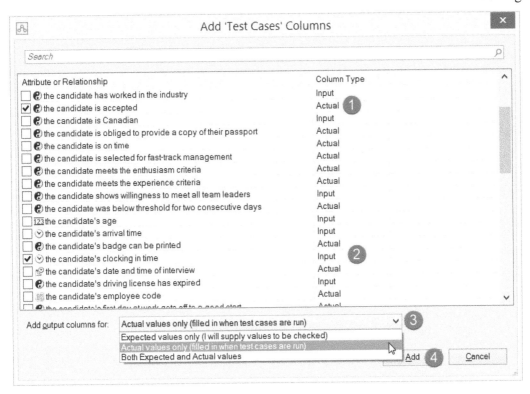

Selecting Data for Tests

Selecting columns: Policy Modeling has detected, for example, that a selected attribute (the candidate is accepted) is an outcome. So you must decide whether just to display the actual outcome, the expected outcome, or both.

1. Policy Modeling automatically fills in the Actual column when you run the test.

2. Policy Modeling lets the rule tester (you) enter the Expected values so they can be compared with the Actual values.

3. For now, simply select Actual in the drop-down. We can add more columns later.

4. Click the Add button. The columns are added to your Excel worksheet.

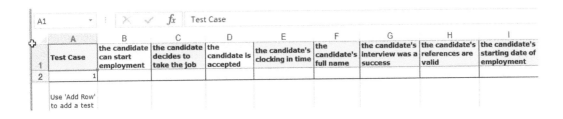

The colours used correspond to the type of information; an attribute that must have data provided is in green, a conclusion is in yellow. The yellow cells will be filled in by Policy Modeling when the test is run.

Enter the following data as an example. Notice the Test Case is #1.

Test Case	the candidate can start employment	the candidate decides to take the job	the candidate is accepted	the candidate's clocking in time	the candidate's full name	the candidate's interview was a success	the candidate's references are valid	the candidate's starting date of employment
1		TRUE		09:00:00	Richard Napier	TRUE	TRUE	24/02/2016

167

Actual Outcome Values

You now have one test case prepared. You can run the testing engine to observe the outcome.

Click the Run button on the ribbon.

The Excel worksheet responds with the message that two outcomes were updated. Looking at Test Case #1 we can see this is the case:

Test Case	the candidate can start employment	the candidate decides to take the job	the candidate is accepted	the candidate's clocking in time	the candidate's full name	the candidate's interview was a success	the candidate's references are valid	the candidate's starting date of employment
1	FALSE	TRUE	FALSE	09:00:00	Richard Napier	TRUE	TRUE	24/02/2016

The test case ran successfully. But maybe the outcome was not what we expected.

Add another test case to the file. Click Add Row.

Notice that Test Case #2 has now been created. Add data according to the second test case shown below:

Test Case	the candidate can start employment	the candidate decides to take the job	the candidate is accepted	the candidate's clocking in time	the candidate's full name	the candidate's interview was a success	the candidate's references are valid	the candidate's starting date of employment
1	FALSE	TRUE	FALSE	09:00:00	Richard Napier	TRUE	TRUE	24/02/2016
2		TRUE		09:00:00	Steve Jobs	TRUE	TRUE	01/01/2016

Run the test cases again.

The results are updated and we see the outcomes.

Test Case	the candidate can start employment	the candidate decides to take the job	the candidate is accepted	the candidate's clocking in time	the candidate's full name	the candidate's interview was a success	the candidate's references are valid	the candidate's starting date of employment
1	FALSE	TRUE	FALSE	09:00:00	Richard Napier	TRUE	TRUE	24/02/2016
2	TRUE	TRUE	TRUE	09:00:00	Steve Jobs	TRUE	TRUE	01/01/2016

By now you should be familiar with the basic principle and vocabulary. Test cases allow us to review the outcomes of executing the policies of the rule Project against test data. The Excel spreadsheet can contain any number of test cases.

Let's examine the different features that provide important functionality. In the next section you will add columns to your spreadsheet, using the Add 'Test Cases' Columns dialog shown below.

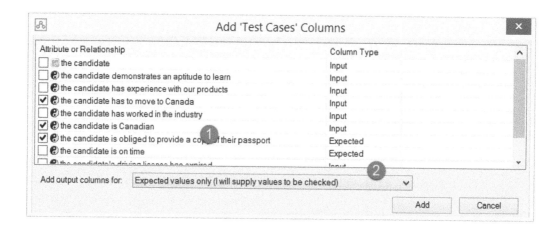

1. This allows you to select the attribute or relationship that you want to include in the worksheet.

2. This selects whether you want to enter *expected* values yourself, or review *actual* values when the tests are run (or both). We will discover the functionality of these two options in the next paragraphs.

Expected Values

If you are following step-by-step, add three more columns to the worksheet using the Add Columns button. You will add two inputs and an *expected value* column. In an expected value column, the rule tester must provide the *expected* result and Policy Modeling will respond after running the test with any variance.

Enter the following information in test case #3. To add a test case click the Add Row button.

Test Case	the candidate can start employment	the candidate decides to take the job	the candidate is accepted	the candidate's clocking in time	the candidate's full name	the candidate's interview was a success	the candidate's references are valid	the candidate's starting date of employment	the candidate has to move to Canada	the candidate is Canadian	the candidate is obliged to provide a copy of their passport
1	FALSE	TRUE	FALSE	09:00:00	Richard Napier	TRUE	TRUE	24/02/2016			
2	TRUE	TRUE	TRUE	09:00:00	Steve Jobs	TRUE	TRUE	01/01/2016			
3		TRUE		09:00:00	Janet Smith	TRUE	TRUE	01/01/2016	TRUE	FALSE	FALSE

In this fictitious scenario, you have indicated that you expect the above value of the attribute on the right-hand extremity (the formatting indicates this is an *expected value* column) when the testing engine runs the test cases.

Run the tests by clicking the Run button.

Policy Modeling responds by telling us that the outcomes have been updated, but that one outcome did not match the expected result.

ate's te of nt	the candidate has to move to Canada	the candidate is Canadian	the candidate is obliged to provide a copy of their passport	Use 'Add expected
/2016				
/2016				true
/2016	TRUE	FALSE	FALSE	

The comment in the relevant cell indicates the expected result for comparison purposes.

Keep Values

Sometimes it is useful to keep a copy of values that were entered in a particular column either for review purposes or comparison. You can use the Keep button to keep a copy of a column.

1. The column that is copied must be selected before clicking the button.

2. Click the Keep button.

3. The copied column (in blue) has no further effect on the test cases, but the remaining column can be modified as normal, if it was an Actual Value column.

Running debug for more information

The testing worksheet you have put in place also allows the rule tester to further review the behavior of a particular test case by reverting back to the debugger. Selecting the test case, click the Debug button. The debug session will be launched using the data in the relevant test case.

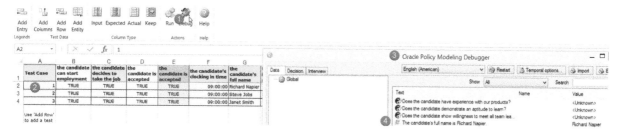

In the example above, the test case #1 has been selected by placing the cursor on the relevant line. After clicking the Debug button, the debugger window is launched with the data from the Excel test case prepopulated in the debug session.

Working with Entities

To experiment using the test case spreadsheet with entities, save your work in the current Project and open the backup copy of the Project from Chapter 3. The rule Project in question uses several entities on the theme of orders and order lines.

To work with entities, the testing Excel spreadsheet needs to be extended to add more tabs. Create a testing spreadsheet now in your Project.

Add your entities to the workbook by clicking the Add Entity button. Select the entities in this Project.

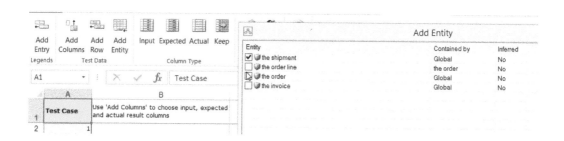

To complete the preparation you will complete the different worksheets. Begin with the Test Cases worksheet:

Test Case	the shipments	the orders	the invoices	the customer id
1				CUSTOMER ONE

In this tab there is only one piece of information used in your rule Project that you will need to enter. The other columns will be formatted as Actual Values. The Policy Modeling testing engine will populate those with the actual values later when running the test. They can also be formatted as Input, in which case you would need to enter the identifying attributes of the relevant lines – an example of which you will see once the basic data entry is complete.

Switch to the next tab and complete the tab in the following way, as an example:

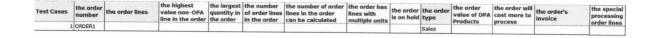

To construct this tab, follow these steps:

- Click Add Column and add all the attribute columns, choosing Active Value as the creation option.

- Complete the two entity-level attributes.

Continue to the next tab, which in my case is the order line. Add all columns as in the previous step.

Test Cases	the order line	the order line amount	the order line product	the order line product is an OPA product	the order line quantity	the order line quantity exceeds one	the order line shipment
all							

Complete the data using the following as a reference – enter the attribute values in the Input columns.

Test Cases	the order line	the order line amount	the order line product	the order line product is an OPA product	the order line quantity	the order line quantity exceeds one	the order line shipment
all	1	100	Product		1		
all	2	10	OPA Product		2		

As you can see, two order lines have been entered and input columns filled with data.

Finally repeat the process for the remaining two entities, which have very little data in input columns.

Test Cases	the shipment	the shipment is marked as delayed
all	1	TRUE

Test Cases	the invoice
all	1

Updating Relationships

Now that the basic data entry is complete, you can update several columns to create a structure similar to the instances created for debugging purposes in the earlier chapter, for example:

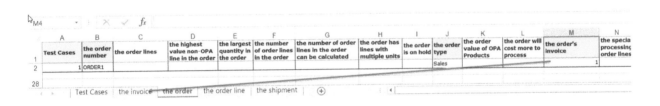

Here, reference 1 refers to the value of the attribute the invoice which is on the invoice tab. Similarly we can update relationships for the order line with identifying data from the shipment tab:

	A	B	C	D	E	F	G	H
	Test Cases	the order line	the order line amount	the order line product	the order line product is an OPA product	the order line quantity	the order line quantity exceeds one	the order line shipment
	all	1	100	Product		1		2
	all	2	10	OPA Product		2		1

Test Cases | the invoice | the order | **the order line** | the shipment | ⊕

Provided you have created enough information to build an appropriate structure you can now do two things:

- Run an instance of the debugger to ensure that you have entered all the requisite data.
- Run the tests and review the results.

Test Cases	the order number	the order lines	the highest value non-OPA line in the order	the largest quantity in the order	the number of order lines in the order	the number of order lines in the order can be calculated	the order has lines with multiple units	the order is on hold	the order type	the order value of OPA Products	the order will cost more to process	the order's invoice	the special processing order lines
1	ORDER1	O1	100	1	1	TRUE	FALSE	(unknown)	Sales	0	FALSE	2	""
2	ORDER2	O2	(uncertain)	2	1	TRUE	TRUE	(unknown)	Sales	20	TRUE	3	O2
3	ORDER3	O2	(uncertain)	2	1	TRUE	TRUE	(unknown)	Sales	20	TRUE	2	O2

The above example shows some output in respect of the order lines.

Getting Test Cases More Quickly

By the time you have finished entering all the data for the above example, you could be excused for being sick of the testing features. But help is at hand! If you are working in the Debugger, remember that the Export button allows you to create a Test Case. If you have a choice scenario in your debugging session, you can send it to a Test Case by selecting Export > Export as Test Case.

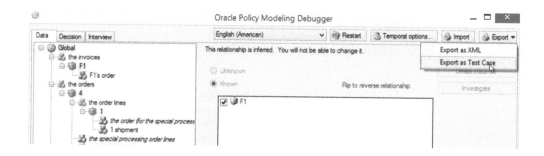

A new Test Case file will be created for you with the scenario already created inside it. The file will contain all of your data from the Debugger, ready to use in the testing engine. Aside from being a neat feature, this helps create template scenarios that you can copy and modify in Excel.

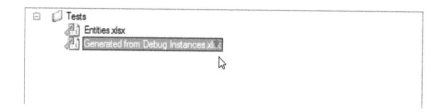

NB: This saves so much time, so remember from now on – there are two formats to export from the Debugger. One for the day-to-day saving of debug instances, the other to turn it into a Test File.

Working with Inferred Entities

The test case model is also capable of testing rule Projects where there are inferred entities involved. As a starting point, save the testing spreadsheet you have been working with and reopen the backup copy you kept from chapter five part three – specifically the Excel-based rule Project where we created inferred instances of entities.

Working with this Project, we can construct a test case to reveal what instances would be inferred with the different choices configured from your inferred instance rule tables.

1. Add the Global attributes.

2. Add the Relationships for the four inferred entities. Tabs will be added to the worksheet. Ensure that you format the cells as Actual Value columns, in order to display the results of the test.

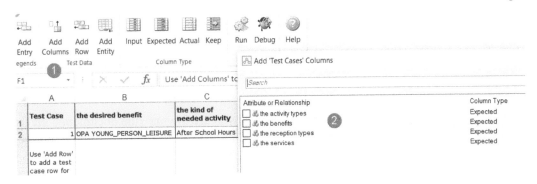

Enter data in the Global attributes, providing appropriate values. Run the test.

The results are posted for review. Note the format – instances are contained in the relevant cells, separated by commas.

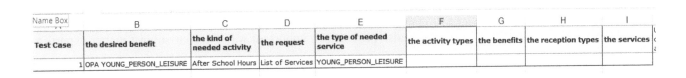

> **NB:** The Debug Export method can be used for Inferred scenarios as well.

Running All the Tests

The Project tab has also a Run button. This will run all the test cases in all the Excel testing files and update the statistics in this window.

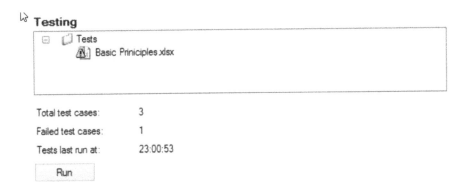

It does not, however, update the Excel files directly (no Actual Values are updated, no comments are added). It only signals an issue through a warning symbol so you know which file is to be investigated. Running the tests from the Excel ribbon, once the file is open, is necessary to learn more.

Working with Data Queried in another System

When working with Test Cases, the tester is sometimes confronted with the challenge of "simulating" data that is coming from an external system that has been queried. For example, your Interview performs policy rules on a Customer, and during the Interview you wish to display Orders made by this customer, but not *all* orders, as this policy only concerns orders placed in the last six months. As you will learn in a later chapter, this is known as an **ExecuteQuery** operation. To simulate the "last six month orders" you can automate the creation of a separate Excel file for this purpose.

Unlike other Test Case files, this one has a fixed name `TestConnectorData`. You can add the queried Entity to Excel in the normal way, and enter data for your scenarios as before.

Why Excel?

The advantage of using Excel as the basis for the tests is the ease with which information can be shared, analyzed and charted, in order to understand regression issues or performance over time. It is inconceivable that an Oracle Policy Automation project file should ever be deployed to end users without significant, documented testing.

You should be as structured in your Test Case Excel files as you are in your rule documents: give each file a pertinent name, and test intermediate goals in separate files rather than putting everything in one single Excel document.

> **NB**: You can add a Test Result column to each Test Case. Executing the tests will display TRUE or FALSE in each row to highlight whether the result is as expected. This makes sorting the cases in Excel very simple.

Summary

Testing your work using Excel testing spreadsheets is a vital part of your Project. Not only does it allow you, the designer, to detect and eliminate issues, it also provides an important way for your subject matter experts to assist, using an easy to understand file format.

Testing files created in this way will prove valuable when making new changes, when upgrading and also when obtaining a Project from another team member, as a quick way to understand the logic of the Project. Using simple Excel functionality like pasting ranges of numbers, copying and pasting random data, you can quickly build a large set of testing files with representative scenarios.

The ability to switch seamlessly from the testing spreadsheet to the debugger is a great timesaver when you need to focus on a specific scenario.

10
Explanations

Explanations for Policy Automation

In many situations, documents must be printed at the end of the Oracle Policy Automation Interview, and passed either to the interviewee (a summary of the interview, and a confirmation of the decision for example) or kept by the interviewer (for filing or annotation). In some cases, these documents must also be shared with external applications such as customer management platforms.

Explanations

This chapter will look at the concept of explanations, whose content is derived from decision reports. These can form part of the documentation provided at the end of an interview. Armed with this information, you will be well-equipped to prepare structured output for printing, display, or storage.

Decision Reports

A decision report is the chain of reasoning behind a particular goal value, expressed as a hierarchy. You have come across this already in previous chapters, for example using the Decision tab in the Debugger. It reveals how a decision was reached and which attributes were involved in reaching it. An **explanation** is an end-user focused decision report, perhaps with unnecessary information filtered out. You will see how the notions of **silent** or **invisible** attributes, as well as **relevance**, can alter what is displayed in Policy Automation explanations.

Forms

There are several other ways to explain outcomes to an end user – in a later chapter you will learn how to create PDF or HTML documents (known in Oracle Policy Modeling as Forms), and indeed these can also contain explanations.

Audit Reports

For more technical or regulatory requirement, Policy Models that use a Connection can also provide full audit reports, which ignore any filtering and provide complete decision reporting on every attribute you choose to audit.

Explanations and Attributes

To begin this investigation of how to prepare explanations for either the interviewer or interviewee (or an external system), you will review a feature that is visible after every debug session; in the different chapters of this book, you have grown used to seeing the following icons at the end of an interview:

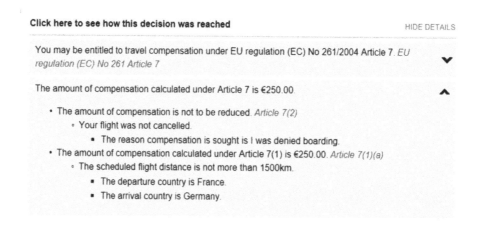

The clickable arrow icons, shown above, provide the ability to expand a line, such as The amount of compensation calculated under Article 7 is €250.00 in order to review the nested information below it. The principle is probably clear from the example – show the reader *why* a particular determination happened, and *why* a conclusion was reached.

The icons are displayed as a direct result of the attribute model you have in your Project. In the above example, using the Project from the previous chapter, we can see that The amount of compensation calculated under Article 7 is a goal in the interview from the icon in the attribute list:

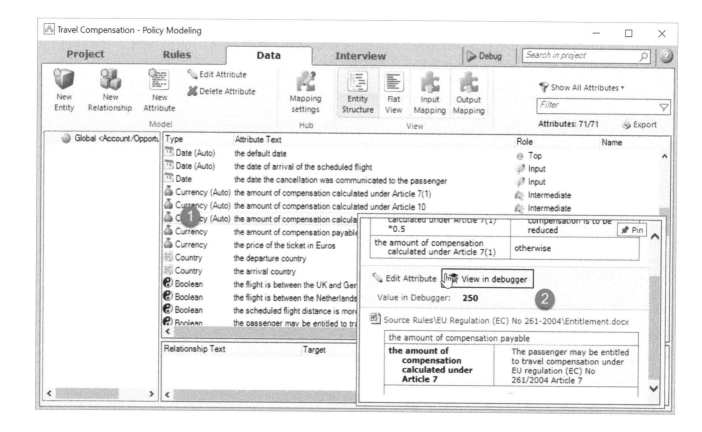

1. Select the Attribute, right click.

2. View the attribute determination, current value in the Debugger, and more.

NB: The example above comes from the Travel Compensation Example Project supplied with Oracle Policy Modeling.

Explanations – Filtering Information

To learn more about the Explanation concept, return to the Project you built in the early chapters of this book, where you determined the outcome of an Interview process for job candidates:

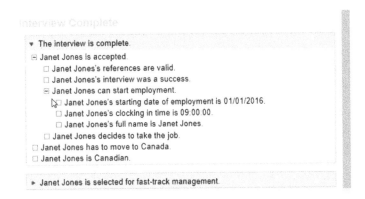

As an example of the purpose of explanations, open the attribute the interview is complete in the Data tab and click the Explanation Options button in the bottom right-hand corner.

Eight different checkboxes are displayed, grouped into two sections. Each section has the same options: true, false, uncertain, unknown, or always. Clicking always checks or unchecks all the other checkboxes.

Silent Explanations

Attributes that have this explanation setting activated for one or more situation are not removed from the interview summary, but the different attributes that provide proof, are.

Our Boolean goal will now be configured. For now we can choose the most obvious checkbox: Always.

The proving attributes will be hidden in all circumstances. When you start a new Debugger session, provided you enter appropriate data, The interview is complete goal is displayed, however the justification (*the explanation*) is not, so there is no clickable icon.

Using Silent for Intermediate Attributes

Using silent or invisible explanation options becomes more useful when considering attributes that are *intermediate*. To illustrate such a scenario, change the settings by removing the Always option for The interview is complete. In the Data tab of Policy Modeling, select the following attribute:

The candidate meets the experience criteria

This is an *intermediate attribute*. The use of silent is for intermediate attributes and allows the interview designer to maintain clarity of result, without showing all the detailed justification of that section – which might be inappropriate for legal or practical reasons.

Click the Explanation Options button and set Silent always.

With your intermediate attribute set, start a new debugger session; if you have saved a session from earlier then you can save time rather than re-entering data.

If you are unsure of where this intermediate attribute is used, the output can be found on the interview summary page by expanding the interview goal The candidate is selected for fast track management.

> **NB:** Recall that in the Data tab of the Policy Modeling you can right-click any attribute to see where it is used and open Word to review the content, as shown at the start of this chapter.

Using the Debugger Data tab, set the outcome of this intermediate attribute to be True. The candidate meets the experience requirements. Your output will look something like the following screenshot:

Interview Complete

▾ Janet Jones is selected for fast-track management.
☐ Janet Jones meets the experience criteria. *Criteria A*
⊞ Janet Jones meets the enthusiasm criteria. *Criteria B*

The modified intermediate attribute is still displayed, however it is no longer possible to expand it – the attribute has been rendered silent.

To further extend your understanding of the usage of this feature, return to the attribute and change the settings to the following, removing the checkmark as shown. The explanation *will be shown* when the outcome is False.

Explanation Options

Choose when this attribute will appear in explanations

Invisible (hide this attribute) if:
☐ True ☐ False ☐ Uncertain ☐ Unknown ☐ Always

Silent (hide proving attributes) if:
☑ True ☐ False ☑ Uncertain ☑ Unknown ☐ Always

OK   Cancel

Set this on both of the following intermediate attributes highlighted:

- the candidate meets the experience criteria
- the candidate meets the enthusiasm criteria

Start the debugger, and enter the relevant data for both of these attributes.

Relevance Revisited

You may be surprised by the results of your work. Although both of the attributes are set with the same values, they do not at first appear to always behave the way you would expect.

Both Attributes are False

For example, when *both* of them are False, the visual result is as expected, as both display the expandable icon for more information:

> ▾ Janet Jones is not selected for fast-track management.
> ⊞ Janet Jones does not meet the experience criteria. *Criteria A*
> ⊞ Janet Jones does not meet the enthusiasm criteria. *Criteria B*

One Attribute is True, the other False

Interview Complete

> ▾ Janet Jones is selected for fast-track management.
> ☐ Janet Jones meets the enthusiasm criteria. *Criteria B*

Note the above example – in this case Criteria B are met, and the expand button is not shown – as we expect.

But where is the *experience criteria*? This disappearance (which can be hard to fathom at first) is the result of the way your rule is written. Here is a reminder of the rule text:

```
the candidate is selected for fast-track management if
        [Criteria A]the candidate meets the experience criteria
            all of the following are satisfied
                    [Criteria A1]the candidate has worked in the industry
                    [Criteria A2]the candidate has experience with our products
    or
        [Criteria B]the candidate meets the enthusiasm criteria
            all of the following are satisfied
                    [Criteria B1]the candidate demonstrates an aptitude to learn
                    [Criteria B2]the candidate shows willingness to meet all team leaders
```

Hidden because of Irrelevance

We have two intermediate criteria, using a grouping operator to express the notion of **either…or**. If one intermediate attribute is true, the other intermediate attribute is *irrelevant* – since Janet Jones is selected for fast-track management because of meeting the other set of criteria. And something that is irrelevant is not shown by default.

Relevance in the Debugger Decision Tab

You can observe identical behavior in the Decision tab of the debug window.

For example, in the above example, where the enthusiasm criteria are met but the experience criteria are not met, selecting View Decision in the right-click menu of the debugger shows the following:

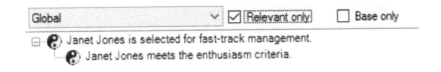

Notice the checkbox marked Relevant only. Unchecking the box shows both of the criteria, the irrelevant set is in grey for easy recognition.

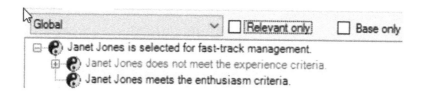

NB: It is important to remember that the notion of relevance permeates Policy Modeling at many levels – not just in your intermediate attribute display, but also for example in interview screens. An interview screen will not be displayed unless it contains something relevant to the interview goal(s).

Relevance in Interviews

To experiment with relevance, return to your Policy Modeling window and move to the Interview tab. As shown in the diagram below:

1. Select a screen in the interview, for example one that you created in Chapter 6.

2. Click the Show Screen If button.

3. Observe the default behavior is to only show the Screen if it is relevant.

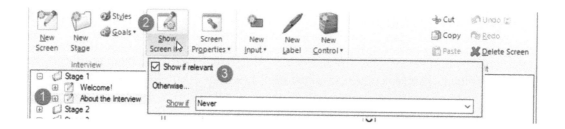

Relevance and Interview Goals

The definition of relevance can be revealed by clicking the Goals button on the Policy Modeling ribbon. Policy Modeling permits the interview designer to specify the goals of the interview from among the different inferred attributes in the Project.

If a goal is selected in this way, then only screens with relevant information will be shown by default.

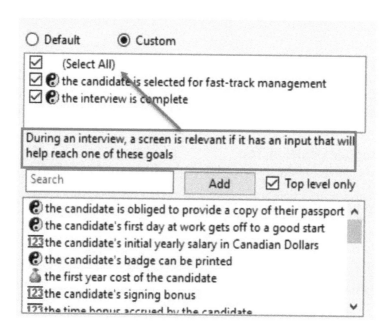

When you create a rule Project and interview, consider carefully what is relevant before you work with the invisible or silent attributes since they will, together, affect the Explanation output.

Structure and Explanation Options

Consider the following rule snippet illustrating several levels of attribute.

Setting the following values for the Explanation Options:

- the interview is complete – silent always.

- the candidate is accepted – silent when true.

> **the interview is complete** if
> > all of the following are satisfied
> > > it is known whether **the candidate is accepted**
> > > it is known whether <u>the candidate has to move to Canada</u>
> > > it is known whether <u>the candidate is Canadian</u>
>
> *Candidate Evaluation Goal*
>
> **the candidate is accepted** if
> > all of the following are true
> > > the candidate's references are valid
> > > the candidate's interview was a success
> > > the candidate can start employment
> > > the candidate decides to take the job

The behavior of the interview is that the interview is complete is always silent, and any nested logic is therefore not displayed – meaning the second attribute explanation options have no effect, since the attribute is already removed from the interview summary.

Invisible Attribute Explanations

Switching from silent to invisible provides an even more radical result. Invisible intermediate attributes are not displayed *at all* in the summary page. Interview Goals that have had their Explanation Options set to invisible will still however display.

Making Sense to the User

Careful attention is needed to ensure that your interview explanations are easily understood. For example, if the following settings are used for two intermediate attributes:

- the candidate meets the enthusiasm criteria – invisible always.

- the candidate meets the experience criteria – no options.

In the situation where the interview summary needs to display both attributes – for example where both conditions are False, then the following output is observed:

> ▼ The candidate is not selected for fast-track management.
> > ⊟ The candidate does not meet the experience criteria. *Criteria A*
> > > ☐ The candidate does not have experience with our products. *Criteria A2*
> > ☐ The candidate does not show willingness to meet all team leaders. *Criteria B2*

There is nothing fundamentally wrong with this text – however you should make sure that this is readable for the end user – the "missing" Criteria B line creates visual confusion – since its parent line is invisible. Sometimes something that is logical is not necessarily very clear for the end-user.

An Explanation Example from A to Z

Consider the following Project, which has been designed to simulate some parts of an online validation system for expenses.

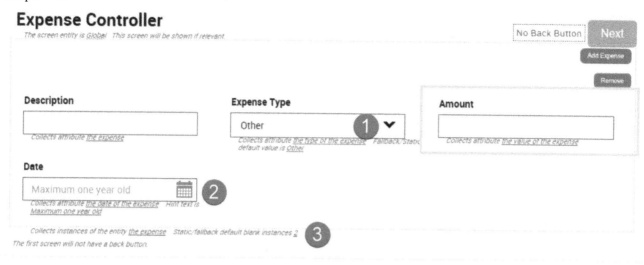

As shown above:

1. Users will enter the expense type.

2. The expense date has hint text to assist the user (see Chapter 7).

3. The Interview will propose two blank instances to help the user begin data entry (see Chapter 6).

Our goal is to display only the Airfare expenses in the Interview Summary Screen. The data model is simple and Input is limited to the items shown:

We infer a small number of Global attributes for our calculations:

Finally in our single Word rule document we have some rules. The writer has created a rule using a common Entity function, and a Boolean attribute to classify data entered as Airfare:

the total cost of all expenses of type Airfare = InstanceSumIf(**the expenses**, **the value of the expense**, **the expense is an airfare**)

the expense is an airfare if

> **the type of the expense** = "Airfare"

Our goal is to display, on the Summary, only the airfare items, and only the description, not the amount.

1. Set the Goal of the Interview to the total cost of the type Airfare.

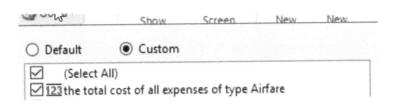

Running the Interview, if we assume that a few lines of data have been entered, both air travel and non-air travel:

The resulting Summary might look something like this, which is definitely not what was intended:

Interview Complete

Click here for the Data Report in HTML

Click here for the Data Report in PDF

▼ The total cost of all expenses of type Airfare is 200.
☐ The value of Flight LHR - AMS is £100.00.
⊞ Flight LHR - AMS is an airfare.
⊞ Car is not an airfare.
⊞ Hotel is not an airfare.
☐ The value of Flight SFO - LAX is £100.00.
⊞ Flight SFO - LAX is an airfare.
⊞ Food is not an airfare.
⊞ Food is not an airfare.
⊞ Car is not an airfare.

There is too much information in the Summary. To remove the unwanted data from this page, first adjust the Explanation options for the following attributes:

1. Make the Expense Value attribute invisible in the Summary by checking the Invisible Always checkbox in the Explanation Dialog:

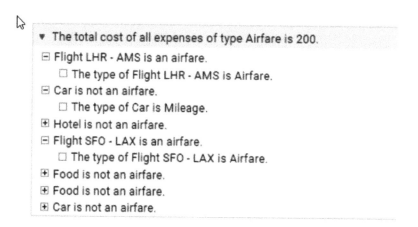

A new Debugger session gives the following output – the *value* has now disappeared. However we still have too much information in the Summary – the unrelated items that are not airfare still display:

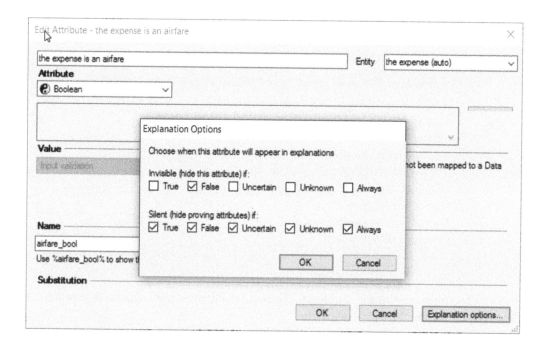

2. Make the other items invisible in the Summary. To do this, return to the Boolean attribute used to identify airfares and change the Explanation Options as follows:

In the image above, non-airfare will be invisible, and the providing Attributes will be always silent. After opening a new Debug session, the result is as follows:

▾ The total cost of all expenses of type Airfare is 200.

☐ Flight LHR-AMS is an airfare.

☐ Flight SFO-LAX is an airfare.

The pertinent data is shown, and only intended information fields are displayed.

Summary

Creating clear and fit-for-purpose explanations for your Interview fulfils several key objectives; clarity, so the user of the interview understands the outcome, compliance, since inappropriate information can be removed from the report, and historical reference, because the explanation is accessible via the different Web Services proposed by Oracle Policy Automation to facilitate the saving of this information in another computer system.

Connections in Projects

Working with Connections

In this chapter, you will discover how to use the Connections in your environment to build mapped Policy Models. Connections are integrations to external applications that have their own data model made up of tables and columns or entities and attributes that you can map in, and out of, a Policy Modeler Project.

Connections

Connections are a vital part of many Policy Automation Projects. A Connection provides rule writers with the capability to bind their attributes and entities to external applications to receive data at the start, to update or create records in an external system at the end of the interview. If their Connection supports the functionality, they can also load dynamic data during an Interview (for example, to pull in relevant order information based on filters).

A policy concerning refunds might use customer, order, and payment information from a Customer Relationship Management platform such as Oracle Siebel CRM. A policy for assessing next-steps in a customer enquiry might leverage data from a cloud-based application such as Oracle Service Cloud. A retail audit might be presented to the user as an Interview containing data from Oracle Engagement Cloud, or from a custom database. Whatever the source of the information, the goal of Connections is to make such application data, and their respective data models, available to the rule writer via the Hub.

In this chapter, we will look at how the rule writer can make use of Connections. In chapter 20, we will look at how a Connection is constructed through a technical example. The complete details of how to write code to make a Connection work are beyond the scope of this book, however a detailed webinar can be found at the following URL https://theopahub.com/main/oracle-policy-automation-siebel-crm-training/ Developers can also find more information about the Connector Framework online at this page http://documentation.custhelp.com/euf/assets/devdocs/cloud18d/PolicyAutomation/en/Default.htm#Guides/Developer_Guide/Connector_Framework/Connector_framework.htm

In this chapter, you will learn the basic vocabulary and steps to use a Connection in Oracle Policy Modeler. Later in this book, you will build and use a Connection with Oracle Service Cloud and observe the differences.

Mapping to a Connection

The first step for a rule writer is to find out what Connections are available in the currently connected Hub.

From the Data tab in an open Project (you don't need to have uploaded the Project but you should be connected to a Hub) click the Mapping Settings button. If you are not already connected to an Oracle Policy Automation Hub, you will be prompted for your username and password.

Available Connections will be displayed in a dialog. The exact name and nature of the Connections will depend on your Hub and the connectivity that has been set up by the Administrator.

NB: Connections are only available if you are connected to a Hub. You can change the URL to which you connect by going to the Project Tab, Hub Pane and editing the address.

In the example above, there is a Connection called Case Management. The name is purely used for identification purposes, therefore administrators should ensure that Connections are given recognizable names. To write a policy in respect of case management for a government service, you select the Case Management Connection.

Retrieving a Data Model

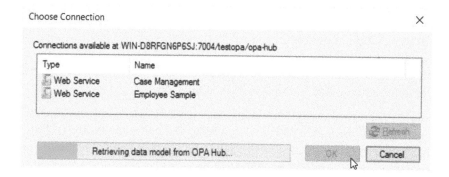

As you can see from the screenshot above, the Policy Modeling retrieves the data model from the OPA Hub. The example shown above is a Web Service – the Hub communicates with the external application that is the source of the Connection through XML.

Once this process is over (and depending on the speed of your network connection and the type of application that is providing the data model, this may take some time), you will be presented with a screen dedicated to the Data Model and the basic settings for your active Project.

Mapping Settings

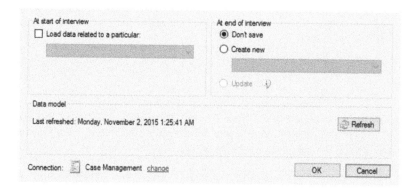

The Mapping Settings dialog box allows the rule writer to align data structures (database views, business components, tables – the exact nature of the underlying application or data source is not visible here, and rule writers can work in abstraction of the technical details) with Policy Modeling entities that are going to be used in rule documents.

For example, in the Case Management application (Oracle Siebel CRM for this demonstration), there is an extensive series of Objects defined. These can be mapped to Policy Modeling entities you create in your Project.

This will facilitate rule writing; instead of working through lots of documentation to determine the structure of the external application, the rule writer can use a visual tool to rapidly view and select external content to map to attributes and entities.

A demonstration is shown in the screenshot below:

1. An object from the Case Management application is selected for mapping into Policy Modeling.

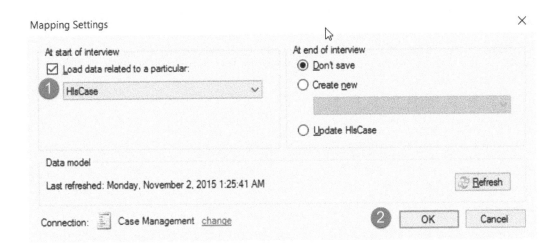

NB: The name and content of the Connection will depend entirely on what has been agreed and implemented by the administrator of the Hub and the technical team responsible for the external application. The objects shown above are for demonstration purposes.

2. Once OK is clicked, the external object is automatically mapped to the parent entity in Policy Modeling (Global) Note the <HlsCase> indicator next to Global in the screenshot below.

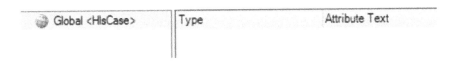

The Global entity is now mapped to the HlsCase object from Oracle Siebel CRM. At the start of an interview or session, data for a particular HlsCase can be loaded into the interview, from the Siebel application. In the End of the Interview section, you can choose to update this Object in the external system, create a new record, or not save the information (in the case, for instance, where your Interview is a simulation and you do not need to save the results to the external application).

NB: HlsCase stands for Homeland Security Case.

Using Connection Mapping in a Project

Now that the initial setup of your Project with a Connection is complete, you are ready to move to the second step – using your Connection to create attributes.

Mapping Fields for Input

Input Mapping means that Policy Automation will *receive* data from an external application, and that data needs to be associated to attributes and entities in your Project.

This step requires a good knowledge of the Connection (the kind of information, the types of data, and so forth) to be able to build an entity model in Policy Modeling.

Switch to the Data tab and click Input Mapping in the ribbon.

The input mapping screen facilitates the process of creating new attributes based on the **Connection Object**.

The screenshot below shows the Input Mapping dialog. On the left are the Objects delivered through the Connection. The names reflect the data source, however their exact format and style will depend on the Connection. Oracle Siebel CRM, for instance, provides **field names** in text format, which makes them easier to understand during the mapping process.

As you move the mouse down the list of Connection fields, Policy Modeling proposes default *attribute text* based on the metadata supplied by the Connection. At the same time, the rule writer can see, on the left-hand side, a list of other *Connection Objects* that they can choose to map to Policy Modeling entities.

The rule writer can adjust the attribute text by clicking on the grey sample and editing it directly.

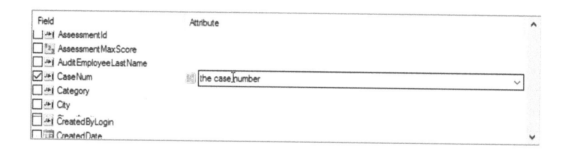

This proves necessary since the sample text provided will, more often than not, require improvement. This is particularly true in non-English language situations where Policy Modeling will give an inappropriate mixture of metadata and locale-based language.

The example above is from a French rule Project. The attribute name proposed is clearly in need of editing. Once the work is completed to map Connection *fields* to Policy Modeling *attributes*, returning to the Data tab for a review shows the list of mapped elements.

Clicking the Entity Structure button on the ribbon displays the results:

Rule writers can also review the current configured state of any attributes by opening the Edit Attribute dialog box and checking the mapping properties:

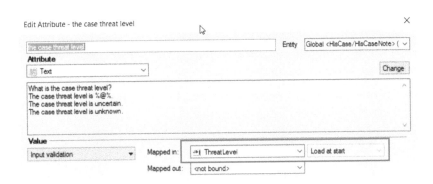

Add Further Entities to Mapping

Further entities can be mapped to *Connection Objects* by highlighting them in the Mapping dialog and selecting the hyperlink Add mapping now to begin the process of creating a new entity mapped to this Connection Object.

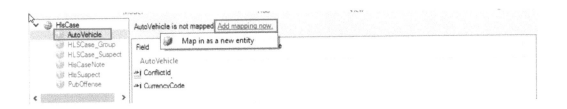

Add Entities for Dynamic Loading of Data

In normal circumstances, a Connection will load data at the start of the Interview (to pre-populate or *pre-seed* various attributes) and will optionally perform submitting the data back to the external application at the end, as described on the previous page.

There is also the possibility, starting with the second release of 2018 (known as Oracle Policy Automation 12 version 18B, or 12.2.11) of loading further data *during the interview*. At the time of writing, this was available as standard in Oracle Service Cloud connections, was possible but required configuration for Oracle Siebel CRM or third-party Web Service connections, and not yet available for Oracle Engagement Cloud connections.

The process of adding extra entities in this way is described below. The loaded data can be filtered and brought into the Interview, even if it is not related to the object already loaded at the start of the Interview (HLS Case in the example above). All data is read-only. This dynamic loading of data is referred to as **ExecuteQuery**.

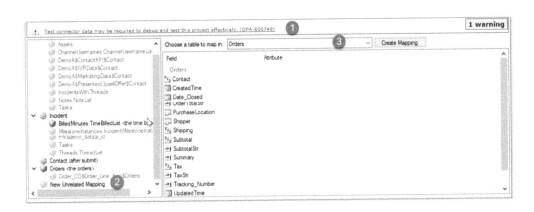

Using the screenshot on the previous page as your guide, notice the following points:

1. As soon as you add your first dynamic loading Entity, this warning will appear. As such it will not stop you from continuing, but to learn its significance for debugging and how to remove it, refer to the chapter on Testing.

2. The New Unrelated Mapping option is only available if your currently chosen connection supports this feature.

3. Selecting a table to map in a clicking Create Mapping adds the Entity to your Project.

Filtering a Dynamically Loading Entity

Once the Mapping has been added, for all intents and purposes you can begin to use the Entity and any Attributes as you would any other – in rules, rule tables, Excel, and so forth. However, when loading unrelated data, it is important to filter the amount of data that is sent to your Interview, and this requires a second step.

An unrelated Entity may display additional choices in the Edit Entity dialog which you are already familiar with. An example is shown below. Note the following observation.

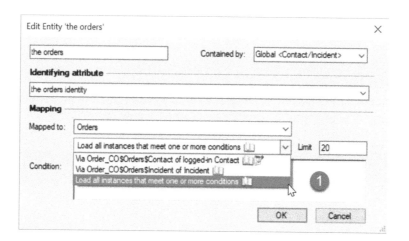

In this example, the Entity in question offers two relationships that are present in the external application. Choosing either of them will revert the Entity normal behaviour; that is, they will provide data used at the start of the Interview only. Retaining the highlighted selection Load all instances that meet one or more conditions signals this data is to be *dynamically* loaded. To facilitate this, another section will appear. You can learn about the key points by referring to the bullet points under the following image.

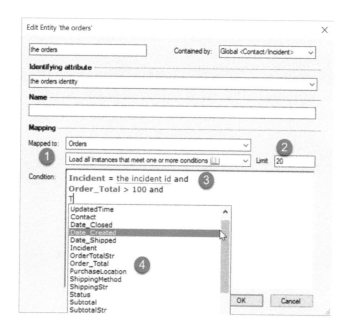

1. The rule designer selects the Load all... option.

2. To avoid loading high volumes of reference data, a limit to the number of records is imposed.

3. A filter expression can be applied (see the next page for more information).

4. Any field – mapped or unmapped – that is present in the Entity can be used as a filter.

The Filter Expression in Dynamic Loading

The syntax used to filter the data in your dynamically loaded Entity is not the same as the syntax you are familiar with. As you are retrieving data from a single Entity, you can only use Fields from one external table in your expression. That is, *no joins are allowed*.

In addition, only a small range of functions are currently supported. Read the observations below the following example to learn more about how to enter your filter expression.

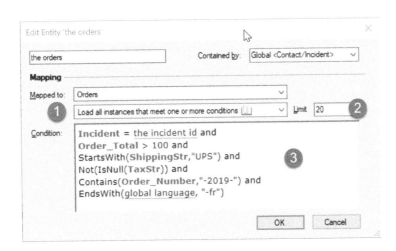

1. Only unrelated Entities need to specify conditions for data loading.

2. Carefully consider – from a usability, and filtering perspective – what might be a practical limit, for the number of rows you wish to return in your query.

3. The example functions shown demonstrate the use of the Condition: feature:

   - Items in blue represent Fields from the external data source. The available list is dependent on the Fields exposed by the Connection.

   - Items underlined represent attributes in your Project.

   - Logical operators (And, Or) are accepted, as well as mathematical signs.

   - StartsWith, Contains and EndsWith allow you to find text strings at different positions in Field values.

   - Not and IsNull allow you to exclude values, and to detect if a value is entered. They can be combined as in the example above.

Syntax Highlighting in Filter Expressions

To assist you in creating your filter expressions, inconsistencies such as confusing Order Total and assuming it is a text field (in this example) are highlighted with a red underline. In addition you can observe details of the error by hovering the mouse over the red underlined area.

all

Incident = the incident id
Order_Total > "100"
Sta ┌Incompatible comparison: Field 'Order_Total' cannot
Not │ be compared with text (OPA-E00758)

Aggregation in Filter Expressions

To avoid having to write `and` or `or` multiple times (as in the example at the top of this page), you can use the Oracle Policy Modeling functions `all`, `any` or longer versions thereof (see the chapter on Functions) to make your expressions more readable. The example at the top of this page could therefore be written as follows, for more clarity.

```
all
    Incident = the incident id
    Order_Total > 100
    StartsWith(ShippingStr,"UPS")
    Not(IsNull(TaxStr))
    Contains(Order_Number,"-2019-")
    EndsWith(global language, "-fr")
```

NB: The Expression you are writing must be syntactically correct before you can close the Edit Attribute dialog.

Create Rules

Once the mapping process is complete, policy rules can be developed using the assigned attribute text in the normal way – in both Word and Excel documents in your Project.

Mapping Fields for Output

Output mapping allows the rule designer to specify what information, if any, is sent back to the external application by the Connection when a Submit button is clicked. Mapped data could be in the form of goal outcomes, entity instances, and so forth.

Mapping the output is done in much the same way as input; there are several different choices:

- No output mapping (don't save back to the Connection).

- Create a new *Connection Object* using attributes mapped onto its fields.

- Update the *Connection Object* that was loaded at the start.

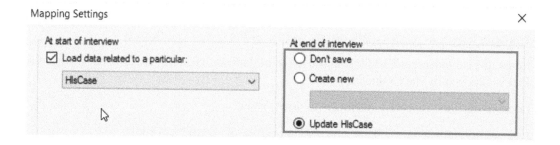

In the case of an update, the rule designer must ensure that the relevant attributes have both input and output mapping properties assigned where desired, as shown in the next screenshot.

The Case Type is loaded at the start of the interview, *and* saved at the submit stage.

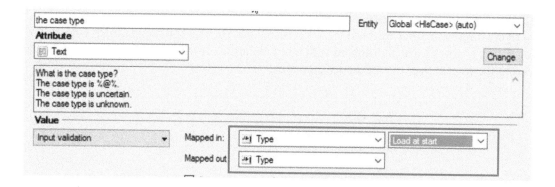

NB: Rule designers can add non-mapped attributes and entities to Projects that include mapped entities.

Adjusting Interview Screens for Mapping

When a Project includes mapping of *output* data, then an error will appear on the Interview tab if there is no Submit button present in the Interview screens:

It is at *Submit* that the Connection will be called to commit the mapped attribute values back into the external application via the Connection.

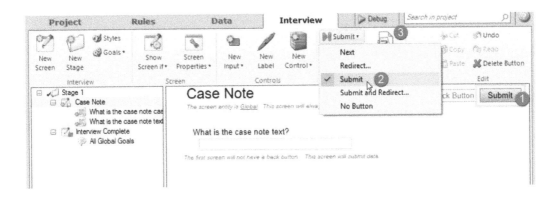

To add a *Submit* button:

1. Select an existing button on an Interview Screen (for example, the Next button).

2. Change the properties of the button using the ribbon as shown.

3. Optionally, a **Form** (see Chapter 9) can be triggered upon Submit, to generate a document at that time.

Mapping Errors

As the rule developer adjusts the input and output mapping of attributes and entities, the removal of mapping may result in errors. These are shown in red and will require changes or removal before the Project can be used.

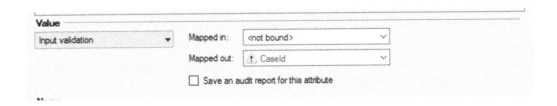

NB: The exact capabilities of a Connection depend entirely on the functionality implemented by the developer. Not all Connections may implement all (input, output) connectivity. Check with the developer before creating mappings. For more examples see chapter 20.

Mapping to Oracle Service Cloud

The mapping of your Oracle Policy Modeling Project with an Oracle Service Cloud instance follows the same basic pattern as the generic example shown. The initial setup is slightly different to that described previously and several other options are available, as described below.

About the Oracle Service Cloud Connection

The Oracle Service Cloud Connection defines the integration between your instance of Service Cloud and your instance of Oracle Policy Automation Cloud Service. Upon connecting to your Oracle Policy Automation Hub and selecting the Connections icon, a Service Cloud Connection should be visible, as shown below. Notice the Type is set to Oracle Service Cloud.

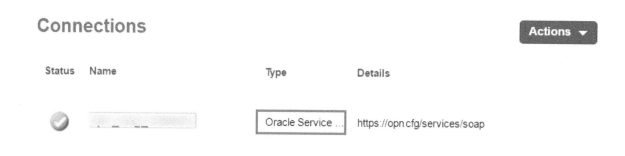

Upon double-clicking the Connection, the following information should be visible:

Shared Secret

As shown above, aside from the instance-specific information relating to your Service Cloud, there is an option called **Show shared secret**. The shared secret is a unique key, which is used in Service Cloud Widgets to ensure that when entering information into a Policy Automation rule set, the data is seeded and / or saved to the correct instance of Service Cloud. A new key can be generated from the Actions menu. In some cases, you may need the shared secret to be able to ensure it is mapped to a Widget in Oracle Service Cloud, or even to edit the shared secret to match an existing Widget.

Initial Mapping

The integration between Oracle Service Cloud and Oracle Policy Automation provides a simple way for Rule designers to leverage the data model of Service Cloud.

The exact choices available are dictated by the underlying data model of the external application. As you might expect, choosing to create an interview, which will be available to anyone, limits what can be done with it – no data can be loaded at the start, and the only option is to create new data in Service Cloud at the end. This would be suitable, for example, for a publicly available website where users are, for example, able to create a new incident by following a process dematerialized in Oracle Policy Modeling screens.

Your Oracle Policy Automation Hub must have a Connection of Type Service Cloud to be able to communicate with your instance of the Service Cloud, as described in the previous pages. The initial mapping dialog has a top-level set of choices, corresponding to the different usage scenarios (an agent working in a contact centre, a customer connected to a portal, or anyone working on an internet site):

Choosing one of the images has an effect on what information will be available for *mapping* in your Project. For example, selecting **Contact Center Staff** will expose the Account object and child objects from Oracle Service Cloud into your Policy Model.

If you select this option, you will be able to map to any data about the logged-in user, and also load data from specific objects in that context, such as an Incident. At the end of the interview you will be able to specify what to do – nothing, update, or create. Selecting one of the other two choices will, in turn, cause the available input and output mapping options to reduce or change in scope. An example of the initial mapping view is displayed on the next page, showing:

1. Input Mapping relating to the logged in user of the Service Cloud instance.

2. Input Mapping options for any other data available in the Connection.

3. Output Mapping available at the end of the Interview.

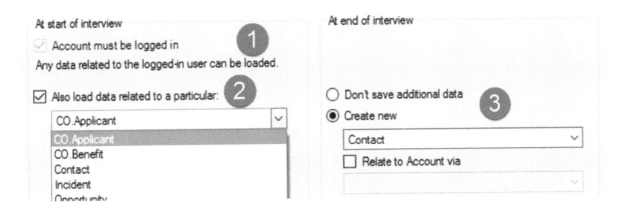

Once this initial choice of content is performed, the Policy Author can proceed to complete the Entity Model based on the data structure in the Oracle Service Cloud instance, for example by creating a new Entity in Oracle Policy Modeler and mapping it to one of the exposed Service Cloud entities, as shown below.

Creating Mapped Entities and Attributes
In this example, an entity has been mapped to the Service Cloud entity Task via a relationship called Tasks of Contact defined in the Connection. The behaviour of the Relationship is detailed in the dialogue.

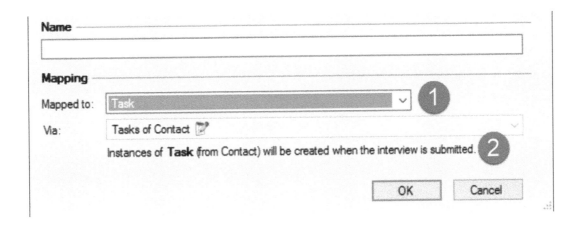

Mapping Relationships

When mapping a new entity in this way, selecting Via allows the rule designer to select how the data will be used, depending on the underlying data model of the Service Cloud application instance.

For example, in the next screenshot, several *different* options for mapping are available. The Service Cloud application provides *several* entity relationships to the Rule author, corresponding to the data model of the Oracle Service Cloud instance and the selected object.

The icon shown next to the relationship indicates whether data will be loaded from ("read" – hence the book icon) or saved into ("written" – hence the pencil) the Service Cloud application in each case. Some relationships will support both operations.

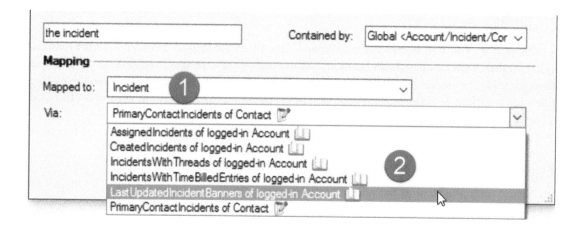

NB: Mapping Entities and Relationships requires a good understanding of the external application, the required fields, and the cardinality of the relationships.

Mapping Fields to Attributes

The process of mapping Fields in Oracle Service Cloud to Oracle Policy Modeling attributes can now be undertaken, much in the same way as shown earlier for a Web Service Connction. The list of fields available will depend on the type of information, and the mapping (input, output) will depend on the type of user (Contact Center, Customer Portal, Anyone) and the underlying data model. In the example below, the type of Attribute is Date and time, so the list of mapping candidates shows only fields matching that type, and the Mapped In option is not available because the entity has not been mapped or the underlying data model does not support inbound mapping.

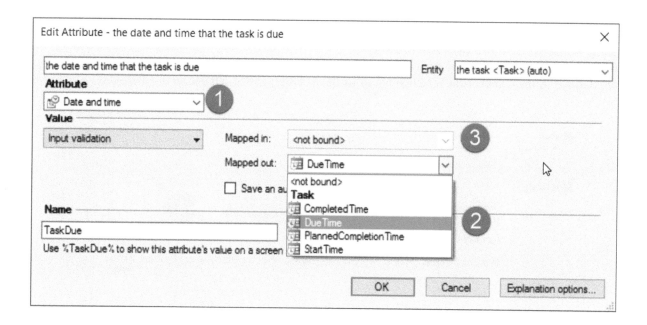

Mapping Required Fields

As you continue working, adding input and output mappings, the Oracle Policy Modeler will signal any incoherence thanks to it's built-in knowledge of the data model, provided by the Connection. For example, if you fail to map a required field, the following message will be displayed:

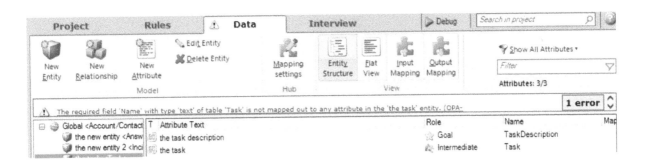

By adding the attribute into the Project the error can be removed. The screenshot shown below demonstrates how the built-in knowledge of Service Cloud from the Connection shows the Rule designer the required fields through a red icon.

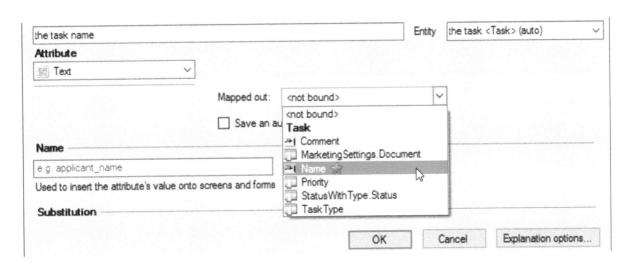

Be aware that just mapping the attribute may not cause the errors to disappear completely – if this is an attribute in an inferred Entity, for example, you will still need to write the Policy rules that infer the information, as you would with any inferred attribute.

Mapping Required Fields for Output

When you have finished mapping initial entities and attributes, it is good practice to verify that all required output mapping has been completed, to ensure than records are created in the Service Cloud instance. For example, you can see in the screenshot below that a required output field has not been mapped to an attribute in the current Project.

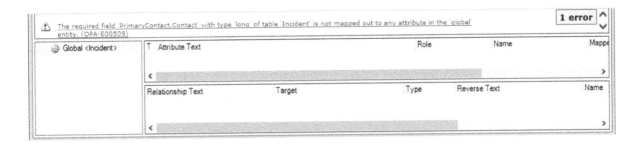

Mapping other Fields for Input

If your chosen option includes data drawn from your Service Cloud instance, ensure that any data is mapped in the Input Mapping option, and that the attributes you need are correctly entered with the correct type as shown in steps one and two below.

Testing a Service Cloud Connection

In the case of a Oracle Policy Automation Project primarily concerned with testing *output* mapping, it can be tested by deploying to the Oracle Policy Automation Hub and executing a Web Determination. In the example below, a contact is being created before being mapped for *output* to Oracle Service Cloud:

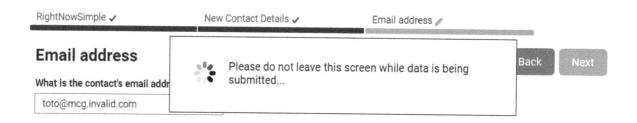

If the connection has been properly established and you have mapped all the required data for output, then the same contact can be found in the Oracle Service Cloud instance:

Connections from Oracle Sales Cloud or Oracle Engagement Cloud

As in the previous examples, the connection to Sales Cloud or Engagement Cloud will follow the same basic principles. The list of connected Tables and Fields is significantly limited compared to the other applications discussed in this chapter. The complete list of currently supported objects can be found, at time of writing, at this URL:

http://documentation.custhelp.com/euf/assets/devdocs/cloud18c/PolicyAutomation/en/Default.htm#Guides/Sales_and_Engagement_Cloud_User_Guide/Engagement_Cloud_data_mappings/Engagement_Cloud_objects_supported_by_OPA.htm

Connections from an External Database or other Data Source

The Connector Framework allows developers to create entity models for almost anything imaginable: legacy databases, Cloud applications, other on-premise software. The development of such a connection is made easier by downloading the Web Service definition from your Oracle Policy Automation Hub.

To download the Web Service definition file, navigate to an existing Connection and select the option shown below from the Action menu. If you do not currently have any connections, simply create a new blank connection in order to access the menu.

Developers can also find example code (in Java, although any language capable of calling a SOAP-based Web Service is acceptable) in the online help at this address:

http://documentation.custhelp.com/euf/assets/devdocs/cloud18d/PolicyAutomation/en/Default.htm#Guides/Developer_Guide/Connector_Framework/WSC_Example_Project.htm

In addition, example XML requests and responses can be found at:

http://documentation.custhelp.com/euf/assets/devdocs/cloud18d/PolicyAutomation/en/Default.htm#Guides/Developer_Guide/Connector_Framework/Connector_framework_WSDL_walkthrough.htm

Connecting to a Static Metadata Connection

In many projects, the availability of the exernal application is something that the Oracle Policy Automation team have no control over. Perhaps the external application is not yet completely ready, or there are elements that are still under development. If the data model is defined, but the application itself is not ready, then the Oracle Policy Automation Hub allows for the creation of a static metadata connection. The goal of such a connection is to allow Rule designers to map and work with Entities and Attributes from the external application, without the external application actually having to be online.

Of course, this "static" connection is not going to provide data of any kind. Its raison d'etre is to provide the metadata only. To understand the basic concept, the following screenshots provide an overview.

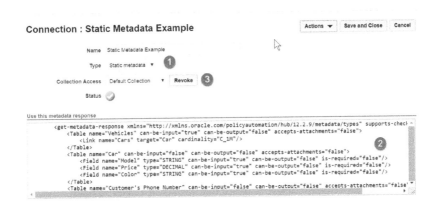

1. The type of connection can be either Static Metadata, Service Cloud or Web Service.

2. The administrator defines the expected output from the external application.

3. The administrator assigns the connection to certain projects (for more information, see the chapter on Hub Administration).

The Rule Designer can now select, map, and work with the connection:

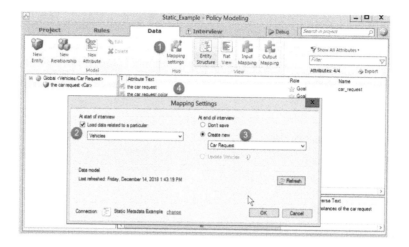

1. The Static Metadata Connection is avalable in the Mapping Settings dialog.

2. The entities defined in the static XML are displayed.

3. Any entities in the XML defined for outbound mapping are also selectable.

4. The Rule designer can build the corresponding entities in Oracle Policy Modeler and work with them.

Summary

Connections provide essential access to external data sources for your Policy Modeler Project. Connections are used in many different ways but the principle of mapping inputs and outputs is common to all of them. As a Rule Designer, you do not have to understand the technical architecture of the integration with an external source; you have to understand how the entities and attributes in your Policy Model map to those in the external application.

Therefore to be successful requires knowledge of both Oracle Policy Automation and the external application. An example of such an external application is Oracle Service Cloud, and you will learn how to deploy connected Interviews into this application in Chapter 19.

A brief overview of the technical structure of a Connection is provided in chapter 21, which focuses on Oracle Siebel CRM as a data source.

Forms

Documents that are printed or viewed at the end of an interview are called, slightly confusingly, **Forms** in Policy Modeler version 12. Forms use Oracle BI Publisher Desktop as their main design tool. As this book is about Oracle Policy Automation, this chapter will focus only on the basic information and steps you need to get a Form working well with Policy Modeler.

If you want to learn more about Oracle BI Publisher Desktop, at the time of writing this URL had lots of useful information: http://www.oracle.com/technetwork/middleware/bi-publisher/overview/index.html.

Starting with version 12.2.7 (May 2017), designers can also choose to use a PDF editor to create their forms. You will also learn how to implement forms built this way in this chapter.

Forms in Policy Automation

With the concept of explanations now in your mind from the previous chapter, you are well placed to discover **Forms**. Forms are PDF files or other standard format documents that are created to support the business process that uses Policy Automation.

Forms for Explanation

One common use for Forms is to provide a written trace of the *explanation* as to the outcome of the interview. Other uses might include:

- Creating a Form to be physically signed or sent to someone.

- Reviewing Answers given in a meeting offline.

- Printing a document to present to the interviewee.

- Sending a PDF to a customer management system as an attachment.

The initial steps to create a Policy Automation Form are as follows. For this exercise, you can begin by using the same Project as in the previous chapter.

> **NB:** Before you begin, however, note that only attributes with *names* will be usable in your Form. Recall that *names* are used to provide *tags* or identifiers for attributes in your Project. These tags are used in all sorts of integration scenarios, of which Form creation is the first one we have met.

In Policy Modeling:

1. Select the Project tab, Forms pane.

2. Add a new Form.

The document that will be added will be in the language of your Project. It is common to wish to prepare different language versions of the same output, for example in a country where there are several official languages or where your audience may speak a number of languages more fluently than the Project language.

Forms

Forms defined here can be added to an interview screen, and generated during an interview.

Name	Template	Explanations	
New Form	New Form_Template.rtf	0	**New**
			Delete...
			Edit...
			Explanations...

Form templates are edited in Microsoft Word, using the Oracle BI-Publisher Desktop for Office.   Download

Form Generation Options

☐ Ensure generated PDFs conform to the PDF/A standard (NOTE: This will cause the form to be generated using the Albany fonts)

In the example shown, the New button only offers Oracle BI Publisher (RTF) as a format. In recent versions, as shown below, two options are provided:

If you need to add different language versions of your Form, you will have to do so manually by following the steps below:

1. Open the Project Folder by going to the Summary Pane of the Project tab and clicking the Project Folder button.

2. Go to the `C:\Users\XXX\Documents\Oracle Policy Modeling Projects\XXX\FormTemplates\` folder.

There you will find a folder name corresponding to the locale of your Project, e.g. fr-FR or en-GB.

3. In the folder, take a copy of the Template File that exists.

4. Create a new folder at the same level as the local folder, with the name corresponding to the new locale you wish to add, for example fr-FR. Paste the file in the new folder. Do not rename the folder or the file.

5. You can now work to create the language-specific version of your Form. *It will not appear in Policy Modeler.*

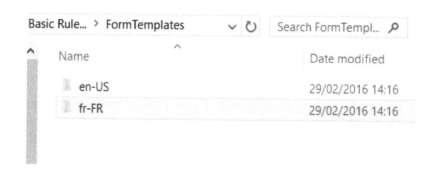

Working with Forms

The next steps assume that you have created a Project, and given names to all the attributes that you want to use in the Form. The steps are identical whether you have chosen PDF or RTF for your Form.

On the Forms pane, click the Explanations button. The Explanations list appears. Note that there is a horizontal scrollbar, so you might have to scroll to see all the attributes in the left-hand portion of the window.

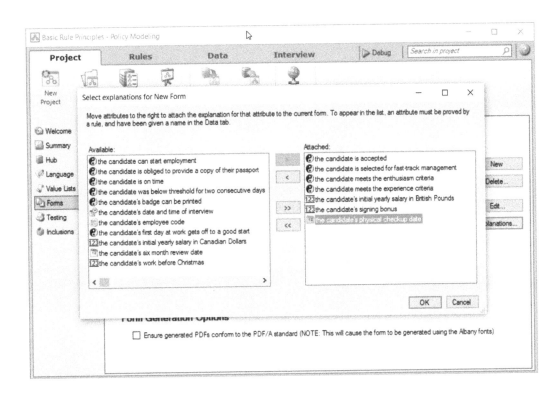

Adding Policy Modeler Attributes to the Form Definition

In this way we can add attributes, which have names, into the list of items attached to the Form. To avoid overloading the page and to reduce traffic on any network involved during the actual delivery of the Form to the end user, only use attributes you actually need.

It should be noted that the data attributes you select are not stored in the Word file – they are stored in an XML file that is placed in the same \FormTemplates\xx-XX folder.

> **NB:** Don't rename the RTF Word template file outside of the Policy Modeler – the file will be deemed to have been removed. If you do rename it inside Policy Automation, then all translated Forms will be renamed also. The XML files will not be renamed.

To follow the next step in this walk-through exercise, select the attributes shown above if you have them.

Working with the Form in Word

The Form is built and edited using Microsoft Word. However it does not use the Policy Modeler ribbon; it uses the BI Publisher Desktop add-on which can be downloaded using the link provided on the Forms pane of your Policy Modeler.

Editing the Form

To edit the Form, select it from the Forms pane and click the Edit button. To be able to build your Form, you will need to load the XML file created for you by Policy Modeler based on the explanations you chose.

In the BI Publisher Desktop Ribbon:

1. Select the Sample Data button.

2. Navigate to the folder for the FormTemplate/xx-XX language you wish to edit.

3. Select the XML file.

4. The Word Dialog confirms the data is loaded.

5. Click the Field button shown below. Do not use the Field Browser button.

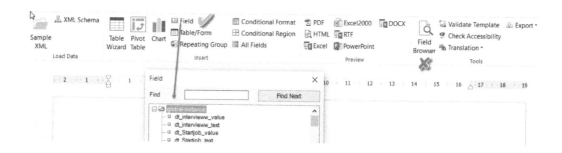

6. The list of attribute text and values appear in the Field dialog.

Creating a Form with Microsoft Word

Since the goal of this guide is to get you started on Policy Automation, this example will remain quite simple – if you need to get deeper into Oracle BI Publisher there is a wealth of documentation and example uses out there on the Internet.

The following simple guidelines will be useful to anyone wishing to use Oracle BI Publisher with Oracle Policy Automation.

Getting Good Sample Data

The sample data generated by the creation of the initial Form is not optimal for working in Microsoft Word as the content is very generic. Clicking the PDF button in the ribbon shows something like this:

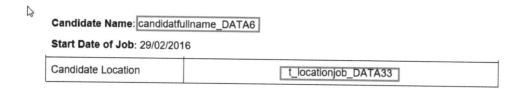

To enhance the display by creating better sample data, follow these steps:

1. Run a debug session of your Project.

2. By either entering or loading up data, fill or determine any attributes you are using in your Word Form.

3. In the debugger, click the Export button.

4. Select the Form you just made.

5. Save the file in a suitable location.

6. Edit your Form by selecting it in the Forms pane and clicking Edit.

7. In Word, using the BI Publisher ribbon, click the Sample Data button.

8. Navigate to the new file you just exported.

Using Sample Data

Now when you are working, you can click the PDF button in the BI Publisher Desktop Ribbon and see the contents of your saved debug session directly in the Word PDF preview, making it much easier to understand how the Form will render in real life when the end user has entered data into an interview session:

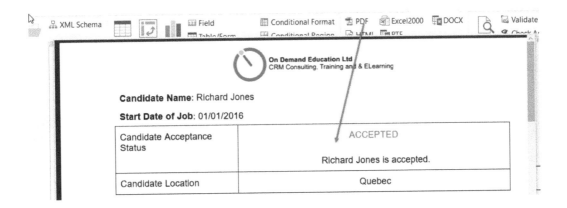

Understanding the XML File Contents

By opening the sample data file that you created a moment ago – for example in your chosen text editor or XML browser – you can also learn important concepts about the data that will actually be available for report creation at run-time. These concepts will help you make decisions about how to display information from Policy Automation as well as what information to use when building logic into your PDF form.

Choosing the Right XML attribute

For example, suppose you wish to create a **conditional region** in your Form, so that certain content is only shown when a condition is met. As an example you will implement the display of ACCEPTED or NOT ACCEPTED depending on the candidate acceptance data. In addition you will format the information in different colours.

By viewing the XML file and finding the attribute in question:

```
    </b_candidate_enthus>
  - <candidateaccepted_value>
        <value state="known">Yes</value>
    </candidateaccepted_value>
    <candidateaccepted_text>Richard Jones is accepted.</candidateaccepted_text>
  - <candidateaccepted type="boolean" question="Is Richard Jones accepted?" inferred="true">
        <value state="known">true</value>
```

You can probably see that your conditional expression in BI Publisher needs to be built based on the candidateaccepted_value (which has a value of Yes or No) and not the candidateaccepted_text, which represents the natural language text of the same attribute.

To implement the new region, here are the basic steps.

- Click the cursor into an empty part of your document.

- Click the Conditional Region button on the BI Publisher Desktop Ribbon. The BI Publisher Properties window will appear.

- Enter values, such as the following.

1. Choose the correct data field as described above.

2. Select the operator for your condition.

3. Select or enter the value as appropriate.

Thus you build your region based on the data type, the text, or the other information you need to create a condition. In this case, if the candidateaccepted_value = Yes then you will display custom green text.

Similarly you could create a second region. If not accepted the value will be No and you can display custom red text.

Candidate Acceptance Status	C ACCEPTED EC C NOT ACCEPTED EC candidateaccepted_text
Candidate Location	t_locationjob_value

Markers in BI Publisher

In the above example, the C and EC markers represent the **condition start** and **condition end** of the conditional region, and the custom text is between the relevant markers. These markers are inserted automatically into your document when you click OK in the BI Publisher dialog to create the conditional region.

The green or red coloured region will display according to the value of the attribute.

Candidate Acceptance Status	NOT ACCEPTED Rachel Jones is not accepted.
Candidate Location	Quebec

In the above example, you can see the following:

- The conditional region for attribute = No.

- The attribute text.

- The job location value.

Numbers and Dates can also be used in conditional regions to create effects similar to this.

Adding Explanations to your Form

The Form you are building now has a useful visual cue for understanding if the candidate has been accepted. Now you will display the proof of the reasoning – you will display the relevant *explanation* from Oracle Policy Modeler.

Creating an explanation comes in several steps:

1. At the top of your Word Form, open the Developer tab and click the Legacy Form and Text Form Field icon to insert a blank Form field (in other versions of Word, insert a blank Form field).

2. Add the following template text to the BI Publisher Properties dialog:

```
<?template@inlines:decision-report?>
<?if@inlines:"attribute-node"?>
<fo:list-block start-indent="{count(ancestor::attribute-node) * 7}mm">
<fo:list-item>
<fo:list-item-label>
<fo:block>*</fo:block>
</fo:list-item-label>
<fo:list-item-body>
<fo:block><xsl:value-of select="@text"/></fo:block>
</fo:list-item-body>
</fo:list-item>
</fo:list-block>
<?for-each@inlines:./attribute-node?><?call-template:decision-report?><?end for-each?>
<?end if?>
<?end template?>
```

3. In the BI Publisher Properties dialog, add Text to display in the Word file. This will help you locate this section again later. It will not print in the final output.

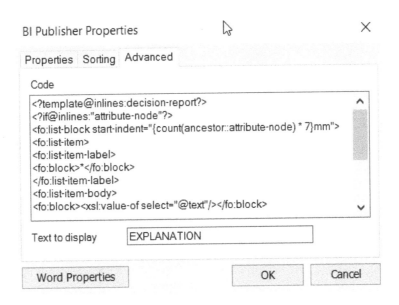

You should now have something like this at the beginning of your Word Form.

EXPLANATION

Candidate Name: candidatfullname_value

Start Date of Job: dt_Startjob_value

NB: The text EXPLANATION does not print or show to the end user. It is just useful to remember not to accidentally delete the otherwise hard-to-see Form field.

---

4. Return to your XML file that you generated from your debugger session, and visualize it in your favorite XML editor or browser.

5. Find the attribute you wish to have the explanation displayed for.

6. Note down the attribute_id of the attribute you wish to display the explanation for, highlighted below as an example.

7. Add a second Form field in the location you wish to have the explanation printed, using the Legacy toolbar as in step 1.

8. In the text Form field, add the following BI Publisher Code:

```
<?for-each:/global-instance/attribute_id/decision-report/*?><?call-template:decision-report?><?end for-each?>
```

9. Replace the attribute_id with the attribute you just obtained from your handy XML file:

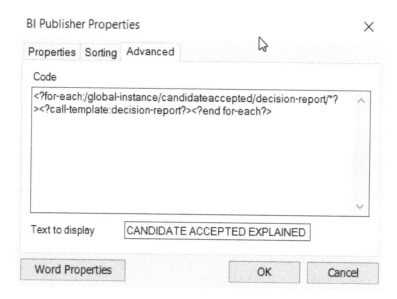

10. As before, add some text to display so you can find the Form field again later.

11. Now, when you preview your PDF file in Word with the BI Publisher Ribbon, using your XML file from the Debugger, you should see something like this:

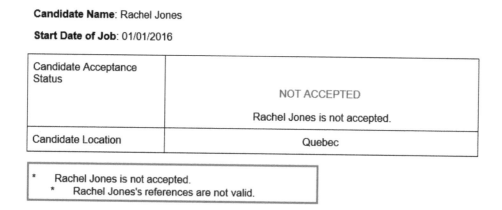

Notice the explanation after the table. You can add as many explanations as you wish to your Forms, but keep in mind the readability of the document and the volume of information that must be transferred across your network to make the document.

That concludes the brief demonstration of the basics of creating, designing, and customizing a PDF form for Oracle Policy Modeling. Now you will bring this to a conclusion by allowing the end-user to access the document at the end of the interview.

> **NB:** The content of your Form will be affected by silent and invisible Explanation Options for your attributes defined in Oracle Policy Modeler. If you need to revise them, see Chapter 9.

Adding a Signature to your Form

Recall from previous chapters that one of the Controls available during the Interview design process is the Signature. Representing an on-screen signature, this may be added to your Form. Adding a signature to your form increases the usefulness of the PDF in many situations, as it may speed up the business process that requires the form; for example, a customer builds and orders using an Interview, signs on their touchscreen, and then downloads the complete contract including their signature, and the same document and signature are sent to an order management system at the end of the Interview as well.

If you have added a signature to an Interview, the process to add it to the Form is as follows:

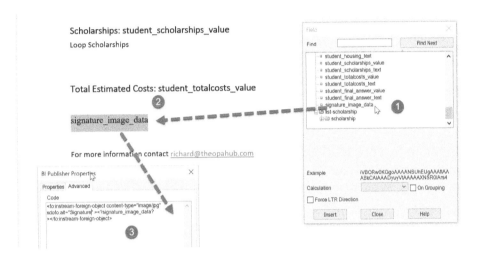

1. Observe that the signature is visible as a special Field, `signature_image_data`

2. Add this Field to the Word RTF document.

3. Double-click the signature and edit the properties, adding the code as shown.

> NB: this code is suitable for a signature assigned to the Global entity in a Screen. If your signature is in an Entity-level attribute, the code is slightly different. Both can be found online at this URL
> http://documentation.custhelp.com/euf/assets/devdocs/cloud18d/PolicyAutomation/en/Default.htm#Guides/Policy_Modeling_User_Guide/Forms/BI_Publisher_code_for_OPM.htm#Signatur

Creating a Form with a PDF Editor

As mentioned at the start of this chapter, it is possible to use a PDF Editor to create Form templates for Oracle Policy Automation. The process is similar with a few minor changes.

Creating a PDF Form Field

To add a field, follow the steps below. As PDF Editors are numerous, the steps below may not reflect your user experience. These example steps were written using Foxit PhantomPDF Editor.

1. Ensure you are in Forms mode.

2. Insert a Field into your PDF document.

3. An empty Field will appear.

4. Using the PDF Form Assistant, select the attribute you wish to insert.

5. Select either the value (formatted for the Project region, or region neutral). the attribute text ("the student's name" or the question text "What is the student's name?" from the radio buttons.

6. Copy the value into the Form Field Name on the PDF.

The following screenshot provides step markers for you to follow.

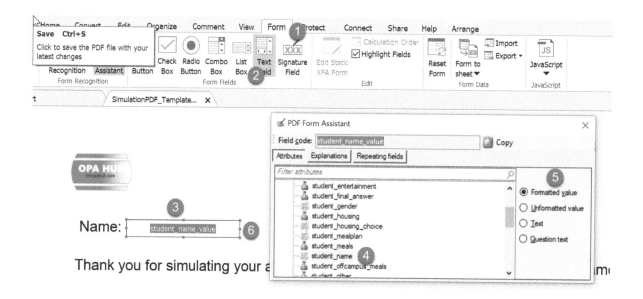

Adding an Explanation to your PDF Editor Form

To add an Explanation to your PDF-based Form requires three steps, in order to build the repeating section that will contain the Explanation. With the screenshot below as your guide, follow these steps:

1. Add the PDF Field as shown above, for which you would like to also display an Explanation (since the field value is not part of the explanation, it makes sense to add it).

2. Add a second Text Field.

3. In the PDF Form Assistant, click the Repeating Fields button

4. Select Start mark and click Copy.

5. Copy the Start mark text into the Tooltip textbox and add a suitable name such as "start".

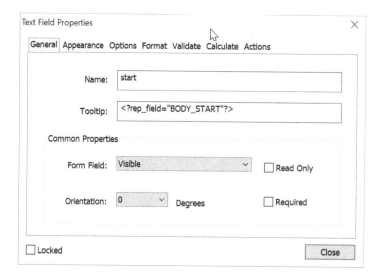

For the second element of the Explanation, you will use several different buttons in the PDF Form Assistant. The steps are as follows:

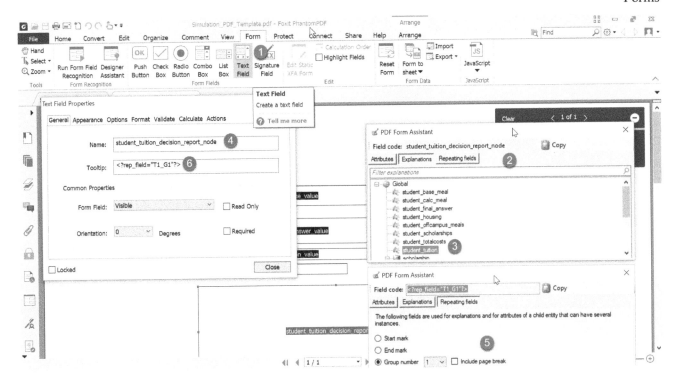

1. Add a Text Form Field to the PDF Form.

2. Select Explanations from the PDF Form Assistant.

3. Select the Explanation you wish to add to the Form.

4. In the Text Form Field, add the Field Code from the PDF Form Assistant.

5. In the PDF Form Assistant, select Repeating field and select Group number.

6. Copy the Group number code into the Tooltip of the Explanation Form Field.

NB: Before adding the End of your Repeating Group, make sure you have left enough space between the start and the end to fully display your Explanation.

You can now add a final Text Field that mirrors the start element you added previously. In the PDF Form Assistant, click the Repeating Fields button, select End mark and click Copy. Copy the end mark text into the Tooltip textbox and add a suitable name such as "end". Your Explanation is now ready for use in the PDF Form.

NB: The Repeating Group concept can also be used to display Entity-based attributes; for example, repeat to show all lines of an order.

Adding your Form to your Interview

Now that you have created a Policy Modeler Form, the requirement is to add Form access to your interview.

- Navigate to the Interview tab in the Policy Modeler.

- Click New Control > Form > Your Form.

- A hyperlink is added to the interview.

- Double-clicking the hyperlink allows you to change the text to something eye-catching as shown below:

The Policy Modeler Ribbon also lets you select the type of output; PDF is the default although there are several others available (Excel, HTML, XML and RTF), and configure the behaviour in several ways as shown and detailed below.

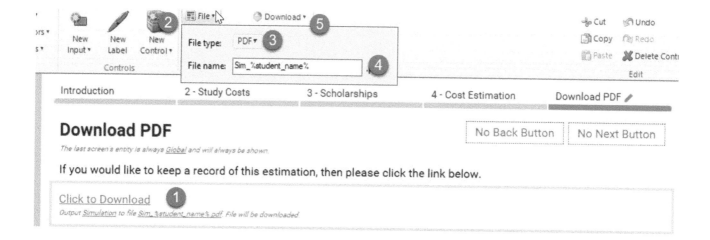

1. The clickable link text is as you defined in the previous step. Ensure that the download link is selected.

2. Click File.

3. File > File Type lets you choose the file type (PDF is the default).

4. File > File Name lets the designer select the file name convention. As you can see above, attributes can be used to create dynamic file names.

5. Click Download to specify if the PDF should appear in a new Browser window, the same window, or directly as a download to disk, when the end user clicks the link.

PDF Form Accessibility

If you choose to produce PDF files and you need to produce PDF/A files that have enhanced accessibility features for users with disabilities, make sure you check the checkbox shown in the screenshot below. This imposes a fixed font and various other embedded features in the PDF file.

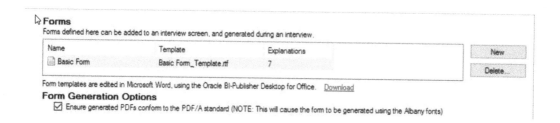

Show If

Your PDF file(s) can utilise logic just like any other Control added to your interview. For example, you may design two different PDF Forms, and only display one to the end-user, dependant on some other attribute such as customer type or similar.

Embedded Fonts in PDF Forms

The built-in Form generator of Oracle Policy Automation now supports the embedding of custom fonts into the Form, making it much easier for organizations to respect their graphical charter all the way through the user experience, for the Interview through CSS rules, and now right into the PDF delivered at the end of the session.

The rule designer can implement this feature during the design of the Form directly from within Oracle Policy Modelling.

TrueType Embedding

In the example below, the rule designer has begun working on a Form, and has formatted some text using a custom TrueType Font.

1. Once the document is saved and the rule designer has returned to the Modeller, the Form appears as normal in the Forms pane.

2. The designer can choose to embed the TrueType Font used in the document. The Font Name appears in the Forms Pane underneath the list of Forms.

3. The rule designer can suggest a substitute on platforms that may not support it.

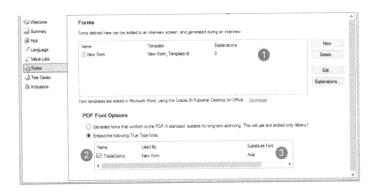

Summary

BI Publisher Desktop allows the creation of rich and complex documents to support the interview process. The skillset you need to work with Forms can be easily achieved by attending an Oracle University Training Course in BI Publisher.

Creating a Form allows the interview to support business processes outside Oracle Policy Automation. The Form can play many important roles: recapping a situation, confirming a status, and motivating an individual to name only three.

Organizations with PDF creation skills can use their own PDF editor to create the template files. Users should note that some features (notably the signature embed) are not yet available for PDF-sourced templates.

Hub Administration

Using the Policy Automation Hub

In this chapter, you will learn about the different administrative tasks related to Policy Automation Hub, such as managing users, managing connections and messages.

About the Hub

The Policy Automation Hub is a web-based application that allows suitably authorised users to perform management tasks such as managing deployments, versions, extracting usage data, and so forth. Its functionality can broadly be divided into three parts: administration of your environment, management of a project repository, and management of project deployment. This chapter looks at the first of those three areas.

Aside from users who log directly into the Policy Automation Hub through a Web page, other users will interact with the Hub through the Oracle Policy Modeling application, by deploying a Project or updating a stored version of a Project. Developers may interact with the Hub using one of the administrative programming interfaces.

Multiple Hubs

Your project may well have more than one Policy Automation Hub, corresponding perhaps to various development, test and production environments. Each Hub has its own users and importantly, its own URL.

The Hub URL

In the case of a Private Cloud installation this might be an internal server running Oracle WebLogic, and in the case of Oracle Policy Automation Cloud Service this will be an external URL you have configured on your Service Cloud Configuration Assistant. As you can see from the screenshot above, Cloud Service sites are categorized by *name* and *site type*. This particular screenshot shows the environment has an upgrade type of *automatic*, and the version number is displayed on the right.

Finding the URL

In both cases the Web interface is fundamentally the same, the content is controlled by license agreement with your provider. For a Cloud Service site, the URL can be found on the Sites menu highlighted in blue on the top right hand corner, and then the Interfaces Tab on the left hand side.

In the case of a Private Cloud installation, the URL will depend on the deployment of the application, although it is typically accessible through a URL such this one:

ⓘ localhost:7002/opa18c/opa-hub/manager

The address is made up of several parts. Firstly the web server name, in this case `localhost`. Then the port number, `7002`. Since the supported platform for on-premise installations is Oracle WebLogic, there will typically be a port number in the 7000+ range. The `opa18c` is the root installation name, which is defined by the administrator during installation and `opa-hub` is one of the applications installed.

> **NB**: In Oracle WebLogic, if your deployment name is `opa18c`, then the Enterprise Application Deployment Name will be `opa18c-opa`.

In both on premise and Cloud Service, the access to the Oracle Policy Automation Hub will look the same as the screenshot shown below. Bear in mind that over the different versions this page has changed quite considerably, so it is not inconceivable that another version might appear in the future.

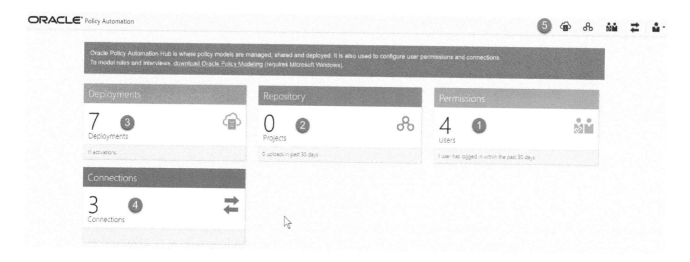

1. Users, Permissions, and related items are managed in this area.
2. The Repository is a storage area for development work.
3. The Deployments section manages active and inactive deployed Projects.
4. The Connections area is used to manage access to external applications that provide data to Oracle Policy Automation.

The icons that are displayed in the Web interface will depend on the level of permission that your active user has, plus whether you have acquired licenses for non-core functionality.

Naming Convention in your Hub

Given that you possibly will have two or more hubs, but that each of those hubs may have different roles in your Project (load testing, regression testing, training, user acceptance and so on), it is important to remember that it will most likely be necessary to adopt strict naming conventions for any Projects you work on (and potentially in other areas too, such as user names and deployments). This book will highlight these areas in the next few chapters but you are, of course, expected to review your own project's naming conventions and guidelines.

On-Premise – Change the About URL Content

In an on-premise installation, administrators can change an application parameter, known as **hub_news_url**, to point users to information about the Hub they are connecting to. The URL points to any valid address. The content of the URL appears in the About menu item, as shown below:

1. The administrator sets the value of the parameter in the database where Oracle Policy Automation was installed to a valid URL, then restarts the WebLogic application.
2. The user clicks the About menu in the Oracle Policy Automation Hub.
3. The custom content is displayed. In this example, the page contains a link to internal resources such as development guidelines.

Licensing for Functionality

When using the Policy Automation Hub, dependant on your license agreement with Oracle Corporation, in addition to core functionality such as user management, you will have access to either one, two or three fundamental features:

- User Management (always present).

- Deployment Tools (always present).

- Versioning and Collaboration Tools (license-based).

- Analytics Workspaces (license-based).

Over and above the licensing aspects, as you are about to discover, a given user may have restricted or no access to parts of the Hub. These features are discussed in the next four chapters of this book. Understanding them is fundamental to being a productive and effective team member in a project.

User Management

Users of the Hub have different roles according to their needs. Some might have full rights to create users and so forth (essentially playing the role of an administrator), whilst others might only be able to review certain deployments and their versions. In addition, to be able to upload information to the Hub, a rule designer needs to have a valid account for the Hub they are connecting to.

This section will walk you through the process of setting up a user for the Hub. When you install the OPA Hub, the only active user is *admin*. There may be a second user, inactive however, called *author* which has limited rights. You are able to create further users with specific rights.

Viewing Users and User Status

To walk through the process, we will view each of the User Screens in turn. Selecting the Permissions tab from the main page shows the All Users page. From here, you can view the details of an existing user (by clicking on the user name) or create a new user by clicking Add User from the Actions menu, as shown below.

Notice that on the left-hand side of the window, Users are one of three areas to manage in respect of access to the application. Users, where the cursor is pointing, usually represent *physical users* whereas API Clients represent *programmatic users* (for example, to allow external applications to communicate with the Hub with a specific identity). Collections are similar to folders, and allow for more granular access control. To get more practical experience, walk through these examples.

Adding a User

Assuming you are working on a new Hub, and the only user available is *admin*. You will therefore be able to create other users. The user is created and a first password assigned by the system. From this page you can add or remove roles as you need:

Add User   Save and Close   Cancel

Username | 1

Full name | 2

Email | 3

Password I03Co60T   ☑ Temporary Password

🔧 ☐ Hub Administrator
     Manage permissions, connections and collections, and review message log   4

✈ ☐ Determinations API
     Perform assessments with Determinations API web services   5

           Collection 🔗 Policy Author   ⚙ Deploy Admin   📱 Mobile User
     6 Default Collection 7 ☐   8 ☐   9 ☐

1. A username must be unique in the Hub. Prefixes such as TEST_ or similar will help others understand the purpose of this user. No white space is permitted.
2. The Full Name allows the user to be associated with a physical member of the team.

3. The email address will receive emails in relation to password resets and similar. By default, a temporary password is proposed.
4. This role allows access to the administration of users, roles, and so on.
5. To be able to access Projects that are deployed as Web Services, this role is required.
6. By default, the system only includes one Collection or "Folder".
7. Anyone wishing to write rules and deploy their work must have this role.
8. A user with this role can manage deployed Projects and choose to activate or deactivate them.
9. Mobile users require a specific permission.

All of these roles will be detailed on the coming pages.

Adding an API Client User

Adding a non-physical user – for example, to clearly identify usage of a programming interface – requires the creation of an API Client user. The process is similar to that described above with some minor changes. Use the screenshot on the next page and the accompanying bullet points to review the functionality available.

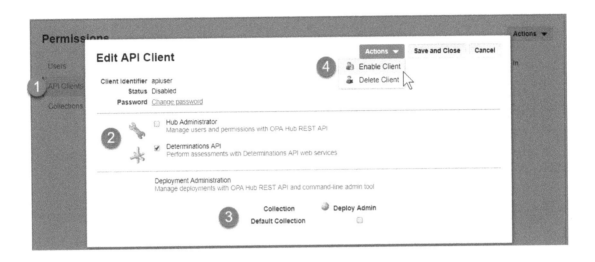

1. An API Client can be created by Hub Administrator role owners.
2. Only three roles in total are available. The first two relate to accessing programming interfaces called the Hub REST API (to automate management tasks) and the SOAP API (to provide Web Service access to Projects).
3. The third role available is, again, required for programmatic access to the REST API and for access to command line tools to automate deployments.

Determinations API

In the above paragraphs, you learned that Web Services allow developers to access Projects using typical SOAP XML. This is called the **Determinations API**. Both physical and API Client users can have this role, as you saw in the User Creation example earlier in the chapter.

Setting up this permission can be broken down into two parts. On one hand, you have seen that a given user may or may not have this permission. On the other hand, you have a global setting which renders the role unnecessary. This option is available from the Actions menu on the Users Tab.

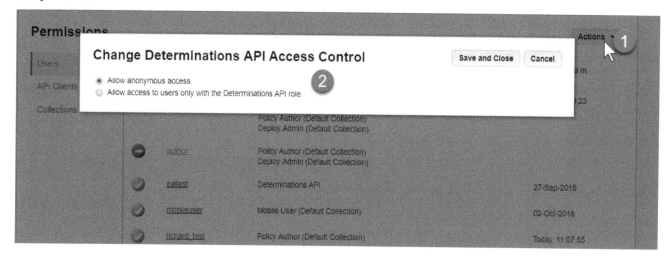

1. Access this global option from the Actions menu in the Permissions Tab.
2. Setting the option to Allow Anonymous Access allows any user to access Projects using SOAP Web Services if they have been deployed with that option set.

> **NB**: Think *very* carefully before allowing anonymous access to your Web Service-enabled Projects.

Resetting Passwords

In addition, from the Actions menu in this user details popup, you can initiate the reset of the user's password, and enable or disable the user. Inactive users are shown with a red icon on the All Users page, as per the example shown in the previous section.

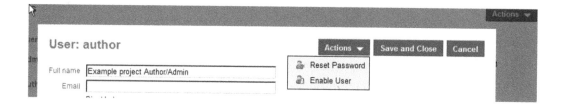

First Use

When the user connects to the Hub for the first time, be it via the Hub web interface or the Policy Modeling, they will need to change their password from the system-generated one. The URL to accomplish this is automatically displayed in the Policy Modeling:

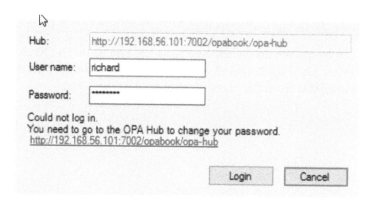

First Use from the Hub

In the event of the user choosing to access the Hub web interface as their first interaction, then they will similarly be asked to change their password.

Password Policies

In the Hub web interface, if your user has sufficient rights (specifically, the Hub Administrator role), they can change the password policies. To do so, select Password Policies from the Permission Tab, Users page.

Users will be affected by your changes, and in the event of a user changing their system-generated password (either as a new user, or following a Password Reset) they will see the following dialog in the event of failing the password policy:

Should a user request a password reset, then the Hub Administrator role permits this through the Actions menu on the User detail page:

The new password will need to be communicated to the end user in a secure fashion, and they will be required to change their password upon first login, in a manner identical to the process for first-time new users.

Identity Management Settings

Customers who have already invested in Oracle Identity Cloud Service (IDCS) can now leverage this centralized tool for password and user management. To enable this feature, a Hub Administrator can return to the Permissions tab and select Identity Management Settings from the Actions menu. Use the image below as a guide on how to enable the functionality. Note the roles and permissions are always managed on the Hub. IDCS replaces user and password management.

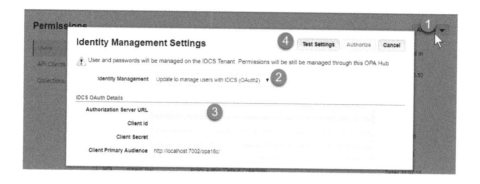

1. Access the option from the Actions menu.
2. Select the Update to manage users with IDCS (OAuth2) option. To revert to default functionality, select Users are managed locally on OPA Hub.
3. Enter the URL and API Key / Secret you obtained from IDCS.
4. Test the settings by clicking the Test Settings button.

Understanding Hub User Roles

More information about the different roles is shown below. You will also learn more about the specifics of some functionality in future chapters.

Policy Author

A Policy Author (assuming that is the only Role they possess) has access to the following functionality.

If the Hub being accessed is licensed for the user of the Repository feature, then the user:

1. Can connect to the Hub to view the current contents of the Repository.
2. Can Download a copy of the latest version of a given Project.
3. Can Upload changes they make to the same Project.

Users will need to have both the correct rights *and* the correct license agreement to use these features. In an environment where the Repository is not licensed, these features will not be enabled.

A user who attempts to use the Deployment button, but who does not have the Deployment Administrator role, will see the following message:

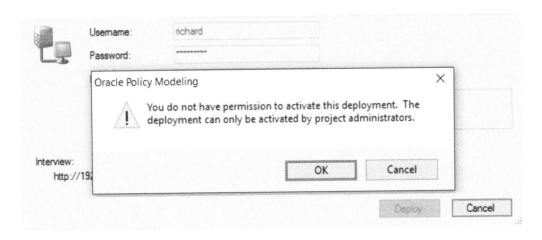

The Policy Author role does not include permission to deploy and activate a Project, thus making it available to the end user. A Policy Author can only register it as deployed. Further permission is required to activate it for the end user population.

Deployment Administrator

Continuing with our previous example, if the Policy Author described above logs into the Hub using a Web Browser, they will see something like the following:

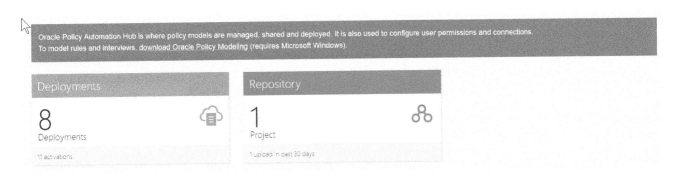

The user interface has removed the various icons corresponding to permissions that are not assigned to the user.

The **deployment administrator** role allows the user to progress beyond the error message shown in the previous paragraph. A Policy Author can access the Deployment section of the Hub, however the Project cannot be deployed, as the example below shows. No deployment is possible, and no access for end-users has been activated.

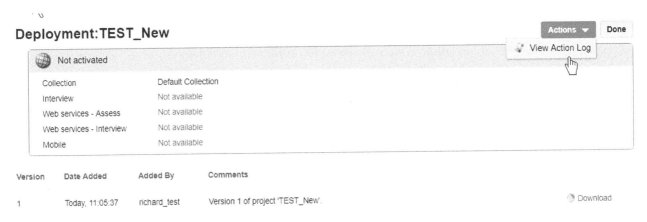

A Deployment Administrator, on the other hand, can deploy and activate the version they have been working on from the Policy Modeling and the Policy Automation Hub. They can access the Deployments, activate or deactivate them. The exact kinds of deployment possible will depend upon your license agreement. In the screenshot below, a deployment administrator can check deployment status, deactivate the deployment and so on.

1. Users with the Deployment Administrator role can activate a deployed Project, to make it accessible to the users.
2. The Deployment can also be deleted.
3. Individual types of deployment can be chosen.
4. The Deployment can be placed in a Collection or "Folder".

Mobile User

Users who wish to access a Policy Model from a mobile device, must have this role. Without this role they are unable to connect the mobile device to the Policy Automation Hub and retrieve the deployments for use. It is important to note that this role is explicitly related to the use of the Oracle Policy Automation App for Android or iOS. End users of the mobile app require this role.

Analysis User

Users with this role have access to the Workspaces icon in the Policy Automation Hub and the ability to create charts and scenarios. Whilst the In-Memory Policy Analytics product is not covered in this book, you can learn about some of the charting facilities in your discovery of the Hub functionality.

Hub Administrator

As you have already seen, the Hub Administrator role gives the user access to the majority of tabs within the Hub: Deployments, Repository, Users, Connections, and Message Logs. You will learn more about these options in due course.

Managing Connections

One of the major changes in the Policy Automation family between version 10 and version 12 is the **Connection** concept. A connection can be considered a generic way to connect to external programs (with a set of functionality that must be implemented by the external application). This differs from the approach of version 10 for example where specific connectors were available for different external applications.

The Connections architecture ensures the same generic approach will allow developers to create integrations using the development platform of their choice through industry-standard web service definitions.

Connector Framework

Connections take the form of a Web Service connection that supports a variety of functionality, of which the following is a subset:

- GetMetaData
- Load
- Save

In addition, the Connector Framework allows developers to implement more advanced functionality such as

- Capture completed interview data, decisions and attachments
- Store and retrieve interview checkpoints
- Perform queries, and load reference data dynamically

Load and **Save** are used at the start and end of connected Projects, to load data mapped as input, or to save data mapped as output into the external system (see Chapter 10 for more information about mapping).

GetMetaData is used to publish information about the entity model in the external application to the Hub, in order to enable access for the rule developers (see Chapter 10 for more information about getting an external model into a Project).

Connections come in several forms, although they all fundamentally share information from an external system with the Policy Automation Hub:

1. Connection to Oracle Service Cloud.

2. Connection to an external application by Web Service (Includes Oracle Sales Cloud, Engagement Cloud, Oracle Siebel, and any custom application).

3. Connection to an in-memory analysis data source.

Create and View Web Service Connections

In a previous chapter, you learned about Connections from the perspective of a Policy Author. In this chapter, you will learn how to configure a Connection in the Hub. In a later chapter, you will see a brief example of the technical details behind a Connection.

View the Connection List

The Connection List Page, accessed by clicking on the Connections tab, shows the currently available list of Connections and their status. The connection status icon may take some time to refresh, depending on the response from the external application. During that time the following icons will appear:

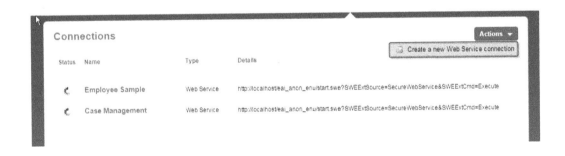

When the applications have responded, the following icons may show in their place:

This indicates a problem of connectivity or functionality in the Connection. Upon seeing this kind of error, users can refer to the Message Log (see later in this chapter) or pass the matter to the technical resources responsible – the underlying Connection may have to be fixed outside of Oracle Policy Automation.

Correctly responding Connections should display the following icons:

Create a Connection

As shown on the screenshot in the previous section, a new Web Service Connection can be added through the Actions menu.

The details of the Connection should be carefully inserted into the Detail page, bearing in mind that any errors are likely to cause a failure in the functionality of the Connection.

> **NB**: To learn more about the Connector Framework and how to try out the sample Web Service Connection, go to the following URL (correct at time of writing)
>
> http://documentation.custhelp.com/euf/assets/devdocs/cloud18d/PolicyAutomation/en/Default.htm#Guides/Developer_Guide/Connector_Framework/Overview_of_connector_framework.htm

Connections are used in many different ways by Oracle Policy Modeling and Oracle Policy Automation. See the chapters on Siebel CRM and Service Cloud for some examples.

View a Connection Detail Page

Selecting a Connection by clicking its name shows the connection details. The exact details will depend upon the external application.

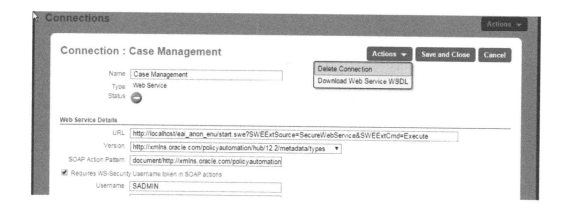

You will notice that the Actions menu also allows for the download of the standard Web Service WSDL which developers can use as a framework for future Connections. In addition, the user can delete a Connection that is no longer required.

The exact fields displayed here will depend on the type of Connection.

Viewing Message Logs

The message logs of the OPA Hub are a good place to start should you notice any failure of Connections. Web service and other messages will be displayed on this page, accessible from the main tabs, and can be transmitted to the relevant technical teams for debugging purposes. Access the Message Log from the User icon in the top right-hand corner of the page.

Collections

When you are working with a large number of rule designers, deployment administrators, and other team members, it quickly becomes clear that greater granularity is needed, beyond the concept of Roles already discussed. The **Collection** is an administrative concept similar in some ways to a Folder, and users of your environment can be assigned Roles to one or more Collections. Thus, one user might be able to deploy work in the Release A folder, but not into the Release B Collection. In the same way, a Connection to another system might be accessible to developers using Release B, but not to those who can only use the Release A Collection.

A Collection can be assigned to users, and Connections can be assigned to Collections.

Edit Permissions for a Collection

The Collection dialog – displayed when creating a new Collection or when editing an existing Collection – has an associated set of permissions that can be granted or rescinded from users of this Hub. This includes both physical and API Client users. In addition, options can be set regarding the types of deployment that are possible in this Collection.

It should be noted that a hierarchy of Collections is not possible. On the next page, use the screenshot as a guide to the different options available when creating a new Collection.

1. Click Actions > Add Collection from the Permissions tab.
2. Collections must have a unique name. As before, consider using a prefix or suffix to better describe the purpose of the Collection.
3. In the same vein, add a Description.
4. Define which deployment channels are used for new deployments in this Collection and if they can be overridden.
5. Select the roles for each user.
6. Select API Client user roles in this Collection.

The increased granularity of permissions allows administrators to provide selected rights to users, no longer for all the policy models on the Hub.

When adding a project to the Repository with this functionality, the model is associated with a Collection. The user of the Policy Modeller will only be able to select a Collection for which he or she has permission as Policy Author, as shown next.

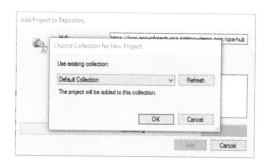

The user must select the Collection from the drop-down list before it can be added to the Hub Repository.

The same principle is used when the policy model is deployed using the Deploy Snapshot option from the menu. The user will only be able to select a Collection for which they have rights to deploy or to deploy as a mobile policy.

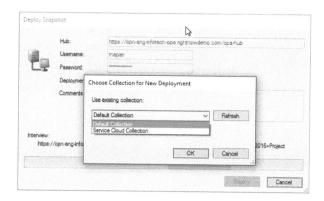

Ediiting or Viewing a User's Permissions

Now that the Collection has been created, the Edit User screen (seen earlier) is updated to allow you to view the complete set of Roles of the user, for each Collection.

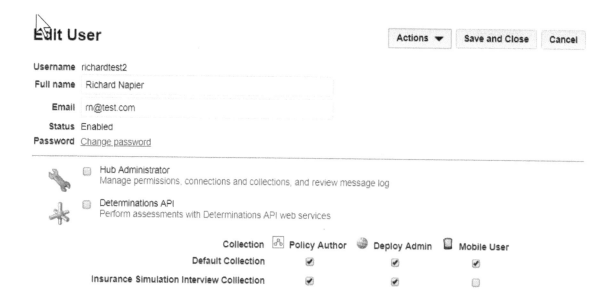

In the example above, the user has different permissions with the various Collections.

Other Considerations

The Hub Administration REST API and Hub Deployment REST API provide non-HTML access to the functionalities of the Hub. Read the chapter on Web Services for more information.

At the time of writing, customers considering whether to use version 10 or version 12 of Oracle Policy Automation can review this page http://www.oracle.com/technetwork/apps-tech/policy-automation/overview/opaprivatecloud-2372566.html . It addresses some typical questions about integration, and the differences in architecture between the two versions.

Although installing the Oracle Policy Automation Hub is beyond the scope of this book, you can find a walkthrough process at the following URL: https://theopahub.com/main/creating-an-opa-hub-self-study-platform-part-one/. The entire process will happily function on a reasonably modern laptop as a virtual machine, or using an Amazon EC2 instance with a medium-sized footprint.

Many of the features discussed in the chapters about the Oracle Policy Automation Hub are license-based. The collaboration features described in the following chapters, for example, or the in-Memory Analytics option, may not be available in your environment.

Summary

The OPA Hub provides a Web interface to conduct the various management and administration tasks necessary to maintain users and deployments. A series of roles allows for the creation of different kinds of user and thus limit access to important functionality such as activating Projects.

Even if you may not be using the OPA Hub on a regular basis, or you may not have access to all the functionality, a good understanding of the different features is a stepping stone to success with Oracle Policy Automation.

Larger projects may have multiple Hubs and many users, so it is critical that the Hub is managed and kept up-to-date from an administration perspective as people join or leave the team, and as Policy Models evolve.

14

The Hub - Collaboration

Collaboration

So far, in this book, you have worked to create rules, interviews, forms and translations to reflect your business policies. But your use of the resulting policies has been confined to the desktop. You have also learned how to deploy them with the Oracle Policy Modeler and how to view the deployment on the Oracle Policy Automation Hub.

In this chapter, you will explore the Hub Collaboration features, the management platform used by Policy Automation to facilitate the deployment of rule Projects. These features impact both those team members in charge of writing business policies, and those in administrative roles.

The Policy Automation Hub Collaboration Features

Logically, collaboration using the Hub can be broken down into two main usage scenarios: using the features of the Hub as a rule writer or designer, and using the Hub as an administrative user.

The basic collaboration features of the Modeler are the following:

- Add a Project to a Hub Repository.
- Download changes from the Project Repository.
- Upload changes to the Project Repository.
- Revert modifications.
- Resolve conflicts.
- Use Inclusions.

The basic collaboration features of the Hub are the following:

- View Repository Versions.
- Manage Repository Versions.

Working with Projects

Opening Projects

Up until this chapter, whenever this book has asked you to open a Project, the assumption has been that it is *stored locally on your computer*, probably in the Documents folder of your Windows User.

As a solitary rule writer, this is perfectly acceptable. But as soon as there are more writers, designers, reviewers and other team players, having the local hard disk of your computer as the main location for storage of Projects becomes a challenge.

In previous versions of Policy Modeling, integrations were offered with popular Version Control Systems such as those produced by Microsoft or Apache. In version 12, the OPA Hub provides not only version management but also a variety of deployment and management tools to facilitate delivery of a rule Project to end consumers.

As a rule writer, the first contact you have with a Hub is perhaps from within your usual Policy Modeling interface. Compare the following two different ways to open a Project.

Open Local Project

In the first screenshot, notice how the Projects are by default being viewed in the Documents folder.

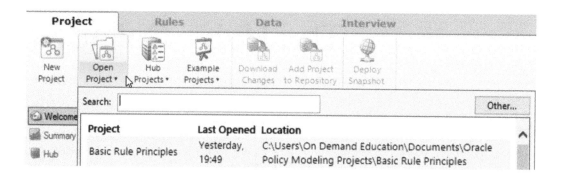

Open Hub Project

In this second example, notice the location is web address.

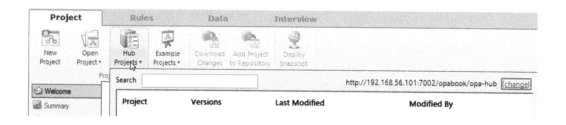

In both cases, the location can be changed – the local disk view has an Other... button, whilst the Hub view has a (change) hyperlink. Policy Modeling is not tied to one location. This makes it easy for you if you have several Hubs, for example for testing or quality assurance.

At the moment, as you can see from the second screenshot, there are no Projects to open on the Hub.

Creating Projects

When you create a Project in Policy Modeling, recall that the Project is saved on your local machine as in the following image.

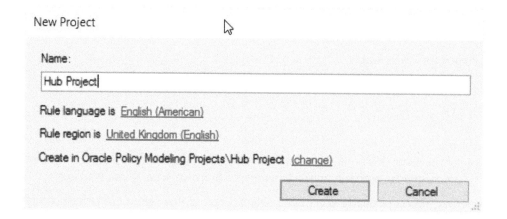

Once you have created your Project, you are able to add it to the Repository on the Hub.

The Repository

The **Repository** is the Hub-side location for all shared Projects that are being developed. Every Hub has a single repository, which is the collection of Projects from all Policy Modellers in the team that have used the Add Project to Repository feature.

Adding a Project to the Repository

Adding a locally created Project to the Hub *copies* the Project files from your local disk to the Hub Repository. From that time on, successful interaction with the Project changes slightly. The Add Project to Repository button is only visible if you have not yet performed this step:

To select this button, you must either

- have created a new Project.

- have opened a Project that you have only ever saved locally.

- have changed Hub location.

Identifying Yourself

As you can see in the screenshot below, the act of adding the Project to the Repository requires you to authenticate yourself, and to add a description.

In the previous chapter, you learned how user management was performed on the Hub. For this example, the screenshot has been taken with the only user name that is created by default during the installation of the Hub, namely admin.

The user is encouraged to provide detail about the work done in the Project. This text is visible to others.

After Adding to the Hub Repository

Once the Add Project to Repository button has been clicked and the dialog successfully closed by clicking Add, the ribbon in Policy Modeling changes, and the Add Project to Repository button is removed, replaced instead by three new buttons ass seen on the right:

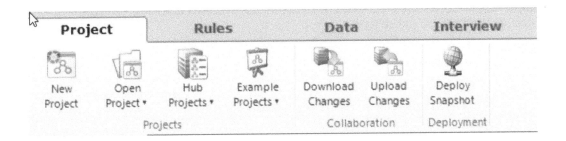

Viewing Hub Details for a Project

If your Project has been successfully added to the Hub, or if you are interested in viewing the current information about a Hub-based Project then the Project tab Hub pane will display the current status and version:

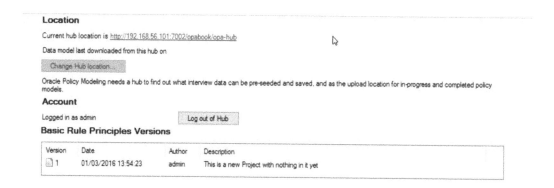

Working with a Project you have never used locally

If you connect to an Oracle Policy Automation Hub and see a Project that you did not create and did not download before, then of course it has been added to the Hub by someone else in your team.

Selecting the Project will create a new local copy for you, on your hard disk – once you confirm the location. Notice how the dialog box below considers that you are *opening* the Project.

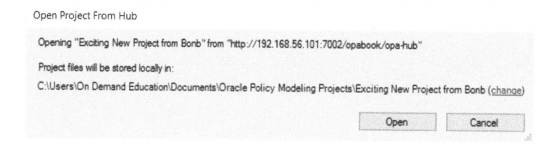

> **NB:** The Add Project to Repository button will not be available, since it has already been added to the Hub Repository by the other team member.

The Policy Automation Hub as Version Tracker

Any team member who *opens* a Project from the Hub in the manner described above is, in fact, engaged in the process of creating a **version** of the Project. In the upcoming pages you will discover the behaviour of the Hub and the Project in different situations.

Working Locally with a Project

You will now have a local copy on your machine. In addition to having the local copy, you will be able to upload any changes you make to the Hub.

For reference, in the following screenshot there have been some changes made to the Project. The nature of the changes will be reflected by the different icons that are displayed in the Policy Modeling (added object, modified object, deleted object, and so forth).

Added Objects

Objects you have added since the upload will display a new icon to indicate their status as additions.

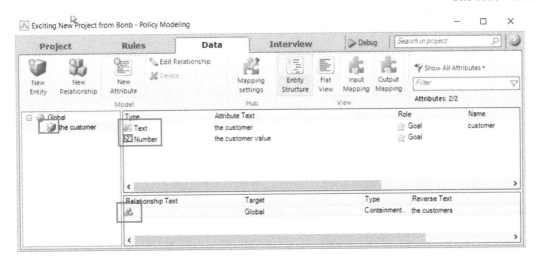

Modified Rules and Interviews

The same icons are used in the different tabs of the Policy Modeling, to display changes in other objects.

Modified rule documents are also highlighted and have a tooltip as well to show that they have been worked on.

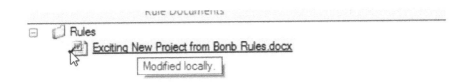

This information is useful to view as you are working on the Project, but this information is critical when you reach the next logical step, and want to upload your changes to the Hub.

Uploading to the Hub

If you have finished making changes to the Project, and your tests are satisfactory, you should now upload those changes to the Repository to update the Hub version. Uploading the changes will record your work as a unique version in the Repository and give you the chance to add descriptive comments at the same time.

Most importantly, the collaborative features will allow you to review the entire Project before uploading, allowing you to make last-minute changes if you wish. The dialog box also mentions the size of the upload.

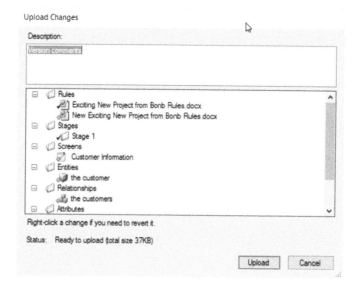

As visible in the screenshot above, all of the items in the Project that have undergone changes are listed. In addition, you can choose to revert to the previous version should you decide not to keep your changes. To revert an object, simply right-click the item and select the context menu.

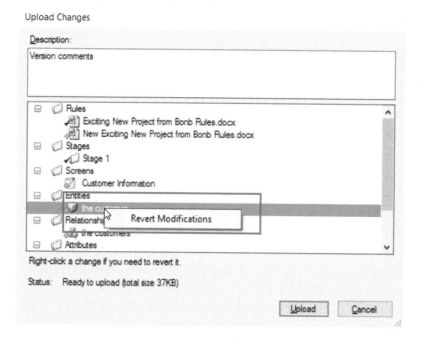

Revert Modifications

Selecting the Revert Modifications menu item shows a final confirmation of the change – given that you would be deleting work you have just done, it seems logical that the process requires you to confirm!

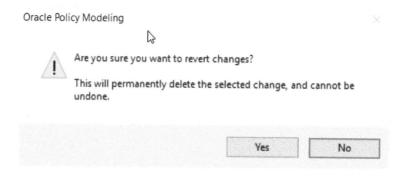

Version History

Once you have completed the upload of your Project to the Repository, you will notice several changes to the user interface of the Policy Modeling. Firstly, on the Hub pane of the Project tab, your new version will be listed complete with the comments you added before completing the upload.

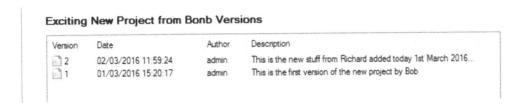

In addition, the icons (green plus, tick mark and so on) have been removed from your Policy Modeling. You have begun working (in the above case) on the future version 3 – a new baseline has been established for changes.

Deleted Objects

If you are working on a version which contained existing items such as attributes, screens or entities that you have *deleted* from the local Project version, as before the Upload Changes dialog will allow you to review the deletions – they will be shown as red crosses.

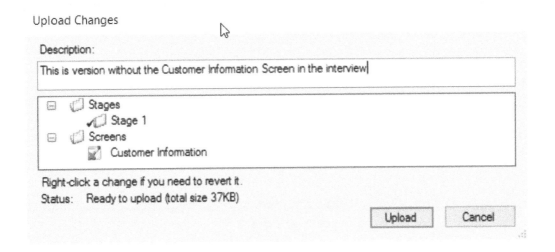

Uploading and Downloading

In a real project environment with multiple users, it becomes more and more important to remember to *upload* changes to the Hub as soon as they have been sufficiently tested, and likewise it becomes very important to *download* any changes before you begin work to ensure that you are working on the very latest version. Recall that you can review the state of a given Project from the Hub pane of the Project tab in the Policy Modeling.

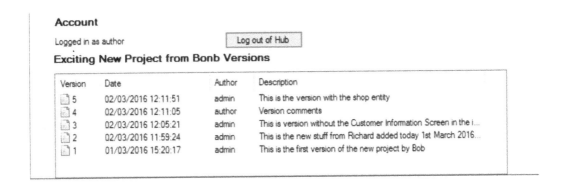

In the above screenshot, author (the logged in user) is able to see that another user – admin – has worked on the Project, illustrating the need to make sure the locally downloaded version is up-to-date before beginning work.

Conflicting with other User Changes

Failing to keep up-to-date with versions, will lead to **conflicts**. For example, working on a local version but not noticing that another version has been uploaded to the Hub will cause an error like this, when the user tries to upload changes:

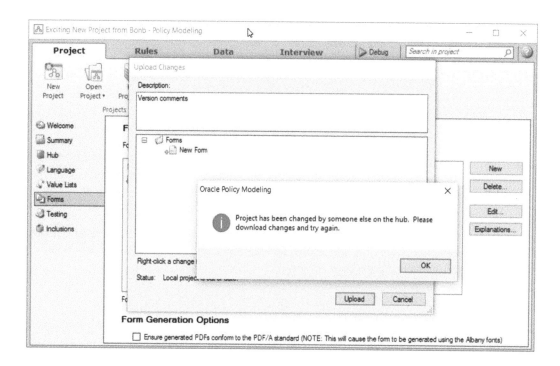

Conflicting with other User Editing Now

Again, failing to pay attention to what team members are doing will cause conflicts. For example, failing to notice that a colleague is also working on the same Project and the same documents *right now*. Policy Modeling warns you this is happening in real-time, if the user is connected to the same Hub – by showing you a **padlock** symbol on the object.

As well as the padlock symbol, you will also see a warning while working on objects, as shown in the next screenshot.

Finally, if you try and upload you will see the following message.

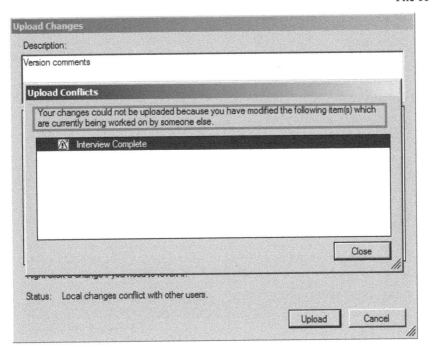

Conflict Detection in Microsoft Word and Excel

In addition to the different icons shown in the section above, further information is presented to users who open documents on their local machine at the same time as others doing the same thing on another local machine: essentially flagging that there is a live conflict of editing.

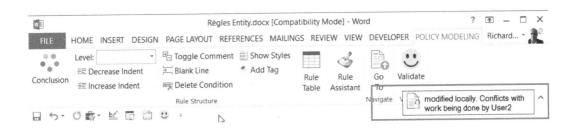

> **NB**: Like any upload / download / synchronization model, the process will work best when *everyone* is playing by the rules and observing strict procedures to ensure the minimum number of conflicts and dead-ends.

Stealing Ownership

In certain circumstances you may need to 'take control' of a conflict situation. If you are uploading some changes and you discover that another user is also making some changes for instance – much like the situation you have seen in the previous paragraph. But if, upon discussion with your colleague, it becomes clear that their changes are either not going to be followed through, or they have decided to abandon them, what can be done?

In that case you can use the feature called **Steal Ownership**. It gives you the right to continue with your upload, and the other user will *have* to download your newer version to synchronize.

If you are working simultaneously on a Project and you see the message illustrated in the previous paragraph, and if you proceed to attempt an upload, you will have two options.

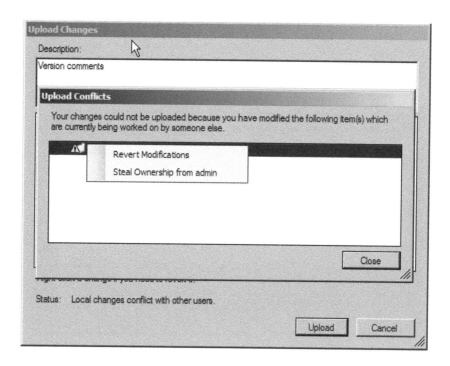

The Steal Ownership from xxx option lets your user take ownership, upload your changes, and obliges the other user to download again.

> **NB**: It goes without saying that this is only to be done with the full knowledge and agreement of the other user. There will be 'edge cases' such as users who have left their office or gone on vacation for a while but like all conflict situations, *dialog* between the users and agreed rules of engagement are of primary importance.

Getting a Hub Project a Second Time

Occasionally, it may be necessary for a user to get the Project from the Hub even after downloading a version to the local machine. For example, to create a second copy locally in order to prototype a change or investigate something, without modifying their existing local version.

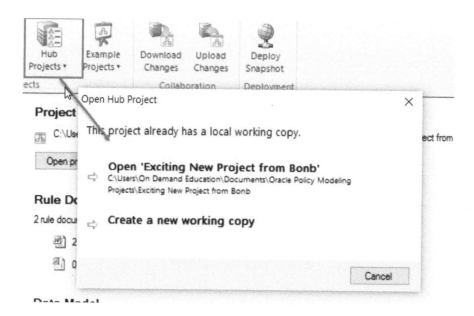

First and most importantly, notice in the above screenshot that the Policy Modeling has detected that you already have opened the Project before. So the first option is, in fact, *not* to do anything unusual and to continue working. The second option however is to create a new copy, essentially a branch.

The second, new working copy is stored in a different folder and you must choose this folder at the point of creating the new working copy, as shown in the screenshot below:

Open Project From Hub

Opening "Exciting New Project from Bonb" from "http://192.168.56.101:7002/opabook/opa-hub"

Project files will be stored locally in:

C:\Users\On Demand Education\Documents\Oracle Policy Modeling Projects\Exciting New Project from Bonb 2 (change)

Open   Cancel

NB: Managing this second parallel version and ensuring that you do not conflict with any other versions is *your* responsibility.

It might be safer only to use this option if you intend to test an idea or concept, before deleting the second copy from your hard disk or otherwise extracting the value. In the example above, the folder name has 2 is appended when compared to the original downloaded version. This is automatic.

Inclusions for a Project

A feature introduced in version 15D of Policy Automation, **inclusions** are similar in some ways to the version 10 functionality known as **modules** – which allowed for parts of a Project to be shared with others. Whereas the version 10 functionality was file-based, with the arrival of the Hub, the transfer of content can be automated and leverages the concept of Projects in the Repository.

Where appropriate, it is good practice to 'reuse' content you have developed. For example, you have worked with colleagues and agreed on a data model that will be used for a series of different rule Projects. So a practical situation would be to share a data model and/or other aspects between these different sets of policies. Inclusions aims to meet that need.

What is an Inclusion?

Firstly, it is important to note that an inclusion is simply a Project uploaded to the Hub. The content of Project A can be imported ("included") in Project B. Logically, inclusions can have inclusions as well. Inclusion creates a reference to Project A that you wish to use in Project B. Your Project B can have many inclusions.

Thus, by clever strategic management, it may be possible to create **component-based** approaches to minimize the effort of having to create new policies from existing structures. As always, you can follow the example below to understand the process and mechanics a little better.

In the screenshot below, you can see a new Project that has just been created. There is no Data model and currently no other content. The Project has not yet been uploaded to the Hub but the user is connected to the Hub.

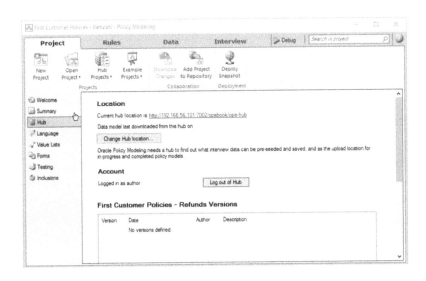

This Project is going to use another Hub Project as an Inclusion.

Adding Inclusions

The empty Project is going to include a Data Model concerning *the customer* and *the customer purchase* since this is the first in a series of policies that will use this model.

- Select the Inclusions pane from the Project tab.

- Click the Add button.

- Select the Hub Project you wish to Include.

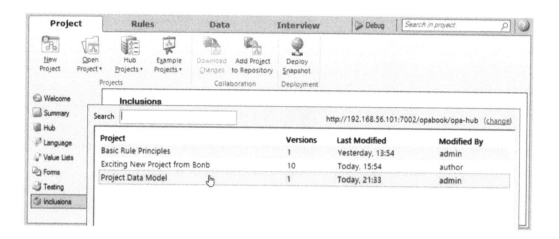

Review the content to ensure it is the right Project.

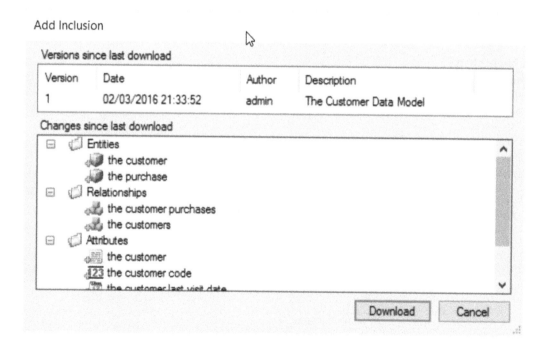

Once the Download button is clicked, the content of the inclusion Project is added to your own Project.

Viewing Inclusions

Viewing included objects in your Project is simple; the style of display used is the same as what we saw when working with versions earlier in this chapter. A combination of tooltips and coloured icons helps to identify the origin of an attribute or object.

Adding an Inclusion from the Hub does not mean it is a static link. Changes can happen in two ways:

Local Changes in your Project
The inclusions may just be the starting point for your new Project – perhaps you wish to add further, Project-specific attributes or other items. Once added, the lack of icons will indicate that they are local.

Changes made by the Author of the Inclusion
In the same way that you make changes and create new versions of a Hub Project, so the Project that you select for inclusion may also evolve. The Inclusions pane on the Project tab of Policy Modeling can be used to check for updates to the included Project. There are several possible alternative actions.

Firstly, review the version that was included in your Project by reviewing the information on the Inclusions pane:

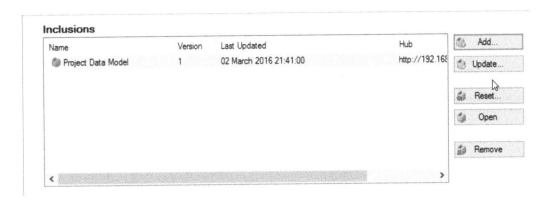

Once the version is ascertained, if you decide to update to the latest version, click the Update button. The screenshot below and the bullet points show you how to work with this **Inclusion Update**.

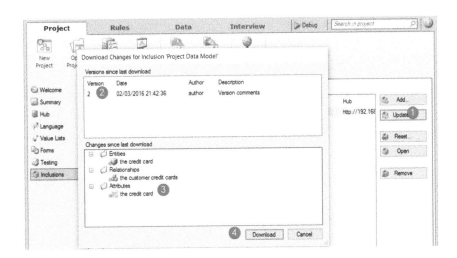

Follow the steps below to update the Inclusion to the version displayed in the Download Changes for Inclusion dialog.

1. Click Update.

2. Understand which version is being downloaded.

3. View the content that has been modified.

In the case above, there are only additions. There may be deletions or modifications – therefore the icons displayed might differ. Refer to the section in this chapter dealing with uploading and downloading to learn about the icons used.

4. Click Download.

The updates are applied to the Project. Local changes are automatically reapplied as well.

NB: You can open the Inclusion Project by clicking the Open button.

Removing Changes to roll back to Inclusion Version

If you have made changes to an object in your Project through inclusion, you may wish to remove your local modifications and revert to the version supplied by the inclusion.

In the screenshot below the designer has modified the attribute the customer store number by adding a Value List and applying it to this attribute. Right-clicking the attribute reveals a new menu option, to revert to the inclusion version:

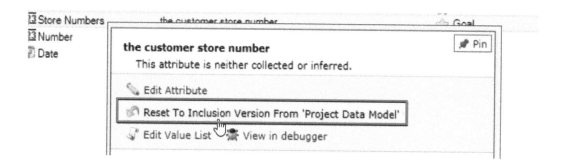

A similar context menu option is available in the Interview tab when viewing locally updated inclusion objects.

NB: Note that in the example above, clicking the Reset To Inclusion Version option will remove the association between the Value List and the attribute. It will not delete the Value List from your Project.

Removing Inclusions

There may be situations when it is necessary to remove an Inclusion. If a lot of work has been done in the destination Project, removing the source Project may have profound effects. Clicking the Remove button in the Inclusions pane, once an Inclusion has been selected, will display the dialog outlining the impact:

Remove Inclusion

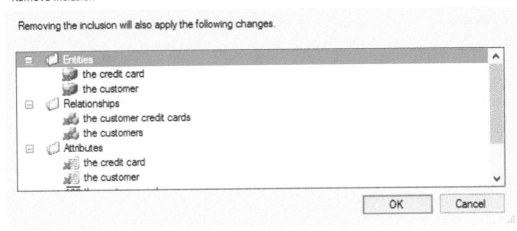

As you can see from the screenshot above, this may result in massive changes to your Project. After clicking OK, for example, this is all that remains of your data model:

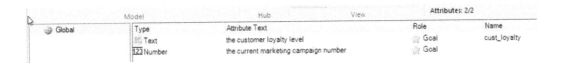

Potential Inclusion Uses

An inclusion does not have to be a complete Project. For example, one inclusion might contain only user interface elements such as defined Styles for an Interview. Another might contain only the entities used across a number of different business cases. A third might include rules which are common to several projects. There are any number of uses for inclusions to act as "containers" of partial projects. When this is combined with the concept of Collections – which you have already investigated in the previous chapter – then you have a quite powerful mechanism for providing different teams of users with different standard styles, common data models, and so forth.

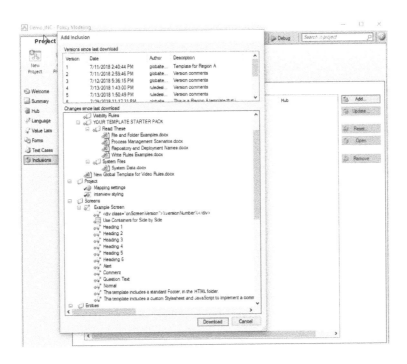

In the example above, an Inclusion has been built as a demonstration to include not only Screen and Styling but also Project mapping information; documentation and various other pieces of information to help a new user get started with a Project.

Viewing the Repository

As you have seen in the previous chapter and these sections, the management of a Project in the OPA Hub can broadly be broken down into two parts, namely the management of the Deployments, and the management of the Repository, where Project versions are stored and managed. Users with the appropriate permissions can therefore also login to the Hub and review, download, and otherwise interact with the Projects they can see in the Repository.

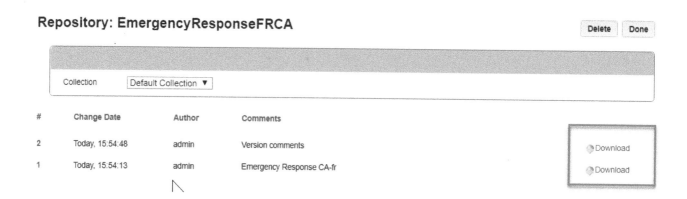

Such access can be useful not just for review purposes, but also in situations where the user no longer has access to the local Project – perhaps due to hardware failure – or they wish to make sure they have the latest development version (for example after a long vacation). They can download the version(s) from the Repository.

Summary

The rule designer has access to a wide variety of built-in version tracking and conflict management tools through the Policy Automation Hub and its collaboration features. In combination with the user and role management functionality you have already seen, project managers can keep track of which work is being done, by which users, for what purpose through the Repository and Collections.

In the next chapter, we shall look at the deployment process through the Policy Modeling and Oracle Policy Automation Hub.

Hub Deployments

Deployments

In this chapter, you will learn the deployment process – how to make a Policy Automation Project visible to end-users and other applications. This can be done in several ways, and for the purposes of clarity we will walk through all of the common scenarios.

About Deployments

Before you look at the different steps and functionality, remember that your organization may have access to multiple Oracle Policy Automation Hubs. Therefore it is not unusual to have to perform the steps to deploy a Project several times – through development, test and production for example. At the current time, there is no unified workflow to progress through these environments. You may find yourself, therefore, repeating steps in different environments. Later in this book, you will discover some programming interfaces that may help you devise your own automated deployment processes.

Backups

The deployment process for Policy Authors ultimately hides much of the process and offers a transparent way to *push* Projects to the Hub. Thus, the physical files that make up your Project are available from the Policy Automation Hub as downloads, should the need arise to recover a specific version of a Project. But the first place that any Project will be stored is on the hard drive of the user of Oracle Policy Modeling. Do not neglect to put in place a process of automated backups of these files, as part of your wider backup strategy. In turn, do not neglect the ability to create a Zip copy of the project at any time, from the Project tab of Oracle Policy Modeling, as you have learned previously.

Making Deployments in Policy Modeling

Before you investigate the deployment features of the Hub Web Interface, it is important to realize that deployment is typically initiated from within the Policy Modeling interface. Provided you have uploaded your Project to the Hub, this button will be readily available from the ribbon:

For this chapter, you can work with the Basic Rule Principles Project from the previous chapters, or pick any Project that has at least one rule in it.

The Deploy Snapshot button will push your current work to the Hub for deployment. The actual Project will not necessarily be available to the user community - that depends on whether the Activate Immediately checkbox is checked or not, and whether your role(s) allow you to do so.

In the following screenshot, you will see the required information, including the Deployment Name. This name will appear in the Hub Web Interface. Care should be exercised not to change the name of a deployment if it has been deployed before – doing so will create a separate deployment record in the administrative interface.

As you learned in Chapter 12, the author of the rule Project will have a user name with specific permissions known as User Roles. The two roles most usually associated with the deployment of Policy Models are the

Policy Author and Deployment Administrator. Both will be able to access the dialog shown below, by clicking the Ribbon button shown on the previous page. Review the points below this screenshot.

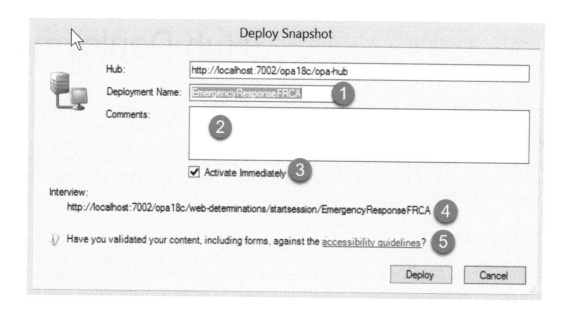

1. The Deployment name, which will also appear in the URL.

2. A good description as to why this version is being deployed, such as bugs fixed, or requirements met.

3. Will this version be immediately accessible to end users? Only the Deployment Administrator will be able to successfully Activate Immediately.

4. The URL to access the Interview.

5. If your organization is implementing WCAG accessibility guidelines, remember to check that content in your Project meets these requirements (for reference, see https://www.w3.org/WAI/standards-guidelines/wcag/).

Once the Deploy button is clicked, the user is validated and the deployment commences, complete with a warning in respect of the deployment name if it is the first time it has been used:

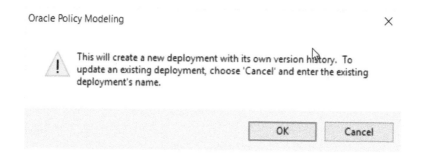

Once the deployment is complete, assuming you are following this example on your own Oracle Policy Automation Hub, you will see that the deployment has finished and the URL is now available. If you click on the URL that is now highlighted you should indeed be able to access your interview.

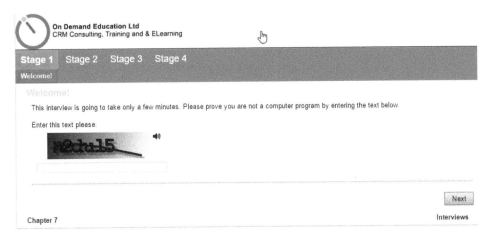

The URL of the interview in an on premise installation is something similar to
http://server:port/installname/web-determinations/startsession/Deployment+Name

When deploying a snapshot in this way, only the Web Determination is available for testing. Mobile and Determination server versions are not yet available. You will discover how to make them available in the next section of this chapter.

Therefore, based on the deployment steps shown above, a Policy Author will need the assistance of a user with a different role, in order to progress deployment to activation as the checkbox shown above will not function. This is a healthy separation of roles. Read the following section of this chapter to understand the next steps in the deployment flow. If you need a reminder of the role concept, check Chapter 12.

Subsequent Deployments

Subsequent use of the Deploy Snapshot button will give you a warning reminding you that the history of deployments, like the history of project versions, is stored by the OPA Hub.

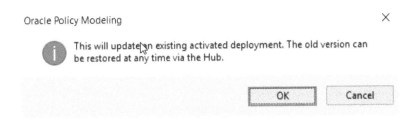

Now that you have discovered the basic deployment functionality available from within Policy Modeling, it is time to discover the administrative interface of the Hub and the different functionalities available to a user with other roles.

Managing Deployments in the Hub

The OPA Hub Web interface also provides a significant number of administrative tools, including deployment management. In the following section you will discover them, in logical order. In this first section, you will review the deployment, as if you had just made it *from the Policy Modeling* (as described in the previous section) - in the OPA Hub interface.

Accessing the OPA Hub

When the OPA Hub is first installed, recall that the only active user is called *admin*. The password will have been entered during the installation. You can find a "self-study" installation script on the Internet at this URL:
https://theopahub.com/main/creating-an-opa-hub-self-study-platform-part-one/

251

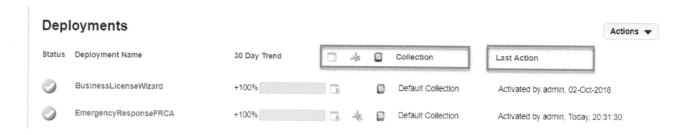

Select the Deployments Icon and view the list of deployments. The Project you deployed earlier in this chapter should be visible, as shown above. Notice the icons in the first highlighted section, which represent Web Determination, Determination Service, and Mobile deployments. At the moment, your Project is only deployed to Web Determinations. Note also the Collection into which the Deployment was made, and when.

Select the Rule Project by clicking the link on the Deployment Name, to show the deployment details as follows:

As you can see in the right-hand menu, the admin user can deactivate or delete a deployment from this page. In addition, this user Deployment Administrator role can activate the other forms of usage – as an Assess Web Service, or Interview Web Service, or as a mobile interview.

Web Service

The Web Service option provides the administrator with the possibility to download the WSDL (the file that defines the manner in which applications can use the web service for your Project). The web service offers different **methods** to work with the Project – this allows external applications to send a request, have it assessed according to your rule Project policies, and then have a response returned.

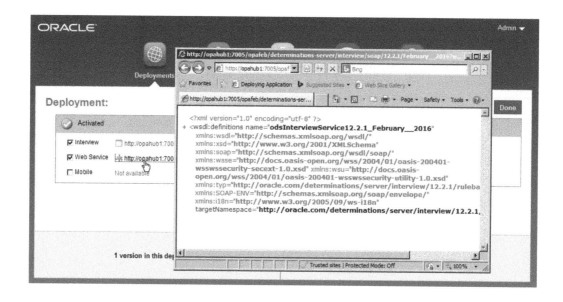

There are several different types of web service usage with different functionality as you learned at the beginning of this book:

- The **Answer Service**, used with Interviews that have Web Service Connections.

- The **Assess Service**, used to request policy execution and return rich structured responses.

- The **Interview Service**, used to build interviews in external applications using the metadata from your Interview Screens.

- The **Server Service**, used to interrogate an OPA Hub for information about policies, versions, and locales currently deployed.

NB: For more information on the different Web Services, see chapter 20.

Mobile Deployment

As you have seen in the chapters about interviews (Chapters 6 and 7), there is a modern user interface for browsers to display your policy interviews (and the interface is constantly being improved with new style sheets and better mobile device rendering).

Licenses

Deploying to a mobile device in this context, however, indicates that there are users who have installed the OPA Mobile Application (for Android or Apple, at the time of writing).

Testing such an interview requires either a physical device (upon which you install the app) or, more likely perhaps, involves the use of a mobile device simulator. A mobile device simulator enables you to test appearances on many different tablets to ensure a good result for all.

NB: Access to the deployment functionality described in this section is subject to license fees, so you may not have the relevant Mobile topic in the OPA Hub Deployment screen shown on the previous page.

There are many different simulators in the public domain, but I have had good results with the following approach for Android devices (for Apple devices things get constrained by the availability of hardware running the relevant operating system and/or payment of developer fees).

Download GenyMotion (https://www.genymotion.com/) Android Simulator and obtain a free personal account or a professional account, whichever is appropriate for your situation. The main advantages of this software are that it is less onerous to install than a full Android Development environment, and it uses Oracle Virtual Box as its emulator engine – which, if you installed the self-study environment suggested in the previous chapter, you already have on your computer.

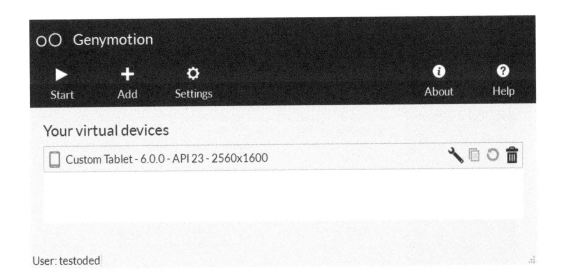

As the screenshot above shows, you can create and add Android emulators to this screen. You should carefully create as many emulators as you have target devices for your users.

You will need to install the Oracle OPA Android App. Installing Google Play Store and downloading the App can be accomplished in just a few minutes, GenyMotion automates almost all of the process. If you need more information about how to set up the Mobile Emulator specifically for the OPA Mobile App, you can find some hints and tips at this URL https://theopahub.com/main/installing-opa-hub-self-study-platform-going-mobile/

Use of the mobile app requires a user who has sufficient permissions to access mobile deployment. Once the details of the Hub are entered, the list of available interviews is refreshed. If you are already connected you can click the Update from OPA Hub now button shown.

> **NB**: The admin user does not, by default, have permission. Read about roles in Chapter 12.

The list of interviews available is displayed. Selecting an interview starts a session. The exact display will, of course, be different depending on the dimensions of your mobile device.

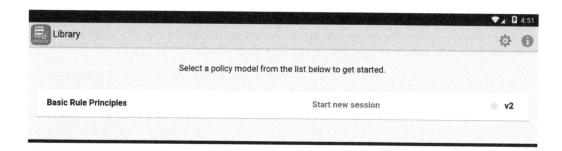

The interview has a very mobile-friendly layout and the style is easy to read. Note the buttons and other user interface elements are large and simple to use.

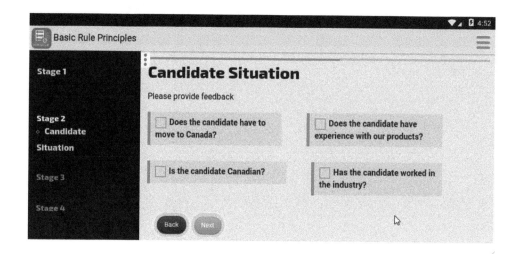

NB: Accessing the OPA Hub from the mobile device requires an up-to-date OPA app, so make sure you have kept the version of the app updated on your emulated device.

At the time of writing, the latest version of the OPA Mobile Application had reduced the differences in the display of a Policy Model (so as to be closer to providing the same user experience as a web Interview).

Viewing the Action Log for a Deployment

A user with sufficient rights can also view the **Action Log**. The Action Log is available from the menu in the top right-hand corner, once a deployment is selected. The Action Log provides a brief list of the different versions and their deployment date.

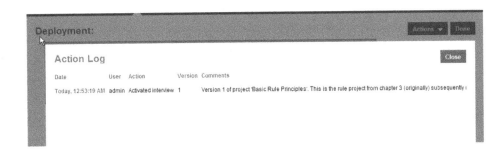

Deployment Management

Over time, the administrator will begin to see the history of deployment for a given Project when viewing Deployment details. For example, from this screen the user can:

1. Download any version.

2. Activate a previous version.

3. Delete an inactive version.

4. Use the Actions menu as described in the previous sections.

The screenshot below illustrates the different features for reference. Note that the currently active version cannot be deleted.

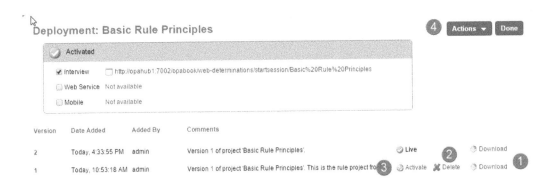

Embedded Interview Deployment

By default, your Interview will be deployed, typically, as a URL that your end-user target population can access like any other Web property. It is possible however that in lots of cases, you wish to embed the Interview in an existing Web Site. This requires two steps. The first step is to enable the feature using the Actions menu on the Deployments page.

1. Select the Actions menu.

2. Click the Add Host button.

3. Enter the host name and port, if appropriate.

The second step is to communicate the format of the embedding process to your Web developers who manage the other Web site. The basic requirement is to initiate the Interview in JavaScript, using something similar to the following code:

```
<script src="https://myserver.com/opa18d/web-determinations/staticresource/interviews.js"></script>  1

</head>

<div style="display: inline-block; width:100%">
    <div id="myInterview" style="width: 100%; display: block; margin-left: auto; margin-right:auto; float: left"></div>
</div>       2

<script>
    var el = document.getElementById("myInterview");
    var webDeterminationsUrl = "https://myserver.com/opa18d/web-determinations";    3
    var deploymentName = "LoanAdvisor";
    OraclePolicyAutomationInterview.StartInterview(el, webDeterminationsUrl, deploymentName);
</script>
```

1. The interviews.js script from your Oracle Policy Automation server is loaded.

2. A DIV is added to the page with dimensions that suit your layout.

3. The same DIV is populated by calling your Deployment Name with StartInterview.

A full set of parameters and potential errors is available here at time of writing
http://documentation.custhelp.com/euf/assets/devdocs/cloud18d/PolicyAutomation/en/Default.htm#Guides/Developer_Guide/Web_Interviews/Integration/Embed_an_interview_in_another_application.htm

> **NB**: It is also possible to use IFRAME tags to embed the Interview, in which case you can copy the URL directly from the Deployment details for your Project.

JavaScript Embeddable Models

Starting in Version 18B, it is possible for Oracle Policy Automation Cloud Service customers to deploy their Project as a single, standalone JavaScript file. This file can be deployed on devices or platforms without the need for those devices to access the Hub.

By their nature, these standalone files have restrictions (no decision reporting, no interviews and no temporal logic for example). They are, however, very well adapted to Internet-of-Things contexts where licensing is required to a large number of devices. The process of accessing this programming interface is straightforward, once the file has been deployed.

1. Load the JavaScript into a Web page, for example.

2. Call the single function `run_DeploymentName`, passing a JSON object as input attributes.

A typical excerpt would look like the following:

```
var myinputdata = {};
myinputdata.firstname = "Richard";
myinputdata.isCandidate = true;
myinputdata.age = 18;
myinputdata.dateofbirth = "1969-07-03";
run_MyDeploymentName(myinputdata);
```

In the example above, `firstname`, `isCandidate`, `age` and `dateofbirth` are the names of attributes in the Project that has been deployed with the name `MyDeploymentName`.

> **NB**: Access to this feature is limited to Oracle Policy Automation Cloud Service customers who have licensed Embeddable JavaScript Models

Deployment Statistics

Various pieces of information regarding the usage of your Hub are available from the Deployment page, through the various charts displayed at the bottom of the page. These are all clickable zones, and give access to the View Statistics options for your Hub. The statistics views let you see usage patterns for your entire Hub, by studying sessions and screens visited for all your deployments. To access the first level of Statistics, click on any graphical zone under the list of Deployments, as shown in the next image.

Chart Access

While viewing Deployment data for your Policy Models, there are three charts that are displayed at the bottom of the deployment information:

1. By default, when accessing this page, the statistics will be Site-wide.

2. Clicking on a zone will display the View Statistics page for the Hub.

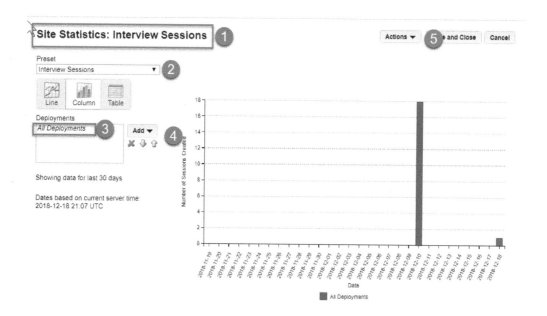

In the above example, statistics are grouped by hour, for the last 30 days, for all deployments.

1. Note the caption is Site Statistics rather than a specific Project.

2. Various predefined Views are available.

3. The statistics are for all deployments, by default.

4. You can change the deployments used for the View.

5. This data can be downloaded from the Actions menu.

To find out more about the options, the following section will help you build charts to meet your own specific needs.

Working with Project Deployment Data in Charts

The Oracle Policy Automation Hub includes simple to use charting facilities that can be helpful in providing an overview of deployment data *per Project* in graphical form as well. These charts can be customized to display data from several versions, and can be configured to display in a variety of different ways. Finally, the chart data can be downloaded for further analysis in an external tool.

Chart Access

While viewing Deployment details for each Policy Model, there are (again) three zones that are displayed at the bottom of the deployment information:

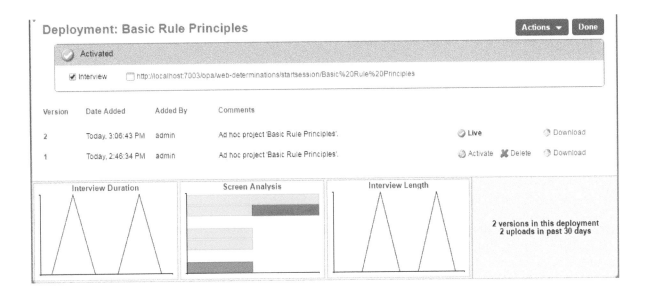

Customizing a Chart

When the user clicks on one of the chart zones shown in the screenshot above, the editing window appears. In the editing window, the following controls are available:

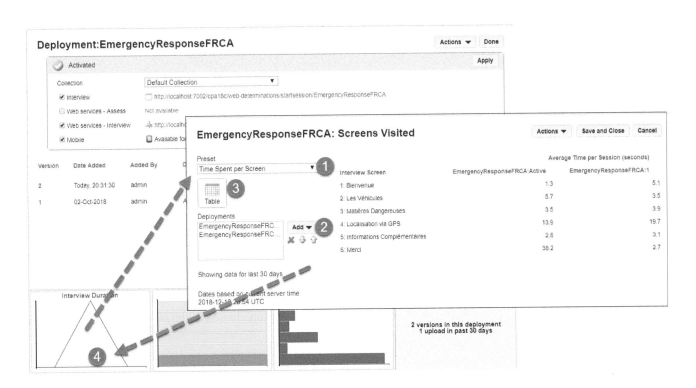

1. Select from a variety of preset Statistics Views. Note that some views are Oracle Service Cloud-specific.

2. Select or Add multiple versions that have been deployed for comparison purposes. In this case, two versions are being compared.

3. Select a Chart Type. The type(s) available depend on the range and type of data viewed.

4. Saving and closing the customized chart will display it in place of the original chart in the zone.

Creating a New Chart

It is also possible to design a custom chart, within the parameters provided by the application. For example, to create a chart that compares three different deployed versions of a Policy Model, over the last thirty days, viewing Interviews by duration.

1. Select the preset Custom... type.

2. Type a short Caption to describe the Chart.

3. Select the Chart type.

4. Select the basic Chart data.

5. Select the Project versions you wish to view in the chart.

6. Select the different types of session to chart: sessions performed by an authenticated agent in Oracle Service Cloud, or anonymous interviews, or Web Service sessions, or a combination

7. Select the timeframe you wish to chart.

An example chart with the above parameters is shown next.

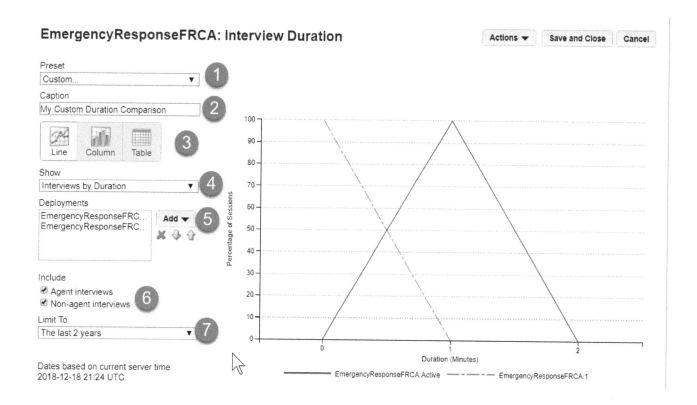

As previously described, once saved, the chart will display in the location chosen at the start of the procedure, as in the example below.

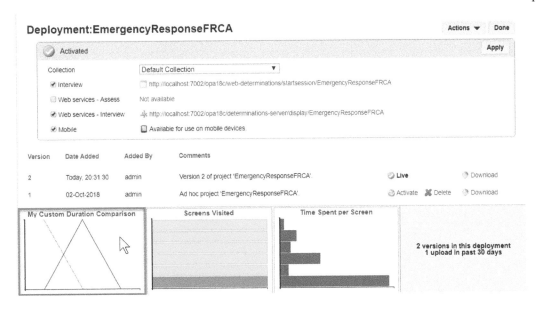

Your custom chart choice is retained even after you logout and log back into the Oracle Policy Automation Hub.

Exporting Chart Data

To export chart data, when in the chart editor, click the Actions button in the top right-hand corner of the page and select Download Chart Data. The Download Data dialog appears:

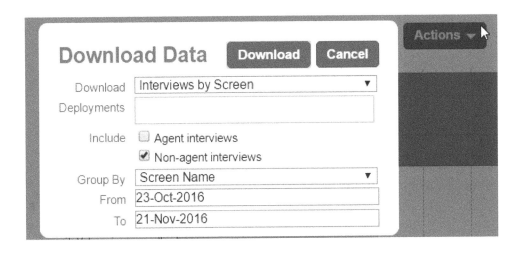

Select from the preset chart types and select one or more deployments, interview types, and a time period. The Group By drop-down list will change according to the type of chart data you are downloading.

Summary

The OPA Hub provides a web interface to conduct the various management and administration tasks necessary to maintain deployments and ensure the correct Policy Models are active. Rule writers interact with this Web Application by deploying Policy Models, and activating them if they have sufficient permission to do so.

Deployment data can be visualized in Chart form, which comes in very handy when presenting high-level data to business audiences.

Languages in Oracle Policy Automation

The language used to write rules may not be your choice. For example, in European governmental organizations, the language is often the official state language.

It should not be forgotten than some states have more than one official language as well (Finland, for example, with Finnish and Swedish languages both officially recognized), which may in turn require the availability of rules, documentation, reports, and more in several languages.

This chapter looks at some of the ways, as a rule designer or consultant, you can improve the chances of this multi-language effort being a success.

Rule Writing – Understanding Language and Region

Choosing a different rule language and region for your Oracle Policy Modeling affects several different aspects, including:

- The language you use to write rules, and the parser that is used.
- The region-defined separators, display of dates and currency, and so on.
- Language-sensitive operators and other terminology.
- The translations you need to provide for end users.

Rule Languages

Version 12 offers a variety of languages for your Project.

The parsers generally have their own limitations and restrictions much as the English-language parser does. It would be impossible to review all the different parsers here (although I do hope the community will step in and contribute to that effort).

This section will simply highlight areas that need frequent attention in such cases.

Gender of Words

Issues may occur with generated text. Take a look at the following examples:

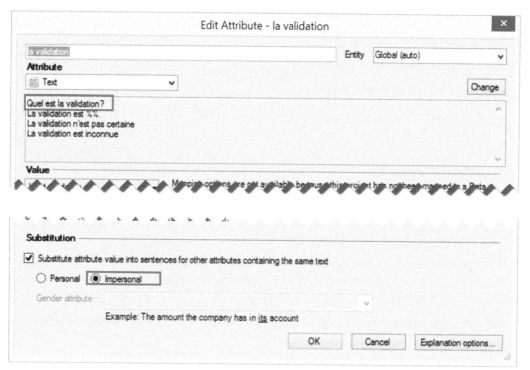

When the attribute is declared as impersonal, the incorrect "Quel" as opposed to "Quelle" (as the word is feminine in gender) is assigned to the interrogative.

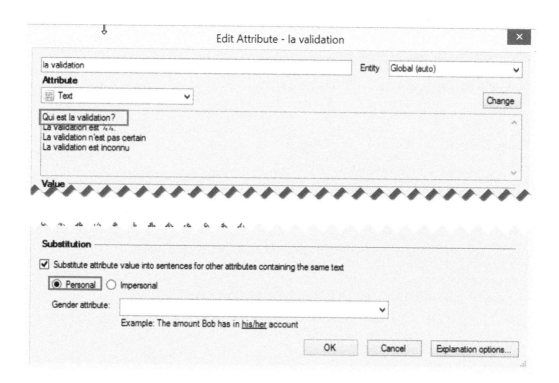

When we choose the alternative, the text is still wrong, of course, since now it uses "Qui" or "Who" as opposed to "What".

As shown above, manual editing of the Interview Screens may be required to provide linguistically acceptable text.

Contractions

In French, for example, the following contractions are normal grammar:

la date du rendez-vous – as opposed to – **la date de le rendez-vous**.

Such contractions are recognized by Oracle Policy Modeling. Some contractions are not, however, especially when involving substitutions. In the previous example we have two attributes, both of which are set up to allow substitution in Interview Screens. In the previous example, we illustrated two attributes "la validation" and "la loi". Introducing a Boolean attribute into the Interview, may result in substitution / contraction errors as shown in the example below.

Values are entered that begin with a vowel, in this case A.

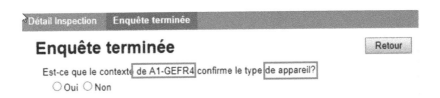

The resulting text on the Interview Screen does not have the correct substitutions ("d'appareil" for example).

Entity Aliases

When referring to one instance of an entity and comparing it to another instance, French and other languages, indicate possession or relationship in different ways to English. For example, these both convey the same basic concept but only the English version uses the apostrophe.

- The driver's teammate.
- Le co-équipier du pilote.

When writing rules that compare instances, such as the following example, showing the use of an alias as well as the contractions "du" instead of "de le":

> **le pilote** qui affiche le meilleur temps aux essais
> ChampPour(le co-équipier du pilote; le co-équipier)
> le temps aux essais du pilote< le temps aux essais du co-équipier

> *the driver with the fastest qualifying times in testing*
> *(ForScope(the driver's teammate; the teammate)*
> *the drivers' time during testing < the teammate's time in testing)*

Such contractions and aliasing may not work in all languages, and you should be on the lookout for such issues.

Adding Verbs to Existing Languages

As mentioned earlier in this book, the parsing engine of Oracle Policy Automation is not limitless in scope – it cannot possibly hope to list and parse all the regular and irregular verbs in any language, let alone all the supported languages.

Unrecognised but Valid Verbs

If you work in a highly-specialised business area, it is likely that you will reach a point where your correctly expressed concept, using an uncommon verb, is simply not recognised by the parsing process. Consider the following example:

The candidate is accepted if
The candidate's dossier parses successfully

Pardon the play on words, but the above test, when correctly formatted, does appear to parse successfully. But upon closer investigation of the attribute, it is clear that the interpretation is not ideal or complete:

> Is the candidate's dossier parses successfully true?
> It is not true that the candidate's dossier parses successfully.
> It is uncertain whether the candidate's dossier parses successfully.

In addition, attempting to use the Change feature in the Edit Attribute dialog reveals that the options provided do not fully solve the problem either:

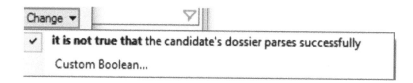

In a situation where a verb is not recognised, and you are going to need this verb multiple times within your Project, then the solution is to add it to the list of Verbs. These verbs are stored transparently in an XML file that will become part of your Project.

1. Navigate to the Languages Pane in the Project Tab.

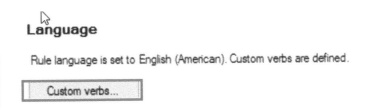

Language

Rule language is set to English (American). Custom verbs are defined.

Custom verbs...

2. Click the Custom Verbs... button.
3. If this is the first time you clicked this button in this Project, you will receive a warning.
4. In the following dialog, note the number of available verbs, and the possibility to scroll through the existing verbs (perhaps, in certain situations, to choose an available alternative).
5. In the case where no verb is available, click the Add... button as shown on the next page:

6. Adding a new verb only normally requires the entry of the infinitive in the top left-hand corner. Upon exiting the data entry field, the other text should automatically be filled in.

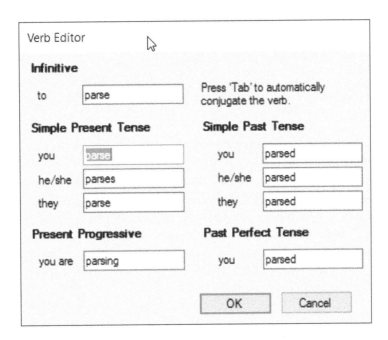

7. You may have to edit some of the text in the case of an irregular verb, however.
8. Returning to the document shown and the start of this example, after Validation the correct verb should be accessible from the menu. Further uses of the verb should be interpreted correctly.

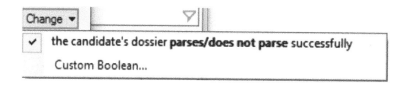

> **NB** : Since the list of verbs is linked to the Project, it is a good idea to establish the list of custom verbs to be added as early as possible in the life of the Project.

Custom Languages

It is possible, should a requirement arise, to create a custom language for use in Oracle Policy Modeling. There are several steps to create one. This may be necessary where rules must be written in a national language, but the language is not currently in the list of supported languages.

Creating a Custom Language

Select Custom when creating a New Project from the list of Languages drop-down. Oracle Policy Modeling will allow you to select an existing language and to create a new customized *branch* – your new language will use the existing language as the basis for structure and syntax. For example, a specific variety of French or another language, along with the name in English and the localized name.

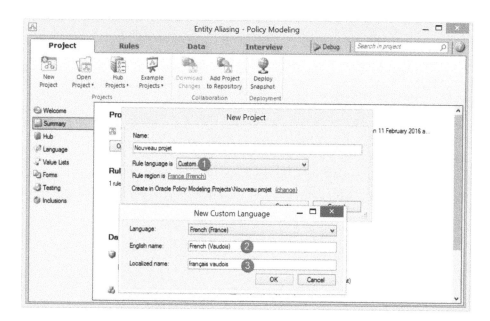

Once the custom language is created in this way, the next step is to customize various aspects of the static text that will be used in the Oracle Policy Modeling.

> **NB**: Creating a customized language does not provide all of the parsing capability of languages supplied out of the box. You may have to simplify some of your sentence forms if the custom language has significant differences to the chosen source language.

Edit Custom Language Strings

As soon as the custom language dialog is complete, a warning message will appear on the Oracle Policy Modeling interface.

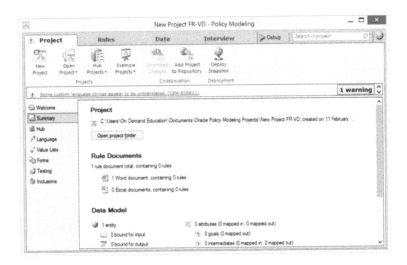

Clicking the warning message shows the following dialog box to configure the custom language text strings.

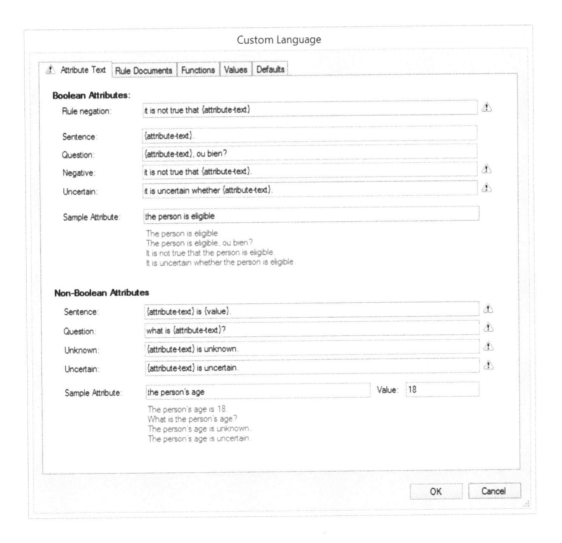

The text shown above will need to be translated and entered here. It should be noted that the different tabs in this dialog box will all require attention from the translator. This is a not inconsequential task, since all the aggregations ("any", "all") and functions of all types must be translated.

No Custom Verbs

Unlike standard languages, custom languages implemented in this way do not currently allow for the storage of a verb list (either standard or custom). Instead, the structure of the sentences will be created from the text entered in the dialog shown on the previous page. The {token} that is present in each sentence must not be modified, but can be placed where required. It is important to note that such a simple structure mapping will not cover all situations and grammatical constructs of a language, but will allow rapid deployment.

Attribute text is customizable even in custom languages.

Reusing a Custom Language

Once the custom language is created and fully localized using the dialog box shown, the language details can be accessed from the Project tab's Language Pane, using the button shown below.

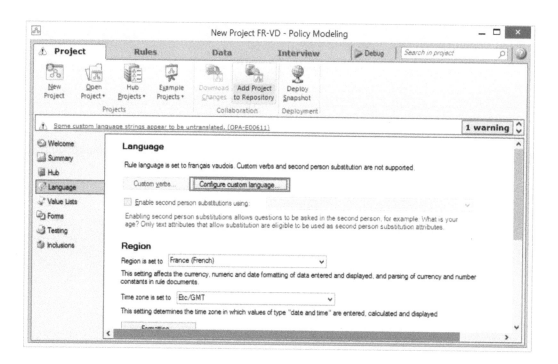

In addition, custom language details are added to a Project file called customLanguage.xml. This file, found in the root folder of your Project, can be copied into the folder of another rule Project to obtain the string values entered in the previously shown Custom Language dialog. The steps are as follows

- Choose the custom language in the Project Creation dialog of the new Project.

- Save the new Project.

- Copy the customLanguage.xml file from the existing file to the new Project.

- Restart Oracle Policy Modeling.

Translation Files

In a situation where the identical rules are applicable and written in one language, yet the user interface must be available in several different languages, Oracle Policy Modeling offers Microsoft Excel-based translation files to assist in the deployment effort. The process is quite straightforward, and represents an acceptable solution for many customers where the desire is to display the Interview in several languages but maintain the rules in only one.

Creating a Translation File

One or more translation files can be added to a rule Project from the Language Pane. Clicking the Add button and selecting a language creates a new file, and adds it to the list of languages available.

Once the file has been added, a number will appear in the Errors column of the Translations list. This represents the number of terms that need to be translated. Double-clicking the file will open it in Microsoft Excel.

Editing a Translation File

The Excel file contains a number of tabs, the content of which needs to be translated. Some tabs relate to content you created (for example, rule text, attribute names, relationship text, screen titles, value lists and so on) and other tabs relate to static content (standard messages to assist the user in using the Interview components and so on). Text that you have not translated yet is shown with a "!" in front of it.

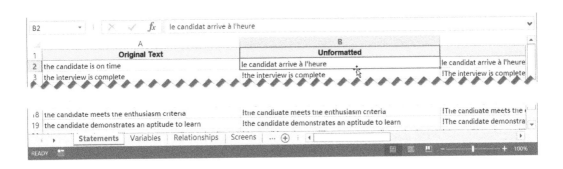

Once you have finished the translation, save the file and return to Oracle Policy Modeling. You should notice that the number of Errors has reduced.

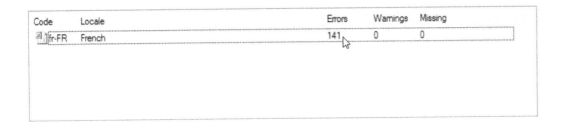

Updating a Translation file

Updates can be made to the translation file at any time. From a management perspective it is clearly not ideal if new text is being added to your Project after the work of translation has begun. If that is the case, the Update All button will allow the translation file(s) to be updated to include any new text that has been added to the Project since the original translation file was generated.

You can see if new text has been added to the Project since the creation of the translation file by looking at the Missing column. In addition, after updating your translation files, comments are added to any errors or warnings in the file.

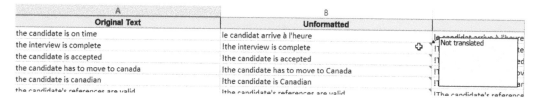

The Update All process adds new text but does not delete old content. So changing items in Oracle Policy Modeling (for example removing an Entity) may mean extra work to remove unwanted content from the Excel file.

Finding Already Translated Text

In the case of a file that has been updated successfully, whose source content (Attributes in your Project, Entities, and so forth) has been repeatedly modified, deleted, and recreated, it is therefore likely that you will reach a point where the following error message appears following an Update All operation.

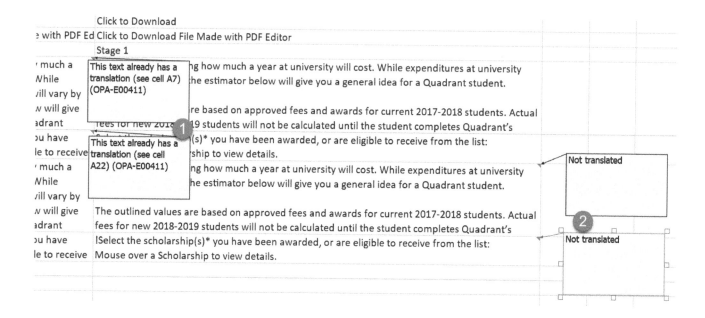

1. In this case, repeated creation and deletion of similar attributes has resulted in the Update All detecting that strings are already translated somewhere else in the Excel Translation File. Recall that the Update All does not delete old content from the File.

2. These strings have been recently added to the Project and require translation.

For reference, the Translations pane of the Project tab would show the items on the left as Warnings, and the items on the right as Missing, as in this image. The total of four Errors is thus derived from these numbers:

Dealing with Substitutions

Your translated text can contain substitution codes. Note that adding substitutions to your Project entities or changing them *after* the generation of the translation files could result in a lot of rework being required to adapt the translated content. To add a substitution, use the `%name%` format that you have seen in the chapter on Interview creation.

Dealing with Language Neutral Terms

To make a piece of text appear as in the original language, simply remove the "!" from the beginning of the phrase. It will appear as-is in the translation. This can be useful for adopted words or items referencing brand names.

Debugging translated interviews

The debugger window contains a drop-down where you may select to see the relevant translation.

Regional Settings

The regional formats you see in Oracle Policy Modeling are visible in your Project and can be accessed via the Languages Pane of the Project tab in the user interface. For example, in my Project, after clicking the Formatting… button I see the following:

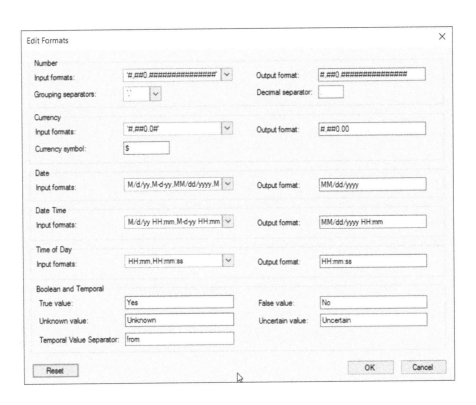

These settings can be modified on a project-by-project basis and will be stored as part of the Project definition, ensuring that the chosen or manually entered formats are passed to Oracle Policy Automation Hub for deployment.

It is important to understand that the addition of a Translation file does not change the Region settings of the Project, and those settings will still be applied.

Second Person Substitution in Translation Files

If your Project has enabled this form of substitution, then you will have an extra column on each of the Statements and Variables Excel tabs, to allow you enter the relevant translations.

PDF Forms and Translation Files

If your project contains PDF forms, it is important to budget time to create translated versions of these documents in order to provide your end users with translated content. If you do not, then the default Form template will be used.

To help you remember to do this, the Oracle Policy Modeling user interface displays a warning message for each Form you have in your Project, as soon as you begin working with one or more Translation files, as shown in the screenshot below.

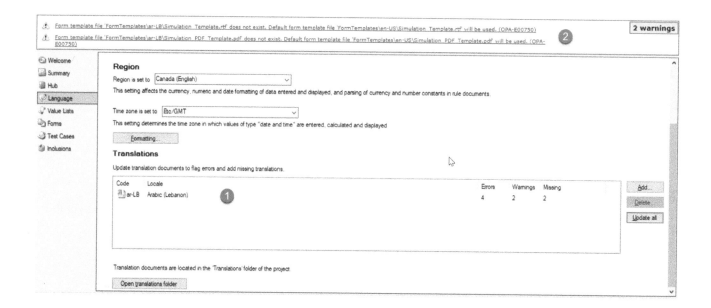

1. Adding a first translation file to the Project...

2. ...triggers the warning messages for each Form already in the Project.

Locale Functions

To be able to detect the **Locale** of an end user is a very powerful capability. For example, perhaps in your Interview, you include a link to your company's website. If your user is currently viewing the ar-LB translation of your Interview, it makes sense to direct them to your Lebanese website rather than the Canadian one; perhaps the products and terms are different in the two locales.

The function looks like this in a typical usage scenario:

<u>the interview locale</u> = CurrentLocale()

the interview language is Arabic if

<u>the interview locale</u> = "ar-LB"

In the first line, the `CurrentLocale()` function is called, and it returns a string of text. The text string is one of the values of the locales in the Locale List (for a complete list at time of writing, see http://documentation.custhelp.com/euf/assets/devdocs/cloud18d/PolicyAutomation/en/Content/Guides/Policy_Modeling_User_Guide/Projects/Locale_codes.htm).

In the second line, the value is compared to `"ar-LB"` and a true or false value is determined. Recall from the chapters detailing Interview creation, that you can:

• Show or Hide Controls, Labels, or Screens based on Boolean attributes.

- Redirect the user at the end of the Interview to another site, the URL of which may contain substitutions.

The above are just examples of how you might leverage the value in your Interview.

Changing language in the Interview

The end user should be able to change language during the Interview process, if multiple languages are available. To enable this feature, go to the Interview tab and the Styles dialog. Use the screenshot on the next page as your guide to both enable the feature and customize its appearance.

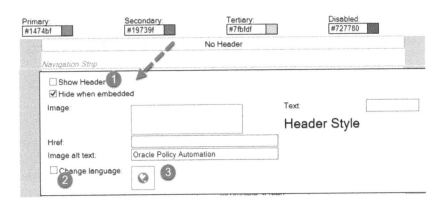

Click the section marked No Header, then

1. Click to Show Header and whether it is also displayed when the Interview is embedded in another page.

2. Click to show the Change language button.

3. Choose an Icon URL or accept the standard icon.

Once your Interview is loaded into the Debugger, observe the new icon and functionality:

Time Zones in Your Projects

When you create a Project in Oracle Policy Modeling, a **Time Zone** can be set at the same time. Below this screenshot, the bullets will explain the impact of the time zone settings.

1. Setting the Time Zone in the Language tab is independent of the Region or Language.

2. Rules using date-time or time of day attributes will be affected by the setting. The current date-time means *the current date time in the selected time zone.*

3. Values displayed in the Debugger will take the time zone into account.

It is important to note that the list of time zones displays the time offset using IANA notation. Thus, a time zone marked as GMT + 12 is actually twelve hours *behind* GMT. You can find out more about this slightly confusing method of displaying time zones in the Oracle Policy Automation documentation at this URL :
http://documentation.custhelp.com/euf/assets/devdocs/cloud18d/PolicyAutomation/en/Content/Guides/Policy_Modeling_User_Guide/Projects/Change_the_time_zone_for_a_project.htm

Region Date and Time Display Formats

The manner in which dates, times, and times of day are displayed are, as you have already learned in this chapter, controlled by your choice of Region for your Project. The display formats for each of the data types are visible within Oracle Policy Modeling, from the Languages pane of the Project Tab, by clicking the Formatting button. An extract of that dialog box is shown below:

It is possible to change these values if required, although in most cases the input and output formats should be in line with regional habits. One possible use might be to add the time zone to the Date Time and Time of Day outputs during a series of tests, in order to help clarify the timezone used and the offset with GMT. For example, the image below shows a setting added to the Output format of Date Time attributes, and the display in the Debugger.

The zzzz causes the *long time zone name* to be displayed. You can also substitute with two letter zz to see the short form (for example AKST) or capital ZZZZ for the time offset, for example -1200.

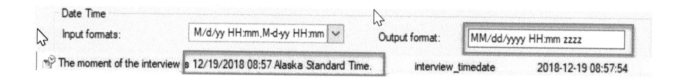

Summary

The use of languages other than English to write rules increases the appeal of Oracle Policy Automation for organizations that may have legal or practical constraints in this regard. Oracle Policy Modeling offers a range of tools to facilitate the creation and testing of language-specific interviews, Forms and other Project components.

Command Line Tools

Command Line Tools in Oracle Policy Automation

Installation of Oracle Policy Automation provides not only the Modeling client application that you are hopefully now familiar with, but also some extra tools – one graphical and several using a command line – that makes migration and batch processing easier.

This chapter looks at how to use those tools successfully and what they can do for you.

Client Side Tools

The **OPMMigrator** is used to upgrade Oracle Policy Modeller Projects that come from earlier versions of the product. **OPMNewProject** allows for the automated creation of Projects on your hard disk. **OPMBuild** automates the build process through a command line. Each of these tools will be reviewed in turn.

Server Side Tools

Although not part of the Oracle Policy Modeler installation, you will discover the Batch Processor in this chapter. This very powerful Java tool allows you to load Comma Separated Value (CSV) files full of input data into the Oracle Policy Determination Server and get the responses. You can also use a database to store the input and output. You will also learn a little about the admin tools available for automating certain Hub-related actions.

Oracle Policy Modeller – OPMMigrator

As noted earlier in this book, the speed of innovation is such that there are regularly new versions of Oracle Policy Automation that arrive on the official download page. As such, you will need to migrate Rule Projects written in older versions to the latest release.

Automatic migration is proposed starting at version 10.4, so if you are working on an earlier version it may be judicious to first migrate to 10.4 in order to benefit from the automatic option.

NB: If you choose to *manually* migrate your 10.3 Project, an excellent checklist is currently available at http://documentation.custhelp.com/euf/assets/devdocs/cloud18d/PolicyAutomation/en/Default.htm#Guides/Policy_Modeling_User_Guide/Projects/Migrate_Policy_Modeling_v_10_project_to_current_version.htm

---

The spectrum of possible migration scenarios for your Projects is very broad: you might be migrating from Version 10.4 or later, to Version 12 with a simple Project containing only a few items, and at the other extreme it may be a complete Project including customised entity collection screens, a version 10 Screen Flow (no longer used in Version 12).

The **OPMMigrator** Tool helps you achieve a successful Project migration and lets you know what has been changed, or left behind during the migration. Let's look at two scenarios, one simple and one complex. In both cases, the task is the same: run the migration tool.

Running the Migration Tool

To run the migration tool, navigate to the folder where the new version is installed on your hard disk. Locate the file called OPMMigrator.exe. Do not double-click the file directly. Instead, open the Windows Command Line utility by pressing the Windows key and typing cmd. Once you have the Command Prompt open, drag the OPMMigrator.exe file onto this window. When you drop the file you will see the following:

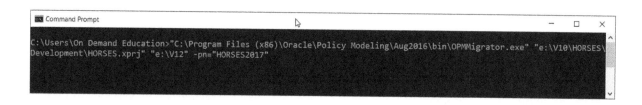

From the above, we can glean the correct way to use the Migrator Tool:

```
OPMMigrator projectpath targetfolder [optionally pn= a new name for the
upgraded project]
```

Simple Migration Output

Taking that into account, a simple command line might look like this, given a project stored in
E:\V10\Horses.xprj and a new file to be stored in E:\V12\Horses2017 with a Project name of HORSES2017.

```
Command Prompt                                                                    —  □  ×

C:\Users\On Demand Education>"C:\Program Files (x86)\Oracle\Policy Modeling\Aug2016\bin\OPMMigrator.exe" "e:\V10\HORSES\
Development\HORSES.xprj" "e:\V12" -pn="HORSES2017"
```

In the case of a small Project file, with only a few elements, there is every chance that the output of this
command line will fit easily onto a small number lines. In the next screenshot, notice that there are a number of
warnings. These warnings indicate that a feature you were using in the old version has not been migrated to the
new version.

```
Command Prompt                                                                    —  □  ×

C:\Users\On Demand Education>"C:\Program Files (x86)\Oracle\Policy Modeling\Aug2016\bin\OPMMigrator.exe" "e:\V10\HORSES\
Development\HORSES.xprj" "e:\V12" -pn="HORSES2017"
04-Nov-2016 03:36:36.360: Migrating project 'HORSES2017' to 'e:\V12\HORSES2017'
04-Nov-2016 03:36:36.460: Migrating screens...
04-Nov-2016 03:36:36.460: Warning: Ignoring data review screen "DefaultScreenOrder: Data Review"
04-Nov-2016 03:36:36.460: Migrating summary screen: Assessment Summary
04-Nov-2016 03:36:36.476: Warning: Ignoring user defined caption(s) on goal control.
04-Nov-2016 03:36:36.491: Migrating 'HORSES2017.xprj'...
04-Nov-2016 03:36:36.507: Migrating 'Interview.xint'...
04-Nov-2016 03:36:36.507: Migrating 'projectDataModel.xml'...
04-Nov-2016 03:36:39.963: Migrating 'New Word Document.docx'...
04-Nov-2016 03:36:42.366: Migrating 'Mardi Deux.user.xml'...
04-Nov-2016 03:36:42.402: Migrating 'Mardi Deux.zip'...
04-Nov-2016 03:36:45.822: Migration successful, created new project in e:\V12\HORSES2017.

C:\Users\On Demand Education>
```

Complex Migration Output

On a larger Project file, for example one with a large number of customised screens, a variety of entities and so forth, the output of the command line can be extremely long. In that case, you should output the command line and then review the associated `migration.log` text file, which is placed in the new `Project` folder.

In such cases, the output is much easier to read in WordPad, Notepad, or a similar editor. An example is shown below. As before, the output highlights a number of functionalities that have not been implemented in Version 12 compared to Version 10, and the Project author would have a significant amount of work to fix all the issues.

The OPM Migrator Tool is therefore a good starting point when you want to get an impression of how much work has to be done.

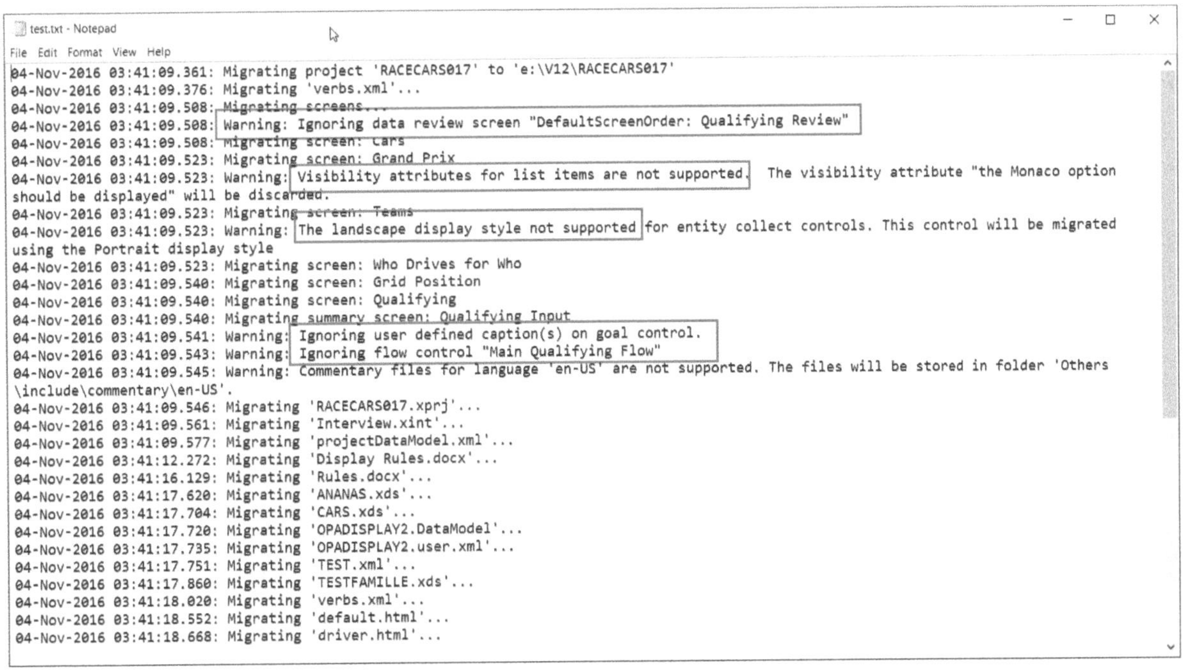

In spite of the fact that the process of upgrading is quick, it is important not to underestimate the actual work that may be required to completely migrate all of the Project components from one version to another. Some of the more complex areas that may take time to accomplish are:

- Reworking Screens in Version 12.

- Reviewing Identifying Attributes for Entities.

- Checking for Functions not available in Version 12.

- Recreating Commentary as Labels.

- Reconstructing Modules using Inclusions.

- Incorporating Screen Flow logic in Version 12 Interviews.

Error Messages from the Tool

Keep in mind that most of the error messages you receive from the command line will not be user-friendly. An example is shown below, and relates to the extra "\" character at the end of the target folder path.

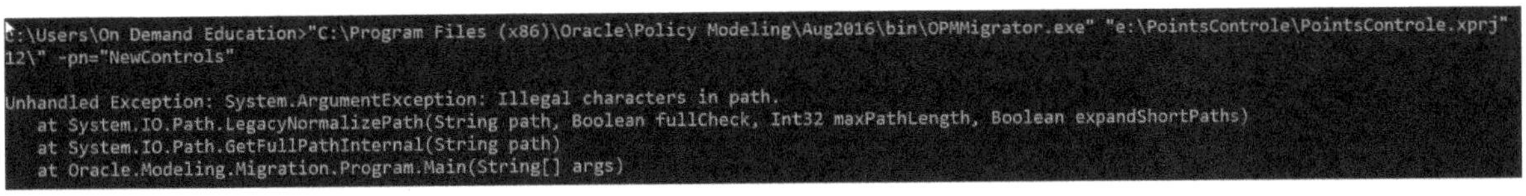

Migrating from version 12.x to 12.y

In contrast to the use of the OPMMigrator to move from version 10 to version 12, moving between different versions – 12.x to 12.y if you like – is very much more straightforward. If you have both versions of Oracle Policy Modeling installed, you can continue to use them side-by-side and when you open a Project made in version 12.x, it will automatically be opened in that version, assuming it is still installed on your hard drive.

Should you uninstall all but the latest version 12, when you now open your Project you will see the following dialogue:

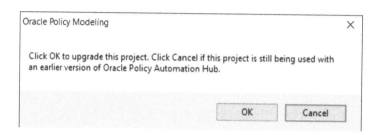

The same message will appear if you connect a Project to an Oracle Policy Automation Hub that has a later version than your Project.

Upgrading a Project to the latest version of Oracle Policy Modeler is a one-way action. Once the Project is upgraded, it will normally only open successfully in that version, so be careful not to upgrade unless you really mean to, or you have kept a copy of the Project to hand as an archive file.

OPA Hub and Modeling Versions

Starting with Oracle Policy Automation 12 version 18D, it is no longer a requirement to upgrade Projects whenever your Hub is upgraded. For example, a Project built in 18D could defer the upgrade to 19A, even after the Oracle Policy Automation Hub has been upgraded to 19A. To switch to the deferred upgrade model, locate the Hub pane of the Project Tab in Oracle Policy Modeling.

1. You must be connected to a Hub version 18D or later.

2. You must be logged in to the Hub.

3. The current version of the Hub is displayed with a link to the documentation.

4. This disables the message requesting an upgrade.

5. If the Hub has been upgraded, the user can download and install the corresponding version of Oracle Policy Modeling.

The process of opening the file in the new version of Oracle Policy Modeling takes only a few seconds and the upgrade is complete. For information, the version number is stored in the **XPRJ file** associated with your Project folder.

Create a New Project from the Command Line

In the latest version of Oracle Policy Modeling, a new tool is included, very similar in style to the Migration Tool, which in this instance allows for the programmatic creation of new Projects. This command line could be incorporated, for example, in a batch file in Windows, or a scripting language.

Creating a Project

To create a Project, navigate to the Oracle Policy Modeling installation folder and locate the OPMNewProject.exe program. It can be run from the command line by supplying the path to the Project, the language, region, and timezone. The only required parameter is the Project Path.

```
OPMNewProject.exe <projectpath> [-lang=<language code> [-region=<regioncode>]
[-timezone=<timezone code>]
```

Thus the following command creates a Project folder and file in c:\data called AutoProject with a set of values to illustrate the optional parameters. Note that the single option -listcodes can be used to obtain the list of valid values for each parameter.

Build a Project from the Command Line

A Project can be built directly from the command line, facilitating automated builds through batch files and other scripting languages.

Building the Project with OPMBuild

To build a Project, navigate to the Oracle Policy Modeling installation folder and locate the OPMBuild.exe program. It can be run from the command line by supplying the path to the Project File:

```
buildtoolpath projectpath [-n <build number> -i] [-h | --diagnostics]
```

The -i parameter indicates an incremental build should occur, not rebuilding any unmodified content and the -n parameter sets the build number visible in the OPA Hub or in the Server Web Service.

Thus the following command builds the Project c:\data\AutoProject with a set of values to illustrate the optional parameters. Note that -h can be used to obtain the list of valid values for each parameter.

The –diagnostics optional parameter prints diagnostic information, ignoring the other parameters.

> **NB:** In both the previous examples, the command line was executed from the folder containing the files. You can run them using a physical path, a relative path, or you can update your Windows Path Environment Variable to facilitate running the tools from other locations.

Interacting with the Oracle Policy Automation Hub

The latest versions of Oracle Policy Automation contain an administration tool to communicate with the Hub to upload or download models, or to configure the Hub from the command line. This and the following section are unique in this book as these tools are part of the *server* installation. However, their usefulness and the need, as a new Oracle Policy Automation user or consultant, to know that they exist, means you need to learn about them.

Their primary benefit is that building and deploying a Project becomes possible without Microsoft Windows, since the tool is available in both Windows and Unix formats.

Connecting to the Hub for Download

The command line tool is available in two forms, for Windows (`admin.cmd`) and for other platforms (`admin.sh`). Here is an example command line for a download.

```
admin.sh download_deployment -huburl=https://myserver/opa-hub –hubuser=richard
-hubpass=password -deployname="My Deployed Name" -version=6 -
deployzip="c:\data\CompleteDeployment.zip"
```

The Command Options

There are a large number of parameters; here is a list of them in more readable format, followed by a screenshot of a typical download command execution.

- The choice of `download_deployment` or `upload_deployment`.

- The URL of your OPA Hub (`-huburl`).

- The user used to connect (`-hubuser`).

- The password for that user (`-hubpass`).

- The name of the deployment to download (`-deployname`).

- The version of the deployment to download (`-version`).

- The name of the zip file to create (`-deployzip`).

The ability to automate the download and upload of deployed Policy Automation content is an important capability that allows customers to migrate rulebases from one environment to another.

Connecting to the Hub for Upload

The command is again available for Windows or other platforms, and the majority of the command line switches are the same. The following are the supplementary parameters, followed by an example of the typical output of an upload command.

- A message that is tagged to the deployment, visible in the Deployments list in the Oracle Policy Automation Hub (`-message="A message"`).

- The deployment will be activated immediately (`-activate`).
  - o If the deployment exists, this will replace the active version (`-confirmReplaceActive`).
  - o If the deployment does not exist, this will create it (`-confirmCreate`).
- `-version` is not used during an upload.

NB: In the above examples, the password is visible in the command line. Take the steps you need in order to ensure that such sensitive information is not visible to others.

Setting Parameters

The `admin.cmd` or `admin.sh` command line tool can also be used to set and read parameters of the Oracle Policy Automation Hub server, reset passwords, and more. Although similar in implementation to the previous examples, they are beyond the scope of this book. For more information, you can consult the System Administrator Guide online for the version you are working with.

The Batch Processor

This tool is also not part of the Oracle Policy Modeller installation, rather it is part of the ZIP file used to install the *server* applications. Nonetheless, it is such a useful feature that I decided to include it in this book.

Secondly, as is the case with the OPMMigrator, this is only relevant for Private Cloud installations. In the ZIP file downloaded from the Oracle Policy Automation Downloads page, extract the file called `determinations-batch.jar`.

The Batch Processor provides a way to run many hundreds or thousands of determinations using CSV files, as part of your testing process, for example.

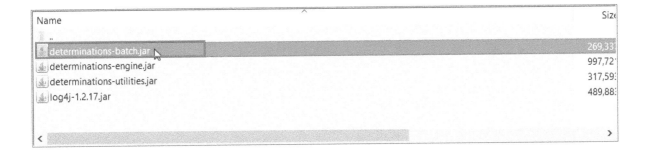

NB: The OPA Download page is currently at: http://www.oracle.com/technetwork/apps-tech/policy-automation/downloads/index.html

---

This file being a Java utility, the basic command line looks a little like the following example, and requires you to have at least the Java Runtime Environment installed on your computer and correctly configured so that it is available as part of your Windows Path.

```
java -jar determinations-batch.jar <command-line parameters>
```

Getting Started with Batch Processor

This utility requires a number of detailed parameters to be set and specified before it will work correctly, in addition of course to the data you are going to use in the form of a CSV file. To understand the process, we will walk through a simple example.

The Prerequisites to using the Batch Determination Utility

To use this utility, aside from the technical requirements mentioned above, the following are the practical steps needed, described in more detail in the coming paragraphs:

- Access to the ZIP file of the compiled Project you wish to use.

- Creation of an XML file to record the configuration information.

- Creation of a CSV file containing the inputs.

Access to the ZIP file of the compiled Project you wish to use

Since the Project will be executed by a runtime engine, and not by the Debugger of your Oracle Policy Modeller, you require only the ZIP archive file. This file can be found in the *output* folder of your Project.

Creation of an XML file to record the configuration information

Although it is possible to pass configuration information through the command line, it is easier and more efficient to create an XML file that contains all the information in one easy-to-edit structure, and pass that to the utility. As you will see in the next few pages, it is not always necessary to have this file in place.

Creation of a CSV file containing the inputs

Your goal is to execute multiple determinations, in a batch. So you need to prepare the data in a batch as a CSV file, or files if you have multiple entities, relations, and so on, that need to be provided as part of the input.

The XML file structure

The XML file contains all the parameters needed by the Batch Determination to understand what to do (for example, which ZIP file to use) and how to use it (for example, how the CSV file maps to the attributes in the Project definition).

The file can be saved as `config.xml` and placed in the same folder as the `JAR` file of the Batch Determination utility, in which case it will be read automatically.

Using a simple Project, we will execute a batch of determinations to see if candidates are accepted. If you plan on working through this example, be sure to check that attribute names and any entity names you use in the batch processing match exactly what you have in your Project.

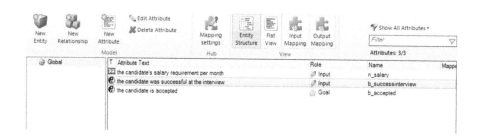

For the purposes of this test of the Batch Processor you will have only one simple rule in your Project:

the candidate is accepted if
      the candidate was successful at the interview and
      the candidate's salary requirement per month < 5000

With these items in place, here is how to use the Batch Processor, step by step. Begin by examining the configuration file example below, written in XML.

The XML Example File

```
<configuration>
<options>
<rulebase>CandidateExample.zip</rulebase>  (1)
<csv>c:\data\input</csv>  (2)
<output type="csv">c:\data\output</output>  (3)
</options>
<mappings>
<boolean-format true-value="Y" false-value="N"/>  (4)
<mapping entity="global" table="candidate" primary-key="#" primary-key-type=
"text">  (5)
<attribute name="n_salary" field="n_salary" output="false"/>
<attribute name="b_successinterview" field="b_successinterview" output="false"/>
<attribute name="b_accepted" field="b_accepted" output="true"/>  (6)
</mapping>
</mappings>
</configuration>
```

In the screenshot above, the following configuration information can be seen. This is just a small sample of the kind of information an XML configuration file might contain:

1. The name / location of the ZIP file, including a full path if not in the same folder as the Batch Determination executable file.

2. The location of the input folder where the CSV file(s) is to be found.

3. The location of the output folder where output will be saved.

4. The values to use when loading or saving Booleans, if they are not "true" and "false" or one of the other acceptable values.

5. The definition of an entity mapped to an input file ("table").

6. The definition of any attributes mapped to a column ("field") in the CSV file and whether they are input or output.

Mapping with Batch Determination by CSV

In a large Project, there will be a large number of CSV files and columns. For example, two entities each with 20 base attributes will make for a lot of mapping information in two separate files. However you can save a lot of time if you name your CSV files with the name of the Oracle Policy Automation entity (so, for example you would name one file candidate.csv and another jobs.csv if you had two entities in your Project).

The Input File

In our example, we are only using the Global Entity, and our XML file maps that to a CSV file called candidate.csv. In practice, you should use the attribute name as the header in the CSV file for each column. The following is a simple example CSV file.

	A	B	C	D	E
1	#	n_salary	b_successinterview	(b_accepted)	
2	1	4500	Y		
3	2	5000	N		
4	3	5050	Y		

In the picture above, note the following points:

1. The identifier column containing unique numbers to identify the candidates. This primary key can also be used in files that include relationships, such as many-to-many or one-to-many.

2. The Y replacing the standard accepted values, detailed in the example XML configuration file shown on the previous page. If we did not have this requirement, we could use one of the accepted value formats such as "YES" or "NO".

   Unformatted times, dates, and numbers are used; the complete list of accepted formats is available in the online documentation for Oracle Policy Automation Batch Processor.

3. The output column is surrounded by brackets.

As a general note, the column identifiers match the attribute *names* (not the attribute *text*), and you use relationship *names*, entity *names* instead of the associated text.

By using the guidelines above, you are building what are known as zero-configuration CSV files. In cases where the naming rules are followed and acceptable values used for Boolean, then the XML file becomes unnecessary. In the case of your simple test, you can maintain the XML file as practice.

Enter three rows of data into your input file, as follows, leaving the output column blank:

#	n_salary	b_successinterview	
1	4500	Y	
2	5000	N	
3	5050	Y	

Running the Batch Processor

With all the files (XML, CSV, and JAR) in place you are now ready to execute the Batch Processor from the Windows command line.

Command Line Parameters

To run successfully, the Batch Processor must be informed of the existence of an XML configuration if zero-configuration is not used. The command line parameter -config should be used as in:

```
Java -jar batch-processor.jar -config config.xml
```

The -config command line parameter is not required if your XML file is named config.xml. Other command line parameters include --rulebase which is required if the rulebase name is not included in a configuration file. Based on the work you have done so far, your command line will look something like the following, and hopefully the logged output will as well.

```
C:\data>java -jar determinations-batch.jar --config config.xml
Starting batch process
Master process started
Batch processor will process 3 cases
100% processed
Waiting for slave processors to finish
Finalising output
Processing completed. Total cases processed: 3. Total cases ignored: 0. Time taken: 0:00:01
```

In the screenshot, the three records are listed as having been processed successfully. Upon opening the output file that you will find in the appropriate folder, you should see something like this:

	A	B	C	D	E
1	#	n_salary	b_successinterview	(b_accepted)	
2	1	4500	Y	Y	
3	2	5000	N	N	
4	3	5050	Y	N	
5					

The output column has been filled in with the correct outcomes for the three cases you submitted.

Going Further

The Batch Processor is an enormously powerful tool, capable of running on multiple processors and handling many thousands of records. It is also capable of reading and writing to and from a database, and managing complex rulebases that contain relationships, inferred entities, and more.

As it is a server-side tool, you many not be able to access it directly, but in a book with a title such as this one, it is important to know that such a concept exists. You may even meet the Batch Processor in another area of Oracle Policy Automation, if you have access to the In-Memory Policy Analysis platform.

Later in this book, you will also learn about the different Web Services that can be used to interact with Oracle Policy Automation Projects; they include a Batch REST API.

Summary

Oracle Policy Modeling and Oracle Policy Automation come equipped with a variety of command line tools to help resolve the most common problems relating to management and control of installation, development, deployment, and migration of policies. Consultants need to be familiar with these tools to be ready to assist and advise how to best leverage their automation capabilities in a project environment.

OPA in Oracle Service Cloud

Deploying in Service Cloud

In this chapter, you will discover how to use the Oracle Policy Automation Cloud Service, along with Oracle Service Cloud Connections in your environment (see Chapter 10) in your Oracle Service Cloud application. There are different ways to deploy your Oracle Policy Automation Project and this chapter will look at them all.

Deploying to Oracle Service Cloud

There are several ways to deploy your rulebase within Oracle Service Cloud. The following pages will illustrate them. They can be broadly described as:

1. Deploying to a suitable page in the Customer Portal for *anonymous* use.

2. Configuring a known *contact* usage where the Customer must log in.

3. Configuring an integration within the *agent* application for internal use; for example, assisting a customer over the telephone.

Anonymous use in the Customer Portal

In our simple example, we are going to embed the interview from Oracle Policy Automation as a publicly accessible page in a mythical "portal" website. Customers will be able to browse the website anonymously, without in any way identifying themselves.

Build the Answer for the Customer Portal

1. Create a new Public Answer in Service Cloud as shown below.

2. In the Answer Tab, Source sub tab, specify the content using an IFRAME tag as shown below.

3. The IFRAME tag is of the format:

```
<iframe height="580" src="https://server/path/web-
determinations/startsession/RightNowSimple" width="100%"></iframe>
```

The `server/path` should be replaced with the values appropriate for your Oracle Policy Automation Cloud environment.

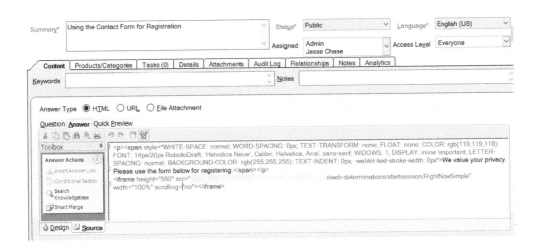

4. Save the Answer record. Make sure that the Answer you have created was using Source mode, as shown above (with the tab in the lower left corner selected) otherwise your IFRAME will not display correctly.

Verify the results in Oracle Service Cloud Consumer Portal

1. Search / Navigate to the Answer record in the Consumer Portal, as an anonymous user using the keyword or text that you entered when creating the Answer above.

Published Answers

Results 1 - 10 of 14

New Contact Registration

We always value your privacy. Please **use** the **form** below to register yourself as a new **contact** along with your marketing preferences.

2. View the details of this Answer and work with the Interview Session as normal. The result will be the same - the Contact is saved in your Service Cloud instance.

Now that you have been able to locate the relevant item in the knowledge base, you will be able to execute the Interview session by clicking on it, to display the IFRAME content discussed earlier.

How do I register as a new *contact* and input my Marketing Preferences?

We always value your privacy. Please *use* the *form* below to register yourself as a new *contact* along with your marketing preferences.

RightNowSimple ✓   New Contact Details ✎

New Contact Details   Back   Next

First name:

Last name:

NB: Instructions on how to upload the various files (PHP, CSS) for the sample OPA Widget, and how to place them on a page in the Customer Portal Development Area, are available in the documentation for your Oracle Service Cloud instance.

Publish the "Answer" to Service Cloud Portal for known contacts

It is also possible to embed an Oracle Policy Automation Rulebase into the Service Cloud Consumer Portal so that "known" (logged-in) contacts can use the Interview Session, launched in the context of the user. Thus, it is possible to pre-seed the Interview with the data from Oracle Service Cloud and, once the determination is completed in Oracle Policy Automation, save the data back into Service Cloud using the Service Cloud Connector described in Chapter 10.

Retrieve the Shared Secret used with the Service Cloud Connection

1. The shared secret can be obtained from the Service Cloud Connection administration page. This is used for the purposes of encrypting the URL parameter "user", as it is launched from within the Service Cloud Consumer Portal. If necessary, a new shared secret can be generated from within this admin page itself. More details can be found in Chapter 10.

Deploy and configure the sample OPA Widget in Service Cloud

2. The relevant artifacts (for OPA Cloud November 2016 Release) and the detailed instructions for installation can be found on the official documentation website at https://documentation.custhelp.com/euf/assets/devdocs/november2016/PolicyAutomation/en/Default.htm#Guides/Developer_Guide/Service_Cloud/Deploy_configure_OPA_sample_widget.htm .

3. Download and Save the file `Oracle_Policy_Automation_Cloud_Examples_Nov2016.zip` from https://documentation.custhelp.com/euf/assets/devdocs/november2016/PolicyAutomation/en/Content/Resources/Files/Oracle_Policy_Automation_Cloud_Examples_Nov2016.zip and unzip or extract the contents of the file to a local folder.

> **NB**: Bear in mind that both of these URLs will probably evolve over time.

4. Verify and, if required, enable the `MOD_CP_DEVELOPMENT_ENABLED` configuration setting for your Service Cloud Instance. This setting is most likely configured by the Oracle team, during the provisioning of your connected OPA Cloud Instance. If necessary, enable this setting under Configuration > Site Configuration > Configuration Settings and change the key value to Yes. This will enable you to work the next steps of configuration within the Customer Portal.

5. Upload the required files to your Oracle Service Cloud instance using any WebDAV client, using the following steps. Suitable tools include Cyberduck V4.4 (free, and recommended by Oracle), WinSCP and a Mapped Network Drive in Windows, to work with and explore the Customer Portal files available at the URL `https://<your_site>/dav`, using the WebDAV protocol.

> **NB**: For the sake of brevity, and to remain focused on Oracle Policy Automation, please refer to the Oracle Service Cloud documentation for the specific process (and best practices) to be followed when uploading the files.

Configure the relevant files

6. Configure/update the Shared Secret value into the file `...\customer-portal\widget\opa-helper.php` by placing it into the **$shared_secret** variable, using any plain text editor.

    a. You will observe from the highlighted code snippet below, that this "shared secret" is used to encrypt the user (contactID) parameter when is passed to the Interview Session through the launch URL. You don't really need to understand the code, just understand that you don't want important URL parameters, such as something that identifies a user, that are readable with the naked eye in a browser.

```
// SET THIS TO THE VALUE OBTAINED FROM OPA-HUB -> DATA SERVICE
$shared_secret = 'XXXXXXXXXXXXXXXXXXXXXXXXXXXXXXXXX'

if ($profile != null)
{

    $contactID = $profile->c_id->value;

    if($contactID > 0 && $shared_secret != '')
    {
        $ts = round(microtime(true) * 1000);
        $plaintext = $contactID . ";" . $ts . ";";
        $token = sha1($plaintext . $shared_secret);
        $security_params = "?user=" .$plaintext .$token

    }
```

b. For Oracle Service Cloud version November 2012 and later, you will need to use Customer Portal framework version 3 and work with different files:

- Upload the directory **OPAWidget** from customer-portal/widget/v3 to dav/cp/customer/development/widgets/custom/opa

- Upload the file opa-helper.php from customer-portal/widget to dav/cp/customer/development/helpers

---

NB: You must have incorporated the "shared secret" before uploading this file, in the same way as shown above.

---

7. Activate the OPA Widget using "Development Mode" in Service Cloud's Customer Portal administration page.

NB: To activate the Widget, you require sufficient permission to open the Customer Portal Administration site at https://<your_site>/ci/admin. You can access it through the "Links" menu or directly via URL

In the application menu bar, select Settings > Set Environment.

- Select Site Mode as **Development** and verify that you *are* actually browsing the development version of the customer portal:

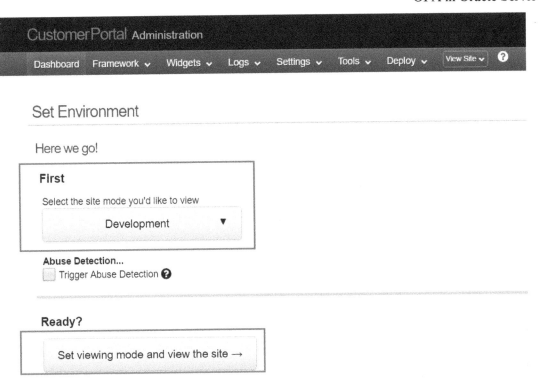

If you have been successful you should now clearly see that you are browsing the portal in development mode:

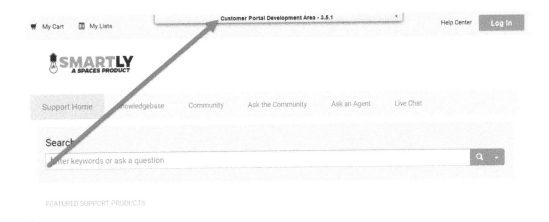

Activate the OPA Widget

Now, you are ready to activate the OPA Widget that you uploaded to your environment.

1. Navigate to the Custom Portal Admin Dashboard page.

2. In the menu bar, select Widgets > Browse Widgets.

3. On the Widgets page, select Custom Widgets, then opa, and then OPAWidget.

4. In the `custom/opa/OPAWidget` view, with version 1.1 selected, click the Activate this version button.

When activated without errors the version drop-down will change to 1.1 (currently in use). In the picture below you can see the 1.1 version is activated.

> **NB**: You will find it easier to use the search function highlighted below rather than scrolling through the myriad of widgets.

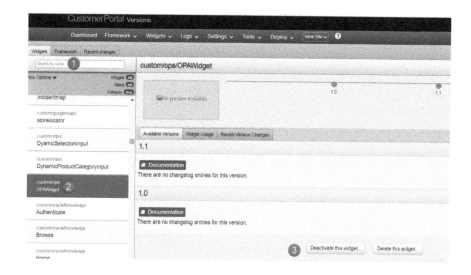

Insert the OPA Widget into the Customer Portal

1. Create a new Public Answer in Service Cloud as shown below.

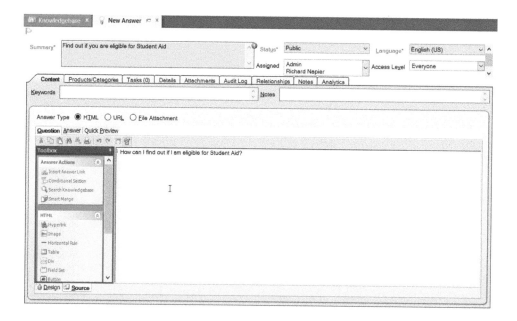

2. Select an appropriate Access Level on your site for this Answer, to ensure that only logged-in users will be able to access this answer from the customer portal. As implemented in the previous steps, a logged-in user is necessary. This will allow the OPA Widget, and your Oracle Policy Automation project, to use information about the logged-in Contact while launching the embedded OPA Interview Session.

3. Save the Answer record and note down the Record ID. We will use this Record ID to ensure that the OPA Widget is visible only when this particular answer is accessed by users in the customer portal. In our case, this ID is *134*.

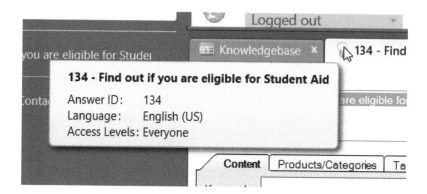

4. Edit the Answer Page design to conditionally include the OPAWidget. The page to be edited is called `detail.php` at the path `/dav/cp/customer/development/views/pages/answers`

5. I used Cyberduck and Notepad++ as the editor with the default character encoding as UTF-8. Cyberduck ensures that every save in the chosen editor was updated into the WebDAV development folder immediately, which is easier than trying to remember to upload the files yourself at the end of the editing session.

6. Include the following code snippet into the file. The recommended position is right after the **rn_AnswerText** `div` tag. In the user interface, the content of your Oracle Policy Automation Interview will be inserted right below the answer text. You must replace the answer ID as is relevant for your site / instance, and in the example below you can see I have changed it to number `134`, and the name of the OPA project whose interview I need to display is StudentBenefits.

```php
<?php if(getUrlParm('a_id') == 134) {?>
<rn:widget path="custom/opa/OPAWidget/"
web_determinations_url="
https://              .rightnowdemo.com/web-determina
policy_model="StudentBenefits"
locale="en-US"/>
<?php } ?>
```

7. Verify the results in Oracle Service Cloud Consumer Portal; note the logged-in user name appears in the Interview. Search / Navigate to the Answer record in the Consumer Portal, for the relevant Answer (in this case number 134).

Student Aid

Published 01/03/2017 12:20 AM | Updated 01/03/2017 12:48 AM

How to determine if I am eligible for Student Aid?

You can use the below wizard to determine if you are eligible for the Student Aid

| Eligibility | Student Details | Immigration Status | Education | Declarations | Conclusion |

Eligibility for Student Aid

H Richard

There are many grants, scholarships, loans and work-study programs available to help students throughout their university studies.

8. View the details of this Answer and work with the embedded Interview Session. You will observe that some of the contact information is pre-seeded as you work through the interview session and the final assessment / determination is saved back into Service Cloud.

The final Incident details are saved in Service Cloud from the Interview session as before.

NB: Please refer to the Oracle Service Cloud Documentation on how to promote these customizations to Staging and then to the Production areas of Service Cloud Customer Portal.

Embed an Oracle Policy Automation Interview in Service Cloud Agent Desktop

If the previous examples of embedding the Oracle Policy Automation Interview experience in the Customer Portal provided you with the capability to deliver better customer service to your end-customers in their Portal website, the Agent Desktop integration described in the next section allows you to provide the same kind of integration to your Contact Center users so they can leverage Oracle Policy Automation when working, for example, over the telephone with the customer.

Create a Custom Workspace (UI) in Service Cloud

If you do not already have a custom **Workspace** in Service Cloud, for the Contact record, you should create one from Configuration > Application Appearance > Workspaces / Workflows

In this example, you can create a custom workspace named `CustomContact` using the steps listed below.

- Copy the Standard Contact Workspace as `CustomContact` into the `Custom` Folder.

- Open this new `CustomContact` Workspace and add a new tab labelled `Student Benefits`

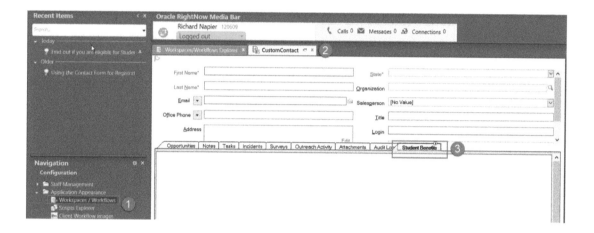

1. Drag and Drop the "OPA" control onto this new tab and specify the control properties that point to the deployed `StudentBenefits` rulebase, the chosen locale for the UI and the refresh behavior.

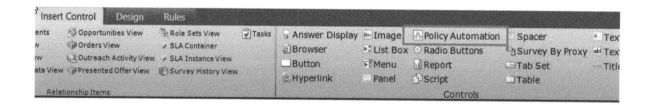

2. You should then configure the control, setting the Policy Model, Locale and the Refresh behavior, so that when a new record is created and saved in the Agent Desktop, the Interview shows correctly. When you have done that, save the Custom Workspace.

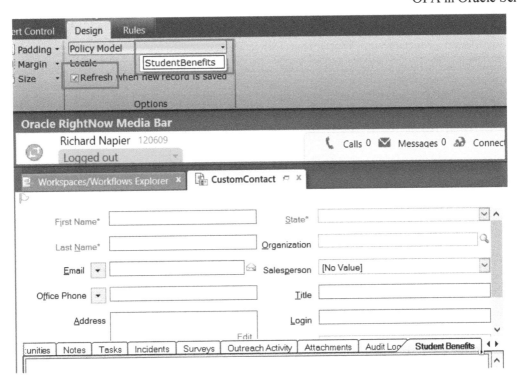

Assign the new CustomContact Workspace to a relevant user assignable Profile

If you added the Oracle Policy Automation Control to a new Workspace, then you will need to assign it to somebody, so that you can test it. If you added it to an existing Workspace you can skip this step and proceed to verify the results.

1. From Configuration > Staff Management.

2. Select Profiles.

3. Open the Profile which should provide access to our CustomContact Workspace.

4. Assign the new Workspace to the Contact record.

5. Click the Magnifying Glass icon to display the popup window and select the Workspace you created.

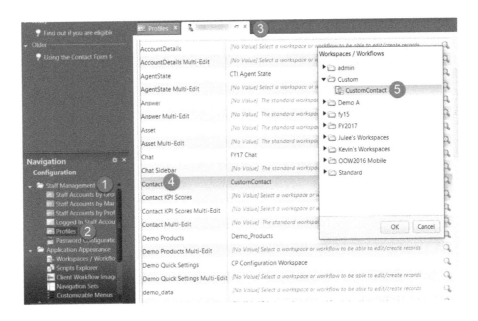

Verify the results in Oracle Service Cloud Agent Desktop UI

Now that the Profile has access to your Workspace, follow these steps to check you have been successful.

1. Login to the Agent Desktop as a user who is assigned the above Profile.

2. Search / Navigate to a known Contact record and navigate to the Student Benefits sub-tab that you added.

You are now able to work through the Oracle Policy Automation wizard and examine the results in the Service Cloud database.

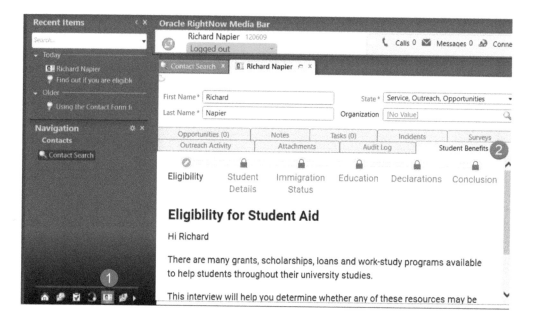

This demonstrates how the benefits of an Oracle Policy Automation rulebase and the included Interview screens can be made available for known Contacts / Users using the Service Cloud Agent Desktop.

Summary

Oracle Service Cloud provides many ways for customers to leverage their Oracle Policy Automation Cloud application through tight integration with scope for anonymous and credentialed users. Easy visual integration means that customers can focus on creating the business rules with Oracle Policy Automation Cloud they need, rather than writing code to meet requirements, and then leverage them in different ways in Oracle Service Cloud. End users are better satisfied as they receive appropriate information in a user-friendly way.

Web Services

Oracle Policy Automation Web Services

In this chapter, you will learn how the Oracle Policy Automation Determinations API gives you access to the functionality of your Rulebases without the need for an interview. The entire process can be driven via XML and standard SOAP Web Services. This chapter will also cover the REST Web Services available that facilitate the administration and deployment of Projects, and the management of your Oracle Policy Automation Hub.

Web Services – Before you Begin

This chapter assumes a basic knowledge of what a Web Service is. The content is aimed at technico-functional audiences; this means both business people and technical people can get value from it. Necessarily, the chapter does not cover all the different possibilities of Web Services, rather it aims to illustrate the following common scenarios

- Using the Assess Method of the Determinations API.
- Using the Answer Method of the Determinations API.
- Using the REST Hub Administration API.
- Using the REST Batch API.

This chapter also assumes, for the purposes of self-study, that you have installed and configured an Oracle Policy Automation Hub or have access to a Public Cloud instance, and that you have access to the following well-known software tools:

- Notepad ++ Freeware Source Code Editor (https://notepad-plus-plus.org/).
- SOAP UI Open Source Edition (https://www.soapui.org/downloads/soapui.html).
- Optionally, Postman App for REST API testing (https://www.getpostman.com/apps).

These are only suggestions and readers may wish to substitute these with other tools.

Determination Server API Overview

The Determinations Server API essentially provides programmers with Oracle Policy Automation Determinations as a Service. As a scalable, centrally-managed platform for accessing Policy goals, it has the advantage of being accessible by anyone or anything that can use HTTP(S) and XML.

Assess Method of the Determinations Server API

For the purposes of this exercise, you should create a simple Project that uses the following attributes if you would like to follow the steps. The content of the Project is extremely generic and designed to be easy to understand.

- An entity named the horse
- An attribute called the horse's status
- A Global attribute called the date of the race

To facilitate writing simple rules that are easy to read, make sure the Relationship text all the instances of the horse is changed to the horses.

Perhaps the most fundamental prerequisite for using the service is that all attributes, entities and relationships that you plan to access, must have **names** specified. This includes the relationship – you might use contracted versions of the actual text, such as `thehorses`. Recall, from earlier chapters, that the **name** is the XML tag used to identify each attribute or component of your Project.

The following rules were added. In an Excel table, the horses are instantiated using typical Entity inference as described earlier in this book.

the race is imminent	the horses	the horse's status
	Bucky	
FALSE	Zorro	"Resting"
	Bucky	
TRUE	Zorro	"Racing"

In the screenshot above, the single condition is used to create the entity instances. In a Microsoft Word document, the following rules are added to provide a Global outcome.

The race is imminent if
  DayDifference (<u>The date of the race</u>; the current date)> 3

You can now proceed to deploy your Project. In the screenshot below from the Oracle Policy Automation Hub application, note the following:

1. The interview checkbox has been deselected, to provide no HTML interface.

2. The Web Service checkbox has been selected, and the URL for the retrieval of the definition file is active.

3. The Apply button saves these changes.

Determinations API Permission

By default, users of the Oracle Policy Automation Hub and Modeller do not have permission to access the Determinations API. To ensure that the user you intend to work with has been set up correctly, verify the Permissions tab of the Oracle Policy Automation Hub and make sure the following checkbox is selected for the relevant user. If you are unsure of the navigation path to reach the User Permissions, refer to chapter 12 for more information.

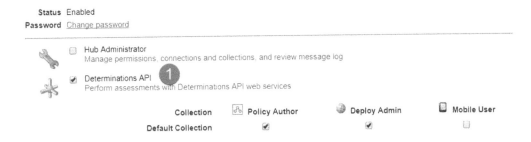

Obtaining the Web Service Definition File

Once the user has sufficient permissions, the Web Service Definition file can be acquired in order to test the service. Clicking the URL shown in the centre image on this page will display a list of URLs, once you have identified yourself with a username and password. Select the most recent version number and download the file.

Available Services for Web Service Demo

Assess Service

- /opa817/determinations-server/assess/soap/generic/11.0/Web_Service_Demo?wsdl
- /opa817/determinations-server/assess/soap/generic/12.0/Web__Service__Demo?wsdl
- /opa817/determinations-server/assess/soap/generic/12.2/Web__Service__Demo?wsdl
- /opa817/determinations-server/assess/soap/generic/12.2.1/Web__Service__Demo?wsdl

Now that you have acquired the necessary Service definition, you can use it to test your Rulebase in SOAP UI Open Source Edition.

Create Project for Determinations Web Service in SOAP UI

Using the screenshot below as a reference, click File > New SOAP Project in SOAP UI.

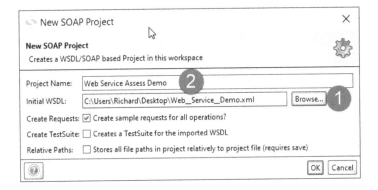

1. Browse to retrieve the file you saved in the previous step.

2. Name the Project something meaningful.

The SOAP UI utility will create sample requests for two different methods, namely `ListGoals` and `Assess` which together form the Service definition.

- `ListGoals` provides a list of top level outcomes provided by the Service.

- `Assess` allows the Rulebase to be actioned in XML.

ListGoals Request in SOAP UI

In order to test the functionality of the Project, you first must make some changes to the request that has been generated for you by SOAP UI. The changes are important as they reflect how the Assess Web Service is used in a real-life scenario. You will add an authentication header to the request.

Using SOAP UI, expand your Project and select the `Request 1` folder of the `ListGoals` method, as shown in the screenshot below.

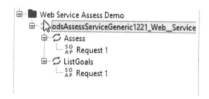

In the SOAP Header of the `ListGoals Request 1`, remove the following line and replace it.

```
<soapenv:Header/>
```

This is an example of the XML that should replace it. Use the correct username and password for your environment, of course.

```
<soapenv:Header>
    <o:Security xmlns:o="http://docs.oasis-open.org/wss/2004/01/oasis-200401-
wss-wssecurity-secext-1.0.xsd">
        <o:UsernameToken>
            <o:Username>XXX</o:Username>
            <o:Password Type="http://docs.oasis-open.org/wss/2004/01/oasis-
200401-wss-username-token-profile-1.0#PasswordText">XXXX</o:Password>
        </o:UsernameToken>
    </o:Security>
</soapenv:Header>
```

The request can now be started in SOAP UI. The response will appear in the window on the right-hand side. An example is displayed on the following page to guide you.

```
<soapenv:Envelope xmlns:soapenv="http://schemas.xmlsoap.org/soap/envelope/" xmlns:typ="http://oracle.com/determinations/server/12.2.1/rulebase/assess/types">
    <soapenv:Header>
        <o:Security xmlns:o="http://docs.oasis-open.org/wss/2004/01/oasis-200401-wss-wssecurity-secext-1.0.xsd">
            <o:UsernameToken>
                <o:Username>     </o:Username>
                <o:Password Type="http://docs.oasis-open.org/wss/2004/01/oasis-200401-wss-username-token-profile-1.0#PasswordText">     </o:Password>
            </o:UsernameToken>
        </o:Security>
    </soapenv:Header>
    <soapenv:Body>
        <typ:list-goals-request show-version="true"/>
    </soapenv:Body>
</soapenv:Envelope>
```

In the above, the request is ready for sending to the Determinations server. Notice that the `ListGoals` method has a small request body with only one attribute, `show-version`, which can be either true or false.

```
<SOAP-ENV:Envelope xmlns:SOAP-ENV="http://schemas.xmlsoap.org/soap/envelope/" xmlns:i18n="http://www.w3.org/2005/09/ws-i18n" xmlns:typ="http://oracle.com/dete
  <SOAP-ENV:Header>
    <i18n:international>
      <i18n:locale>en_US</i18n:locale>
      <i18n:tz>Etc/GMT</i18n:tz>
    </i18n:international>
  </SOAP-ENV:Header>
  <SOAP-ENV:Body>
    <typ:list-goals-response>
      <typ:version-info>                                              1
        <typ:deployment-version>1</typ:deployment-version>
        <typ:version-uid>281f89c1-493d-45dc-8470-f727b2824f50</typ:version-uid>
        <typ:build-time>2017-09-20T20:33:10Z</typ:build-time>
      </typ:version-info>
      <typ:entity entity-id="global">          2                3
        <typ:attribute id="3793c0bb-ba3c-4c5b-9736-fc922b419ce7" text="What is the cost of horse feed?" type="number"/>
      </typ:entity>
      <typ:entity entity-id="thehorse">          4
        <typ:attribute id="h_status" text="What is the horse's status?" type="text"/>
        <typ:attribute id="h_start" text="Is the horse ready to start?" type="boolean"/>
      </typ:entity>                              5
    </typ:list-goals-response>
  </SOAP-ENV:Body>
</SOAP-ENV:Envelope>
```

1. If you set the value to `true` as in the example, then the response will include version information and deployment dates and build time.

2. The global entity is displayed.

3. The attribute that is `the cost of the horse feed` does not have a name defined. This means a system-generated key is used instead. Any attributes or other elements you wish to manipulate in XML should have a *name* defined in the Oracle Policy Modelling application. This attribute is shown for educational purposes as your Project does not contain any attribute of this nature.

4. The entity the horse has a defined XML name `thehorse`.

5. The horse's status and readiness are the entity-level attributes that can be obtained by request with the Assess method.

> **TIP:** More examples of `ListGoals` and other Service methods can be found on https://theopahub.com

---

ListGoals Response

`ListGoals` is used to obtain a list of the entity and global goals in a Rulebase. Essentially, it allows the developer to discover what outcomes can be obtained for what objects. Once this information has been obtained, the `Assess` method can be used to actually obtain outcomes for specific data provided.

Assess Request in SOAP UI

Make the same changes to the header of the Request for `Assess` as you did in the previous example. All your requests must be authenticated, unless you have switched off authentication (which is most unlikely to be the case in a real world scenario).

Changing the Assess Request Body

Now that you have been able to obtain information about the goals in the Project, you will make an assessment request using actual data.

To make a simple `Assess` request using XML, the body of the request can be stripped down to a minimum of XML. Whilst the request will not be as complex as an example generated by SOAP UI, it will be a fully functional example of the Assess method.

In the next image, notice the following elements:

1. The outcome section is used to describe how the outcome of the request will be presented. In this case, the horse entity is included, and the two attributes are requested to be **value-only**.

2. In the main section, the Global attribute `race_date` is entered using the standardized date format. This constitutes the only input being provided.

```
/soapenv:Header>
   <soapenv:Body>
      <typ:assess-request>
         <typ:config>
            <typ:outcome>
               <typ:entity id="thehorse">
                  <typ:attribute-outcome id="horse" outcome-style="value-only"/>
                  <typ:attribute-outcome id="h_status" outcome-style="value-only"/>
               </typ:entity>
            </typ:outcome>
         </typ:config>
         <typ:global-instance>
            <typ:attribute id="race_date" >
               <typ:date-val>2017-09-20</typ:date-val>
            </typ:attribute>
         </typ:global-instance>
      </typ:assess-request>
   </soapenv:Body>
</soapenv:Envelope>
```

Assess Response

Upon starting the request, a valid response should be returned in the SOAP UI utility. An annotated example is shown below, based on the Project example used so far.

```
<SOAP-ENV:Body>
   <typ:assess-response>
      <typ:global-instance>
         <typ:attribute id="race_date" type="date">
            <typ:date-val>2017-09-20</typ:date-val>
         </typ:attribute>
         <typ:entity id="thehorse" inferred="true">
            <typ:instance id="0x5536fa10c4186418">
               <typ:attribute id="horse" type="text" inferred="true">
                  <typ:text-val>Bucky</typ:text-val>
               </typ:attribute>
               <typ:attribute id="h_status" type="text" inferred="true">
                  <typ:text-val>Racing</typ:text-val>
               </typ:attribute>
            </typ:instance>
            <typ:instance id="0x98067f5980814a79">
               <typ:attribute id="horse" type="text" inferred="true">
                  <typ:text-val>Zorro</typ:text-val>
               </typ:attribute>
               <typ:attribute id="h_status" type="text" inferred="true">
                  <typ:text-val>Racing</typ:text-val>
               </typ:attribute>
            </typ:instance>
         </typ:entity>
      </typ:global-instance>
   </typ:assess-response>
</SOAP-ENV:Body>
```

1. The date value you entered is shown.

2. The horse entity instances are described according to the outcome of the Project (refer to the Excel spreadsheet shown earlier to review the rules used).

3. The values of the entity attributes are provided. No detail is provided. They have been inferred by your Project.

Assess Outcome Style

In your first request, you set outcome style to `value-only`. Two other choices are possible, both of which provide more detailed information in their response.

Base-Attributes

- Change the outcome style for the horse `status` to `base-attributes`, replacing `value-only` using the image at the top of this page as your guide.

- Run the request again.

You should notice the response contains more information. Specifically, the race date is referenced as the attribute needed for the status of the horse to be correctly inferred. An example is shown below. The indented XML shows the date was the base attribute which contributed to the horse status being set to `Racing`.

```
        <typ:attribute id="h_status" type="text" inferred="true">
    I    <typ:text-val>Racing</typ:text-val>
          <typ:decision-report report-style="base-attributes">
             <typ:attribute-node id="dn:2" entity-id="global" instance-
                 <typ:date-val>2017-09-20</typ:date-val>
             </typ:attribute-node>
          </typ:decision-report>
       </typ:attribute>
```

Decision-Report

The final choice of the outcome style is decision-report. Replace the XML tag value as before, this time with `decision-report` and rerun the request a third time. The output should be more verbose, since it now contains the detailed decision report for the horse status.

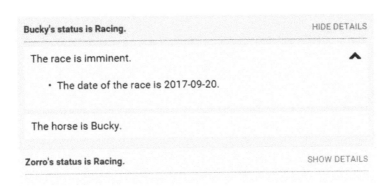

```
1
  <typ:text-val>Racing</typ:text-val>
 <typ:decision-report report-style="decision-report">
    <typ:attribute-node id="dn:0" entity-id="thehorse" instance-id="0xd52d03975507d
       <typ:text-val>Racing</typ:text-val>
       <typ:attribute-node id="dn:1" entity-id="global" instance-id="global" hypoth
         <typ:boolean-val>true</typ:boolean-val>
        <typ:attribute-node id="dn:2" entity-id="global" instance-id="global" hyp
           <typ:date-val>2017-09-20</typ:date-val>
        </typ:attribute-node>
      </typ:attribute-node>
      <typ:attribute-node id="dn:3" entity-id="thehorse" instance-id="0xd52d039755
         <typ:text-val>Bucky</typ:text-val>
         <typ:already-proven-node id="dn:1"/>
      </typ:attribute-node>
    </typ:attribute-node>
 </typ:decision-report>
```

Decision Report and Explanations

The arrow highlights the area of the XML response that contains the report on how the decision was reached. In this case, the horse has a status of `Racing` because the race is imminent (the `true` value shown) and the date of the race was used to decide if the race was imminent or not.

Although not easy to read, at first, this structure is a logical tree very similar to the **explanations** you see at the end of an HTML Interview. Here is the same Project shown as an Interview for reference.

Bucky's status is Racing.	HIDE DETAILS
The race is imminent.	⌃
• The date of the race is 2017-09-20.	
The horse is Bucky.	
Zorro's status is Racing.	SHOW DETAILS

The Answer Service

The Answer Service is only available for Oracle Policy Automation Projects that load or save data via a Connection. If you need a refresher as to what a Connection is, refer to chapter 10.

Obtaining the Answer Web Service Definition

The process to obtain the definition file is identical to that for the Assess Service. The file can then be loaded into SOAP UI as a new SOAP Project in exactly the same way. The structure of the SOAP request is different, however, given the need to comply with the structure of the Connection that the Project is expecting to use.

The Answer Service Methods

GetInputDataDefinition

This method provides a list of the input data required to use the Project. The input data listed will be in the Oracle Policy Automation format, not the format of the external application that has connected to this Project. This method can be useful to understand what work will have to be done in the external application to map external data. An example is shown next, where the Project has three fields in one table.

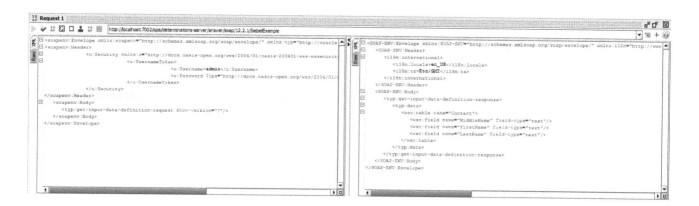

GetAnswer Method

The `GetAnswer` method, as its name suggests, allows the caller of the Web Service to obtain the output from the Project. The request must provide the data structure corresponding to the needs of the Project, which you normally have acquired from the `GetInputDataDefinition` method as described in the previous paragraph.

It can be useful to use this method to test sending data to Oracle Policy Automation according to the defined structure but in the absence of the application that is supposed to send the data (perhaps the application is offline or not yet available), and you wish to test the Web Service in the meantime.

Below is a simple example of the `GetAnswer` Method in SOAP UI, being tested. In the screenshot, note the data in the input conforms to the output of the previous method.

The Interview Service

The Interview Service shares one method with the Answer Service, `GetInputDataDefinition`. The other methods of this Web Service are dedicated to providing *developers* with the necessary functionality to create their own Interview user interface using whatever platform (Java, Silverlight, Android app development) they choose.

Since this service is dedicated to providing the means to create an external user interface, most of the method requests and responses will use not only the *data* definition but also the **screens**, **controls** and interview status (complete, on the first page, on the last page, navigation forwards or backwards and so on).

The process to obtain the definition file is identical to that for the Assess Service. The file can then be loaded into SOAP UI as a new SOAP Project in exactly the same way. The structure of the SOAP request is different, however, given the specific goal of this technical Web Service.

The Interview Service Methods

The interview service includes the following:

GetInputDataDefinition

This method works in the same way as in the Answer Service, for Interviews that leverage a Connection.

StartInterview

This method starts the interview with data, and returns an XML rendition of the screen and controls that the Interview should display as the first page. The developer can parse this output and transform it into whatever interface they choose.

In the screenshot below, notice the following points:

1. Almost all the functionality of the Interview service is focused on the user interface. Thus, the screen id is displayed here. A developer can choose to render this screen in whatever programming language they desire.

2. The Interview is composed of stages, which are referenced here along with information about whether the screen has been visited before in this interview, and so on.

3. Each control corresponds to one item of information to be edited or viewed by the user.

> **NB**: The `StartInterview` method returns an HTTP Session Id, which the developer must use in subsequent calls in respect of the same interview session.

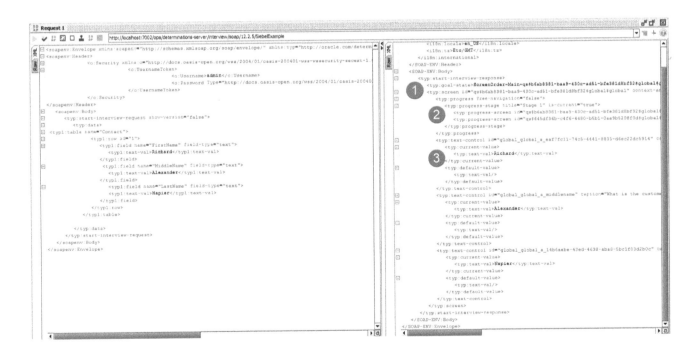

The response to the `StartInterview` method also contains a Session Id, visible in SOAP UI highlighted on the right.

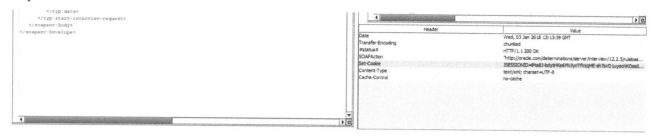

Investigate

This method is called repeatedly, in order to find out if data entered by the user in the screen has caused any goals to be met or attribute values to change (for example, the custom user interface provided by the developer lets the user enter their name and press the Next button. The `investigate` method might return the next relevant screen and content).

There are several different ways to call this method, relating to forward or backward navigation, or to the addition of data to the session. In all cases, however, as mentioned above, the request should be accompanied by the relevant Session Id retrieved from the `StartInterview` response, as shown below.

GetFiles

The developer may wish to provide a custom user interface to allow the interviewee to attach files. This method encodes the files for storage in the data source defined in the Connection.

GetSessionData & SetSessionData

These methods obtain or set the data for the Interview session, comprising the tables and columns and associated data defined for the global entity instance, as well as contained entities and their attributes and relationships.

SnapshotSession & RestoreSession

These methods allow the developer to provide save and resume functionality if the Connection used in the Interview supports it (for more information see the example in chapter 20 in reference to Siebel. Note that this functionality is also referred to as a **Get and Set Checkpoint**).

EndInterview

This method ends the interview session using the Session Id obtained in the `StartInterview` method.

A Real-life example of the Interview Service

As you probably have realized, implementing a new User Interface for Oracle Policy Automation is a complex task undertaken by developers. Hopefully this brief overview lets you understand the functionality provided.

The Interview Service can be seen in action if you have deployed the Oracle Siebel CRM Innovation Pack 15 integration with Oracle Policy Automation 12. In that specific example, the User Interface is (re)built using Siebel CRM Open UI JavaScript, rather than the standard Oracle Policy Modelling HTML interface.

Oracle Policy Automation REST Services

Starting with the August 2017 release, Oracle Policy Automation provides access to a variety of administrative features through a REST interface. The access to these features is through a specific user type, known as an integration user. Integration users must access the REST API using **OAuth2 tokens**.

REST API resources might form part of your automation strategy; by using the different resources at your disposal you can extract, detail and modify information about users and deployments. Whatever you use it for, first you should create an **Integration User** with special permissions to clearly limit access.

Implementing an Integration User

The Oracle Policy Automation Hub allows for the creation of an integration user, with permissions to access the REST API for user management and deployments. The screenshot below highlights the option in the Actions menu and provides an example. Note the integration user has several checked options relating to REST API.

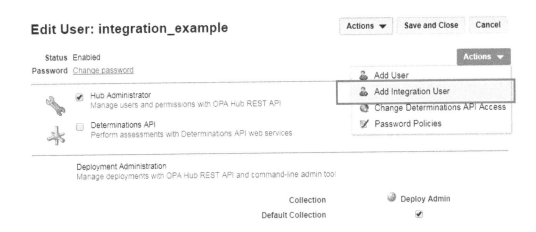

Once the user has been created, then you can begin implementing processes and scripts that leverage this special user in order to automate common tasks such as creating users, downloading and uploading Projects (potentially, therefore, moving Projects from one environment to another), and other features provided by the REST API.

> **NB**: To use the Batch Assessment REST API, the Determinations API check-box should also be checked. This feature may be license-based, so check with your accredited account representative before attempting to use it.

In the following examples, SOAP UI will be used to demonstrate some of the core functionality. To follow these examples, ensure you have an Oracle Policy Automation Hub running, an integration user set up as in the previous example, and that you begin by selecting File > New REST Project. Enter the URL shown below, with (of course) modifications to reflect your own server and port.

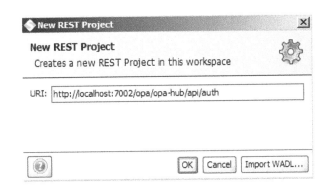

Obtaining OAuth2 Authorisation

Before using any of the different REST API functions, it is necessary to obtain an Access Token. With your new REST project open in SOAP UI, click the Auth button on the base of the main Window.

Using the screenshot below, refer to the different steps to configure the authorisation request.

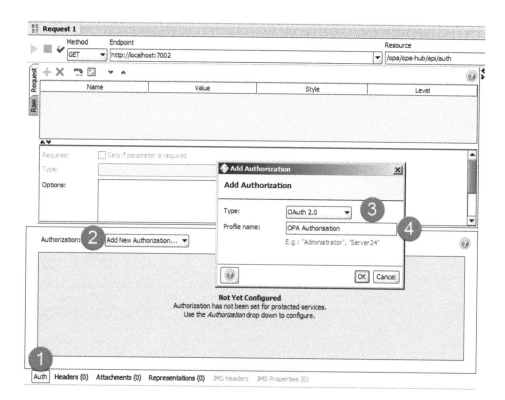

1. Click the Auth button.

2. Select Add New Authorisation…

3. Select OAuth 2.0.

4. Give your Authorisation a friendly Profile Name.

Once you have clicked OK, the second stage will appear. Now that you have specified the type of Authorization, you must provide credentials to access the relevant service. Select Get Token.

As before, in the following screenshot refer to the bullet points detailed underneath.

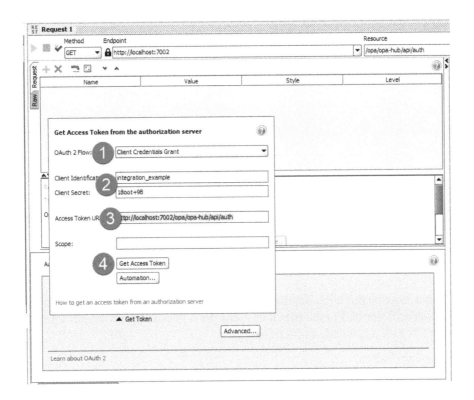

1. Choose the Client Credentials Grant option. With the Oracle Policy Automation REST API, a client (you) can provide credentials in order to be granted access.

2. Enter the username and password for your integration user (created earlier in this chapter).

3. Enter the URL of your server as before, complete with the /api/auth element.

4. Click the Get Access Token button.

If you have been successful in getting this far, you should now have an Access Token.

1. The token should display in the manner shown below.

2. You are now free to access any of the other resources provided by the REST API.

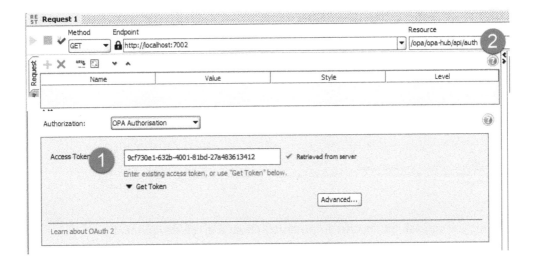

This introduction does not intend to show you, in detail, every single call that is possible using the REST API. Full documentation is available at the following URL (you may need to replace the reference to "august2017" with the version you are working with):

http://documentation.custhelp.com/euf/assets/devdocs/august2017/PolicyAutomation/en/Default.htm#Guides/Developer_Guide/Administration/Overview_Hub_REST_API.htm

Working with Users

The REST API has three basic areas of functionality. For example, you can view and manipulate users, as part of an automated documentation or administration strategy. An example is shown below.

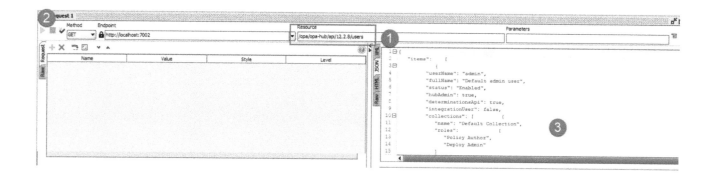

1. The resource must match the URL details provided in the documentation, and you must have acquired an Access Token as described in the previous steps. In this example, we simply list users. This resource is the base URL for all user-related functionality.

2. Click the green Run button.

3. Observe the formatted output. Make sure you select JSON in the list of tabs on the left hand side of the window.

Working with Deployments

In the same fashion as the users listed above, the REST API allows you to access details about deployments or a specific deployment. For example, the following screenshot shows a list of deployed Projects on the Hub. Make sure that when you call this service, you have checked the resource URL for your version. The resource URL can be edited in the zone highlighted in red.

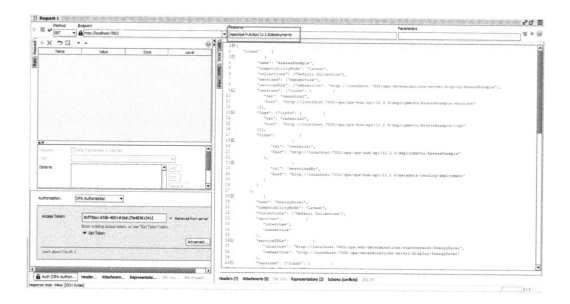

In the same fashion, you can ask for specific information about a given deployment:

1. The resource URL contains the name of a specific deployment.

2. The returned detailed information can be parsed for further study.

Working with Batch Assessments

The third form of REST API available in Oracle Policy Automation is the Batch Assessment API.

Essentially a wrapper for the Assess Service you saw earlier, customers who have purchased the necessary licenses for this module can launch batch assessments of their Projects using the REST API.

The same process as shown earlier is used to obtain an **Access Token**. Although there are several different ways to work with this programming interface, for demonstration purposes you will launch a number of data sets as a *batch*. This example will use a simple Project with only one **outcome**, and just a small number of input attributes. This example calculates whether a person caught speeding should lose their license based on a variety of simplistic criteria. The outcome is a Boolean attribute, and the input is represented by a series of text and number attributes such as the speed, and the nature of the road, and so on. In JSON format, the input data for your request to the Batch Assessment might look something like this:

```
{
    "outcomes" : [
        "boolloselicense"
    ],
    "cases" : [
        {
            "@id" : 1,
            "driverspeed" : 120,
            "driverlocation" : "on urban district street",
            "gender" : "male",
            "drivername" : "Stirling"

        },
        {
            "@id" : 2,
            "driverspeed" : 130,
            "driverlocation" : "on urban district street",
            "gender" : "female",
            "drivername" : "Janet"
        }
    ]
}
```

The order of the information shown is important when sending it to the Batch Processor. In the following screenshot, each bullet is accompanied by some explanatory text to describe how to use this information to run a Batch Assessment.

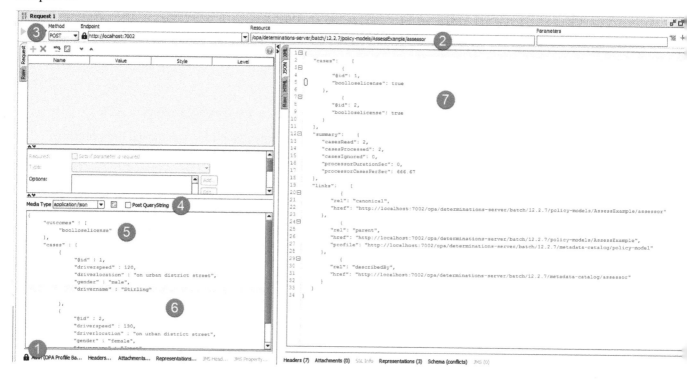

1. An Access Token is required, as shown earlier in this chapter.

2. The resource URL is unique to the Batch Assessment REST API, and contains the name of the Project you wish to execute in Batch mode.

3. The `POST` method must be selected.

4. The Request must be of type `application/json` and pasted into the area shown.

5. Outcome(s) are specified first.

6. Data sets (of which there may be many in a batch) are specified next.

7. When the green arrow is clicked, the response in JSON format will list the data sets or cases and the outcome for each case.

Accessing the REST Services

In order to access the REST services, developers can either use SOAP UI for simple tests as in this chapter, or can implement their own code using whatever platform they are familiar with.

For example, in the screenshot on the following page, Microsoft Visual Basic is used to call the REST service and supply a username and password, and retrieve the Access Token which is required for all further interaction with the REST services, in conformity with the OAuth2 mechanism.

```vbnet
Function GetCredentials(username, password, site) As String
    ' Build the URL
    Dim URI As String = site & "auth?"
    Dim querystring As StringBuilder = New StringBuilder
    querystring.Append("grant_type=client_credentials&")
    querystring.Append("client_id=" + username + "&")      ①
    querystring.Append("client_secret=" & password)

    URI = URI + querystring.ToString
    'Prepare the POST
    Dim req As WebRequest = WebRequest.Create(URI)          ②
    req.Method = "POST"
    ' Add parameters to post
    req.ContentType = "application/json"
    req.ContentLength = 0
    Dim data() As Byte = Encoding.ASCII.GetBytes("")
    Dim os As Stream = req.GetRequestStream
    os.Write(data, 0, 0)
    os.Close()
    'Do the post and get the response.
    Dim resp As WebResponse = req.GetResponse             ③
    If (resp Is Nothing) Then
        Return Nothing
    End If
    Dim sr As StreamReader = New StreamReader(resp.GetResponseStream)
    Dim stringoutput = sr.ReadToEnd
    'extract access token from the response
    Dim tempPost = New With {Key .access_token = ""}       ④
    Dim token = JsonConvert.DeserializeAnonymousType(stringoutput, tempPost)
    Return token.access_token    ⑤
End Function
```

1. The service URL is constructed out of a series of elements (`site`, `client_id` and `client_secret`) presented to the user.

2. The Web Request is prepared and formatted correctly as an HTTP POST.

3. The Web Response is obtained and checked for content.

4. The Access Token is extracted from the response in JSON format.

5. The Access Token, now in string format, is returned.

As a further example, using the Administration REST API, it is possible to retrieve the ZIP file containing a deployed Project, and save it programatically (perhaps prior to migrating it to another environment).

```vbnet
Dim querystring As StringBuilder = New StringBuilder
URI = URI + querystring.ToString
Dim req As HttpWebRequest = HttpWebRequest.Create(URI)
req.Headers.Add("Authorization", "Bearer " & GetCredentials(username, password, site))
req.Accept = "application/zip"  ①
req.Method = "GET"
req.ContentLength = 0
Dim resp As WebResponse = req.GetResponse  ②
If (resp Is Nothing) Then
    Return Nothing
End If
Dim memStream As MemoryStream
Using rdr As System.IO.Stream = resp.GetResponseStream
    Dim count = Convert.ToInt32(resp.ContentLength)
    Dim buffer = New Byte(count) {}
    Dim bytesRead As Integer
    Do
        bytesRead += rdr.Read(buffer, bytesRead, count - bytesRead)
    Loop Until bytesRead = count
    rdr.Close()
    memStream = New MemoryStream(buffer)
End Using
'Folder must exist
Using filestrm As FileStream = New FileStream("c:\temp\" & deployment & ".zip", FileMode.Create)
    memStream.WriteTo(filestrm)  ③
End Using
Return "File Downloaded to temp folder"
Function
```

1. The request asks for a ZIP file.

2. The response is obtained.

The response is converted from Base 64 into a physical file and saved to the disk of the user.

Swagger

Development teams often use tools such as Swagger to document and expose information about REST-based application programming interfaces. Both the Batch and the Deployment REST services provide swagger files, which can be imported into Swagger editor for a concise view of all the resources and methods available.

Note that this feature, and the amount of information returned, will be affected by the Oracle Policy Hub settings in respect of Determinations API access. If no authentication is required, or if a valid authorization is sent with the request, then the full document will be received. If authentication is not sent, an abridged document is sent.

Below, you can see an example screenshot from a locally installed Swagger Edit, after the import of the Batch API swagger file. The URL is based on the installation of your Oracle Policy Automation server applications and will be structured as follows: https://X/determinations-server/batch/Y/swagger.json where X represents the root of your installation and port number, and Y represents a valid version number such as 12.2.7.

1. Click File > Import URL and enter the URL of the service.

2. The raw contents of the Swagger definition are displayed.

3. You can provide an authorization token (using the method described in this chapter) directly here.

4. You can review any parameters and output description.

5. You can test any service method by clicking Try it Out.

> **NB**: As a useful byproduct of using Swagger, it will also generate CURL commands which you can use, and any output can be downloaded and saved to your hard disk for reference.

Other Ways to Consume Web Services

The breadth of Oracle Corporation's Cloud strategy means that customers now have many ways to consume Oracle Policy Automation Web Services. The most notable example thereof is the Oracle Integration Cloud Service.

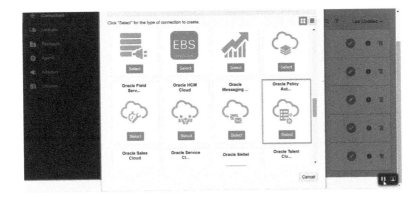

Amongst the myriad different connection possibilities, Oracle Policy Automation integrations can be created using an intuitive drag and drop interface.

Summary

The various Web Services and interfaces of Oracle Policy Automation facilitate integration into the wider information technology environment at you, or your customers' sites. By permitting access to both Metadata and Data services, designers can build Policy Modelling Projects that map directly to third-party applications and developers can integrate Oracle Policy Automation into their on-premise and Cloud applications.

Administrators can implement automation to build easy-to-use interfaces to help create users, deploy Projects, run test cases, and more, using the REST API.

OPA in Oracle Siebel

Deploying in Oracle Siebel

In this chapter, you will discover how to use Oracle Policy Automation with Oracle Siebel CRM. Since Oracle Siebel CRM is primarily an on-premise solution, the integration style is slightly different to that described in the previous chapter.

Given that this book is dedicated to Oracle Policy Automation and not to Oracle Siebel CRM, this chapter will concentrate on highlighting the basic concepts in order to familiarise you with the architectural elements and the overall process. This will be very useful if you are working on a project that has both Oracle Siebel CRM and Oracle Policy Automation. It will not, however, go into the technical details of how to code the different elements of the solution.

Siebel CRM Versions

At the time of writing, Siebel Innovation Pack 16 was the most widely deployed in production, so this chapter references this version. Siebel CRM Innovation Pack 15 uses a different integration technique involving similar concepts. Later versions of Siebel such as Innovation Pack 17 or Siebel 2018 can use the methods shown here.

Siebel CRM Connection Architecture

Every Connection that you build (whether it be for Siebel CRM or another application) will handle some or all of the following communication methods. In the case of Siebel CRM, each of them will typically be handled by a Workflow Process. Much of the Workflow Process structure will be generic, encouraging reuse and reducing configuration overheads when you add new Connections; however, methods such as `Load` and `Submit` will typically need to be configured for the specific entities you intend to send or receive.

Let's take a moment to review the core services needed for a Connection, as defined by the Connector Framework. Broadly they can be divided into two parts:

Metadata Services

CheckAlive
This generic Method is a communications "Ping" to inform Oracle Policy Automation that your Connection to Siebel is alive.

The example Siebel Workflow Process is entirely generic and can be reused for each Connection you implement.

Connections that respond successfully to the CheckAlive are shown with a Green Tick in the Connections list.

GetMetaData

This step, specific to your chosen Siebel Integration Object (the equivalent of an entity hierarchy in OPA), returns to Oracle Policy Automation an abstraction of your Siebel data model so that Rule Designers can map their Attributes and Entities to the corresponding Siebel concepts.

Rule Designers see your Metadata in their Modeller when they select your Connection. Recall that these steps are covered in chapter 10.

The GetMetaData service is used in many different places in both Oracle Policy Modeling and during integrations, in order to verify the data model of the external system.

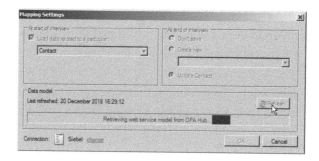

For example – as shown above – clicking the Refresh button on the Mapping Settings dialog calls GetMetaData to refresh the model.

Data Services

Load

`Load` calls Siebel, providing an identifier, and Siebel queries its database. The resulting data is reformatted according to the Oracle Policy Automation definition and sent back so that the information retrieved can be displayed or manipulated in Oracle Policy Automation by your rules.

This is known in Oracle Policy Modelling as **Inbound Mapped, Load at Start**.

Submit

`Submit` sends data back to Siebel for updating. In Oracle Policy Modelling, this equates to **Outbound Mapped**, and sends data back to Siebel.

Once the update is complete, Siebel may send back notification to confirm that the data has been received. This can be displayed in Oracle Policy Automation. Attributes in Oracle Policy Modelling set up in this way are said to use **Inbound Mapped, Load After Submit.** This allows the Interview designer to display the value of an attribute on the Screen following a Submit.

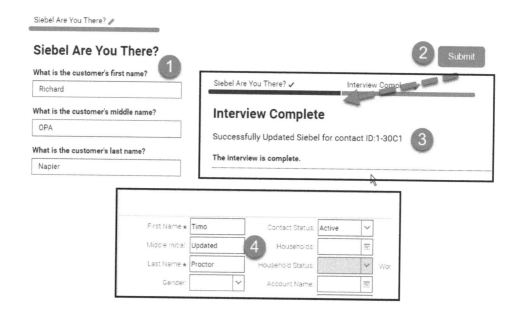

In the example shown above, the following points illustrate a simple example of mapping.

1. When the Interview starts, some attributes are Inbound mapped, Load at Start. The information is displayed in the relevant Screen controls. The user can update some of the attributes and proceed in the Interview.

2. The user navigates through the Screens and clicks Submit.

3. An attribute is set to Inbound Mapping, Load after Submit. The Siebel integration populates this attribute and it is displayed to the user after the Submit.

4. The Siebel CRM application has been updated with the changes made in the Interview.

Optional Services

ExecuteQuery

`ExecuteQuery` performs a supplementary query on demand during an Interview. For example, when an Interview requests reference data to display certain products. This is subject to limitations on the query type and the volume of data. The configuration of an entity to support this functionality is explained in chapter 13. From a technical standpoint, the ExecuteQuery is very similar to the Load service.

SetCheckPoint

This method will store an Interview snapshot in Siebel for recovery later and continuation. The data is stored in Base 64 encoded string format. Note that `SetCheckPoint` requires a table and columns in your Siebel CRM database to store these strings. Other applications can support these services if they implement a storage area for the checkpoint information.

GetCheckPoint

This method retrieves a session data string from Siebel and opens the Interview with the saved input data already in place, ready to continue the process.

Designing interviews with CheckPoints

As described in earlier chapters, the Rule designer sees the **CheckPoint** capability in the Modeller when building the Interview. Get and Set checkpoints are not required for a Connection to work correctly. In the screenshot shown below, the Checkpoints option is available because Oracle Policy Modelling has opened a Project with a valid Connection that supports these concepts. The designer can select how and when checkpoints will be saved to Siebel (or another application).

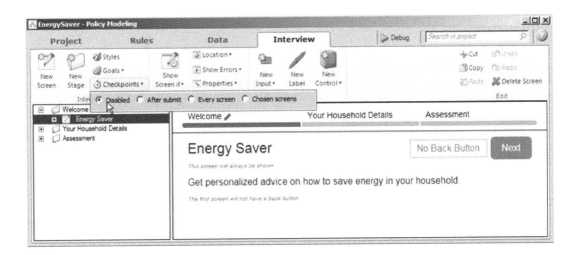

The checkpoint information is stored in the data source serviced by the Connector. In the case of Siebel CRM, developers will need to ensure a table and Business Component is available to receive this information.

To resume an Interview from a checkpoint, the Interview URL changes from a standard http://server:port/opa/web-determinations/startsession/ProjectName?id=1234 to http://server:port/opa/web-determinations/resumesession/EnergySaver?id=1234 This example assumes that the checkpoint is first created in the `startsession` URL and then recalled later using the `resumesession` URL.

The example below shows a typical Siebel database table and the stored Session Id. The `DECISION_TEXT` column contains the encoded checkpoint information.

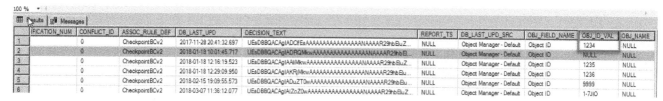

	IFICATION_NUM	CONFLICT_ID	ASSOC_RULE_DEF	DB_LAST_UPD	DECISION_TEXT	REPORT_TS	DB_LAST_UPD_SRC	OBJ_FIELD_NAME	OBJ_ID_VAL	OBJ_NAME
1		0	Checkpoint BCv2	2017-11-28 20:41:32.697	UEsDBBQACAgIADOfEsAAAAAAAAAAAAANAAAAR29hbBuZ...	NULL	Object Manager - Default	Object ID	1234	NULL
2		0	Checkpoint BCv2	2018-01-18 10:01:45.717	UEsDBBQACAgIADRQMkwAAAAAAAAAAAAANAAAAR29hbEl...	NULL	Object Manager - Default	Object ID	NULL	NULL
3		0	Checkpoint BCv2	2018-01-18 12:16:19.523	UEsDBBQACAgIAAlIMkwAAAAAAAAAAAAANAAAAR29hbEuZ...	NULL	Object Manager - Default	Object ID	1235	NULL
4		0	Checkpoint BCv2	2018-01-18 12:29:09.950	UEsDBBQACAgIAAKRjMkwAAAAAAAAAAAAANAAAAR29hbElu...	NULL	Object Manager - Default	Object ID	1236	NULL
5		0	Checkpoint BCv2	2018-02-15 19:09:55.573	UEsDBBQACAgIADuZT0wAAAAAAAAAAAAANAAAAR29hbElu...	NULL	Object Manager - Default	Object ID	9999	NULL
6		0	Checkpoint BCv2	2018-03-07 11:36:12.077	UEsDBBQACAgIAlZcZ0wAAAAAAAAAAAAANAAAAR29hbBuZ...	NULL	Object Manager - Default	Object ID	1-7JIO	NULL

> **NB**: Customers who migrate from the Siebel / Oracle Policy Automation 10 integration will already have such a table in their database. Other customers will need to either create it from scratch, or use the table provided in the version 10 integration as an example.

Using Oracle Policy Automation with Siebel CRM

The basic steps for integrating these two applications are as follows:

1. Download and install the various items listed in the Oracle White Paper entitled "Combining Siebel IP 2016 and native OPA 12.x Interviews". This can currently be downloaded from the following URL, with an accompanying ZIP file : https://blogs.oracle.com/opa/combining-siebel-ip-2016-and-native-opa-12x-interviews-answer-service

2. Configure the Siebel Workflow Process engine and Inbound Web Services to handle the transfer of information between the applications.

3. Build an appropriate User Interface to allow the user to interact with Oracle Policy Automation from inside Siebel. This might be through an Interview (the user of Siebel CRM views and works with an Interview in much the same way as described in the previous chapter concerning Oracle Service Cloud), or through a data-only mechanism (for example the user clicks on a button, and a data Field is updated in Siebel with a response from Oracle Policy Automation).

> **NB**: If you are looking for a detailed, technical description of the installation and implementation of Oracle Policy Automation and Oracle Siebel CRM IP16, you can find a complete webinar on the OPA Hub Website https://theopahub.com/main/oracle-policy-automation-siebel-crm-training/

Installing the Siebel Objects

If you have downloaded the previously mentioned ZIP file, these are the important steps needed to perform on the Siebel CRM environment. This should be performed on a development environment and will require Siebel Administrator permissions to be able to access many of the screens listed.

- Import the Archive `OPAGenericWSConnector.sif` into Siebel Tools. This SIF file contains Workflow Processes and Integration Objects.

- Perform a Full Compile and release your repository file to Server and Client.

- Publish and Activate the OPA Get Checkpoint, OPA Load For PUB Sample Intake Contact, OPA Process Submit Data, OPA Set Checkpoint, and OPA Submit For PUB Sample Intake Contact Workflow Processes.

The above steps provide the following functionality to Siebel, in order:

1. The proxy objects in Oracle Siebel CRM which map to the requests and responses defined in Oracle Policy Automation are created, to enable communication.

2. The objects are made accessible to the other parts of Siebel CRM by means of a compilation.

3. The example Workflow Processes are needed to move the data in and out of Siebel, based on the information received from Oracle Policy Automation. They can be copied and modified to form the basis of your own customized integration.

Creating the Oracle Policy Automation Connection to Siebel CRM

The next step in the integration is to allow the Workflow Processes to be initiated from outside Oracle Siebel CRM. Like many Siebel CRM integrations this is achieved through an Inbound Web Service.

The White Paper provides a simple example, which uses the Contact entity (a similar entity was used in many of the screenshots in the previous chapter). To continue with this example configuration, you must now import the sample Web Service into your Siebel CRM.

1. Import into Siebel CRM the supplied example Inbound Web Service, and adjust the URL to the URL of your Siebel CRM system, as you would normally do.

2. Add a new Connection to this Web Service from within the Oracle Policy Automation Hub application. This will allow you to test whether the communication between these systems is functioning.

The screenshot shown on the following page highlights the numbered areas listed here:

1. The URL of your Siebel EAI Object Manager Component.

2. The version number cited in Integration Object User Properties in your Siebel Repository.

3. The prefix you add to the Inbound Web Services to distinguish them (for example if you build several different connections to Siebel CRM). In this case the prefix used is Conn_.

4. If you authenticate connections to Oracle Policy Automation using OAuth, how the information will be added to your Oracle Policy Automation requests.

5. How you will authenticate connection to Oracle Siebel CRM (typically a Siebel or LDAP user depending on your Siebel CRM configuration).

The configuration of this Connection is critical. If the configuration of your Web Service and Connection has been successful, the Oracle Policy Automation Hub will display a green check mark as in this screenshot.

Once the green checkmark is visible, rule designers who connect to this Hub should be able to see and access your Connection as part of the design process as described in chapter 10.

> **NB**: If you are using Siebel CRM with a later version of Oracle Policy Automation than that used to create the Zip, don't forget to update the Integration Objects User Properties or simply ensure you import the up-to-date external Web Service definition into Siebel Tools

Testing the Connection with Siebel

As the Connection architecture is usually implemented in Siebel CRM with Workflow Processes and Inbound Web Services, testing each of the above-mentioned steps is typically performed using SOAP UI or another testing tool in order to visualize the requests and responses. Errors can be seen quickly and changes made to the relevant elements in Siebel CRM.

Workflow Process designers familiar with Siebel can leverage their knowledge to manipulate the requests and responses using tools they know already, such as Business Services, EAI XML Converters, XLST Transformations and eScript code. They can add content to the Workflow Processes to notify of successful changes in Siebel. The sample ZIP file contains such an example, shown below. Note the "Successfully Updated Siebel…" message in the Response. This response could use the Input Mapping, Load after Submit feature, described earlier, to provide feedback to the end user of Siebel.

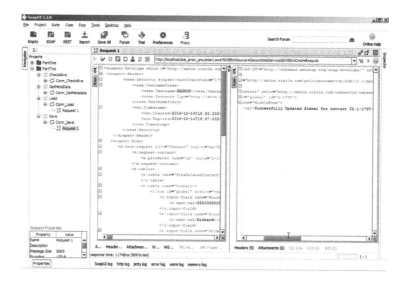

Displaying the Integration

The display of the Interview, or the triggering of other Oracle Policy Automation Web Services (as described in chapter 19), can be achieved with standard a Siebel CRM configuration, such as (but not limited to):

- Symbolic URL embedding of the Interview.

- Open UI and Oracle Policy Automation JavaScript embedding.

- Adding buttons to trigger a Workflow Process.

Summary

Oracle Siebel CRM is the most powerful and configurable CRM system available today. Its sophisticated Integration Architecture, robust development tools, and modern user interface allow developers to implement integrations with Oracle Policy Automation that provide complex data storage, retrieval, and transformation.

Siebel's preeminence in the Public Sector is consolidated by a sophisticated series of integration options to Oracle Policy Automation. This chapter has outlined the different areas of technical configuration that are typically impacted upon by a basic Siebel CRM Integration with Oracle Policy Automation. Many more integration options are commonly envisaged using the techniques described later in this book and in the Siebel documentation.

Custom Controls

About Custom Controls

The term Custom Controls has been in the Oracle Policy Automation vocabulary since version 10. However, starting in 2017, the manner in which custom controls are developed has been considerably updated and streamlined. The language used for these modern custom controls is JavaScript. The objective of this chapter is not to concentrate on the details of how to program in JavaScript, rather, it aims to guide you to a level of understanding where you know what is possible (and advisable) with each functionality.

What are Custom Controls used for?

Custom Controls can be separated into two main functionalities in Oracle Policy Automation. Both of these work directly on the Interview, changing the user experience in some way.

Styling Extensions

Custom Styling lets the developer change the colour, background, and many more elements of the Interview and the user Controls. These styling options go beyond what is accessible to the Rule Designer in the Oracle Policy Modeling application.

Control Extensions

The developer can also customize the behaviour of visible controls – these changes in behaviour might be (for example) displaying a Google Map, or providing new ways to view, interact or edit data in an Interview. With the language used for this being JavaScript, developers can leverage jQuery and its myriad of available plugins to create just about any new experience imaginable.

When should I implement this?

Bear in mind that these changes are customizations, designed by developers and implemented using a programming language that manipulates the Browser. As such, the risks associated with this (bugs, browser-incompatibility, accessibility issues, and so on) mean that you should only undertake such work if there is no way of achieving a similar outcome using standard configuration features. There are also a set of guiding principles that are accessible at this URL:

http://documentation.custhelp.com/euf/assets/devdocs/cloud18d/PolicyAutomation/en/Default.htm#Guides/Developer_Guide/Web_Interviews/Styles_and_scripts/Overview_of_interview_styling_and_behavior.htm

Create a Styling Extension

Implementing any customized behaviour requires the developer to create new JavaScript files that reside in the /resources directory of the current Project.

The simplest way to create the /resources directory is to access the Styles... dialog in the Interview tab of the Oracle Policy Modeling application, Clicking the Custom Files... button shows the dialog displayed below. Clicking OK creates the folder and opens it in Windows Explorer.

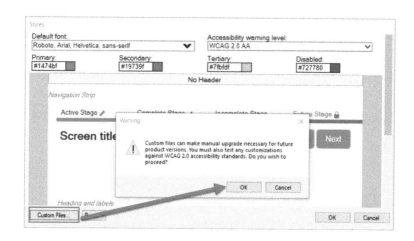

The structure of a custom JavaScript file used to change the styling of an Interview is shown on the next page.

Custom Styling Extension Template

In the resources folder, using Windows Notepad or a similar application, create a text-based file that has the following structure. You might use this as a general template for self-study purposes. Over the following pages, you will implement several examples of Custom Styling Extensions; each time you will construct a file based on a template similar to this.

```
OraclePolicyAutomation.AddExtension({
    style: {
        objecttype: {
            className: "css class name",
errorclassName: "error css class",
            propertyname: "property value"
        }

    }
});
```

In the template shown above, there are four main areas to be worked on:

Object Type
The Object Type identifies the element you are trying to restyle. This could be the Interview content, the "Next" button, or a specific type of element such as a Calendar input Control.

Class Name
The style details (color, background, or indeed any Cascading Style Sheet content) should be in a separate file, with the extension CSS.

Error Class Name
The style details to use when a control is in an error state (for example, a user has entered an invalid date) should be in a separate file with the extension CSS.

Property Name
In simple cases, where only one aspect is changed, in certain controls it is possible to change the value without a separate style sheet.

To make it easier to understand how each of the above areas can be used, you will create a new Project in Oracle Policy Modelling and add the following:

1. Add three **Attributes**:

    o   the customer's name (a text attribute).

    o   the date of purchase (a date attribute).

    o   the amount of the invoice (a number attribute).

2. Add One New **Screen**

    o   Add all of the attributes to the Screen.

    o   Add a Signature Control.

3. Add One **Rule** in Microsoft Word.

the interview is complete if

all

the customer's name is known
the date of purchase is known
the amount of the invoice is known

Your Interview should look like the following screenshot (if you have built it according to the instructions above). Note that, in the example, some of the labels have been changed to make them easier to read.

Custom Styling Extension Example: Signature Control

In your /resources folder, create a new file called example.js and open it in Notepad ++. The name of the file should, outside of an example like this one, have a unique name which indicates its purpose. Similarly, the file should have a header detailing the developer and useful metadata to understand what the file is for.

Add the following text.

```
OraclePolicyAutomation.AddExtension({
    style: {
        signatureInput: {
            inkColor: "magenta"
        }
    }
});
```

Note the format of the text, which will be familiar to anyone used to working with JavaScript objects. In this first example, the signatureInput key indicates that the following instructions will relate to that Control type. The inkColor property is set to magenta, or bright pink. Save your file and use the debugger to test your work. The signature Control should now look like this, when you sign it.

Custom Styling Extension Example: Calendar Control

The second example will work with the Calendar Control. In order to achieve the objective of restyling the Calendar, you will use a CSS file.

Edit the JavaScript file in the /resources directory in your Project. Use the example on the next page to guide you.

> **NB**: You can only have a single Style extension file in each Project, but it can contain many different Control styling elements, as the following examples will demonstrate.

```
OraclePolicyAutomation.AddExtension({
    ① style: {
        signatureInput: {
            inkColor: "magenta"
        }, ②
        calendarInput: {
            className: "my-calendar-input",
            iconColor: "red",
        }
    }
});
```

In the example above, note the following points when you are editing your JavaScript file.

1. There is only one style extension permitted per project.

2. But it can contain many different styled Controls. Note the comma at the end of each section.

This example uses an external CSS file to centralize the CSS classes used, which can make for easier management and editing of styles. In a separate file in the /resources directory, add the following CSS Class. The file should have the extension .css. After you have edited the file, save it.

```
.my-calendar-input {
    font-size : 25px;
}
```

Now run the debugger again and test your Project. The signature Control should function as before, however you now have a styled Calendar Control with a red icon and a larger font size for the date, if you enter one using the Control.

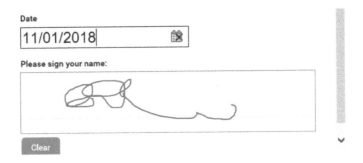

Custom Styling Extension Example: Text Control with Error Styling

The third example will once again require you to edit the JavaScript file and add a styling element. This time you will include styling for when the user inadvertently enters some invalid text in the Name Control of your Interview.

First, edit the customer's name attribute and define a regular expression and an error message.

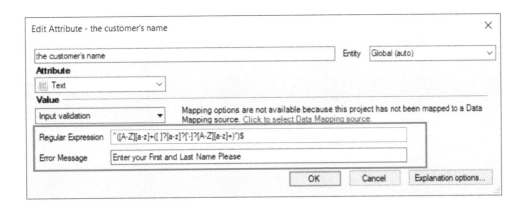

NB: If you want to copy and paste, the regular expression is available at https://regexr.com/ under the Community heading, labelled "First / Last name" : ^([A-Z][a-z]+([ ]?[a-z]?['-]?[A-Z][a-z]+)*)$

Finally, edit your JavaScript file to include another section, using the screenshot on the next page as your guide.

```
OraclePolicyAutomation.AddExtension({
    style: {
        signatureInput: {
            inkColor: "magenta"
        },
        calendarInput: {
            className: "my-calendar-input",
            iconColor: "red"
        },①
        textInput: {
          ② errorStyle: {
                backgroundColor: "#fcc"
            }
        }
    }
});
```

1. Do not forget to add the comma before you start the new section.

2. The errorStyle key allows the Control to adopt a specific look and feel when an error occurs.

Debug your work and observe the behaviour. As a side-effect, notice that the `amount` Control also uses the same styling if it is left blank. This may or may not be the required behaviour. In the final example, you will adjust this.

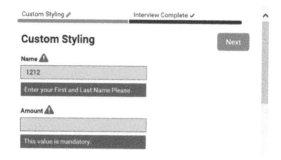

Custom Styling Extension Example: Input Styling with Functions

The final example in this section will use a JavaScript function to implement conditional styling. Edit your JavaScript file to look like this final version.

```
OraclePolicyAutomation.AddExtension({
    style: {
        signatureInput: {
            inkColor: "magenta"
        },
        calendarInput: {
            className: "my-calendar-input",
            iconColor: "red"
        },
        textInput: function (control) {         1
            if (control.getDataType() === "number") {
                var v = control.getValue();
                if (v != null && v < 0)
                    return {                    2
                        style: {
                            color: "red"
                        }
                    }
            } else           3
            if (control.getDataType() === "text") {
                return {
                    errorStyle: {
                        backgroundColor: "#fcc"    4
                    }
                }
            }
        }
    }
});
```

1. In this case, the styling of the Control is turned over to a JavaScript function. So we use `return` to send back the relevant styling.

2. In the first instance, numbers are styled red if they are negative.

3. Otherwise...

4. Text fields will use the error styling you added in the previous section.

Once you have edited the file, check your JavaScript file carefully and test it using the Debugger in Oracle Policy Modelling when you are ready. The end result should showcase all of the examples so far:

Hopefully you will be able to note the following user experience enhancements enabled in your Project:

1. The text field, when an error is present, is shaded pink.

2. The calendar has a red icon and large font size.

3. The numeric amount, if negative, is shown in red.

4. The signature Control uses a pink ink color.

> **NB**: There are many more objects, Controls, properties and techniques that can help you style your user experience. The complete reference, at the time of writing, is at
> http://documentation.custhelp.com/euf/assets/devdocs/cloud18d/PolicyAutomation/en/Default.htm#Guides/Developer_Guide/Web_Interviews/Styles_and_scripts/Interview_extensions_reference.htm

Custom Controls – Control and Interview Extensions

The JavaScript approach you discovered in the previous section can also be used to implement new behaviors. For example, you might replace a standard list of options with a dynamic list retrieved from another application or service. You might also replace an address hyperlink with an embedded map provided by Google, Bing or another mapping service. In a sense, you can create a user experience that is as unique as your rulebase.

The JavaScript template for Control Extensions

Just as with the previous examples, working with a template can help you understand how to design your new functionality. Exactly how the template is defined depends on the type of extension you wish to work on:

- Interview Extension (Header, Navigation, Footer).

- Control Extensions (Labels, Text Controls, Calendar Controls, and so on).

Both templates use a format similar to that used in the previous section. Here is an example of an Interview Extension, designed to customize the behavior of the Header.

```
OraclePolicyAutomation.AddExtension({
    customHeader: function (interview) {
        return {
            mount: function (el) {}
            update: function (el) {}
            unmount: function (el) {}
        }
    }
});
```

1. The `customHeader` keyword identifies this extension as targeting the Header.

2. The `interview` object, and various properties, are accessible in your script.

3. The mount, update, and unmount keys allow you to program start, update and end behavior.

The Label Control Extension template looks like this:

```
OraclePolicyAutomation.AddExtension({
    customLabel: function (control, interview) {    (2)
        return {
            mount: function (el) {}
            update: function (el) {},    (3)
            unmount: function (el) {}
        }
    }
})
```
(1) at customLabel

1. The customLabel keyword identifies that this script will customize one or more label Controls.

2. The interview object and the control object are both accessible in your script.

3. The mount, update, and unmount keys are ready to receive your custom behavior script.

A Simple Control Extension Example

The objective of this example is to highlight typical areas for consideration when delivering custom JavaScript code for your Project. Items of interest are highlighted and discussed at the end of the series of screenshots. Of course, in a publication such as this, only the most important areas are indicated. You can find a complete technical reference online by clicking the Help icon in the Oracle Policy Modelling application.

Using the Custom Control JavaScript, or indeed the Custom Styling JavaScript, does not preclude also using the experimental RuleScript feature described earlier in this book. You should, as always with customization such as this, ensure that your code does not break any functionality already present in the standard interface, and you should rigorously test your code with each new release of the software.

```
/**
 * Richard Napier The OPA Hub Website November 2018
 * Educational Example of Custom Label Google Map Extension
 * I will remember this is for demonstration purposes only
 */
OraclePolicyAutomation.AddExtension({
    customLabel: function (control, interview) {
        return {
            mount: function (el) {
                if (control.getProperty("name") == "xMap") {    (1)

                    var script_tag_addition = document.createElement('script');
                    script_tag_addition.setAttribute('src', 'https://maps.googleapis.com/maps/api/js?key=YOURKEYHERE&callback=initMap');    (2)
                    script_tag_addition.onload = initMap;
                    script_tag_addition.defer = true;
                    script_tag_addition.async = true;
                    document.body.appendChild(script_tag_addition);

                    var div = document.createElement("div");    (3)
                    div.id = "lblmap";
                    div.style.visibility = 'visible';
                    div.style.height = '500px';
                    div.style.width = '870px';
                    el.appendChild(div);

                    var latmap = Number(interview.getValue("cl_lat"));    (4)
                    var longmap = Number(interview.getValue("cl_long"));

                    var iconBase = '${resources-root}/images/';    (5)
                    var icons = {
                        fire: {
                            icon: iconBase + 'firedept.png'
                        },
                        flood: {
                            icon: iconBase + 'waterfalls.png'
                        },
                        accident: {
                            icon: iconBase + 'caution.png'
                        },
                        other: {
                            icon: iconBase + 'police.png'
                        }
                    };
```

1. In this case, the code will only execute for a single custom Label control whose name has been identified in the Oracle Policy Modeller as `"xMap"`. All other Controls will be unaffected. Recall that Controls can have custom Properties added in the Interview ribbon. The `mount` keyword means this code will run upon loading the Screen.

2. Custom JavaScript can call external JavaScript libraries, in this case Google Maps. You will require an API Key and Quota to use these libraries.

3. Your JavaScript code can also create new HTML tags, for example in this case a rectangle to contain a map.

4. Attributes of your Rulebase are available to you if they are present on the Interview Screen you are customizing.

5. You can store images in a subfolder, and reference them using this syntax.

```
function initMap() {          6
    var mapOptions = {
        center: new google.maps.LatLng(latmap, longmap),
        type: interview.getValue("cl_type"),
        zoom: 8,
        mapTypeId: google.maps.MapTypeId.ROADMAP
    };

    var map = new google.maps.Map(document.getElementById("lblmap"), mapOptions);   7

    var features = [{
        position: new google.maps.LatLng(latmap, longmap),
        type: interview.getValue("cl_type")
    }
    ];

    features.forEach(function (feature) {
        var marker = new google.maps.Marker({
            position: feature.position,
            icon: icons[feature.type].icon,
            map: map
        });
        marker.addListener('click', function () {          8
            infowindow.open(map, marker);
        });
    });

    var infowindow = new google.maps.InfoWindow({
        content: interview.getValue("cl_name") + " declared an incident of type " + interview.getValue("cl_type") + " here.<br> Estimate of damage is " +
            interview.getValue("val_inventory") + " PLC."
    });

    }

  }
},
update: function (el) {},          9
```

6. Callbacks such as this one can be triggered in your code. This function is executed following the loading of Google Maps into your custom Screen.

7. Google Maps and other plugins (such as jQuery plugins, since Interviews can leverage jQuery) can be loaded.

8. Event handlers can be added to trigger special behavior. Here, a click handler is added to the map marker.

9. In the case of a label, which is not used for user data entry, no update code is required. Other controls such as Calendars and Text Boxes may need to use the `update` or `validate` keys to implement further behavior when the user makes changes.

```
unmount: function (el) {

    if (control.getProperty("name") == "xMap") {          10
        var map = document.getElementById("lblmap");
        map.remove();
    }

    }

    }

  }
})
```

10. Your code should always remove your custom Control. Here the map is removed when the Screen is no longer displayed, using the `unmount` key. Some browsers may not support remove().

The final result, deployed on an Oracle Policy Automation server platform looks like the following screenshot, with the Google Map replacing a Label and being displayed with a clickable interface:

Control Extension – Entity Container Example

A special type of Control is used to contain others. For example, when building the user interface Screen to display entity instances, you build a repeating section inside a container, as in the example below.

The two attributes are displayed inside an Entity Container. At runtime, the effect is as follows:

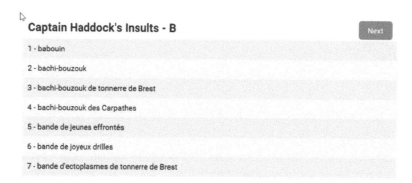

The screenshot above only shows the first seven rows in the Container. Clearly this is not going to be very useful for the end user, since there is no scroll bar, pagination, or other method to find something in the list.

Container Control Extensions provide the developer with the ability to create new experiences for the user in these situations. The basic structure of the file is as per previous examples, and once again the JavaScript developer will choose to leverage external components to provide a quick solution.

The script looks like this. Comments are on the following page:

```
/**
 * Educational Example of Custom EntityContainer Extension
 * I will remember this is for demonstration purposes only
 */
OraclePolicyAutomation.AddExtension({
    customEntityContainer: function (control, interview) {
        console.log("Get Array Reference");
        var myInterview = interview._session.config.data[1].instances
// ASSUMES ONLY 1 ENTITY
        if (control.getProperty("name") == "xEntity") {
// IF MORE THAN ONE CONTAINER ON THIS PAGE ONLY EXECUTE ON THE RELEVANT ONE
            return {
                mount: function (el) { // START BUILDING THE LIST CONTROL
                    console.log("Beginning customEntityContainer jqGrid");
                    var myDiv = document.createElement('div');
                    myDiv.setAttribute("id", "mySpecialDIV");
                    console.log("Styled customEntityContainer");
                    el.appendChild(myDiv);
                    var myFlatList = [];
                    var myObject;
                    for (i = 0; i < myInterview.length; i++) {
// ITERATE THROUGH INSTANCES OF ENTITY
                        myObject = new Object();
                        myObject.insult =
myInterview[i].attributes[0].value.toString()
                        myObject.insult_text =
myInterview[i].attributes[1].value.toString()
                        myFlatList.push(myObject);
                        console.log("Flattened the list" + i);
                    }
                    $("#mySpecialDIV").jsGrid({
// INSERT THE LIST WITH JQUERY
                        width: "80%",
                        height: "400px",
                        sorting: true,
                        paging: true,
                        pageIndex: 1,
                        pageSize: 10,
                        pageButtonCount: 10,

                        data: myFlatList,

                        fields: [{
                                name: "insult",
                                type: "text",
                                width: 20,
                            }, {
                                name: "insult_text",
                                type: "text",
                                width: 150
```

```
                            }
                      ]
                });
                console.log("Finished customEntityContainer");
            },
            update: function (el) {},
            unmount: function (el) {
                var myDiv = $('#mySpecialDIV');
                myDiv.remove();
                console.log("Removed the customEntityContainer");

            }
        }
    }
  }
});
```

The code uses only the *mount* and *unmount* sections because, in this case, the information is read-only and no code is required to refresh the list if other elements on the page are updated.

The documentation for jsGrid is available online at http://js-grid.com/ In this example, pagination is set at 10 rows per page, with clickable links for every 10 rows. The grid displays the two columns side by side.

Going Further with Control and Interview Extensions

A large number of commented educational examples, videos, and code samples are available on the OPA Hub Website. They are free for educational purposes, and there are new articles regularly. Some of those already examined are as follows:

- Text Input and Full Input Extensions.

- Label Input (Google Maps, Google Places, Geocoding, other Labels).

- Custom Date Input Extensions.

- Entity Container Extensions (Simple, Filtered, Charts).

- Entity Collect Extensions.

- Interview Header Extensions.

- Dynamic Option Extensions.

- REST Search Extensions (Siebel, Airlines, Trains, Airports, and many more).

You can find these, and more at https://theopahub.com/main/category/interviews/javascript-extensions/ If you want to use templates to get started yourself, you can download a Template Builder from https://theopahub.com/main/extension-code-generators-for-javascript/

Summary

The Oracle Policy Modeling application, being based on the modern standards of HTML5, JavaScript and CSS, is easily extended using official customization principles called Styling Extensions and Control Extensions. JavaScript developers, aided by Oracle Policy Modelling experts and User Experience teams, can deliver responsive, flexible and appealing user interfaces for their end users.

Mobile for Oracle Policy Automation

Oracle Policy Automation provides end users with flexible and powerful decision-making tools. It's not surprising, if the need arises, for these users to take Oracle Policy Automation with them, wherever they are. On the road, at the customer, in a place where connectivity is limited or non-existent. This chapter looks briefly at the different options available to help meet the needs of this population.

What Mobile Options are Available?

Custom Controls can be separated into two main functionalities in Oracle Policy Automation. Both of these work directly on the Interview, changing the user experience in some way.

Oracle Policy Automation Mobile App

The Oracle Policy Automation Mobile app is available for Android and iOS platforms at time of writing. The application is built around several key concepts that underpin the user experience.

Mobile User Role

Recall from the earlier chapter about user roles, that in order to be able to take advantage of the Mobile App, a user must have the Mobile User role, *and* the Project that should be accessible to this user should be deployed as a Mobile determination, as in the following image:

Deployment:CopyrightPermissions		Actions ▼ Done
⊘ Activated		Apply
Collection	Default Collection ▼	
☑ Interview	☐ http://localhost:7003/opa18d/web-determinations/startsession/CopyrightPermissions	
☑ Web services - Assess	⚓ http://localhost:7003/opa18d/determinations-server/display/CopyrightPermissions	
☐ Web services - Interview	Not available	
☑ Mobile	☐ Available for use on mobile devices.	

Mobile Deployed Projects

Once the user has downloaded the app onto their device, the next step to take advantage of any Mobile-deployed Project is to establish the Connection to the Oracle Policy Automation Hub, so that their credentials may be verified. The user experience is familiar :

The primary purpose of this login sequence – aside from verifying roles and permissions – is to synchronize the device with the Hub. Synchronize has two components:

1. Download any Projects that are deployed for Mobile use that this user can access, in order to be able to run the project.

2. Download any Assessments that have been assigned to this Service Cloud user.

It is important therefore to wait until the synchronization is finished, before proceeding. The user is shown a progress dialog similar to this one, from iOS:

Mobile Assessments

Once the synchronization is complete the user is taken to the Asessments screen.

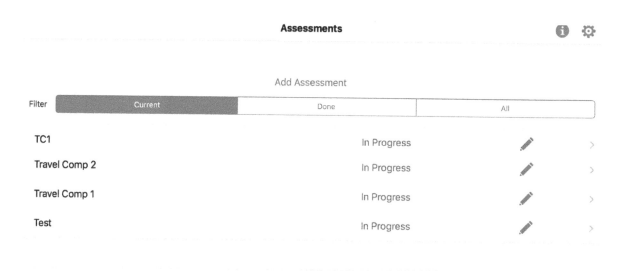

The user can filter the list by Assessment status, by clicking one of the blue buttons (in the screenshot above, the Current button has been selected).

Executing the Assessment on the Mobile Device

The Assessment can be accessed by clicking the Start button, or by clicking the pencil icon to return to an unfinished assessment. The user experience is, in Latest Version interviews, completely identical to the normal HTML Interview.

1. The Home icon returns the user to the Assessment list. Tapping this icon saves the Interview and it can be resumed later from the Assessment list.

2. If the Project has translations, they are available here.

3. Stages are displayed in the standard way.

4. Screen lists are displayed if the Interview has been configured to show them.

5. If the Oracle Service Cloud Connection is in place, the data can be submitted to Service Cloud.

The Mobile Assessment leverages the functionality of the device. For example, in the following image the Browser file upload has been replaced with the iOS add Photo dialog.

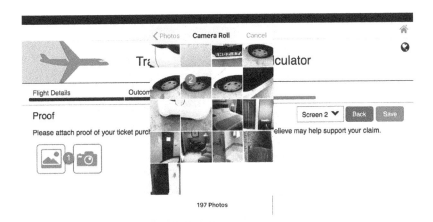

1. Click to take a photo or to select an existing photo.

2. Shows the iOS Camera Roll and related functionality.

Oracle Service Cloud Mobile Assessment

In the case of an Oracle Service Cloud and Oracle Policy Automation Cloud Service integration, the user may undertake any assigned Assessment and submit their work, using the Service Cloud Connection as described in a previous chapter. If they are offline (with no Internet connection) at the time of completion, then the Assessment is placed in a Queue ready for submission later, when Internet connection has been restored.

At the time of writing, this functionality was available only with Oracle Service Cloud. Users can create and execute ad hoc assessments as the need arises. For ad hoc assessments, no results are uploaded, and there is no management of the assessment in Service Cloud.

The user of the Mobile App cannot remove an Assessment that has been created for them in Oracle Service Cloud. In addition, the Mobile App regularly scans to see if new Assessments are available, and these are added to the Assessment list. Any cancelled assessments (in Service Cloud) will automatically be removed from the Assessment List in the Mobile app.

Once the user has completed the Assessment in the Mobile app, the Assessment can be submitted to to Oracle Service Cloud. This can be done at the end of the interview:

Mark this assessment for upload?

Yes   No

It can also be done at a later time, by swiping the Assessment in the Assessment list. The Assessment is now ready for upload:

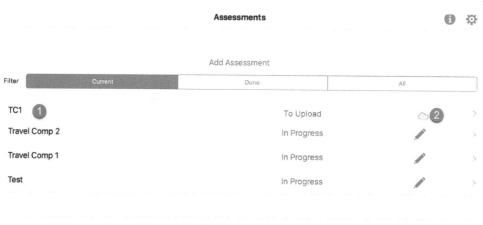

The upload will be performed the next time the user synchronizes the device with the OPA Hub; as described previously, this happens in the background on a regular basis, or when the app is launched. A manual synchronization can also be performed by swiping down the screen from the Assessment list:

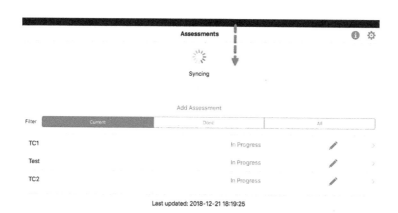

Only Service Cloud-initiated Assessments – that is, they were created in Oracle Service Cloud – offer the capability to download data to the Mobile app and upload determinations back to Oracle Service Cloud.

The status of the assessment is shown by a variety of icons in addition to those described in the previous sections.

Ad Hoc Assessments

Regardless of whether Oracle Service Cloud is used or not, Mobile Assessments can be added by clicking Add Assessment at the top of the page. The user can then select one of the available Projects and name the assessment for their own reference.

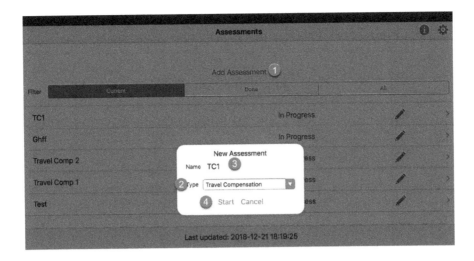

1. Click Add Assessment.
2. Select the Mobile Project.
3. Name the Assessment.
4. Start the Assessment.

Oracle Policy Automation Mobile SDK

For customers looking to leverage the basic principles of the Oracle Policy Automation Mobile App, and take it further, perhaps by implementing new kinds of connectivity or new user interface elements, the Mobile Software Development Kit (SDK) offers a robust, cross-platform development solution.

The SDK provides a Mobile Application Archive that developers can use in their integrated JDeveloper 12c (12.2.1.3.0) development environment. Examples are provided of both simple, mobile Assessments as well as more advanced synchronization to the Oracle Policy Automation Hub.

Developing a Mobile application is beyond the scope of this book, but you can find initial steps on the Oracle OPA Blog at this address: https://blogs.oracle.com/opa/opa-mobile-sdk-get-started

JavaScript Embeddable Models

Earlier in this book you learned of the possibility – for Oracle Policy Automation Cloud Service customers – to deploy a Project as a standalone JavaScript file. Whilst this is not a Mobile solution in and of itself, the prospect of being able to execute a JavaScript function to obtain Oracle Policy Automation determinations is a stepping stone on the (albeit rather long) road to creating a mobile experience built from scratch. Given that the JavaScript is completely independent and does not require any connectivity with the Oracle Policy Automation Hub, it provides the developer with an easy-to-program way of executing logic on the device without Internet connectivity. Of course, the Embeddable Model has restrictions and will require significant effort to integrate it with a custom Mobile solution, but in an era when Browsers can create their own databases, and complex Customer Relationship Management solutions like Oracle Siebel CRM use this to provide offline capability, adding Oracle Policy Automation into this offline scenario is an intriguing possibility.

Mobile Browser

Last and by no means least, when Internet is available, the user can open the mobile Browser and conduct an interview online.

Summary

Mobile devices and Oracle Policy Automation are a very good mix – end user productivity in the field can be increased by having the power of policy determinations available wherever they are. The range of solutions, from fully standardized app to software development kit (to name but two) ensures that Policy Automation will be present wherever it needs to be.

What Next?

What Next?

Hopefully, you have found this book useful. It would be great if it has fulfilled its goal of helping you to get started with OPA. It is, however, only natural that you should consider this the beginning of your Oracle Policy Automation journey.

There are several items that should be on your checklist as you progress to mastery of the product and all of the fantastic functionality it has to offer your organization or your customer's organization.

- Develop Strategies to Optimize your Work.
- Get Further Training.
- Get Certification.
- Get Talking.

Develop Strategies to Optimize your Work

Unlike other expert systems that rely on programming skills to develop rules, Oracle Policy Modelling's unique approach means Microsoft Word and Excel are the primary tools used to create and manage rule content. This creates a fantastic opportunity for the business to engage fully in the process of delivering the IT system of which Oracle Policy Automation forms a key part.

This use of common business tools does, however, require careful handling. In one sense, the ease of use and flexibility promoted by Word and Excel is a double-edged sword which I hinted at back in Chapter 1.

As your vision of Oracle Policy Automation matures, you will find that you increasingly become aware of the need to implement a strategy capable of maintaining the enthusiasm and engagement of all your rule designers, whilst also ensuring that the rules delivered are as clean and tidy as they can be. Essentially, therefore, you will need to adopt techniques familiar to programmers, known as refactoring. This concept was largely defined by Martin Fowler. He states:

"Refactoring is a controlled technique for improving the design of an existing code base. Its essence is applying a series of small behavior-preserving transformations, each of which is "too small to be worth doing". However the cumulative effect of each of these transformations is quite significant."

> **NB**: *From Wikipedia* "Martin Fowler (born 1963) is a British software developer, author and international public speaker on software development, specializing in object-oriented analysis and design, UML, patterns, and agile software development methodologies, including extreme programming. His 1999 book Refactoring popularized the practice of code refactoring."

I have had the pleasure of working with Dr Jason Sender of the University of Oxford, who was Rules Architect for nearly four years on the most complex Rulebase used by the Legal Aid Agency in the United Kingdom, which is used to determine capital and income eligibility of applicants.

His dissertation, entitled "The Application of Design Patterns to Oracle Policy Automation", is a fascinating read and after discussion with him, he has kindly agreed that parts of it might be republished both here and in a less detailed format on my OPA Hub Website. Amongst other topics, Dr Sender studied Refactoring Techniques, applying them to Oracle Policy Automation where appropriate. A short introduction is provided in the sections that follow.

How to Apply Object-Oriented Design Patterns to OPA?

At a broad level, it is possible to apply design patterns from Object-Oriented Design to OPA. Since OPA does not have objects and classes in the same sense as an object-oriented programming language, we should not expect a straightforward application of Fowler's design patterns to OPA. Not all of the patterns will be technically applicable, and even some of those will be unfeasible or without any great impact. Dr Sender's work discusses the application of the most common patterns. (If you would like to read further on this matter, please feel free to contact Jason using the information at the end of this chapter.)

Improving your design Approach to OPA Rulebases

Object-Oriented languages come equipped with advanced development environments and a plethora of automation tools to help the refactoring effort. Oracle Policy Automation uses Microsoft Word and Excel, and is classified as a Production Rules System rather than a fully-fledged object-oriented language. As Fowler states (since it is particularly relevant to our daily lives as Oracle Policy Automation Consultants or Architects):

"There are also many languages where you don't have tools, so knowing how to do it yourself is still important."

The Application of Object-Oriented Refactoring to Oracle Policy Automation

This short introduction to Dr Sender's work focuses on simple refactoring techniques that everyone can adopt, and which bring clarity and maintainability to Oracle Policy Automation rules. Each technique is shown with an example, and a citation from the site https://refactoring.com/ run by Martin Fowler.

Extract Variable Rule

Extract Variable Rule is an Oracle Policy Automation reworking of Fowler's Extract Method, since Oracle Policy Automation does not have Methods. Let's start with a practical example. Have you ever seen something like this in an Oracle Policy Automation Word document?

the total amount received = the deposit + the security + the normal payment + the overpayment

By applying the `Extract` Method, *"You have a code fragment that can be grouped together. Turn the fragment into a method whose name explains the purpose of the method."* we find ourselves with a revised version that looks a little like the example below.

the total amount received = the initial payments + the regular payments

the initial payments = the deposit + the security

the regular payments = the normal payment + the overpayment

The gain in readability and ease of maintenance should be obvious. Now that Dr Sender has gotten us on the right track, let's take a few more examples from his work. These revolve around the removal of conditional expressions from Microsoft Word or Microsoft Excel tables.

Extract Rules from Rule Table

Extract Rules from Rule Table is a more meaningful OPA rebranding of Fowler's `Decompose Conditional` Method which is described thus:

"You have a complicated conditional (if-then-else) statement. Extract methods from the condition, then part, and else parts."

As an example in Oracle Policy Automation, the following table shows a starting point where conditions and premises meet convoluted conclusions:

the charge	
the quantity + the winter service charge + the winter rate	the current date < the start date of summer or the current date > the end date of summer
the quantity + the summer rate	**otherwise**

Now, here is the table, following an application of the `Decompose Conditional` refactoring technique:

the charge	
the winter charge	the date is not summer
the summer charge	**otherwise**

the date is not summer if
>   the current date < the start date of summer or
>   the current date > the end date of summer

the winter charge = the quantity + the winter service charge + the winter rate

the summer charge = the quantity + the summer rate

Reduce Complexity and Duplication

The aim of `Extract Rules from Rule Table` is to reduce code duplication and/or duplicated conclusion values. It should be noted that it can add a level of indirection (i.e., flexibility) too, but its main use would be to extract duplicated rules from a complicated Word rule table, not, as in the example above, to extract only the conditions and conclusions of a single row (which, arguably, would add indirection at the cost of more code, unneeded flexibility, and complexity).

Flexibility vs Reduction

In certain situations, flexibility is needed, even if it creates *more* content. For example, instead of hard-coding a value in (e.g., an amount) in 20 different conclusions of a rule table, you could set a variable equal to the amount and put the variable in the rule table, as this would add the 'flexibility' to change the amount if needed. We could say it adds a level of indirection – but it does create more lines in Word and therefore complexity.

We refactor to simplify code and increase clarity – if it does not do so in a given situation then that refactoring technique is probably not needed in that situation. Not every refactoring technique will be appropriate in every situation, indeed many refactoring techniques are inverses of each other.

Consolidate Conditional Expressions

"You have a sequence of conditional tests with the same result. Combine them into a single conditional expression and extract it."

Consider the following Word Table representing a sequence of tests:

the disability amount	
0	the seniority < 2
0	the month's incapacitated > 12
0	the person is part time
0	otherwise

By separating the conditions into a single expression and extracting it from the table using `Consolidate Conditional Expressions` refactoring technique, the result would resemble the following example:

the disability amount	
0	the person is not eligible for disability
0	otherwise

the person is not eligible for disability if
the seniority < 2 or
the month's incapacitated > 12 or
the person is part time

The readability and maintainablity benefits should be immediately obvious.

Parameterize Methods
Replace Parameters with Specific Methods

"An object invokes a method, then passes the result as a parameter for a method. The receiver can also invoke this method. Remove the parameter and let the receiver invoke the method."

Sometimes the refactoring seems simple but when applied to large scale projects the benefits are still tangible. Consider the example below:

the base price = the quantity * the item price
the discount level = the given discount level
the final price = the discounted price
the discounted price = the base price * the discount level

The four lines above in reality could be slimmed down to the following, with no loss of readability or maintainability, using `Replace Parameters with Methods` refactoring:

the base price = the quantity * the item price
the final price = the discounted price
the discounted price = the base price * the given discount level

Going Further in Refactoring and other Design Principles

Dr Sender offers a variety of custom training sessions in line with his work on refactoring Oracle Policy Automation rules in order to maximise the quality, maintainability and readability of rulebases. He can be contacted through his LinkedIn profile.

Get Further Training

Oracle University Training

A potential next step should be to get trained at Oracle University – they provide training on Oracle Policy Automation. At the time of writing, there are three courses available:

Introduction to Oracle Policy Automation

Described as the first step for analysts and non-technical users – a one day course on version 12. The course is detailed, at the time of writing, at this address https://education.oracle.com/pls/web_prod-plq-dad/db_pages.getpage?page_id=609&get_params=dc:D93644,clang:EN

Oracle Policy Modelling for Policy Experts

This three-day course provides many hands-on exercises with the product, and is recommended for anyone who will work within, or with, an Oracle Policy Modelling 12 team. The course outline is currently online at https://education.oracle.com/pls/web_prod-plq-dad/db_pages.getpage?page_id=609&get_params=dc:D98213,clang:EN

Oracle Policy Modelling Essentials Rel. 10.4

This five-day course equips you with the skills you need for capturing, analysing and maintaining business policies. Currently focussed on version 10, check with your Oracle University representative to see if the course is running with a trainer conversant in version 12, or if an updated course is due soon. Certification is available for this course; more information is currently online at https://education.oracle.com/pls/web_prod-plq-dad/db_pages.getpage?page_id=654&get_params=p_id:67

Independent Training

As a consultant and trainer, I deliver customized and customer-driven training on many aspects of the Oracle Policy Automation platform: Policy Modelling, Policy Automation Integration with Oracle Siebel CRM and many more. I deliver training on areas not covered by the Oracle University courses, in English or in French where required. I can be contacted on my website https://theopahub.com/main.

Get Certification

You should strongly consider getting certified on one of these paths. Certification confirms your value in the marketplace and contributes to the establishment of a strong community.

Oracle Policy Automation 10 Rule Developer Essentials Exam: 1Z0-534
(http://www.oracle.com/partners/en/products/applications/policy-automation-exam-1z0-534/index.html)

Oracle Policy Automation Cloud Service 2017 Implementation Essentials Exam: 1Z1-345
(http://www.oracle.com/partners/en/products/cloud-solutions/opacloud-1z1-345/index.html)

Get Talking

Don't forget that the Internet is home to a number of good OPA websites – outlined in the Preface – where you can learn and discuss things with others.

Together with another Oracle Policy Automation cheerleader, my great friend Raj, and a happy band of guest authors from around the world, I am lucky to run the website https://theopahub.com. This website offers a Blog, an Events Calendar, Jobs List, and fun interactive Quizzes and other learning videos for anyone who wants to learn more about Oracle Policy Automation. It's free and I encourage you to register.

There are a number of excellent resources online, including these forums:

https://cloudcustomerconnect.oracle.com/resources/742fffc5fa/summary Policy Automation for Service Cloud

https://community.oracle.com/community/groundbreakers/oracle-applications/industries/oracle_policy_automation/oracle_policy_automation_-_general_discussion/content Oracle OPA Community

https://blogs.oracle.com/opa/welcome-to-the-oracle-policy-automation-blog The Oracle OPA Blog

Get Example Projects

Remember that the Oracle Policy Modeling application comes with a large number of Example Projects. You've used a few of them in this book. They are a really excellent way to discover use cases and techniques since they come from the software designers! The OPA Hub Website uses often them to explain useful solutions to business scenarios.

And Finally

All that remains is for me to say *thank you for reading*.

The fourth edition of this book for 2019 once again allowed me to draw on the large community of OPA gurus for support, ideas, and help. Thanks go to Orlando R, and of course Davin, Jasmine, Phil in the UK, and Paul F.

The third edition of this book, in 2018 benefitted from generous input from the finest minds in the OPA universe. My heartfelt thanks go out to Dr Jason Sender, Jason Stoddart, Alex H, Pascal S and Sylvie A.

I especially acknowledge my friend and colleague Raj's assistance with the second edition of the book and the Service Cloud integration sections.

I also want to thank Thomas N, Myriam B, Laurent P and all the many students and customers who share my interest in OPA, CRM, and everything in-between, and who helped provide ideas used in this book.

And finally, thanks once again to my enlightened (and enlightening!) publisher-cum-mentor James, without whom this book would never have seen the light of day.

Nice, January 2019

Index

Index

Index

Index

Getting Started with Oracle Service Cloud [OSvC]

Richard Napier

Oracle Service Cloud (OSvC) is Oracle's flagship cloud-based customer service product.

Oracle Service Cloud (formerly RightNow) helps businesses to understand their customers, and the complete customer service solution provides the tools and technologies that help companies adapt to customers' changing needs.

In this practical, accessible, full-colour book, join leading trainer Richard Napier as he takes you on a journey into the universe of Oracle Service Cloud. A universe that includes Incidents, Answers, Administration, and the Business Automation of the Agent Desktop and your Customer Portal. This book is a superb standalone resource or perfect complement to your Oracle University Service Cloud (RightNow) Training and covers the real-world use of Workspaces, Workflows, Guided Assistance, Chat, and More. Test yourself with over 50 challenging questions to make sure you are ready for OSvC!

Get to grips with OSvC quickly and easily…

> Set up Users, Profiles and Workspaces to personalize your agents' work environment

> Create Business Rules and Workflows to improve quality, standardize responses, and increase accuracy when working with customers

> Create a customized, branded Customer Portal

> Build Outreach Campaigns and Surveys

> Create and Manage Answers in your Knowledgebase

> Create Custom Objects and Custom Reports

> Prepare for interviews or exams

> Filled with Colour Illustrations and Tips

Oracle Siebel
Open UI
Developer's Handbook
[2016 Edition]

The Oracle Data
Relationship
Management 11 Guide

Successful Implementation
Essentials

Jeff Flak
Edward J. Cody

Oracle Hyperion
Financial Reporting 11
A Practical Guide

Edward J. Cody
Eric M. Somers

The Definitive
Guide to
Oracle FDMEE

Tony Scalese

Oracle FDMEE
Scripting:
Essential Elements

Tony Scalese

WHERE
DATA
IS
WEALTH
Profiting from data storage
in a digital society

J. BRUCE DALEY